ReadyGEN®

Teacher's Guide

GRADE 1

PEARSON

Glenview, Illinois • Boston, Massachusetts • Ch

Acknowledgments of third-party content appear on page TR67, which constitutes an extension of this copyright page.

PEARSON

ISBN-13: 978-0-328-85182-9
ISBN-10: 0-328-85182-5
7 16

Program Authors

Pam Allyn

Executive Director and Founder, LitLife and LitWorld

Elfrieda H. Hiebert, Ph.D.

Founder, President, and CEO of TextProject, Inc.
University of California, Santa Cruz

P. David Pearson, Ph.D.

Professor of Language, Literacy and Culture
Graduate School of Education,
University of California, Berkeley

Sharon Vaughn, Ph.D.

Executive Director, The Meadows Center for
Preventing Educational Risk
H.E. Hartfelder/Southland Regents Chair
University of Texas at Austin

ReadyGEN

Learning Resources

TRADE BOOKS

- 12 full-length, authentic trade books
- Balance of literary and informational texts
- One set of 12 for teachers at Grade K

NEW! Audio, highlighting, bookmarking, and note-taking capabilities make every trade book come alive.

TEXT COLLECTION

- A collection of texts that offer students an opportunity to continue exploring the unit topic through a variety of genres—poems, biographies, and more
- Big Books at Kindergarten and Grade 1, Unit 1

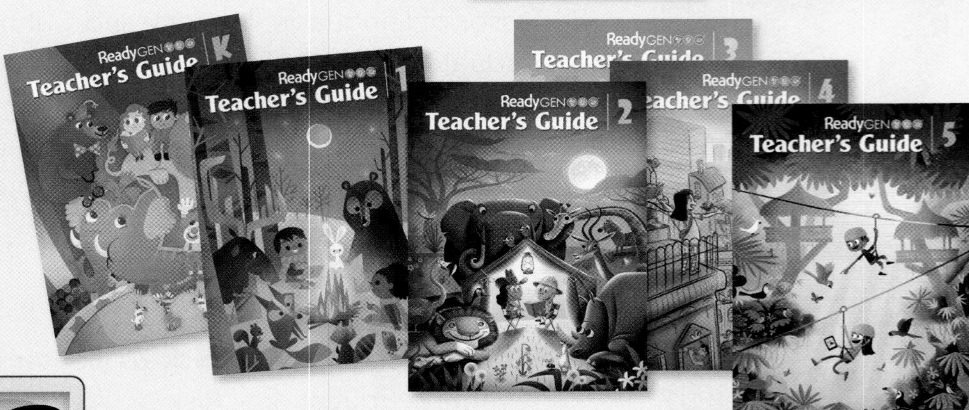

TEACHER'S GUIDE

- One volume per unit
- 6 volumes, Grades K–2
- 4 volumes, Grades 3–5

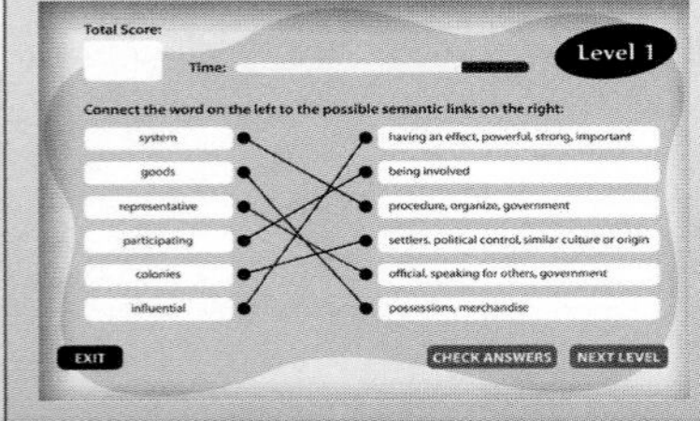

NEW! Foundational Skills instruction appears in every lesson. Interactive word analysis games allow students to practice foundational skills anytime, anywhere and a collection of readers and interactive tools further support instruction.

IMPLEMENTATION GUIDE

- Tips for successful implementation
- Annotated lessons
- Standards correlations
- Classroom management suggestions

SCAFFOLDED STRATEGIES HANDBOOK

- Scaffolded strategies to unlock text, writing, and performance-based assessments
- Activities and routines to support reading, writing, and vocabulary acquisition
- Support for English Language Learners, struggling readers, and accelerated learners

ASSESSMENT STUDENT BOOK AND TEACHER'S MANUAL

- *ReadyGEN* Assessment Overview
- Baseline Assessment
- End-of-Unit Assessments
- Answer key, rubrics, and reproducibles

Learning Resources

SLEUTH

- Short texts for close-reading practice
- Close-reading routine follows Super Sleuth Steps:
  Look for Clues,
  Ask Questions,
  Make Your Case,
  Prove It!
- Performance tasks to demonstrate comprehension
- Kindergarten Sleuth selections are found in the Teacher's Guide

READER'S AND WRITER'S JOURNAL

- Reading and writing response opportunities
- Practice for vocabulary
- Hands-on, close-reading practice

READER'S AND WRITER'S JOURNAL TEACHER'S GUIDE

- Answer key for the student journal

LEVELED TEXT LIBRARY

- 60 topically related texts per grade
- 10 texts per unit, Grades K–2
- 15 texts per unit, Grades 3–5
- Wide range of reading levels to ramp up reading

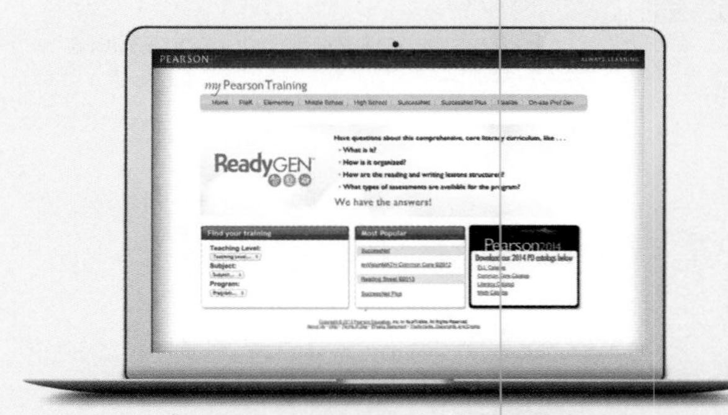

ONLINE PROFESSIONAL DEVELOPMENT myPearsonTraining.com

24/7 access to online videos and tutorials.

ONSITE PROFESSIONAL DEVELOPMENT

With the *ReadyGEN* tiered approach, you can choose the service pathway that best supports your desired learner outcome goals.

- Access ReadyGEN resources anytime, anywhere at PearsonRealize.com.

Comprehensive Literacy Workshop

Reading

1

WHOLE GROUP 30–40 minutes

READING

- Built-in Foundational Skills Mini-Lesson
- Build Understanding
- Close Read
  - Benchmark and By-the-Way Vocabulary Instruction
- Reading Analysis
- Focused Independent Reading
  - Students participate in purposeful, self-selected reading while the teacher transitions to Small Group Time.

2

SMALL GROUP 30–40 minutes

SMALL GROUP OPTIONS

- Additional instruction, practice, or extension as needed in the areas of fluency, foundational skills, and reading and language analysis.

INDEPENDENT LITERACY WORK

- Student-selected grade-level text
- Leveled Text Library
- Decodable and Practice Readers

READYGEN INTERVENTION

- Extra support for struggling readers.

SCAFFOLDED INSTRUCTION

The Scaffolded Strategies Handbook works in tandem with your *ReadyGEN* Teacher's Guide to provide a comprehensive system of scaffolded instruction, useful strategies, and practical routines that will guide you in supporting the needs of all students. The Scaffolded Strategies Handbook provides explicit support in unlocking each *ReadyGEN* text, writing task, and performance-based assessment.

Writing

WHOLE GROUP 30–40 minutes

WRITING
- Each lesson focuses on one of the writing types critical to college and career readiness.
  - Set the Purpose
  - Teach and Model
  - Prepare to Write
  - Independent Writing Practice

CONVENTIONS MINI-LESSONS
- provide instruction for critical grammar skills that students can apply in their speaking and writing.

3

Performance-Based Assessment

What Are My Students Reading?

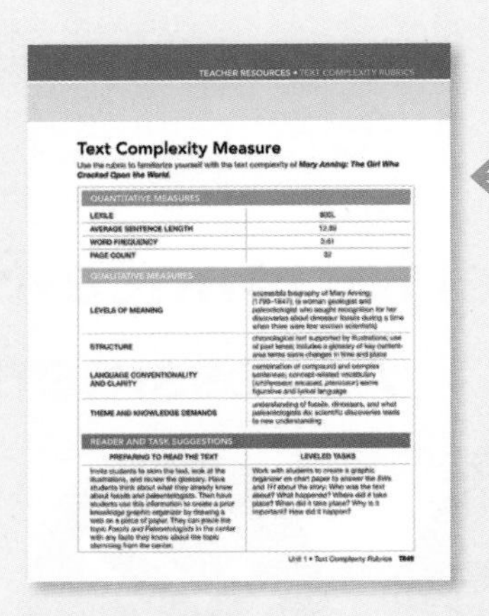

TEACHER RESOURCES • TEXT COMPLEXITY RUBRICS

Text Complexity Measure

QUANTITATIVE MEASURES	
LEXILE	[illegible]
AVERAGE SENTENCE LENGTH	[illegible]
WORD FREQUENCY	[illegible]
PAGE COUNT	[illegible]
QUALITATIVE MEASURES	
LEVELS OF MEANING	[illegible]
STRUCTURE	[illegible]
LANGUAGE CONVENTIONALITY AND CLARITY	[illegible]
THEME AND KNOWLEDGE DEMANDS	[illegible]
READER AND TASK SUGGESTIONS	
PREPARING TO READ THE TEXT	LEVELED TASKS
[illegible]	[illegible]

ReadyGEN provides text complexity rubrics for all core selections to identify potential stumbling blocks in texts and provide support in clearing those obstacles.

TEXT	LEVEL	INSTRUCTIONAL PURPOSE
Trade Books	On or above grade level	Students and teachers engage in multiple close readings of and discussions about *ReadyGEN*'s full-length, authentic literary and informational texts.
Text Collection	On or above grade level	Students and teachers engage in multiple close readings of and discussions about *ReadyGEN*'s shorter pieces of authentic text.
Sleuth	Grade level	During Small Group, students read short selections to sharpen their close-reading skills; they look for clues, ask questions, make their case, and prove it.
Independent Reading	Text appropriate to student reading level	Students select books and practice reading independently with “just right” text.

ReadyGEN's overall progression of complexity of text, within and across grades, facilitates students' learning of academic vocabulary, close reading, and foundational skills, and further deepens content knowledge and comprehension.

TEXT	LEVEL	INSTRUCTIONAL PURPOSE
Leveled Text Library	Text appropriate to student reading level	Students select topically related readers for extra reading practice at their own reading level.
Kindergarten Student Reader	Text appropriate to student reading level	Students practice phonics skills and reread for fluency.
Decodable Readers (Grades 1–3)	Text appropriate to phonics skills	Students practice phonics skills and reread for fluency.
Practice Readers (Grades 4–5)	Text appropriate to word analysis skills	Students practice word analysis skills and reread for fluency.
Kindergarten I Can Read selections	Text appropriate to student reading level	Additonal text allows students to practice reading, as they work through the Reader's and Writer's Journal.

Grade-level Text Scaffolded for All

ReadyGEN provides educators with a variety of scaffolding strategies that promote instructional equity and access to rigorous text for all students.

Support for every learner

On-the-spot scaffolds

- address common stumbling blocks encountered by ELLs and struggling readers and writers.
- allow for proven interventions on an as-needed basis.
- strategic support and extension mini-lessons provide options for engaging independent learners during Small Group Time.

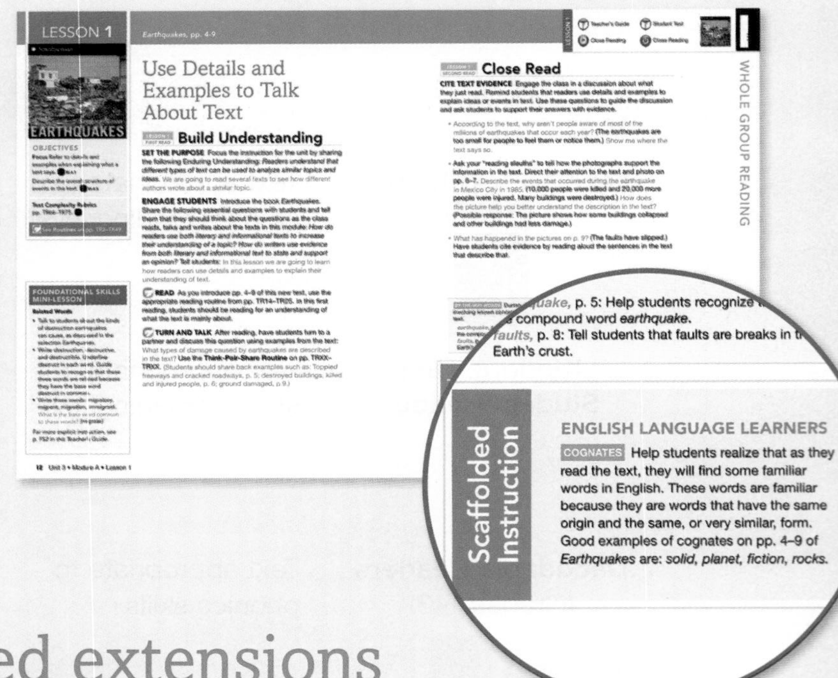

Strategic, targeted extensions

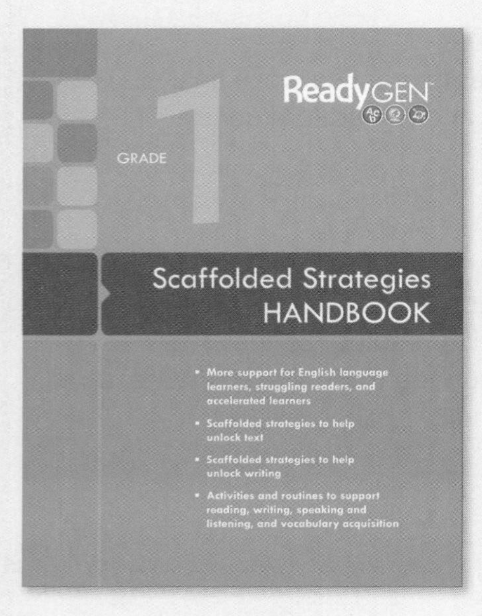

The Scaffolded Strategies Handbook, which is intended to work in tandem with this Teacher's Guide, was designed to meet the intent of the Council for the Great City Schools "Framework for Raising Expectations."

The Handbook provides support for working with students one-on-one, in pairs, and in whole or small groups, and is divided into three parts. Each section offers support strategies personalized to *ReadyGEN* learning activities. Turn to pages xviii–xix in this Teacher's Guide to see how the Scaffolded Strategies Handbook accelerates learning for all.

All texts are aligned to be appropriately complex, ensuring that all students interact with suitable grade-level texts.

QUANTITATIVE MEASURES	
LEXILE®	1010L
AVERAGE SENTENCE LENGTH	14.18
WORD FREQUENCY	3.35
PAGE COUNT	30
QUALITATIVE MEASURES	
LEVELS OF MEANING	straightforward explanations of topic
STRUCTURE	introduction; details interspersed with examples, reinforced by photos and diagrams; glossary and index at end
LANGUAGE CONVENTIONALITY AND CLARITY	domain-specific vocabulary defined in text and glossary
THEME AND KNOWLEDGE DEMANDS	basic knowledge of the causes, locations, and effects of earthquakes
READER AND TASK SUGGESTIONS	
PREPARING TO READ THE TEXT	LEVELED TASKS
Discuss earthquakes with which students may be familiar and the effects of those earthquakes.	Discuss earthquake-related terms, such as *Richter scale, plates,* and *faults.*

Intervention and extensions to meet individual needs

ReadyGEN provides further scaffolded instruction for students who need additional support with critical print skills, vocabulary, reading, and writing competencies that will enable them to fully meet the challenges of college and careers.

- Targeted foundational skills instruction provides a strong base for beginning and struggling readers and writers at the early elementary grades.
- Vocabulary and comprehension lessons help students at all levels develop the necessary skills to succeed both in and out of school.
- Fluid entry and exit points make intervention lessons accessible and user-friendly.

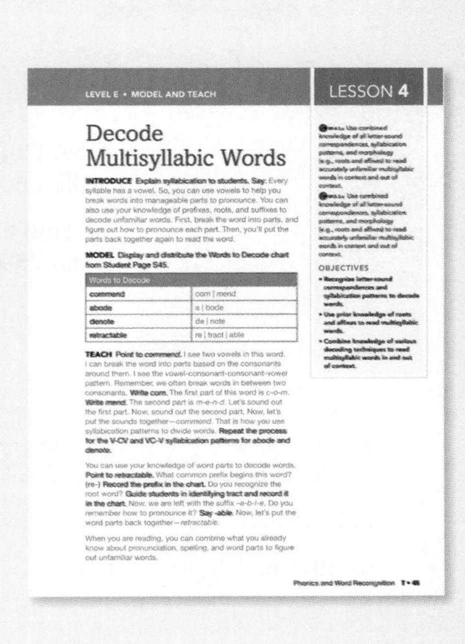

LEVEL E • MODEL AND TEACH

LESSON 4

Decode Multisyllabic Words

INTRODUCE Explain syllabication to students. Say: Every syllable has a vowel. So, you can use vowels to help you break words into manageable parts to pronounce. You can also use your knowledge of prefixes, roots, and suffixes to decode unfamiliar words. First, break the word into parts, and figure out how to pronounce each part. Then, you'll put the parts back together again to read the word.

MODEL Display and distribute the Words to Decode chart from Student Page S45.

Words to Decode	
commend	com | *mend*
abode	a | bode
denote	de | note
retractable	re | tract | able

TEACH Point to commend. I see two vowels in this word. I can break the word into parts based on the consonants around them. I see the vowel-consonant-consonant-vowel pattern. Remember, we often break words in between two consonants. **Write com.** The first part of this word is *c-o-m.* **Write mend.** The second part is *m-e-n-d.* Let's sound out the first part. Now, sound out the second part. Now, let's put the sounds together—*commend.* That is how you use syllabication patterns to divide words. **Repeat the process for the V-CV and VC-V syllabication patterns for abode and denote.**

You can use your knowledge of word parts to decode words. **Point to retractable.** What common prefix begins this word? (re-) **Record the prefix in the chart.** Do you recognize the root word? **Guide students in identifying tract and record it in the chart.** Now, we are left with the suffix *-a-b-l-e.* Do you remember how to pronounce it? **Say -able.** Now, let's put the word parts back together—*retractable.*

When you are reading, you can combine what you already know about pronunciation, spelling, and word parts to figure out unfamiliar words.

OBJECTIVES

- Recognize letter-sound correspondences and syllabication patterns to decode words.
- Use prior knowledge of roots and affixes to read multisyllabic words.
- Combine knowledge of various decoding techniques to read multisyllabic words in and out of context.

Phonics and Word Recognition

MODULE A

TEXT SET

ANCHOR TEXT

Stellaluna
Lexile AD550L
Literary Text

SUPPORTING TEXT

"Dragons and Giants"
Lexile 460L
Literary Text

SLEUTH

"How Polar Bears Hunt"
Lexile 260L

"A New Family"
Lexile 350L

Leveled Text Library
Lexile BR–370L

TEACHER RESOURCES

MODULE B

TEXT SET

ANCHOR TEXT

Time to Sleep
Lexile 140L
Informational Text

SUPPORTING TEXT

What Do You Do With a Tail Like This?
Lexile 620L
Informational Text

SLEUTH

"A Happy Ending"
Lexile 360L

Leveled Text Library
Lexile BR–370L

www.PearsonSchool.com/ReadyGen

Assessment

FORMATIVE ASSESSMENT

HOW ARE MY STUDENTS DOING?	HOW DO I SCAFFOLD AND SUPPORT?

READING

Reading Keystones in every lesson assess children's understanding of key language, structures, and ideas. These keystones help you check children's progress toward the Performance-Based Assessment.

- Benchmark Vocabulary practice
- Text Analysis practice/application
- Write in Response to Reading

Use the Unlock the Text section of the ***Scaffolded Strategies Handbook.***

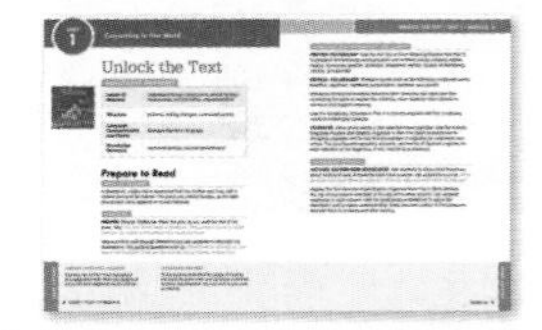

WRITING

Writing Keystone Checklists throughout the unit assess children's opinion, narrative, or informative writing. These checklists help you determine how children are progressing toward the task in the Performance-Based Assessment.

	Achieved	Notes
Express a clear statement of opinion.		
Provide reasons to support the opinion.		
Develop the reasons with facts, details, examples, and quotations from the text.		

Use the Unlock the Writing section of the ***Scaffolded Strategies Handbook.***

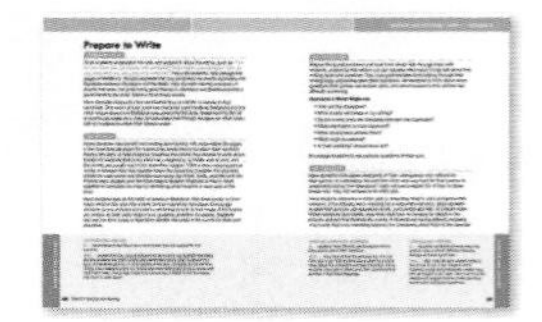

FOUNDATIONAL SKILLS/STANDARDS MASTERY

Baseline Assessments are used at the onset of the year to help determine children's instructional needs. The ***Reader's and Writer's Journal*** includes weekly practice opportunities for word analysis and other key skills.

Check Progress formative assessments are at the end of every Foundational Skills section in each unit to assess children's word analysis skills.

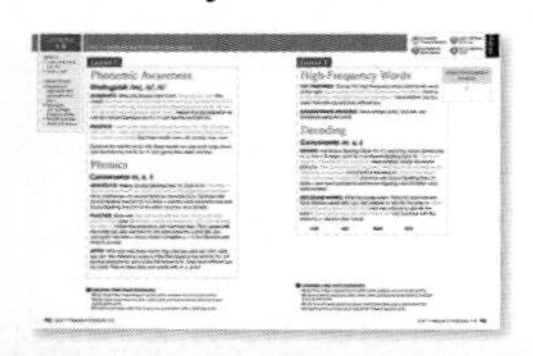

Once performance data from the Baseline Assessment, the *Reader's and Writer's Journal,* and the Check Progress formative assessment is gathered, use ***SuccessReady*** for children who need standards support.

PERFORMANCE-BASED ASSESSMENT

Every Module

Each module culminates in a **Performance-Based Assessment** that can be used to measure children's mastery of standards.

UNIT 1 • MODULE A **Write About Friendship**

TASK: Children will think about the friendship between the birds and Stellaluna. Then they will illustrate and write sentences about how the characters showed their friendship when they first met and then later in the story.

UNIT 1 • MODULE B **Write Questions and Answers**

TASK: Children will use facts from *Time to Sleep* and *What Do You Do With a Tail Like This?* to write questions and answers about animals.

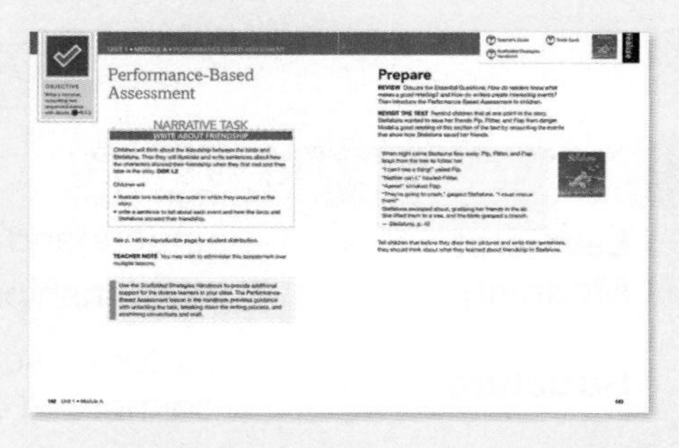

END-OF-UNIT ASSESSMENT

The **End-of-Unit Assessment** is found in the ***Assessment Book.*** This test presents engaging literary and informational passages. Children answer selected-response and technology-enhanced comprehension and vocabulary questions.
They also respond to narrative, informational, and opinion writing prompts. Use this assessment to give you additional information on students' progress and to inform your instruction.

Accelerate Learning for All

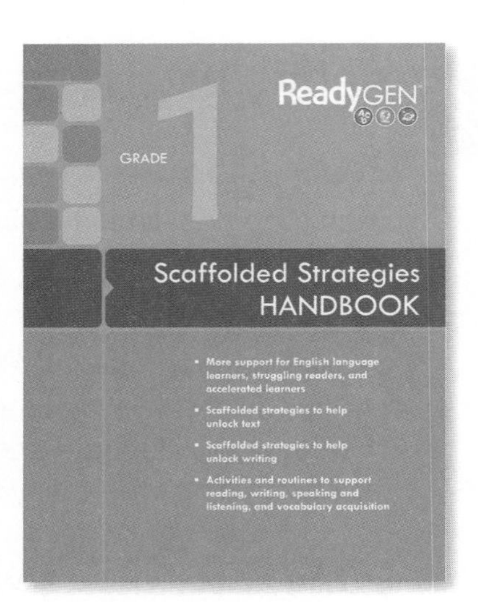

1. What makes the text challenging?

Use the Text Complexity Rubrics in the Scaffolded Strategies Handbook to familiarize yourself with potential "stumbling blocks" for each text in this unit.

QUALITATIVE MEASURES	
Levels of Meaning	understand human behaviors in animal fantasy; relationships and friendship; characterization
Structure	pictures; setting changes; connected events
Language Conventionality and Clarity	dialogue; figurative language
Knowledge Demands	nocturnal animals; bat and bird behavior

2. What types of scaffolds will my students need?

Based on your students and the text complexity rubrics, determine the support students will need to overcome the challenges in the texts. Use the resources in the Scaffolded Strategies Handbook to support

- English language learners
- struggling readers
- accelerated learners

3. How can the Scaffolded Strategies Handbook help?

Unlock the Text

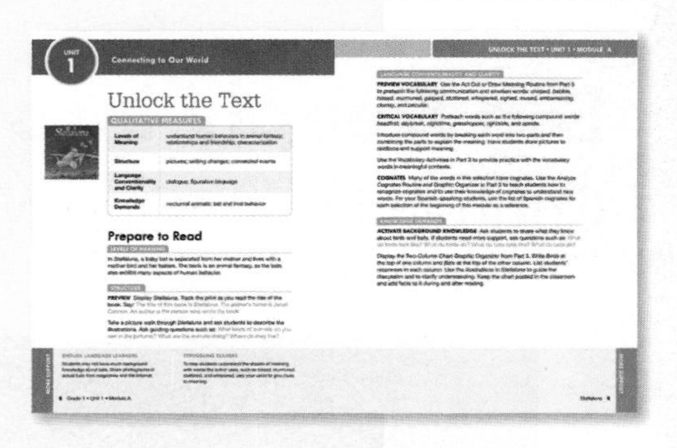
Connecting to Our World

Unlock the Text

Prepare to Read

Use Prepare to Read to

- ensure text readiness
- support knowledge building
- provide language and concept development

Use Interact with Text to

- examine language and structure
- monitor and support comprehension
- help students access content

Use Express and Extend to

- support academic conversations
- integrate developmental writing tasks

Unlock the Writing

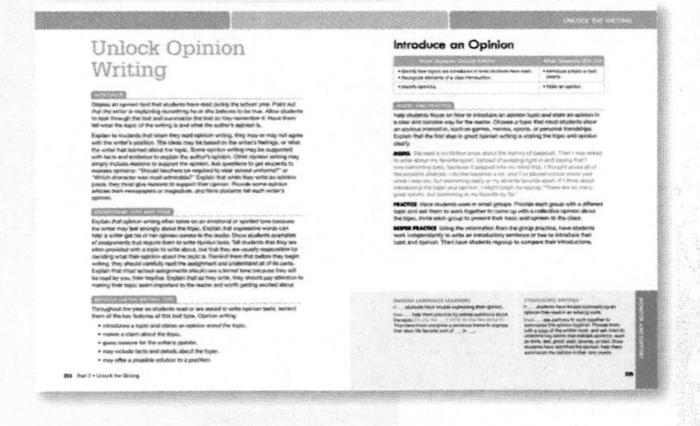
Unlock Opinion Writing

Introduce an Opinion

Use the scaffolded lessons for module performance tasks to

- unlock the task
- support the process
- talk it through

Use scaffolded opinion, informative and narrative writing lessons to

- unlock the mode
- provide a deeper understanding of the process
- extend the writing

Routines and Activities

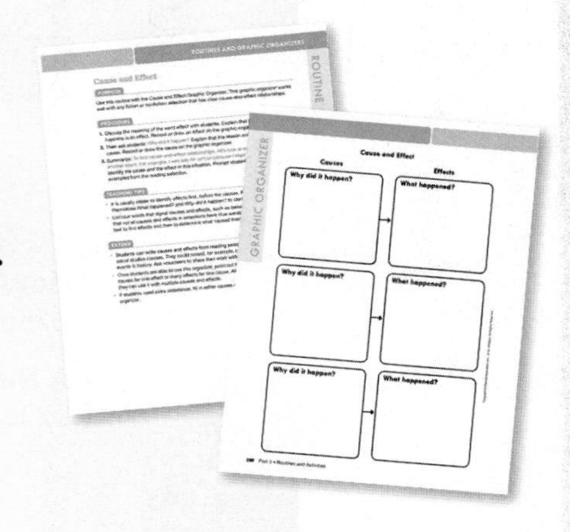
Cause and Effect

Use the routines to scaffold learning in reading, writing, speaking and listening.

Use the activities to support language and word study and to accommodate linguistic differences.

More Support for ELLs

Use the visuals to provide support for content.

Use the passage, vocabulary, and questions to build background knowledge.

Use the close reading questions to dig deeper into vocabulary and structure.

Path to College and Career Readiness

Dig Deeply into Complex Text

Connecting to Our World

TEXT SET

PEARSON realize

ANCHOR TEXT

Stellaluna
Lexile AD550L
Literary Text

SUPPORTING TEXT

"Dragons and Giants"
Lexile 460L
Literary Text

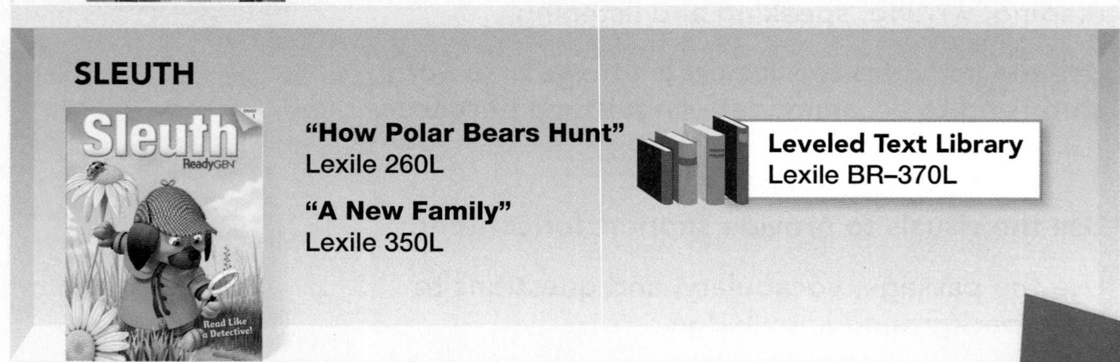

SLEUTH

"How Polar Bears Hunt"
Lexile 260L

"A New Family"
Lexile 350L

Leveled Text Library
Lexile BR–370L

Enduring Understandings

- **Readers** understand that they improve their comprehension by identifying story elements.
- **Writers** understand that details play a role in explaining the events in a story.
- **Learners** understand that living things depend on one another.

"Knows"

ESSENTIAL QUESTIONS

How do **readers** know what makes a good retelling?

How do **writers** create interesting events?

"Dos"

MODULE GOALS

Readers will retell stories, including key details.

Writers will write a narrative story in which they recount one or more sequenced events.

EXPLORE CONTENT **Learners** will recognize that there are relationships among living things.

PERFORMANCE-BASED ASSESSMENT

NARRATIVE TASK: WRITE ABOUT FRIENDSHIP

Children will think about the friendship between the birds and Stellaluna. Then they will illustrate and write sentences about how the characters showed their friendship when they first met and then later in the story.

Vocabulary to Unlock Text

Generative Vocabulary

ReadyGEN provides systems for understanding how words work. Teach **generative vocabulary** as children dig deeply into complex texts. Focus on sets of rare Tier II and Tier III words that unlock meaning, build knowledge of critical content domains, and help children internalize word-learning strategies. Go to www.PearsonSchool.com/ReadyGEN to read more about generative vocabulary instruction in *ReadyGEN.*

BENCHMARK VOCABULARY Benchmark Vocabulary words are important for understanding concepts within a text. These can be defined as

- words needed to deeply comprehend a text.
- words from other disciplines.
- words that are part of a thematic, semantic, and/or morphological network.
- words central to unlocking the Enduring Understanding of the text.

BY-THE-WAY WORDS By-the-Way Words are sophisticated or unusual Tier II and Tier III words for known concepts that can be stumbling blocks to comprehending a text. They should be defined quickly during reading, but instruction should not interfere with the fluent reading of the text. These are addressed during Close Reading and can be defined as

- words that don't require lengthy discussion within a particular text.
- words supported by the text for meaning.
- words that are more concrete.

Generative Vocabulary in Speaking and Writing Children should demonstrate a deep understanding of vocabulary by using those words and words generated from them in conversation, writing practice, and the Performance-Based Assessments.

Additional Vocabulary Support

For Spanish cognates, see the *Scaffolded Strategies Handbook*.

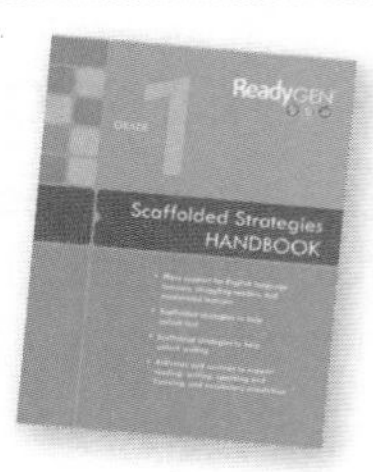

ANCHOR TEXT *Stellaluna*

Literary Text Use this chart as a starting point for your class to generate related words. There may be more words in each cluster than those listed here.

Benchmark Vocabulary	Possible Morphological Links	Possible Semantic Links	Narrative Links
escaped		fled, ran, survived	*Plot*
survived	survivor, survival	live, continue, endure	*Plot*
trembling		shake, shiver	*Actions or Movement*
embarrassing	embarrassed	upsetting	*Character*
clumsy	clumsily	awkward, accident-prone	*Character*
limb		branch	*Setting*
land	landing	set down, reach	*Actions or Movement*
perched	perch	sit	*Actions or Movement*
nighttime		dark, night	*Setting*
crash	crashed	smash, hit	*Action or Movement*
rescue	rescuer	free, save, release	*Plot*
clutched	cling	grabbed, snatched	*Actions or Movement*
grasped	grab	caught, clutched	*Actions or Movement*
headfirst			*Character*
daybreak		dawn, first light	*Setting*
obey	obedience	follow, observe	*Communication*
rules	ruler	laws, standards	*Communication*
behaved	behavior	act, conform	*Character*
safe	safety	secure, unhurt	*Plot*
mused		wondered, awed	*Communication*
wondered	wonderful	thoughtful	*Communication*
mystery	mysterious	secret, riddle	*Plot*
wingspan		size, reach	*Character*
tropical	tropics	climate, weather	*Setting*

Vocabulary to Unlock Text

SUPPORTING TEXT "Dragons and Giants" ***from Frog and Toad Together***

Literary Text Use this chart as a starting point for your class to generate related words. There may be more words in each cluster than those listed here.

Benchmark Vocabulary	Possible Morphological Links	Possible Semantic Links	Narrative Links
brave	bravery	courageous, unafraid, dare, challenge	*Character*
mountain		hill, peak, summit, valley, climb, view	*Setting*
snake		reptile, lizard	*Plot*
together		both, partners	*Character*

Additional Vocabulary Support

For Spanish cognates, see the *Scaffolded Strategies Handbook.*

UNIT 1 • MODULE A Overview

Readers understand that they improve their comprehension by identifying story elements.

READYGEN LESSONS	READING INSTRUCTIONAL FOCUS Text Talk / Close Read / Text Analysis	INDEPENDENT READING Process and Strategy
LESSONS 1–3 *Stellaluna*	Identify Elements of a Story	**P** Engagement and Identity **S** Comprehension
	Use Illustrations and Details to Describe Characters	**P** Engagement and Identity **S** Comprehension
	Use Details to Understand Characters	**P** Engagement and Identity **S** Comprehension
LESSONS 4–5 "Dragons and Giants"	Retell a Story's Events in Order	**P** Engagement and Identity **S** Comprehension
	Understand the Words Authors Use	**P** Engagement and Identity **S** Vocabulary Knowledge
LESSON 6 *Stellaluna* and "Dragons and Giants"	Compare Characters	**P** Independence **S** Fluency
LESSONS 7–9 *Stellaluna*	Understand That Authors Choose Words to Tell a Story	**P** Independence **S** Vocabulary Knowledge
	Identify and Describe the Setting of a Story	**P** Independence **S** Critical Thinking
	Use Illustrations to Understand a Story	**P** Engagement and Identity **S** Fluency
LESSON 10 *Stellaluna* and "Dragons and Giants"	Understand the Ending of a Story	**P** Engagement and Identity **S** Critical Thinking
LESSON 11 *Stellaluna*	Identify the Central Message of a Story	**P** Engagement and Identity **S** Comprehension
LESSON 12 "Dragons and Giants"	Identify the Central Message of a Story	**P** Stamina **S** Decoding and Word Recognition
LESSON 13 *Stellaluna*	Discuss Informational and Literary Texts	**P** Stamina **S** Decoding and Word Recognition

P = Process Focus **S** = Strategy Focus

Connecting to Our World

Writers understand that details play a role in explaining the events in a story.

WRITING INSTRUCTIONAL FOCUS	INDEPENDENT WRITING
Tell Beginning, Middle, and End	Write About Story Events
Character Details	Write About Characters' Relationship
Use Character Details	Write About Characters and Events
Tell Beginning, Middle, and End	Write Events in Order
Use Character Details	Write Details About Characters
Event Details	Write About a Story Event
Use Character Details	Write About a Character
Setting Details	Write About a Setting
Event Details	Write Event Details
Writing Process: Plan	Plan a Narrative
Writing Process: Draft	Write a Narrative
Writing Process: Revise and Edit	Revise and Edit a Narrative
Writing Process: Publish	Publish a Narrative

PERFORMANCE-BASED ASSESSMENT

Children will think about the friendship between the birds and Stellaluna. Then they will illustrate and write sentences about how the characters showed their friendship when they first met and then later in the story.

UNIT 1 • MODULE A Planner

Suggested Pacing

READING
30–40 minutes

- Build Understanding
- Close Read
- Benchmark Vocabulary
- Text Analysis

SMALL GROUP TIME
30–40 minutes

- Focused Independent Reading
- Small Group Options

WRITING
30–40 minutes

- Narrative Writing
- Independent Writing Practice

LESSON 1
Teacher's Guide, pp. 12–21

READ Trade Book Read the entire book.
Stellaluna

BENCHMARK VOCABULARY
escaped, survived

READING ANALYSIS Retell a Story

WRITING Write About Story Events

LESSON 2
Teacher's Guide, pp. 22–31

READ Trade Book Read the entire book.
Stellaluna

BENCHMARK VOCABULARY
trembling, embarrassing, clumsy

LANGUAGE ANALYSIS Word Choice

WRITING Write About Characters' Relationship

LESSON 6
Teacher's Guide, pp. 62–71

COMPARE
- *Stellaluna*
- "Dragons and Giants"

BENCHMARK VOCABULARY
nighttime, crash, rescue

READING ANALYSIS Compare Characters

WRITING Write About a Story Event

LESSON 7
Teacher's Guide, pp. 72–81

READ Trade Book pp. 5–10
Stellaluna

BENCHMARK VOCABULARY
clutched, grasped

LANGUAGE ANALYSIS Word Choice

WRITING Write About a Character

LESSON 11
Teacher's Guide, pp. 112–121

READ Trade Book pp. 36–45
Stellaluna

BENCHMARK VOCABULARY
mused, wondered, mystery

READING ANALYSIS Central Message

WRITING Write a Narrative

LESSON 12
Teacher's Guide, pp. 122–131

READ ***Text Collection*** pp. 5–15
"Dragons and Giants"

BENCHMARK VOCABULARY
together

READING ANALYSIS Central Message

WRITING Revise and Edit a Narrative

LESSON 3
Teacher's Guide, pp. 32–41

READ Trade Book Read the entire book.
Stellaluna

BENCHMARK VOCABULARY
limb, land, perch

READING ANALYSIS Characters

WRITING Write About Characters and Events

LESSON 4
Teacher's Guide, pp. 42–51

READ *Text Collection* Read the entire story.
"Dragons and Giants"

BENCHMARK VOCABULARY
brave

READING ANALYSIS Retell

WRITING Write Events in Order

LESSON 5
Teacher's Guide, pp. 52–61

READ *Trade Collection* Read the entire story.
"Dragons and Giants"

BENCHMARK VOCABULARY
mountain, snake

LANGUAGE ANALYSIS Categorize Words

WRITING Write Details About Characters

LESSON 8
Teacher's Guide, pp. 82–91

READ Trade Book pp. 4–11
Stellaluna

BENCHMARK VOCABULARY
daybreak, headfirst

LANGUAGE ANALYSIS Sensory Details

WRITING Write About a Setting

LESSON 9
Teacher's Guide, pp. 92–101

READ Trade Book pp. 30–33
Stellaluna

BENCHMARK VOCABULARY
obey, rules, behaved

READING ANALYSIS Story Events

WRITING Write Event Details

LESSON 10
Teacher's Guide, pp. 102–111

COMPARE Read the end of each text.
- *Stellaluna*
- "Dragons and Giants"

BENCHMARK VOCABULARY
safe

LANGUAGE ANALYSIS Story Endings

WRITING Plan a Narrative

LESSON 13
Teacher's Guide, pp. 132–141

READ Trade Book pp. 46–47
Stellaluna

BENCHMARK VOCABULARY
wingspan, tropical

LANGUAGE ANALYSIS Fiction and Nonfiction

WRITING Publish a Narrative

LANGUAGE AND FOUNDATIONAL SKILLS IN THIS MODULE

Conventions Print Uppercase and Lowercase Letters; Spell Words Phonetically; Write Complete Sentences; End Punctuation: Periods, Question Marks, Exclamation Points; Capitalize Sentences; Capitalize Names of People; Use Complete Sentences **Phonics** Consonants *m*/m/, *s*/s/, *t*/t/, *c*/k/, *p*/p/, *n*/n/, *f*, *ff*/f/, *b*/b/, *g*/g/; Short *a*: *a*/a/; Short *i*: *i*/i/

PERFORMANCE-BASED ASSESSMENT

Teacher's Guide, pp. 142–149

NARRATIVE TASK: WRITE ABOUT FRIENDSHIP

Children will think about the friendship between the birds and Stellaluna. Then they will illustrate and write sentences about how the characters showed their friendship when they first met and then later in the story.

Center Options

During Small Group Time, children can use independent center activities to practice and apply standards while you work with individuals or groups. Options for activities focusing on both concepts and learning objectives for this unit are included here.

READING CENTER

- Have children share a character description from an independent reading book with a partner.
- Have children draw three pictures that show the beginning, middle, and end of an independent reading book.
- Log into Pearson Realize and use the instruction in the Comprehension Focus and Vocabulary Focus sections of the Reading Mat activity for this module. Then have children read EnVision Math Problem-Solving Mat for Topic 12, *Farm animals* and complete the accompanying graphic organizer.

DOK L2

WRITING CENTER

- Have children draw detailed pictures of two characters to include in a story. Then have them write a sentence about the relationship of the two characters.

Write in Response to Reading

- Have children complete the appropriate Write in Response to Reading prompts, found within pp. 1–39 of their *Reader's and Writer's Journal.*
- Have children log into TikaTok and write their own question-and-answer book about an interesting animal they choose. Have them go to www.tikatok.com.

DOK L2

DIGITAL CENTERPIECES

STUDENTS AS AUTHORS

Powered by TikaTok

Children write their own books connected to the unit topic. They log into **www.tikatok.com**, respond to prompts, insert images, and produce a book to keep.

STUDENTS AS THINKERS

Children use EnVision Math Problem-Solving Mats to practice comprehension and vocabulary. They apply what they learn as they complete a unique online activity.

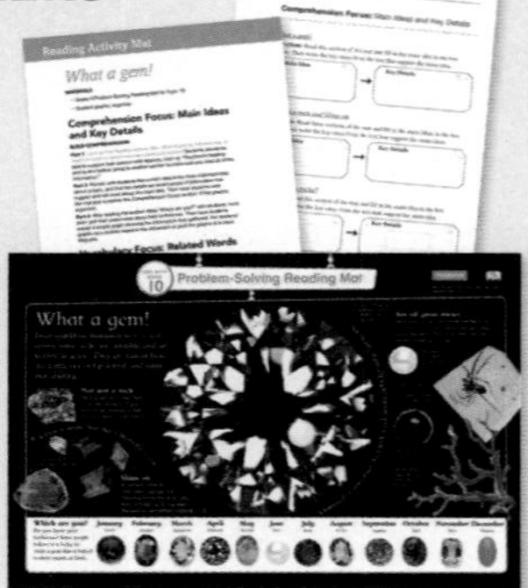

MODULE GOALS

Readers will retell stories, including key details.

Writers will write a narrative story in which they recount one or more sequenced events.

Learners will recognize that there are relationships among living things.

WORD WORK CENTER

- Have children add words and phrases to the class word wall that relate to characters.
- Have children create "Setting" vocabulary lists. As they read books during independent reading, have them add interesting words to their lists that help them describe a setting.
- Have children find examples of words that show sequence or time passing in their independent reading books and add these examples to a class list of words.

DOK L1

RESEARCH CENTER

- Have children research one of the animals they have read about: bats, birds, frogs, and toads.
- Have children write two facts about the animal they researched using a computer or tablet.
- Have children find a picture on the Internet to go with the facts they have written about the animal they researched. The facts and pictures could be collected and placed in a class book.

DOK L2

STUDENTS AS WORD WORKERS

Children play online foundational skills and generative vocabulary games to strengthen their word analysis skills and build their vocabulary.

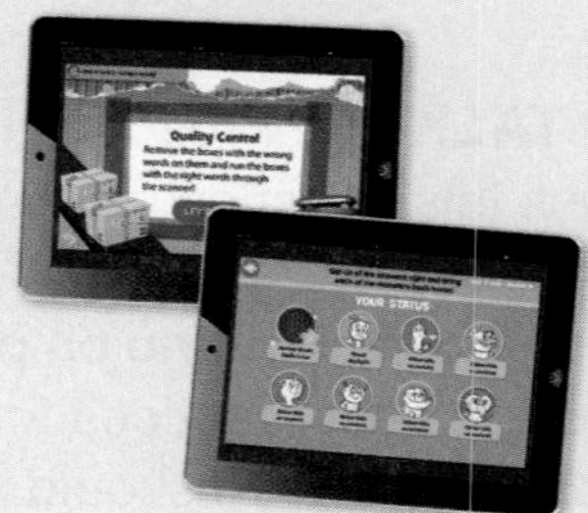

STUDENTS AS READERS

Children use online leveled texts to practice reading at their independent levels. Texts are related to the unit topic and offer a range of levels to meet every child's needs.

OBJECTIVES

Focus Identify and understand story elements of a text. RL.1.3

Use text evidence to answer questions during a close reading. RL.1.1

Text Complexity Rubrics
pp. TR48–TR54.

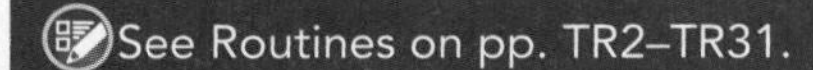
See Routines on pp. TR2–TR31.

Identify Elements of a Story

LESSON 1
FIRST READ

Build Understanding

SET THE PURPOSE Focus your instruction for the unit by keeping the following Enduring Understanding in mind: *Readers understand that they improve their comprehension by identifying story elements*. We are going to read several stories to practice identifying story elements. Story elements are *who* the story is about, which is called a character, *where* the story takes place, which is called the setting, and *what* happens, which are the important events in the story.

EXPLORE POETRY We are going to read a book about a bat. Listen to this poem. Read the poem "Batty" in the *Text Collection*, p. 44. When are bats awake? Why would the baby bat be afraid of the light?

ENGAGE CHILDREN Introduce the book *Stellaluna*. Use this time to review and model basic print concepts, including proper book orientation and the arrangement of print on the page. Then point to the bat on the front cover and explain that this is a made-up story about made-up characters. Share the following Essential Questions with children to focus their ideas. Tell them that they should think about the questions as the class reads, talks, and writes about the stories in this module: *How do readers know what makes a good retelling? How do writers create interesting events?* Tell children: Today we are going to learn how to talk about the elements of a story called *Stellaluna*. Remember the elements of a story that we talked about: character, setting, and important events.

READ As you introduce this story, use the appropriate reading routine from pp. TR8–TR19. In this first reading, children should be gaining a general understanding of what the story is mainly about.

TURN AND TALK After reading, have children turn to a partner and discuss this question using examples from the story: Tell me who the characters are. Who is the story mostly about? Use the **Think-Pair-Share Routine** on pp. TR2–TR3, making sure children are using best practices for speaking and listening outlined in the routine. (Children should share examples such as: Stellaluna, p. 5 or Mother Bat, p. 5.)

FOUNDATIONAL SKILLS MINI-LESSON

Consonants *m*/m/, *s*/s/, *t*/t/

- Show the Picture Card *moon*. Let's say *moon*. Now let's say the first sound in *moon*: /m/.
- Show Sound-Spelling Card 15. Point to *m*. The letter m stands for the sound /m/, which you hear at the beginning of *mountain*. Write *mat*. What is the first sound in *mat*? What letter stands for the sound /m/? *(m)*
- Repeat the above procedure for *s* and *t*, using Picture Cards *sun* and *ten* and Sound-Spelling Cards 21 and 23.
- Read these words: *tag, mat, sad, man, tan, sat*. Have children write the letter that spells the first sound.

For more explicit instruction, see p. FS2 in this Teacher's Guide.

Close Read

CITE TEXT EVIDENCE Engage the class in a discussion about what you just read. Review the elements of a story with children: characters, setting, and important events. Then remind children that readers can identify elements of a story. Use these questions to guide the discussion and ask children to support their answers with evidence.

- Who are some of the characters we meet at the beginning of this story? Point to these characters on page 4 and say their names with me. (Stellaluna and Mother Bat) **DOK L1**
- Where does the story take place? Tell me more about this place. (In a forest; it is warm and many animals live there.) **DOK L1**
- Why did Mother Bat drop Stellaluna? (An owl swooped down and struck her.) Let's reread this part of the story on page 6. The story says, "the powerful bird swooped down upon the bats." Mother Bat could not escape from the owl and she dropped Stellaluna. **DOK L2**
- What are some words that we read that tell about Stellaluna's wings? (*baby, limp, useless*, like "wet paper") How do you know that Stellaluna cannot fly on her own? (Stellaluna's baby wings are "as limp and useless as wet paper." Stellaluna falls into the forest when her mother drops her.) **DOK L2**

BY-THE-WAY WORDS During close reading, define the following words for children involving known concepts that can be stumbling blocks to comprehending the story.

scent, p. 6: Explain to children that *scent* is another way to say "smell."

spied, p. 6: Tell children that *spied* means "saw" or "noticed."

Scaffolded Instruction

ENGLISH LANGUAGE LEARNERS

MULTIPLE-MEANING WORDS Help children understand that sometimes *bat* means "a wooden stick, used for hitting a ball," but in this case *bat* means "a small animal that flies." Tell children that often they can figure out the correct meaning of a word by reading the words around it or by looking at the illustrations.

STRATEGIC SUPPORT

ASK QUESTIONS If children have difficulty understanding what happens to Mother Bat and Stellaluna at the beginning of the story, reread p. 6 and ask clarifying questions, such as: *What does the owl do when it sees Mother Bat? What does Mother Bat do? What happens to Stellaluna when the owl attacks?*

OBJECTIVES

Determine the meanings of unknown words.
 L.1.4

Retell a story.  RL.1.2

BENCHMARK VOCABULARY

- escaped, p. 34
- survived, p. 34

BENCHMARK VOCABULARY

- Find and read aloud the sentences from the story with the words *escaped* and *survived*.

  Use the **Benchmark Vocabulary Routine for Literary Text** on pp. TR28–TR31 to teach the meanings of the words.

- Use the information on pp. 2–5 to discuss other words connected to each of the Benchmark Vocabulary words.

PRACTICE Have children use p. 2 in the *Reader's and Writer's Journal* to show contextual understanding of the Benchmark Vocabulary. Monitor children's vocabulary development.

Reading Analysis

TEXT TALK

 **Keystones** Reading and Writing Keystones are a quick check to

- assess children's understanding of key language, key text structures, and key ideas.
- indicate children's progress toward the Performance-Based Assessment.
- inform your Small Group Time decisions.

RETELL A STORY Explain to children that retelling a story can help a reader understand the important events. A good retelling tells who the characters are and what happens in the beginning, middle, and end of the story. It shows that the reader understands what the story is about. Provide the Three-Column Chart on p. TR40.

MODEL Let's look at page 6 where the author tells what happens right before Stellaluna loses her mother. What happens first? I can look at the picture and go back into the text. I read that Mother Bat smells fruit and goes to search for it. I'm going to write this under *Beginning* on my chart.

Retell a Story		
Beginning	Middle	End
Mother Bat goes to search for fruit.	An owl chases Mother Bat.	Mother Bat drops Stellaluna.

PRACTICE/APPLY Have children work in small groups to complete the graphic organizer by writing or dictating events for each column. Use the **Small Group Discussion Routine** on pp. TR6–TR7 to have children discuss the beginning, middle, and end of the story. Check understanding by asking children to share or by circulating among children or groups.

Reader's and Writer's Journal

Generative Vocabulary Games

Leveled Text Library

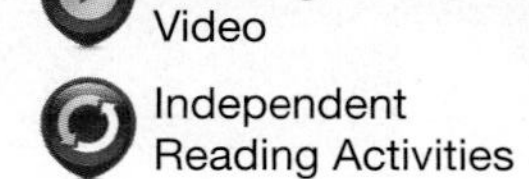

Independent Reading How-To Video

Independent Reading Activities

Small Group Time

STEP 1 Focused Independent Reading

BUILD ACCOUNTABILITY Prepare children to read their **self-selected texts.** Announce the two focus points to the class, and help children make a plan for their reading. Children will apply both focus points to their self-selected texts.

TODAY'S PROCESS FOCUS	
☑ Engagement and Identity	☐ Independence
☐ Stamina	

Tell children to choose a book they think they will enjoy reading. Encourage them to choose a book whose illustrations or characters they find interesting. As they choose a book, have children think about some of their favorite stories and why they enjoyed them.

TODAY'S STRATEGY FOCUS	
☐ Vocabulary Knowledge	☐ Critical Thinking
☐ Fluency	☑ Comprehension

Guide children in applying the content of today's Reading Analysis lesson to their self-selected texts. We learned that authors use illustrations and details to help describe characters, settings, and events in a story. Today as you are reading, look for these story elements. Place a sticky note next to the characters, settings, and events you like best. Alternatively, have children log into Pearson Realize to find an Independent Reading Activity that is appropriate for the story they are reading.

MONITOR PROGRESS

- **Process Focus:** Have children draw pictures of what happens in their chosen story in a daily reading log. Children should also dictate or write about whether they are enjoying their book and give reasons for their response.
- **Strategy Focus:** Have children review with you the sticky notes they placed in their book. Ask them to explain which ones are characters, which ones are settings, and which ones are events. Alternatively, have children log into Pearson Realize and review with you the Independent Reading Activity they completed for their book.

For further guidance, see the **Independent Reading Routine** on pp. TR12–TR19.

While children are reading independently, use the Small Group Options on pp. 16–17.

INDEPENDENT LITERACY WORK

Text Club (pp. TR20–TR23)

Leveled Text Library

Center Options (pp. 10–11)

Use **Write in Response to Reading** on p. 2 of the *Reader's and Writer's Journal* to check children's understanding of key ideas in *Stellaluna*.

Phonics: Decodable Readers

GUIDED READING OPTIONS

Use the **Leveled Text Library** to choose appropriate texts based on children's needs.

Use ***ReadyUp! Intervention*** for children who require additional instruction with this lesson's reading and foundational standards or with prerequisite standards.

STEP 2

Small Group Options

Based on formative assessments of children's progress, use the following options to provide additional instruction as needed.

PHONICS

For children who need support with this week's Phonics skills, use pp. FS2–FS5 in this Teacher's Guide.

UNLOCK THE TEXT

For children who need support in accessing key ideas, key language, and key structures in ***Stellaluna***, use **Unlock the Text** in the *Scaffolded Strategies Handbook*, pp. 8–13.

CONFERENCE

For independent reading accountability, **conference** each day with two or three children to discuss **self-selected texts** and support their reading.

READING ANALYSIS SUPPORT

For children who struggle with retelling story events in ***Stellaluna***, use this **Support Reading Analysis Mini-Lesson**.

RETELL A STORY Help children retell *Stellaluna* by asking guiding questions, such as: Who are the characters? Where do they live? What events have happened so far? As children answer your questions, encourage them to elaborate by asking follow-up questions, such as: What happened next? Then what happened? Tell me what happened at the end of the story. Have children draw and label pictures of the story events and use their drawings to retell the story to a partner.

Invite children to retell the events from page 12 when Mama Bird feeds Stellaluna an insect for the first time. Use the **Think-Pair-Share Routine** on pp. TR2–TR3.

Ask and answer questions about key details in a text. RL.1.1

Retell events in a story in order. RL.1.2

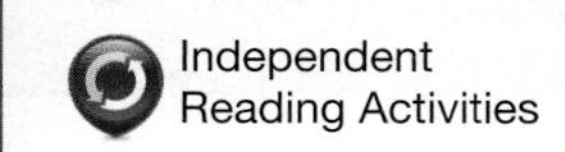

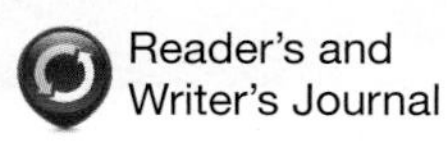

Games

READING ANALYSIS EXTENSION

For children who can easily retell story events in ***Stellaluna***, use this **Extend Reading Analysis Mini-Lesson.**

RETELL A STORY Have children use their graphic organizer to retell the story of *Stellaluna* to a partner. Then have children discuss the following questions:

- What happens on page 18 after Mama Bird tells Stellaluna that she is teaching Mama Bird's children bad things? (Stellaluna promises to obey and behave like a bird.)
- What happens on page 30 when Stellaluna falls asleep hanging by her thumbs when she is far from home? (Another bat flies by and tells her she is upside down.) Why is that an important event? (Stellaluna begins to understand that she is supposed to act like a bat.)
- How do the birds act when they visit Stellaluna's bat family? (On pages 40–42, they behave like bats by hanging upside down and trying to fly at night.)

Ask and answer questions about key details in a text. RL.1.1
Retell events in a story in order. RL.1.2

FLUENCY

For fluent reading accountability, use this **Oral Reading Fluency Quick Check.** ☑ **Today assess 2–3 children.**

MODEL APPROPRIATE RATE Explain that reading at an appropriate rate means reading at just the right speed—not too fast and not too slow—in order to keep the listener interested. Have children follow along as you model reading aloud from *Stellaluna,* first very quickly, then too slowly, and finally at an appropriate rate. Review why a reader wouldn't want to read too slowly or too quickly. Then choral read with children a portion of a leveled text at an appropriate rate.

Read on-level text orally with accuracy and appropriate rate. RF.1.4.b

QUICK CHECK

MONITOR PROGRESS

If . . . children are reading too slowly,

then . . . have them practice reading aloud with a partner in order to gain confidence with the story.

If . . . children are reading too quickly,

then . . . remind them to slow down so the listener is better able to understand and imagine what is being read to them.

OBJECTIVE
Recount a narrative's beginning, middle, and end. W.1.3

Narrative Writing

Tell Beginning, Middle, and End

SET THE PURPOSE A narrative is a story. It has a beginning, a middle, and an end. Explain that events in a narrative happen in order, or in sequence. One thing has to happen before something else happens. Provide an example of beginning, middle, and end that children can relate to, such as the task of brushing one's teeth and the order in which this event occurs.

Reread p. 5, p. 14, and p. 44 of *Stellaluna* with children. Talk about the beginning, middle, and end of the narrative. Guide discussion with the following questions.

- What happens at the beginning of this story? (Mother Bat names her baby and takes her out to search for food each night. They are attacked by an owl, and baby Stellaluna falls from her mother into a bird's nest far below.)
- What does Stellaluna learn in the middle of the story? (She learns how to be like the birds in the nest, eating bugs and staying awake during the day. She learns to fly, and after flying far from the bird's nest, she meets other bats and finds her mother again.)
- What do Stellaluna and the birds realize at the end of the story? (They are the same and different, but they can still be friends.)

TEACH AND MODEL Through discussion, help children notice words in the story that help readers understand sequence. Have children look at the beginning of the story on p. 5 and then on p. 14.

In a warm and sultry forest far, far away, there once lived a mother fruit bat and her new baby.

At the beginning of the story, the writer uses the word *once* to tell readers that this is just the beginning.

Stellaluna learned to be like the birds. . . . Her bat ways were quickly disappearing.

The writer uses words, such as *quickly disappearing,* to help readers understand that time is going by.

Explain that when children are writing narratives of their own, they should write the events in the order in which they happen so that readers can follow the story.

Write About Story Events

PREPARE TO WRITE Explain to children that learning to write is a skill that is related to learning to read. While children are learning to write, have them practice modeling examples of good writing from the stories they read. By identifying the beginning, middle, and end in many stories, children will become familiar with plot patterns and be able to start shaping their own narrative plots.

ORGANIZE A NARRATIVE Explain that you will model telling the different story elements for a familiar fable, "The Tortoise and the Hare."

In the story "The Tortoise and the Hare," two animals decide to race each other. At the beginning of the race, the hare is fast and the tortoise is slow. Then the hare decides to take a nap before he crosses the finish line. At the end, the tortoise crosses the finish line before the hare. I can draw a picture to go with each part of the story. I will draw the pictures in the order of how the events happened. Then I can write a sentence to go with each part of the story.

WRITE AND ILLUSTRATE A NARRATIVE Draw illustrations to show the beginning, middle, and end of the short story you retold. The illustrations do not need to be elaborate, but they should support what happens at the beginning, middle, and end of the story. Then write simple sentences next to each picture. (Possible sentences: The hare and the tortoise decide to race. The hare takes a nap. The tortoise wins the race.) Review with children that events happen in order in a story.

Writers always include a beginning, middle, and end when they write a narrative. It is important to use these story elements so our writing makes sense and is fun to read!

Scaffolded Instruction

STRATEGIC SUPPORT

BEGINNING, MIDDLE, AND END For children who struggle with identifying the beginning, middle, and end of a story, have them draw illustrations to show the events of another familiar story such as, *The Three Little Pigs*, *The Ugly Ducking*, or *Cinderella*. Provide a graphic organizer, such as the Story Sequence A chart, to help children better visualize the order of key events for their retelling.

OBJECTIVES

Recount a narrative's beginning, middle, and end. W.1.3

Identify and print uppercase letters. L.1.1.a

Independent Writing Practice

WRITE Have children think about the narrative *Stellaluna*. They will identify the beginning, middle, and end of the story by drawing an illustration for each part. Then they will choose one part of the story to write a sentence about. Have children

- revisit the narrative *Stellaluna*, flagging pages they feel tell about the beginning, middle, and end of the story. Children will use the illustrations to help them identify what is happening on each page.
- illustrate an event that occurs at the beginning, middle, and end of the narrative.
- choose one event and write or dictate a sentence about that event on p. 3 of their *Reader's and Writer's Journal*. Provide a sentence frame for children to use to help them with their writing: *In the beginning, ____; In the middle, ____;* or *In the end, ____.*

CONVENTIONS For children who struggle with identifying and printing uppercase letters, use the Conventions Mini-Lesson on p. 21. Tell children to print their letters neatly when writing stories or other types of writing.

DIGITAL OPTIONS If available, guide children in using tablets or computers to type their sentences and then print them out. Then, on the same sheet of paper, have children draw a picture above or below the text to illustrate what their sentences are about.

Share Writing

Have children share their illustrations and sentences with a partner. Have them discuss how the beginnings, middles, and ends were similar or different from each other. Then have listeners share with the reader whether they understood the story, if they liked it, and why.

Conventions Mini-Lesson

Identify and Print Uppercase Letters

TEACH AND MODEL Review with children the difference between lowercase and uppercase letters. Write a few children's names on the board and point out the uppercase letters that are used at the start of their names. Explain that uppercase letters are also found at the start of sentences.

One by one, Pip, Flitter, Flap, and Stellaluna jumped from the nest.	An uppercase letter is used at the beginning of each characters' name.
One by one, Pip, Flitter, Flap, and Stellaluna jumped from the nest.	An uppercase letter appears at the start of a sentence.

PRACTICE Have children turn to p. 10 in *Stellaluna* and identify characters' names that begin with uppercase letters. On a separate sheet of paper, have children practice writing the uppercase letters that begin each character's name: *S, F, M,* and *P*. For more practice in writing uppercase letters, have children complete the activity on p. 3 in the *Reader's and Writer's Journal*.

Scaffolded Instruction

ENGLISH LANGUAGE LEARNERS

UPPERCASE LETTERS Children may still be learning how to identify and form letters. Provide magnetic uppercase letters for children to practice identifying each letter. Then have them practice writing the uppercase letters that correlate with each letter they identified.

OBJECTIVES

Focus Use illustrations and details in a story to describe its characters. 

Use key events and details to describe story elements. RL.1.3

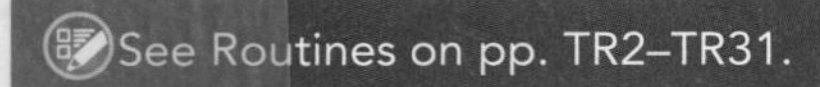
See Routines on pp. TR2–TR31.

Use Illustrations and Details to Describe Characters

LESSON 2 FIRST READ

Build Understanding

SET THE PURPOSE Explain to children that as they revisit *Stellaluna,* they will continue to explore the following Enduring Understanding: *Readers understand that they improve their comprehension by identifying story elements.* We are going to continue reading *Stellaluna* to learn how the author creates interesting characters. Remember that characters are the people or animals in a story.

ENGAGE CHILDREN Remind children that *Stellaluna* is a fantasy, which is a made-up story. Explain that even though it is a made-up story that could never happen, there are facts about real fruit bats in *Stellaluna*. Go through the story and show children the illustrations. Use the illustrations to point out details about the characters in the story. Help children recognize that using the illustrations can help them to talk about the characters in the story. Remind children of the Essential Questions: *How do readers know what makes a good retelling? How do writers create interesting events?* Tell children: We are going to learn how readers can show that they understand what a story is all about by how they retell the story.

READ To review important events and characters, read aloud the entire story of *Stellaluna*. Use the appropriate reading routine from pp. TR8–TR19. In this reading, have children focus on understanding what is happening and what the characters are doing.

TURN AND TALK After reading, have children turn to a partner and discuss this question using examples from the story: What did you learn about the characters from the pictures? Use the **Think-Pair-Share Routine** on pp. TR2–TR3. (Children should share examples such as: Stellaluna's mother survived, p. 35; Stellaluna learned that she could see at night, p. 37; Stellaluna eats fruit, not bugs, p. 39.)

FOUNDATIONAL SKILLS MINI-LESSON

High-Frequency Words; Consonants *m*/m/, *s*/s/, *t*/t/

- Display the High-Frequency Word Card *I*. Have children read the word. The word *I* has just one letter, *I*. Have children write *I* and then use it in sentences.
- Use Sound-Spelling Cards 15, 21, and 23 to review consonants *m, s,* and *t*. Have children identify each letter and the sound it stands for. Then write these words: *mat, sat, Sam, Tam*. Have children identify the first letter in each word and its sound.

For more explicit instruction, see p. FS3 in this Teacher's Guide.

LESSON 2
SECOND READ

Close Read

CITE TEXT EVIDENCE Engage the class in a discussion about what you just read. Remind children that readers use illustrations and details in a story to describe its characters. Use these questions to guide the discussion and ask children to support their answers with evidence.

- How do Stellaluna and Mother Bat feel when they see each other again? (happy, relieved, surprised) How do you know that Mother Bat is happy to see Stellaluna? Show me where the text and the pictures say so. (On pages 34–35 Mother Bat "wrapped her wings around" Stellaluna. Together, Mother Bat and Stellaluna hang upside down by their feet.) **DOK L3**
- Look at the picture on page 37. What is Stellaluna doing? (flying in the dark) How does Stellaluna figure out she can fly in the dark? Let's look back at what Mother Bat tells her. Mother Bat explains that Stellaluna is a bat, and bats can see in the dark. When Stellaluna tries, even though she is afraid, she learns that she can fly at night! **DOK L2**
- What is Mother Bat trying to teach Stellaluna? (Mother Bat is trying to teach Stellaluna how to behave like a bat.) What are some things that fruit bats do? (They hand upside down, fly at night, and eat fruit.) **DOK L2**

BY-THE-WAY WORDS During close reading, define the following words for children involving known concepts that can be stumbling blocks to comprehending the story.

delicious, p. 34: Tell children that *delicious* is another way to say "very good tasting."

mango, p. 38: Explain to children that a mango is a fruit that is green and red on the outside and yellow on the inside.

Scaffolded Instruction

ENGLISH LANGUAGE LEARNERS

KEY DETAILS Help children understand that often they can figure out a phrase by reading the other words and sentences around it. Point out the phrase *she stuffed herself full* on p. 38. Then read the text on the page. Help children recognize that the phrase "ate as much of the fruit as she could hold" explains the meaning of "she stuffed herself full."

STRATEGIC SUPPORT

KEY DETAILS Help children who have difficulty understanding that Mother Bat is teaching Stellaluna bat ways. Have them use the illustrations to answer questions about bats, such as: *How do bats rest in trees? When do bats fly? What do bats eat?*

OBJECTIVES

Identify and use words and phrases in stories. RL.1.4; L.1.6

Use words acquired from texts. L.1.6

BENCHMARK VOCABULARY

- grasped, p. 42
- embarrassing, p. 22
- clumsy, p. 24

BENCHMARK VOCABULARY

- Find and read aloud the sentences from the story with the words *embarrassing, clumsy,* and *grasped.*

  Use the **Benchmark Vocabulary Routine for Literary Text** on pp. TR28–TR31 to teach the meanings of the words.

- Use the information on pp. 2–5 of this Teacher's Guide to discuss other words connected to each of the Benchmark Vocabulary words.

PRACTICE Have children use p. 4 in the *Reader's and Writer's Journal* to show contextual understanding of the Benchmark Vocabulary. Monitor children's vocabulary development.

Language Analysis

TEXT TALK

WORD CHOICE Explain that authors use interesting words to describe characters' feelings and actions. As a class, record words the author uses to describe the characters' feelings in the story. Provide Web A on p. TR44.

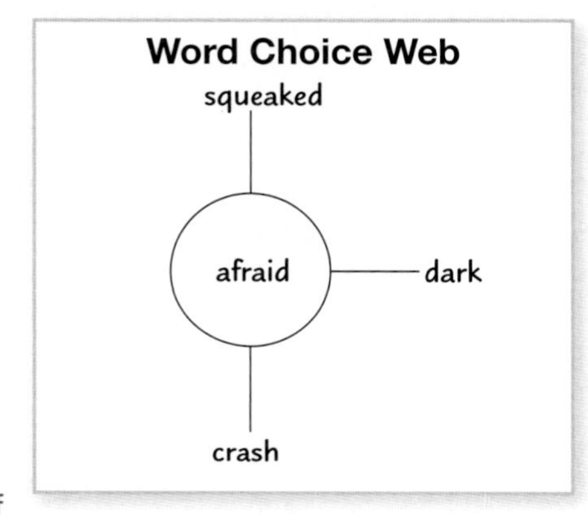

MODEL Let's look at page 36. "But it's nighttime," Stellaluna squeaked. "We can't fly in the dark or we'll crash into trees." I think Stellaluna is feeling afraid right now. I'm going to write that word in the middle of the word web. I can look for other interesting words that help me understand why Stellaluna is feeling afraid, such as *squeaked, dark,* and *crash*. Let's write these words on the spokes of the web.

PRACTICE/APPLY Have children work independently or in small groups to complete the graphic organizer. Use the **Small Group Discussion Routine** on pp. TR6–TR7 to have children discuss how the illustrations and details help describe the characters in the story. Check understanding by asking children to share or by circulating among children or groups.

Small Group Time

STEP 1 Focused Independent Reading

BUILD ACCOUNTABILITY Prepare children to read their **self-selected texts.** Announce the two focus points to the class, and help children make a plan for their reading. Children will apply both focus points to their self-selected texts.

TODAY'S PROCESS FOCUS	
☑ Engagement and Identity	☐ Independence
☐ Stamina	

Tell children to choose a book they think they will enjoy reading. Have them page through the illustrations in several books and choose a book whose characters they wish to know more about. Have children form a question about a character before reading and then try to answer the question during reading.

TODAY'S STRATEGY FOCUS	
☐ Vocabulary Knowledge	☐ Critical Thinking
☐ Fluency	☑ Comprehension

Guide children in applying the content of today's Language Analysis lesson to their self-selected texts. We learned that authors use illustrations and details to help describe characters in a story. Today as you are reading, pay attention to the characters in the book and the words the author uses to describe them. Make a note of which characters you like best. Alternatively, have children log into Pearson Realize to find an Independent Reading Activity that is appropriate for the text they are reading.

MONITOR PROGRESS

- **Process Focus:** Have children draw pictures of the characters in the story in a daily reading log. Children should dictate or write to tell what they know about these characters.
- **Strategy Focus:** Have children explain what characters they chose as their favorite and why. Alternatively, have children log into Pearson Realize and review with you the Independent Reading Activity they completed for their book.

For further guidance, see the **Independent Reading Routine** on pp. TR12–TR19.

While children are reading independently, use the Small Group Options on pp. 26–27.

INDEPENDENT LITERACY WORK

Text Club (pp. TR20–TR23)

Leveled Text Library

Center Options (pp. 10–11)

Use **Write in Response to Reading** on p. 4 of the *Reader's and Writer's Journal* to check children's understanding of key ideas in *Stellaluna*.

Phonics: Practice Readers

GUIDED READING OPTIONS

Use the **Leveled Text Library** to choose appropriate texts based on children's needs.

Use ***ReadyUp! Intervention*** for children who require additional instruction with this lesson's reading and foundational standards or with prerequisite standards.

STEP 2 Small Group Options

Based on formative assessments of children's progress, use the following options to provide additional instruction, practice, or extension as needed.

PHONICS

For children who need support with this week's Phonics skills, use pp. FS2–FS5 in this Teacher's Guide.

UNLOCK THE TEXT

For children who need support in accessing key ideas, key language, and key structures of ***Stellaluna,*** use **Unlock the Text** in the *Scaffolded Strategies Handbook,* pp. 8–13.

CONFERENCE

For independent reading accountability, **conference** each day with two or three children to discuss **self-selected texts** and support their reading.

LANGUAGE ANALYSIS SUPPORT

For children who struggle with understanding the author's word choices in ***Stellaluna,*** use this **Support Language Analysis Mini-Lesson.**

WORD CHOICE Help children work through the web by asking questions that relate to times they felt afraid. Continue modeling to find words the author chose to explain characters' feelings in *Stellaluna*. Read aloud the story on p. 8. Ask: What are some other words the author uses to show that Stellaluna is feeling afraid? Let's look at the pictures on pages 8 and 9 for help. I think she is afraid and trying to feel safe. Help children identify the words *clutched, trembling,* and *cold*. Continue to fill in the web together.

Invite children to choose another page and have them look at the pictures and find words that are used to describe characters. Use the **Think-Pair-Share Routine** on pp. TR2–TR3.

Ask and answer questions about key details in a text. RL.1.1

Describe characters in a story, using key details. RL.1.3

Identify and use words that appeal to the senses. RL.1.4

LANGUAGE ANALYSIS EXTENSION

For children who easily understand the author's word choices in *Stellaluna,* use this **Extend Language Analysis Mini-Lesson.**

WORD CHOICE Have children work together to find words the author chose to explain other characters' feelings. Choose one or two of the words they find to create new Word Choice Webs. Encourage children to refer to their webs as they write and talk about the story.

- Read aloud the story on p. 26. Point out the following words in the story: *sun is setting, lost,* and *dark*. What do the author's words suggest about how the birds are feeling? (The birds are feeling anxious.) Have children create a web for *anxious*.
- Then read aloud the story on p. 5 and the last paragraph on p. 32. What words does the author use to show that Mother Bat loves Stellaluna? (*soft, tiny, crooned, carry, clutched*) What words did the author use on page 32? (*sniffing Stellaluna's fur, whispered, my baby*) Have children create a web for *love*.

Ask and answer questions about key details in a text. RL.1.1
Describe characters in a story, using key details. RL.1.3
Identify and use words that appeal to the senses. RL.1.4

FLUENCY

For fluent reading accountability, use this **Oral Reading Fluency Quick Check.** ☑ **Today assess 2–3 children.**

MODEL EXPRESSION Explain to children that reading with expression helps to keep the listener interested in the story. If you don't read with expression, the story can get very boring, and you don't enjoy it as much. Turn to p. 36 and read aloud the first sentence with expression: "But it's nighttime," Stellaluna squeaked. "We can't fly in the dark or we will crash into trees." Point out the quotation marks. Explain that quotation marks show that a character is talking. Which character is speaking? (Stellaluna) How does she feel? (scared) Have children follow along in the book as you read Stellaluna's words again. Then have them read the quotation with you. Encourage children to read aloud as if Stellaluna is speaking the words.

Read fluently with expression RF.1.4.b

QUICK CHECK

MONITOR PROGRESS

If . . . children are struggling to read with expression,

then . . . have them choose a page of *Stellaluna* to read to a partner in order to practice expression.

If . . . children are reading with expression in the wrong areas,

then . . . review with them the purpose of quotation marks and what they indicate.

OBJECTIVE
Write narratives recounting details.
W.1.3

Narrative Writing

Character Details

SET THE PURPOSE Talk about the central message of *Stellaluna*: friendship. Point out that even though birds and bats are different, the characters in *Stellaluna* found ways to be friends. Explain that the writer helps readers understand the friendship between the birds and the bats by choosing words carefully. Reread p. 14 of *Stellaluna* with children. Point out how Stellaluna and the baby birds showed that they were building a friendship. Guide the discussion with these questions:

- What does Stellaluna do to fit in with the baby birds? (She stayed awake all day and slept at night and she ate bugs.) When we become friends with others, we often do the things they like to do to show that we are interested in them. Stellaluna showed that she wanted to be liked by the birds by doing some of the things they do.
- What do the baby birds do to better understand Stellaluna and her bat habits? (They try hanging from their feet.)

Point out the phrase "learned to be like" and the word *curious*. Explain that the writer chose these words to help readers understand that the baby birds and Stellaluna were becoming friends with one other.

TEACH AND MODEL Through discussion, help children notice words in the story that help readers notice character details. Read aloud p. 26 and p. 42 of *Stellaluna*. Provide the following models:

The three anxious birds went home without her.

The word *anxious* gives readers an understanding that the baby birds are worried about Stellaluna.

"They're going to crash," gasped Stellaluna. "I must rescue them!"

The writer uses these details to help readers understand that Stellaluna considers the baby birds to be her friends.

Write About Characters' Relationship

PREPARE TO WRITE Explain to children that writers spend time creating the characters for their narratives even before they begin writing their stories. They think about the relationships the characters will have with one another in a book. Once the writer decides how the characters will interact with each other, words are chosen carefully to help readers understand the relationship between the characters. Encourage children to ask themselves the following questions as they prepare to draw and write about the characters in a story:

- Who is the story about? Are these characters real or imaginary?
- If these characters could talk, what would they say?
- Will these characters be friends?
- Will these characters agree or disagree?
- Will these characters solve a problem together? How will they solve it?

ORGANIZING A NARRATIVE Explain that you will model writing a few sentences about Stellaluna and the baby birds. You will choose words carefully to help readers understand what kind of friends they are to each other. As you model describing the characters in a narrative, have children listen for words or phrases you use to explain the characters' relationships:

Stellaluna quickly flew into action when the birds began to fall in the dark sky. She grabbed each of them and flew them up to the safety of a tree branch. She spread her wings and huddled around them to protect them. "Hold tight little birds. You are safe with me," she said.

Review with children how the words *quickly, grabbed, safety, huddled around,* and *protect* helped them understand that Stellaluna was concerned about her friends rather than just letting them figure out flying in the dark on their own. Point out that children will want to choose their words carefully when writing about characters as well.

WRITE A NARRATIVE Explain to children that as they write their narrative, they need to include words to describe the characters so the reader will know more about who the characters are and what they feel. Once children have decided on who they want to draw or write about, they can begin thinking about their narrative and what details they would like to include.

Scaffolded Instruction

STRATEGIC SUPPORT

CHARACTER DETAILS For children still struggling with choosing words to describe characters, have them draw a character to show what a character is like or how the character feels as you read a story. The illustrations do not need to be elaborate, but should portray what the character is like or something that happened to the character. Review with children their word choices, verifying that they used the correct types of words to describe the character they chose.

OBJECTIVES

Write details about characters. W.1.3

With guidance, use technology to produce and publish writing and to collaborate with others. W.1.6

Identify and print lowercase letters.

Independent Writing Practice

WRITE Have children think about the relationship between Mother Bat and Stellaluna. How does the writer choose words that help readers understand the relationship between Stellaluna and her mother? Have children

- revisit the narrative *Stellaluna*, flagging pages that show the relationship between Stellaluna and her mother.
- draw a picture that helps others understand the relationship between Stellaluna and her mother.
- write or dictate a sentence on p. 5 of the *Reader's and Writer's Journal* that tells about the relationship between Stellaluna and her mother.

CONVENTIONS If you wish to teach children about identifying and printing lowercase letters, use the Conventions Mini-Lesson on p. 31. Have children check that they have used lowercase letters correctly in their writing.

DIGITAL OPTIONS If available, have children use tablets or computers to type out their sentences and print them. Then, on the same sheet of paper, have them draw a picture to illustrate what their sentences are about.

Share Writing

Have children share their illustrations and sentences with a partner. Have them discuss which words in their sentences help others understand what Stellaluna and her mother were feeling. Then have volunteers suggest other words the writer could have used in order to help the reader understand what Stellaluna and her mother were feeling.

Conventions Mini-Lesson

Print Lowercase Letters

TEACH AND MODEL Review with children the difference between lowercase and uppercase letters. Point out that lowercase letters are used for most words in sentences. They are not used at the beginning of character names or sentences.

The dark leafy tangle of branches caught Stellaluna as she fell.

Lowercase letters are used for most words in sentences. However, the first letter of the first word in a sentence and the first letter of proper nouns, such as names, must be uppercase.

PRACTICE Have children turn to p. 20 in *Stellaluna* and identify which parts of the character names are written in lowercase letters. Then have children practice writing lowercase letters on p. 5 of their *Reader's and Writer's Journal.*

Scaffolded Instruction

ENGLISH LANGUAGE LEARNERS

LOWERCASE LETTERS English language learners may still be learning how to identify and form letters. Provide magnetic lowercase letters for children to practice identifying each letter. Then have them practice writing the lowercase letters that correlate with each letter they identified.

LESSON 3

OBJECTIVES

Focus Use key details from the text to understand characters. RL.1.7

Use text evidence to answer questions about key details.
 RL.1.1

See **Routines** on pp. TR2–TR31.

Use Details to Understand Characters

LESSON 3 FIRST READ

Build Understanding

SET THE PURPOSE Focus the instruction for the unit by sharing the following Enduring Understanding: *Readers understand that they improve their comprehension by identifying story elements.* Characters—the people or animals in a story—are one story element. Today, we are going to see how the characters in *Stellaluna* relate to one another. Relating to another person can mean being friends, sharing, helping each other, and having fun together.

EXPLORE POETRY Read the poem "The Little Birds" in the *Text Collection*, p. 44, and discuss it with children. Why do baby birds beg? Why do they appear to be all mouth?

ENGAGE CHILDREN Have children page through *Stellaluna*, using the illustrations to remind them of the events and characters. Remind children to think about the Essential Questions as they read, talk, and write about the texts in this module: *How do readers know what makes a good retelling? How do writers create interesting events?* Tell children: We are going to learn how authors help readers understand the characters in a story.

READ Read aloud the entire story of *Stellaluna.* Encourage children to try to read along silently. Pause when necessary to cue children to turn the pages. As you read, use the appropriate reading routine on pp. TR8–TR19. Have children focus on details that tell what the characters are like and how they feel.

TURN AND TALK After reading, discuss the following event using examples from the text: Now we are going to look more closely at what Stellaluna does after she falls. Have children open their books to page 12. Try reading this sentence with a partner. Indicate the sentence that begins "Finally,..." With your partner, explain why Stellaluna acted this way. Use the **Think-Pair-Share Routine** on pp. TR2–TR3. (Children should explain that Stellaluna was hungry and was hoping to be fed.)

FOUNDATIONAL SKILLS MINI-LESSON

Short *a*: *a*/a/

- Show the Picture Card *ant.* Let's say *ant.* Now let's say the first sound in *ant:* /a/.
- Show Sound-Spelling Card 1. Point to *a.* The letter *a* stands for the sound /a/, which you hear at the beginning of *astronaut.* It also stands for the middle sound in *mat,* /m/ /a/ /t/. Let's write *a* and say its sound.
- Write *bat. Stellaluna* is a story about a bat. The middle sound in *bat* is /a/, /b/ /a/ /t/. What is the middle sound in *bat?* What letter stands for that sound?
- Write these words: *mat, sat, Sam, Tam.* Have children identify the sounds in each word.

For more explicit instruction, see p. FS4 in this Teacher's Guide.

LESSON 3 SECOND READD

Close Read

CITE TEXT EVIDENCE Engage the class in a discussion about what you just read. Remind children that readers use details from the text to help them understand story elements, such as characters. Use these questions to guide the discussion about Stellaluna, the three baby birds, and Mama Bird, and ask children to support their answers with evidence.

- Why does Stellaluna think she can fly? (She says she is just like the birds.) Let's find details that would make Stellaluna think that. She learned to act like the birds by eating bugs and sleeping at night. She promised Mother Bird she would not hang by her feet. **DOK L2**
- Have children turn to page 10. Read the last sentence with me. Depending on children's abilities, have them read along silently with you or echo read the sentence. Is Pip being loud or quiet? (quiet) Why does Pip want the others to be quiet? (He doesn't want Mama Bird to know Stellaluna is there.) **DOK L2**
- Have children turn to p. 12 and read the sentence aloud with expression, emphasizing the word *plop*. Have children echo read the sentence. You can see that the word *plop* looks different. This slanted type is called italics. Why do you think the author put this word in italics? (The author wants us to read the word in a louder voice.) The word *plop* stands for a sound. How does it help you imagine what is happening in the story? (It helps me imagine what it sounds like when Mama Bird drops a grasshopper into Stellaluna's mouth.) **DOK L2**

BY-THE-WAY WORDS During close reading, define the following word for children involving known concepts that can be stumbling blocks to comprehending the text.

crawly, p. 12: Help children recognize the word *crawl* in *crawly* and understand that *crawly things* are things that crawl, like insects.

Scaffolded Instruction

ENGLISH LANGUAGE LEARNERS

CRAFT AND STRUCTURE Help children understand two of the sound words on p. 10: *Flump!* and *Shhh!* Say "flump!" as you drop a stuffed animal or doll into a chair. Point out the next sentence, which says that Stellaluna landed headfirst in a nest. For *Shhh!*, explain that saying *Shhh!* is a way of telling someone to be quiet. Demonstrate bringing your finger to your lips to emphasize the meaning.

STRATEGIC SUPPORT

CLOSE READING If children have difficulty understanding the baby birds' early reactions to Stellaluna and Mama Bird, read p. 10 and ask clarifying questions such as: *What does Flap say when Stellaluna falls into the nest? What does Flitter say? How do the birds feel about what just happened?*

OBJECTIVES

Identify and use words from stories. 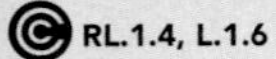

Use illustrations and details to describe characters and their relationships. RL.1.7

BENCHMARK VOCABULARY

- limb, p. 42
- land, p. 44
- perched, p. 44

BENCHMARK VOCABULARY

- Find and read aloud sentences from the text with the words *limb*, *land*, and *perched*.

Use the **Benchmark Vocabulary Routine for Literary Text** on pp. TR28–TR31 to teach the meanings of the words.

- Use the information on pp. 2–5 of this Teacher's Guide to discuss other words connected to each of the Benchmark Vocabulary words.

PRACTICE Have children use p. 7 in the *Reader's and Writer's Journal* to show contextual understanding of the Benchmark Vocabulary. Monitor children's vocabulary development.

Reading Analysis

TEXT TALK

CHARACTERS Explain that describing characters and their relationships can help readers understand why things happen in a story. Provide the T-Chart on p. TR39. Label the columns *Birds* and *Stellaluna*. Model filling in the first items in each column.

Characters

Birds	Stellaluna
Let Stellaluna join the nest	Agrees to act like a baby bird
Hang upside-down with her	Invites the baby birds to meet her family
Fly with her to meet her family	Saves the baby birds when they can't fly at night
Hug her	Says she and the baby birds are friends

MODEL Let's talk about the characters in *Stellaluna*. At the end of the book, Stellaluna says she and the young birds are friends, even though they are very different. I'm going to look for details that help me understand why Stellaluna and the birds feel the way they do. First, I'll look for things the birds do for Stellaluna. At the beginning of the story, they let Stellaluna join the nest. They also try hanging upside-down from the nest. Maybe they want to know what it's like to be Stellaluna! I'm going to write these details under *Birds* on my chart.

PRACTICE/APPLY Have children work independently or in small groups to complete the graphic organizer by writing or dictating one or two more details in each column. Use the **Small Group Discussion Routine** on pp. TR6–TR7 to have children discuss why the characters are friends. Check understanding by asking children to share or by circulating among children or groups.

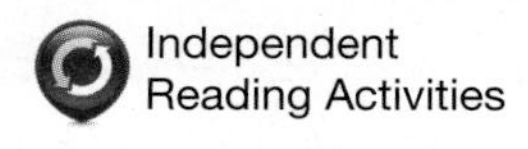

Small Group Time

STEP 1 Focused Independent Reading

BUILD ACCOUNTABILITY Prepare children to read their **self-selected texts.** Announce the two focus points to the class, and help children make a plan for their reading. Children will apply both focus points to their self-selected texts.

TODAY'S PROCESS FOCUS	
☑ Engagement and Identity	☐ Independence
☐ Stamina	

Tell children to choose a book they think they will enjoy reading. Some children may have had enough reading experiences to name a favorite author. Encourage others to look at book covers and titles to choose a book that is on a topic that interests them. You may also allow children to choose a book that appeals to them visually.

TODAY'S STRATEGY FOCUS	
☐ Vocabulary Knowledge	☐ Critical Thinking
☐ Fluency	☑ Comprehension

Guide children in applying the content of today's Reading Analysis lesson to their self-selected texts. When you read today, look for details that tell you something about how a character acts. Use colored tabs to mark each detail or picture you notice. Write the name of the character on the note. Alternatively, have children log into Pearson Realize to find an Independent Reading Activity that is appropriate for the text they are reading.

MONITOR PROGRESS

- **Process Focus:** Have children record their reading in a daily reading log. Children should write or dictate one sentence telling something they liked about their book and draw a picture to illustrate their sentence. Have children find the title page of the book and copy the title and author into their reading log.
- **Strategy Focus:** Have children review with you the colored tabs they placed in their book. Ask them to explain what each detail or illustration tells about the character. Alternatively, have children log into Pearson Realize and review with you their Independent Reading Activity.

For further guidance, see the **Independent Reading Routine** on pp. TR12–TR19.

While children are reading independently, use the Small Group Options on pp. 36–37.

INDEPENDENT LITERACY WORK

Text Club
(pp. TR20–TR23)

Leveled Text Library

Center Options
(pp. 10–11)

Use **Write in Response to Reading** on p. 7 of the *Reader's and Writer's Journal* to check children's understanding of key ideas in *Stellaluna.*

Phonics: Practice Readers

GUIDED READING OPTIONS

Use the **Leveled Text Library** to choose appropriate texts based on children's needs.

Use ***ReadyUp! Intervention*** for children who require additional instruction with this lesson's reading and foundational standards or with prerequisite standards.

STEP 2 Small Group Options

Based on formative assessments of children's progress, use the following options to provide additional instruction, practice, or extension as needed.

PHONICS

For children who need support with this week's Phonics skills, use pp. FS2–FS5 in this Teacher's Guide.

UNLOCK THE TEXT

For children who need support in accessing key ideas, key language, and key structures in ***Stellaluna,*** use **Unlock the Text** in the *Scaffolded Strategies Handbook,* pp. 8–13.

CONFERENCE

For independent reading accountability, **conference** each day with two or three children to discuss **self-selected texts** and support their reading.

CLOSE READING SUPPORT

For children who struggle with close reading, use this **Support Mini-Lesson for *Sleuth*.**

SLEUTH WORK Read aloud "How Polar Bears Hunt" on pp. 8–9 of *Sleuth*. Then discuss the following questions with the group. Have children use text evidence to support their answers.

LOOK FOR CLUES Find the first detail in the story that describes the place where polar bears live. What does it say about where they live? (Polar bears live where it is cold.)

ASK QUESTIONS What else would you like to know about polar bears and how they hunt? Have children dictate a list of questions they would like to ask.

MAKE YOUR CASE Find words that together mean *mothers* in the text. (*Mama bears*) Let's reread the paragraph that has the words in it.

PROVE IT! What do mama bears teach their cubs? (how to hunt) How do polar bears hunt? (They look for clues in the ice. Seals use cracks in the ice to come up for air, sun, and heat. Bears eat seals.)

Ask and answer questions about key details in a text. RI.1.1

CLOSE READING EXTENSION

For children who are adept or excel at close reading, use this **Extend Mini-Lesson for *Sleuth*.**

SLEUTH WORK Have children read "How Polar Bears Hunt" on pp. 8–9 of *Sleuth*. Then discuss the following questions with the group. Have children use text evidence to support their answers.

LOOK FOR CLUES What do polar bears eat? (seals) What do the baby birds in Stellaluna eat? (bugs)

ASK QUESTIONS What questions would you ask to compare the animals in "How Polar Bears Hunt" and *Stellaluna?* (Answers will vary.)

MAKE YOUR CASE How are mother polar bears and Mama Bird in *Stellaluna* alike? (They help their young get food.) Have children find details in the words or illustrations to support their answers.

PROVE IT! How do mother polar bears help their children get food? (They teach their children to hunt seals.) How does Mama Bird help her children get food? (She flies away and brings back bugs for them.) Ask children to point to the sentences in the texts that helped them answer the questions.

After children discuss the *Sleuth* work, direct them to pp. 8–9 of their *Reader's and Writer's Journal* to further explore "How Polar Bears Hunt."

Ask and answer questions about key details in a text. RI.1.1

OBJECTIVE

Retell an event in a narrative, using character details.
W.1.3

Narrative Writing

Use Character Details

SET THE PURPOSE Remind children that the elements of a story are characters, setting, and events. Explain that the elements answer the following questions:

- Who is in the story? (characters)
- Where and when is the story taking place? (setting)
- What is happening in the story? (events)

Tell children that today they will focus on including details to describe characters in their writing.

TEACH AND MODEL When a writer writes a story, he or she uses details that tell how the characters feel. Explain that the writer does not always convey a character's feelings directly using sentences such as "The birds felt surprised" or "The mother was scared." Instead, writers help readers understand a character's feelings by telling

- how the character acts.
- what the character says.
- how the character looks.

Point out that in *Stellaluna*, the illustrations convey how the characters look at key points of the story.

Provide the following models from p. 6 and p. 8 of *Stellaluna* that tell how characters act and what they say:

Dodging and shrieking, Mother Bat tried to escape, but the owl struck again and again, knocking Stellaluna into the air.

Dodging and *shrieking* are details that tell how Mother Bat acted when she was attacked. They help readers understand she is scared.

Wrapping her wings about her, she clutched the thin branch, trembling with cold and fear. "Mother," Stellaluna squeaked. "Where are you?"

These details show that Stellaluna is lost and frightened after her mother drops her.

Write About Characters and Events

PREPARE TO WRITE Explain that you will retell one of the scenes from *Stellaluna*. You will act as the writer, using details to help readers understand what is happening and how the characters feel during the events. Tell children you will retell the scene on pp. 14–16 in which Mama Bird comes home to find Stellaluna and the birds hanging off the edge of the nest.

First, model asking and answering questions about the story elements in *Stellaluna*.

- Who is in the story? (Mama Bird, the three baby birds, Stellaluna)
- Where and when is the story taking place? (the nest, in the daytime)
- What is happening in the story? (Mama Bird returns to the nest. She finds Stellaluna and the birds hanging upside-down. She scolds Stellaluna.)

MODEL NARRATIVE WRITING Read your story aloud as you write. Stop periodically to invite children to provide suggestions for details to add to your writing. Point out that although you are retelling only one event from the story, the actions are still told in order.

Mama Bird flew into the nest and gasped when she saw it was empty. Where were her baby birds? She quickly found them hanging upside down at the edge of the nest. Mama Bird squawked loudly. "Get back in the nest right away!" she said. Then Mama Bird scolded Stellaluna for teaching her babies such bad habits. Stellaluna promised she would behave herself from now on.

CHARACTERS IN WRITING Discuss the details you used in your writing that helped children understand how Mama Bird feels in the story.

- How does Mama Bird feel when she arrives at the nest? (afraid, surprised) What detail tells you she feels that way? (She gasps.)
- What does Mama Bird say and do to show she is angry? (squawks loudly, tells Stellaluna and the birds to get into the nest right away, scolds Stellaluna)

STRATEGIC SUPPORT

STORY ELEMENTS Use the illustration on page 15 of *Stellaluna* to help children understand how you answered the questions about the characters, setting, and events in your retelling. After you ask each question, point out the aspect of the illustration that helps provide the answer. You may also wish to reinforce the link between each question and the related story element by repeating the words *character, setting,* and *event* as you discuss the illustration and your answers.

OBJECTIVES

Write a narrative.
 W.1.3

Use technology to produce and publish writing and to collaborate with others. W.1.6

Print all upper- and lowercase letters.
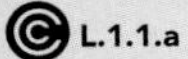 L.1.1.a

Independent Writing Practice

WRITE Ask children to think about one of the events they found interesting in *Stellaluna*. Then have children retell this event in their own words. Begin by having children answer the following questions:

- Who is in this event?
- Where does the event take place?
- What is happening in the event?
- What details can I include to tell about the characters?

Have children dictate or write three sentences on p. 10 of their *Reader's and Writer's Journal* to tell what happened during the event they chose to retell. Tell them to circle three words that give readers details about the characters.

CONVENTIONS If you wish to review using uppercase and lowercase letters correctly, use the Conventions Mini-Lesson on p. 41.

DIGITAL OPTIONS If available, have children practice using presentation software such as PowerPoint for their retellings. Have children type or dictate each sentence into a separate slide, then allow them to decorate each slide with related images, such as birds, insects, bats, and trees.

Share Writing

Ask volunteers to share their writing with the class. Ask the class to identify the details that tell something about the characters.

Writing Keystone Checklist

Writing About Story Elements

Use this checklist to assess children's narrative writing. If children need additional support writing about story elements, use the Unlock Narrative Writing beginning on p. 272 of the *Scaffolded Strategies Handbook*.

	Achieved	Notes
Identify the beginning, middle, and end of a story.		
Tell about the relationship between characters.		
Give details that describe characters.		
Tell about setting in a story.		
Tell about story events.		

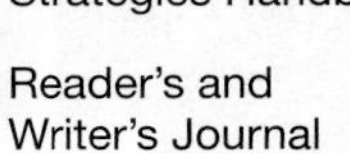

Conventions Mini-Lesson

Print Uppercase and Lowercase Letters

TEACH AND MODEL Review with children the difference between uppercase and lowercase letters. Review the uses of uppercase letters:

- The first letter of a character's name is uppercase.
- The first letter of the first word of a sentence is uppercase.
- The word *I* is always an uppercase letter.

When night came Stellaluna flew away. Pip, Flitter, and Flap leapt from the tree to follow her.

Point out that *Stellaluna*, *Pip, Flitter,* and *Flap* all begin with an uppercase letter. Note that *When* also begins with an uppercase letter because it is the first word in the sentence.

The bird landed on Brad's arm. "I will name you Bella," Brad said.

Point out the words *Brad* and *Bella* to children. Ask them to tell why each word starts with an uppercase letter. Do the same for *The* and *I*.

PRACTICE Have children turn to p. 18 in *Stellaluna* and identify character names. With partners, have children take turns saying the uppercase letters and lowercase letters in each of the character names on the page. You may wish to clarify for children that when a character name has two words, as in Mama Bird, both words begin with an uppercase letter. Ask partners to identify the other words with uppercase letters on the page (*All, Soon, One, Their, I'm, I*) and tell why the words begin with an uppercase letter. For more practice in writing uppercase and lowercase letters, have children turn to p. 10 of their *Reader's and Writer's Journal.*

Scaffolded Instruction

ENGLISH LANGUAGE LEARNERS

UPPERCASE AND LOWERCASE LETTERS To help English language learners better associate uppercase and lowercase letters with one another, play a matching game with magnetic letters or letter tiles. Have children match the uppercase letter with the correct lowercase letter. Then have children write both cases of letters on a sheet of paper.

LESSON 4

OBJECTIVES

Focus Retell a story using key details. RL.1.2

Identify events and the order in which they happen. RL.1.3

Text Complexity Rubrics
pp. TR48–TR54.

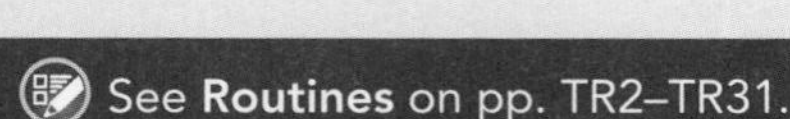
See **Routines** on pp. TR2–TR31.

Retell a Story's Events in Order

LESSON 4 FIRST READ Build Understanding

SET THE PURPOSE Focus the instruction for the unit by sharing the following Enduring Understanding: *Readers understand that they improve their comprehension by identifying story elements.* Story elements are the characters, setting, and the events of a story. We can identify characters, setting, and events to retell a story.

ENGAGE CHILDREN Introduce the story "Dragons and Giants." Display the cover page on p. 5 of the *Text Collection* and explain that this story comes from a bigger book called *Frog and Toad Together*. Point to Frog and Toad in the illustration and tell children that these are the characters in the story. Remind children to think about the Essential Questions as they read, talk, and write about the story: *How do readers know what makes a good retelling? How do writers create interesting events?* Tell children: In this lesson we are going to learn how readers can use characters, setting, and events to retell the story.

READ As you read "Dragons and Giants," use the appropriate reading routine from pp. TR8–TR19. Have children follow along as you read. Encourage them to read p. 7 with you and then on their own. In this first reading, children should be gaining a general understanding of what the story is mainly about.

TURN AND TALK After reading, have children turn to a partner and discuss this question using examples from the text: What did you learn about the events from the illustrations? Use the **Think-Pair-Share Routine** on pp. TR2–TR3 and make sure children are using best practices for speaking and listening as outlined in the routine. Tell children that they can ask and answer questions about what the speaker says to get more information or to clarify something they do not understand. (Children should share examples such as: Frog and Toad look afraid of the big snake, p. 9; Frog and Toad look afraid of the rocks, p. 11; Frog and Toad are not really brave, p. 15.)

FOUNDATIONAL SKILLS MINI-LESSON

High-Frequency Words, Short *a*

- Display the High-Frequency Word Cards for *I*, *see*, and *a*. Have children spell each word and then read it. Then ask them to use the words in sentences.
- Use Sound-Spelling Card 1 to review short *a*. Have children identify the letter and the sound it stands for. Write the words *at*, *mat*, and *Sam*. Ask children to say the sound for each letter and then blend the sounds to read the words.
- Have children turn to *Decodable Practice Reader R1B*, p. 9. Tell them to read the title and then take turns reading the book with a partner.

For more explicit instruction, see p. FS5 in this Teacher's Guide.

LESSON 4 SECOND READ

Close Read

CITE TEXT EVIDENCE Engage the class in a discussion about what you just read. Tell them to take turns speaking. Remind children that readers identify characters, setting, and events to retell a story. Use these questions to guide the discussion, and ask children to support their answers with evidence.

- What have Frog and Toad been reading about? (brave people) Why is this important to the story? I read that Frog wonders if he and Toad are brave, so they go outside to find out. The book is the reason Frog and Toad go on an adventure. **DOK L2**
- What do Frog and Toad decide to do first to prove they are brave? Let's read those sentences together. Have children chorally read the first three sentences on p. 8 with you. **DOK L1**
- What do Frog and Toad see first as they climb the mountain? (They see a dark cave and a big snake.) Point to the words that tell this. How do Frog and Toad react? Why? (They jump away because they are afraid.) **DOK L2**
- How do you think Frog and Toad feel at the end of page 11? Why do you think so? (They feel scared because big rocks are coming toward them.) Let's find a word on the page that tells how they feel. Children should point to and read the word *trembling*. **DOK L2**

BY-THE-WAY WORDS During close reading, define the following words for children involving known concepts that can be stumbling blocks to comprehending the text.

dragon, p. 6: Tell children that a dragon is a big animal that is supposed to look like a snake with wings and claws. It often breathes out fire and smoke.

avalanche, p. 10: Have children examine the illustration on p. 10 as you explain that an avalanche is when a lot of rocks, snow, or ice quickly fall down the side of mountain.

Scaffolded Instruction

ENGLISH LANGUAGE LEARNERS

MULTIPLE-MEANING WORD Explain to English language learners that the word *cried* has more than one meaning. In this text, *cried* means "to shout." Remind children that they can use surrounding words, illustrations, or other clues, such as an exclamation point, to help them figure out which meaning is correct.

STRATEGIC SUPPORT

KEY DETAILS Help children understand why the snake says "Hello lunch" on p. 9. Explain that some real snakes eat frogs and toads. The snake in the story wants to eat the characters Frog and Toad, so they run away.

OBJECTIVES

Determine the meaning of and use academic and domain-specific words in a text. RL.1.4; L.1.6

Retell a story using story elements. RL.1.2

BENCHMARK VOCABULARY

- brave, p. 6

BENCHMARK VOCABULARY

- Have children find and read the sentence from the text with the word *brave*.

Use the **Benchmark Vocabulary Routine for Literary Text** on pp. TR28–TR31 to teach the meaning of the word.

- Use the information on pp. 2–5 of this Teacher's Guide to discuss other words connected to the Benchmark Vocabulary word.

PRACTICE Have children use p. 11 in their *Reader's and Writer's Journal* to show contextual understanding of the Benchmark Vocabulary. Monitor children's vocabulary development.

Reading Analysis

TEXT TALK

RETELL Remind children that when readers retell a story, they tell about the characters, setting, and events. A good retelling tells about what happens in the beginning, middle, and end. Provide Story Sequence A graphic organizer on p. TR37.

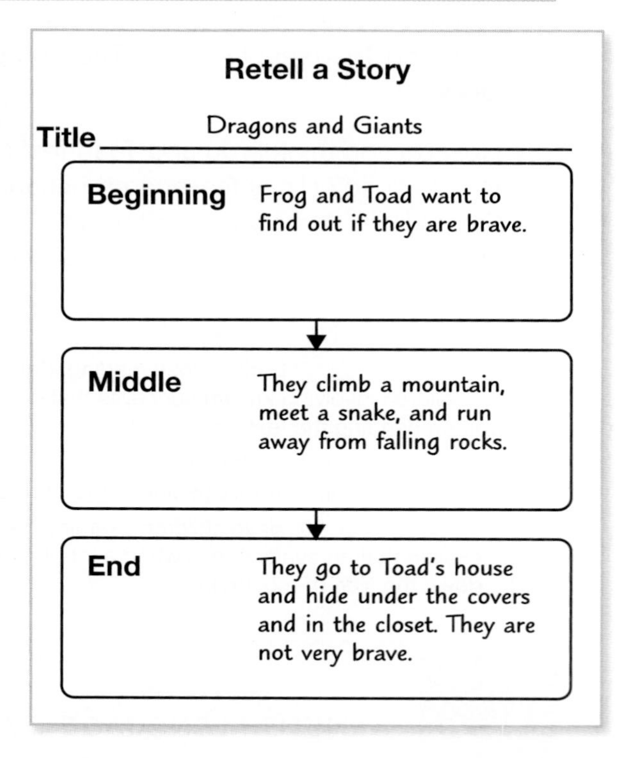

Retell a Story
Title Dragons and Giants
Beginning
Frog and Toad want to find out if they are brave.
Middle
They climb a mountain, meet a snake, and run away from falling rocks.
End
They go to Toad's house and hide under the covers and in the closet. They are not very brave.

MODEL Let's look at pages 6 and 7 to figure out what happens at the beginning of the story. What are Frog and Toad doing? I can go back and read about it. I read that they are reading a book about brave people. What do they decide to do? They decide to find out if they are brave! I'm going to write that in the first box of my graphic organizer.

PRACTICE/APPLY Have children work independently or in small groups to complete the graphic organizer by writing, dictating, or drawing events for each box. Use the **Small Group Discussion Routine** on pp. TR6–TR7 to have children discuss details about what happens in the middle and at the end of the story. Check understanding by asking children to share or by circulating among children or groups.

Small Group Time

STEP 1 Focused Independent Reading

BUILD ACCOUNTABILITY Prepare children to read their **self-selected text.** Announce the two focus points to the class, and help children make a plan for their reading. Children will apply both focus points to their self-selected text.

TODAY'S PROCESS FOCUS	
☑ Engagement and Identity	☐ Independence
☐ Stamina	

Display a variety of storybooks with illustrations. Tell children to select a book they think they will enjoy reading. Have them preview a few books by reading the title and examining the cover picture to determine if the book might be interesting.

TODAY'S STRATEGY FOCUS	
☐ Vocabulary Knowledge	☐ Critical Thinking
☐ Fluency	☑ Comprehension

Guide children in applying the content of today's Reading Analysis lesson to their self-selected texts. We learned that readers use characters, setting, and events to retell stories. Today as you are reading, identify the characters and setting. Write or draw notes about the pages that tell about the most important events at the beginning, in the middle, and at the end. Alternatively, have children log into Pearson Realize to find an Independent Reading Activity that is appropriate for the text they are reading.

MONITOR PROGRESS

- **Process Focus:** Have children draw a picture of their favorite part of their book. Then have them dictate or write a short phrase or sentence in their daily reading log that tells what they like about their book.
- **Strategy Focus:** Have children review with you the notes they made about the events. Ask them to use their notes to retell the beginning, middle, and end of their book. Alternatively, have children log into Pearson Realize and review with you the Independent Reading Activity they completed for their book.

For further guidance, see the **Independent Reading Routine** on pp. TR12–TR19.

While children are reading independently, use the Small Group Options on pp. 46–47.

INDEPENDENT LITERACY WORK

Text Club (pp. TR20–TR23)

Leveled Text Library

Center Options (pp. 10–11)

Use **Write in Response to Reading** on p. 11 of the *Reader's and Writer's Journal* to check children's understanding of key ideas in "Dragons and Giants."

Phonics: Decodable Practice Readers

GUIDED READING OPTIONS

Use the **Leveled Text Library** to choose appropriate texts based on children's needs.

Use ***ReadyUp! Intervention*** for children who require additional instruction with this lesson's reading and foundational standards or with prerequisite standards.

STEP 2

Small Group Options

Based on formative assessments of children's progress, use the following options to provide additional instruction, practice, or extension as needed.

PHONICS

For children who need support with this week's Phonics skill, use pp. FS2–FS5 in this Teacher's Guide.

UNLOCK THE TEXT

For children who need support in accessing key ideas, key language, and key structures in **"Dragons and Giants,"** use **Unlock the Text** in the *Scaffolded Strategies Handbook,* pp. 14–19.

CONFERENCE

For independent reading accountability, **conference** each day with two or three children to discuss **self-selected texts** and support their reading.

READING ANALYSIS SUPPORT

For children who struggle with retelling **"Dragons and Giants,"** use this **Support Reading Analysis Mini-Lesson**.

RETELL Help children retell the middle events of the story. Have them turn to p. 8 and ask guiding questions, such as: Where do Frog and Toad go? What do Frog and Toad do to find out if they are brave? Do Frog and Toad act brave? How do you know? As children answer the questions, have them find the words in the story that tell that information. Then have them draw a picture showing the event and write a label. Continue with the rest of the things that happen when Frog and Toad try to find out if they are brave. Have children use their drawings to retell the middle events.

Invite children to retell the end of the story on pp. 14–15 by drawing pictures of what happens. Then help them put the beginning, middle, and ending together to retell the whole story in their own words using their drawings. Use the **Think-Pair-Share Routine** on pp. TR2–TR3.

Retell a story using key details. RL.1.2

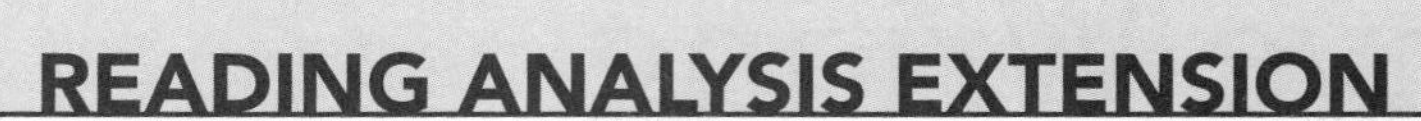

READING ANALYSIS EXTENSION

For children who can easily retell **"Dragons and Giants,"** use this **Extend Reading Analysis Mini-Lesson.**

RETELL Have children use their completed graphic organizer to retell "Dragons and Giants" to a small group. Then have them discuss the following questions:

- Why do Frog and Toad decide to find out if they are brave? (They are reading a book about brave people.)
- How do Frog and Toad react to meeting the snake? (They jump away. Toad starts shaking.) What does Toad say? ("I am not afraid!") What do Frog's and Toad's words and their actions tell about them? (Frog and Toad are not acting very brave, but they are shouting that they are not afraid.) Point to the illustration and words that helped you figure that out.
- Why do you think meeting the snake would show how brave Frog and Toad are? (Possible response: The snake is bigger than they are, so they might be afraid of it. When someone is brave, they are not afraid.)

Ask and answer questions about key details in a text. RL.1.1
Retell a story using key details. RL.1.2

FLUENCY

For fluent reading accountability, use the **Oral Reading Fluency Quick Check.** ☑ **Today assess 2–3 children.**

MODEL APPROPRIATE RATE Explain that reading at an appropriate rate means reading at just the right speed—not too fast and not too slow. Have children follow along as you model reading aloud p. 6 from "Dragons and Giants," first very quickly and then very slowly. Review why a reader would not want to read too slowly or too quickly. Then choral read with children a portion of a leveled text at an appropriate rate.

Read grade-level text with appropriate rate. RF.1.4.b

QUICK CHECK

MONITOR PROGRESS

If . . . children are reading too slowly,
then . . . have them practice reading aloud with a partner who can provide cues for the reader to speed up.

If . . . children are reading too quickly,
then . . . remind them to slow down because listeners have a hard time understanding any of the words.

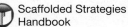

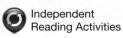

OBJECTIVE

Recount a narrative's beginning, middle, and end. W.1.3

Narrative Writing

Tell Beginning, Middle, and End

SET THE PURPOSE Review the concept of a narrative's beginning, middle, and end. Remind children that events in a narrative happen in order, or in sequence. Then tell them that they will be writing about an event from a story.

Display the illustrations in "Dragons and Giants." Talk about the beginning, middle, and end of the narrative. Guide the discussion with the following questions.

- What happens at the beginning of the story on page 6? (Frog and Toad are reading a book about brave people. Frog and Toad wonder if they are brave, so they decide to find out.)
- What happens in the middle of the story? (Frog and Toad run from a snake, an avalanche, and a hawk. Each time they say they are not afraid.)
- What happens at the end of the story? (Frog and Toad run back to Toad's house and decide to stay inside where they are brave together.)

TEACH AND MODEL Through discussion, help children notice how the writer helps readers understand and follow the sequence of events in the story. Provide the following models from pp. 8, 9, 10–12, and 13 of "Dragons and Giants" that show details about the events.

Frog and Toad went outside. "We can try to climb this mountain," said Frog.	The writer tells where the characters are and what they plan on doing: climb a mountain.
They came to a dark cave.	The writer tells the next place that the characters go. When the writer identifies a new location, readers can then understand that a new event is happening or about to happen.
They climbed higher, and they heard a loud noise. . . . They came to the top of the mountain.	The writer uses the words *higher* and *top* to show that the characters have worked their way up the mountain.
Then they ran down the mountain very fast. . . . They ran all the way to Toad's house.	The word *then* indicates the text event in the order it happened. The writer identifies the next place the characters go: Toad's house.

Write Events in Order

PREPARE TO WRITE Explain to children that they can use the books they read as examples for writing events in their own stories. By identifying the beginning, middle, and end in many stories, children will become familiar with plot patterns and be able to write their own order of events as they develop their own narrative writing.

WRITE A STORY Explain to children that you will model writing your own short story about Frog and Toad. Then you will list the events in order.

I am going to write and illustrate a new story about Frog and Toad. The beginning of my story will start when Frog and Toad run into a big snake. Listen closely to what happens. *Frog and Toad meet a big snake at the top of the hill. They stop and stare at it. The snake opens its mouth. Frog and Toad try to back away before the snake can eat them. They trip on some rocks and tumble down the hill. It wasn't the best way to get away from the snake, but it worked.*

IDENTIFY THE ORDER OF EVENTS Work with children to create a list of the events that happen in the new story. Then model writing a short sentence about each event.

1. meet a snake
2. try to back away
3. trip on rocks and tumble down a hill

Let's write a sentence that tells about each event. Then we can discuss what we can draw for each event.

Beginning: First, Frog and Toad see a big snake.
Middle: Then they try to get away from the snake when it opens its mouth.
End: Last, Frog and Toad fall down the hill when they trip on some rocks.

Explain to children that the words *first, then, when,* and *last* help readers follow the order of events in stories.

Scaffolded Instruction

STRATEGIC SUPPORT

ORDER OF EVENTS Children may have difficulty identifying the order of events of a story that does not use sequence words. Try telling the model story using the words *first, next, then,* and *last*. Then have children identify the order of events using those words. Reinforce the idea of sequence, or order, by pointing to the numbers on the list as you work with the class to identify the order of the events.

OBJECTIVES

Write notes about the order of events in a story. W.1.3

Draw a story event and then write a sentence about it.

With guidance, use technology to produce and publish writing and to collaborate with others. W.1.6

Spell words phonetically. L.1.2.e

Independent Writing Practice

TAKE NOTES Have children look through "Dragons and Giants" to identify the events that happen. As a class, take notes about the order of events in the story. For example:

1. read a book
2. start climbing a mountain
3. see a snake
4. hear and run away from an avalanche
5. see hawk
6. run home and hide

WRITE Have children draw an illustration for one part of the story and then write a sentence that tells what happened during that part of the story on p. 12 of their *Reader's and Writer's Journal*.

CONVENTIONS If you wish to teach children about spelling words phonetically, use the Conventions Mini-Lesson on p. 51. Encourage children to listen to the sounds of the words as they write them.

DIGITAL OPTIONS If available, have children use computers or tablets to type their sentence. Then print out their writing for children to illustrate.

Share Writing

Have volunteers share their illustrations and sentences, identifying if the event happened in the beginning, middle, or end of "Dragons and Giants." As a class, arrange children's work in order of the events in the story.

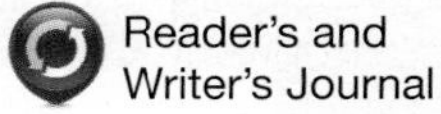

Conventions Mini-Lesson

Spell Words Phonetically

TEACH AND MODEL Explain that the sounds in a word may give writers good hints about how the word is spelled. Tell children that as they learn to correctly spell words, they can begin to spell words by listening to the sounds in the words. Read aloud this sentence: *Toad stayed in bed.* Have a volunteer write the sentence phonetically.

Phonetic Spelling: Tod stad in bed.

Point out that the word *Toad* has the long *o* sound, but it uses a special spelling pattern. Continue with the word *stayed*. Then point out how the words *in* and *bed* are spelled the way they sound.

PRACTICE Say these sentences one at a time: *A cat can jump. Sam ran fast.* Repeat each word and have volunteers write that word. For more practice with phonetic spelling, have children answer the question on p. 12 of their *Reader's and Writer's Journal*. Remind them to use the sounds they hear in the words to best answer the question.

Scaffolded Instruction

ENGLISH LANGUAGE LEARNERS

PHONETIC SPELLING English language learners may struggle with phonetic spelling if they are still learning the sounds for each letter or groups of letters. Work with children to find pictures in magazines, or draw their own, to represent the sound(s) each letter makes. Children can make flashcards or a poster of letters and their sounds. For example, children can find a picture of a dog or draw a picture for the sound /d/ spelled *Dd*.

OBJECTIVES

Focus Understand an author's word choice. RL.1.4

Use text evidence to answer questions about a story. RL.1.1

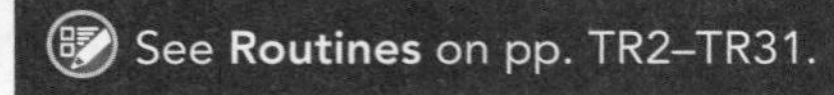
See **Routines** on pp. TR2–TR31.

Understand the Words Authors Use

LESSON 5 FIRST READ Build Understanding

SET THE PURPOSE Focus the instruction for the unit by sharing the following Enduring Understanding: *Writers understand that details play a role in explaining the events in a story.* Stories have details that tell about characters, setting, and events. Writers choose certain words to help readers better understand the events of a story.

ENGAGE CHILDREN Have children page through "Dragons and Giants" beginning on p. 5 of the *Text Collection* to remind them of the characters and events. Then ask children to point to the first sentence on p. 6. Identify the features of the sentence by explaining that the first word is written with an uppercase letter and the last word is followed by a punctuation mark. Have children identify those features in other sentences in the book. Remind children to think about the Essential Questions as they read, talk, and write about the story: *How do readers know what makes a good retelling? How do writers create interesting events?* Tell children: In this lesson we are going to look more closely at the details in the story.

READ As you read "Dragons and Giants," use the appropriate reading routine from pp. TR8–TR19. Have children follow along as you read. Encourage them to read aloud sentences with you and then on their own. In this reading, have children focus on interesting details or words.

TURN AND TALK After reading, have children turn to a partner and discuss this question using examples from the text: What are Frog and Toad afraid of? Use the **Think-Pair-Share Routine** on pp. TR2–TR3. Tell children to describe the things and events in the story with relevant details from the words and illustrations. (Children should identify a snake, p. 9, an avalanche, pp. 10–11, and a hawk, p. 12.)

FOUNDATIONAL SKILLS MINI-LESSON

Consonants *m*/m/, *s*/s/, *t*/t/; Short *a*

- Show Sound-Spelling Cards 15, 21, and 23 to review *m*/m/, *s*/s/, and *t*/t/. Have children name the picture and the sound the picture name begins with. Then have them identify the letter that spells that sound.
- Review short *a* using Sound-Spelling Card 1.
- Say words from "Dragons and Giants" one at a time and ask children to name the letter that spells the first sound. Use these words: *said, Toad, mountain, saw, mouth, top.*

For more explicit instruction, see p. FS5 in this Teacher's Guide.

LESSON 5
SECOND READ

Close Read

CITE TEXT EVIDENCE Engage the class in a discussion about what you just read. Tell them they can ask questions of their own to clear up any confusion about the text. Remind children that readers use details to better understand a story. Use these questions to guide the discussion, and ask children to support their answers with evidence.

- Look at how the author tells about Frog and Toad's trip back down the mountain on page 13. What do they run past as they go down? (They run past the places they saw on the way up: the place with the avalanche, the place with the snake.) Let's read that part together. **DOK L1**
- Ask your "reading sleuths" to explain if Frog and Toad are brave. Direct their attention to the text and illustration on pp. 14–15. What do Frog and Toad do when they get to Toad's house? Let's read those sentences together. Have children chorally read the sentences. What does the illustration show? (It shows what the words say.) What do Frog and Toad's actions tell about them? (They are afraid and not very brave.) **DOK L3**
- Why is the end of the story funny? (Frog and Toad think they are being brave, but they are hiding in the closet and under the covers.) When I think about what brave means and then think about what Frog and Toad are doing, I realize that their actions are not brave. Even though they say they are not afraid, their actions show the opposite. **DOK L2**
- Let's read what Frog and Toad say to each other at the end of the story. Have children read the dialogue with you. What does Frog and Toad's conversation tell about their friendship? (Possible response: They are good friends because they help each other feel brave.) Read the words or phrases that help you come to that conclusion. Children can point out *glad, happy,* and *a brave friend like you*. **DOK L3**

Scaffolded Instruction

ENGLISH LANGUAGE LEARNERS

VOCABULARY CLUES Make sure children understand the vocabulary clues that show and tell how frightened Frog and Toad are when they are outside. On p. 9, Toad was *shaking*. On p. 11, Frog was *trembling*. They scream, "We are not afraid" as they run away. Act out the meanings of the words *shaking* and *trembling*. Explain the contradiction of Frog and Toad yelling they are not afraid yet they run away.

STRATEGIC SUPPORT

HUMOR If children have difficulty understanding the humor at the end of the story, review the meaning of the word *brave*. Then discuss the illustrations on the last pages of the story. Ask why Frog and Toad are hiding—are these actions that brave people do?

OBJECTIVES

Determine the meaning of and use academic and domain-specific words in a text.

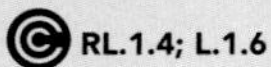 RL.1.4; L.1.6

Categorize words from a text to better understand their meanings.

 L.1.5.a

BENCHMARK VOCABULARY

- mountain, p. 8
- snake, p. 9

BENCHMARK VOCABULARY

- Have children find and read sentences from the text with the words *mountain* and *snake*.

  Use the **Benchmark Vocabulary Routine for Literary Text** on pp. TR28–TR31 to teach the meanings of the words.

- Use the information on pp. 2–5 of this Teacher's Guide to discuss other words connected to each of the Benchmark Vocabulary words.

PRACTICE Have children use p. 13 in their *Reader's and Writer's Journal* to show contextual understanding of the Benchmark Vocabulary. Monitor children's vocabulary development.

Language Analysis

TEXT TALK

CATEGORIZE WORDS

Tell children that words can be put into groups, or categories. Some words can be in categories based on what the words do: name things, show action, or describe. Provide a Three Sorting Circles graphic organizer on p. TR41. Label the circles "Words That Name," "Words That Show Action," and "Words That Describe."

Categorizing Words

Words That Name

cave, mountain, shadow, hawk, Frog, Toad, rock, place, avalanche, snake, house

Words That Show Action

came, fell, jumped, flew, screamed, ran

Words That Describe

dark, big, wide

MODEL Let's look at page 9 and find words that can fit in one of the categories. I see the words *dark cave*. The word *cave* names a place, so I'm going to write that in the "Words That Name" circle. Where should I write *dark?* The word *dark* describes, or tells about, the cave. So I will write *dark* in the "Words That Describe" circle.

PRACTICE/APPLY Have children work independently or in small groups to complete the graphic organizer using words from pp. 9–13. Use the **Small Group Discussion Routine** on pp. TR6–TR7 to have children discuss how these words make the story better and more interesting. Check understanding by asking children to share or by circulating among children or groups.

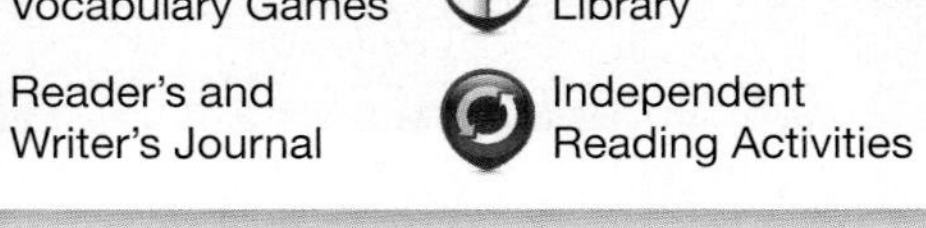

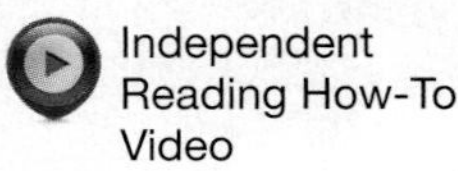

Small Group Time

STEP 1 Focused Independent Reading

BUILD ACCOUNTABILITY Prepare children to read their **self-selected texts**. Announce the two focus points to the class, and help children make a plan for their reading. Children will apply both focus points to their self-selected texts.

TODAY'S PROCESS FOCUS	
☑ Engagement and Identity	☐ Independence
☐ Stamina	

Tell children to select a book they think they will enjoy reading. Have them choose a few books with interesting titles or cover illustrations. Ask children to quickly look at the pictures inside to determine which book interests them the most.

TODAY'S STRATEGY FOCUS	
☑ Vocabulary Knowledge	☐ Critical Thinking
☐ Fluency	☐ Comprehension

Guide children in applying the content of today's Language Analysis lesson to their self-selected texts. We learned that the words *dark, big,* and *wide* are words that describe. They can be put in the same category, or group, to show how they are alike. Today as you are reading, I would like you to find words that can fit into the category *Words that Describe*. When you find a word, write it on a sheet of paper in a list and keep reading. Alternatively, have children log into Pearson Realize to find an Independent Reading Activity that is appropriate for the text they are reading.

MONITOR PROGRESS

- **Process Focus:** Have children record their reading in a daily reading log by drawing a picture of their favorite part. Then have them use their drawing to tell you about their book.
- **Strategy Focus:** Have children review with you the words they found. Ask them to explain why the word fits in the *Words That Describe* category by telling what the word describes in the book. Alternatively, have children log into Pearson Realize and review with you the Independent Reading Activity they completed for their book.

For further guidance, see the **Independent Reading Routine** on pp. TR12–TR19.

While children are reading independently, use the Small Group Options on pp. 56–57.

INDEPENDENT LITERACY WORK

Text Club (pp. TR20–TR23)

Leveled Text Library

Center Options (pp. 10–11)

Use **Write in Response to Reading** on p. 13 of the *Reader's and Writer's Journal* to check children's understanding of key ideas in "Dragons and Giants."

Phonics: Decodable Practice Readers

GUIDED READING OPTIONS

Use the **Leveled Text Library** to choose appropriate texts based on children's needs.

Use ***ReadyUp! Intervention*** for children who require additional instruction with this lesson's reading and foundational standards or with prerequisite standards.

STEP 2 Small Group Options

Based on formative assessments of children's progress, use the following options to provide additional instruction, practice, or extension as needed.

PHONICS

For children who need support with this week's Phonics skill, use pp. FS2–FS5 in this Teacher's Guide.

UNLOCK THE TEXT

For children who need support in accessing key ideas, key language, and key structures in **"Dragons and Giants,"** use **Unlock the Text** in the *Scaffolded Strategies Handbook*, pp. 14–19.

CONFERENCE

For independent reading accountability, **conference** each day with two or three children to discuss **self-selected texts** and support their reading.

LANGUAGE ANALYSIS SUPPORT

For children who struggle with categorizing words in **"Dragons and Giants,"** use this **Support Language Analysis Mini-Lesson.**

CATEGORIZE WORDS Help children begin by adding words they know to the categories in order to better understand the concept of each category. Remind children that "Words That Name" can be people, places, animals, or things. What names for things in the classroom can we add? Write children's suggestions. Continue explaining the other categories and prompting children to identify words they know that fit in it. If necessary, provide clues for specific words they will know, such as *pencil, dance,* and *tall*. Then return to the story to help children find words to add to each category.

Invite children to discuss with a partner why each word fits in the category it is in. Use the **Think-Pair-Share Routine** on pp. TR2–TR3.

Sort words into categories to understand the concept of the categories. L.1.5.a

LANGUAGE ANALYSIS EXTENSION

For children who can easily categorize words in **"Dragons and Giants,"** use this **Extend Language Analysis Mini-Lesson.**

CATEGORIZE WORDS Have children continue adding words to their Three Sorting Circles graphic organizer by looking for words in other books to fit in the categories. When children have at least three new words in each category, ask them to construct simple sentences using one word from each category. Provide a model for children.

- I want to choose one word from each group to make a sentence. I choose the words *hawk, flew,* and *big*. What sentence can I make that uses these words? *The big hawk flew*. What other words can we add to this sentence to make it more interesting? *The big hawk flew in the sky*.

Discuss how to put the words in the correct order. Challenge children to create silly sentences using the words in their categories: *The silly snake skipped*. *The small rock crawled*.

Sort words into categories to understand the concept of the category.
L.1.5.a

READING ACTIVITY MATS

For comprehension and vocabulary practice, use the **Reading Activity Mat** Graphic Organizer on Pearson Realize.

COMPREHENSION FOCUS Work with children in small groups to build comprehension skills by using the EnVision Math Problem-Solving Reading Mat *Farm animals*. Follow the teaching plan on the instruction page that accompanies the student graphic organizer on Pearson Realize.

VOCABULARY FOCUS Work with children in small groups to build their vocabulary skills by using the EnVision Math Problem-Solving Reading Mat *Farm animals*. Follow the teaching plan that accompanies the graphic organizer.

If children need more time to complete the activity, have them log in to Pearson Realize during Small Group Time in subsequent lessons throughout the module.

OBJECTIVE

Write a narrative that recounts details about characters.

 W.1.3

Narrative Writing

Use Character Details

SET THE PURPOSE Remind children that a story has characters, setting, and events. The characters are who or what the story is about. The setting is when and where the story takes place, and the events are what happen in the story. Writers use details to tell more about these parts of a story. Tell children that today they will focus on using details to describe characters in their writing.

TEACH AND MODEL Writers use details to tell what characters look like, what they say, what they do, and how they feel. These details help readers better understand the characters. Explain to children that readers can use the details in a story to make up their minds about the characters.

Provide the following models from pp. 6, 13–15 of "Dragons and Giants" that show details about Frog and Toad's friendship.

"Frog and Toad were reading a book together."	The writer does not directly say that Frog and Toad are friends. He writes about an activity that Frog and Toad do together to show they are friends.
"We are not afraid!" screamed Frog and Toad at the same time.	The writer uses the phrase *at the same time* to give readers a clue that Frog and Toad are experiencing the adventure together, like friends do.
"Frog, I am glad to have a brave friend like you," said Toad. . . . "And I am happy to know a brave person like you, Toad," said Frog.	The writer uses what the characters say to show how they feel about each other.
They stayed there for a long time, just feeling very brave together.	The word *together* explains that Frog and Toad are good friends.

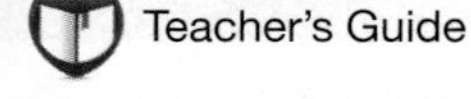

Write Details About Characters

PREPARE TO WRITE Explain to children that you will write a few sentences about Frog and Toad's friendship. Instead of writing about their friendship directly, tell children that you will show their friendship through details about what they say and do. Tell children you will write a new ending to "Dragons and Giants" that show details about the characters and their friendship.

WRITE A NARRATIVE Read your writing aloud as you write. Stop occasionally to ask children to provide details to add to your writing. Remind them to think about what details would best tell about Frog and Toad's friendship.

Listen to my story as I write: Frog and Toad reach Toad's home safely. Frog asks, "Are you okay, Toad? I was worried that you were going to fall down that steep mountain."

"I'm fine, Frog. How are you? I thought that snake was going to eat you for lunch. I was ready to grab you and pull you to safety if he tried!"

DISCUSS DETAILS Review with children how the dialogue in your story between Frog and Toad helps readers understand their friendship. Underline *are you okay*. What can you tell about Frog because he asks this about Toad? (Frog cares about Toad because he wants to make sure he is okay.) Continue with the word *worried* and the phrase *pull you to safety*. Ask children to discuss how the writer's word choice helps "show" details about Frog and Toad's friendship rather than "tell" about it.

Scaffolded Instruction

STRATEGIC SUPPORT

CHARACTER DETAILS Children may have difficulty identifying and understanding words or phrases that show that two characters are friends. Have a discussion about what friendship means and what friends do and say to each other. Capture words and phrases that children suggest in a list. Review the list to emphasize the different ways writers can explain how and why people are friends.

OBJECTIVES

Write a narrative that recounts details about characters.  W.1.3

With guidance, use technology to produce and publish writing and to collaborate with others. W.1.6

Spell words phonetically. L.1.2.e

Independent Writing Practice

BRAINSTORM As a class, make a list of activities, games, or other adventures that Frog and Toad might do together as friends. Children will use that list to help them draw a picture and write a sentence about Frog and Toad's friendship.

WRITE Have children draw and write about Frog and Toad's friendship. Children can use ideas from the list the class worked on together or they can think of their own. Have children

- draw a picture that shows Frog and Toad doing something together as friends.
- write or dictate a sentence on p. 14 of the *Reader's and Writer's Journal* that tells about the picture and Frog and Toad's friendship.

CONVENTIONS If you wish to teach children about spelling words phonetically, use the Conventions Mini-Lesson on p. 61. Encourage children to listen to the sounds of the words as they write narratives or other kinds of writing.

DIGITAL OPTIONS If available, have children use computers or tablets to type their sentence. Then print out their writing for children to illustrate on the same page.

Share Writing

Ask volunteers to share their writing with the class. Discuss the words in the sentences that help readers understand that Frog and Toad are friends.

Conventions Mini-Lesson

Spell Words Phonetically

TEACH AND MODEL Remind children that the sounds in a word may give writers good clues about how the word is spelled. Tell children that they can learn to correctly spell words by listening to the sounds in the words. Read aloud this sentence: *They came to a dark cave.* Have volunteers write the words *came* and *cave* phonetically.

Phonetic Spelling: They cam to a dark cav.

The words *came* and *cave* have the long *a* sound. That means you say the name of the letter *a* when you read each word.

PRACTICE Read aloud the second sentence on p. 9 of "Dragons and Giants": *A big snake came out of the cave*. Then have volunteers write the words *big, snake, came,* and *cave*. After volunteers have written the words phonetically, write the correct spellings. Point out that e at the end of *snake, came,* and *cave* is silent, but it tells readers to say the name of the letter *a*. For more practice with phonetic spelling, have children answer the question on p. 14 of their *Reader's and Writer's Journal*. Remind them to use the sounds they hear in the word to best answer the question.

Scaffolded Instruction

ENGLISH LANGUAGE LEARNERS

PHONETIC SPELLING Engage English language learners in understanding how long vowels say their names. Provide picture cards of objects with long vowels, such as *rake, bike, five, cone, bone, slide,* and *cube*. As children identify each object, have them identify the vowel that says its name. For example, children should identify the letter *a* when they say *rake*. Then write the name of the object and point to the letter that spells the long vowel sound.

OBJECTIVES

Focus Compare the adventures and experiences of characters in stories. RL.1.9

Use details in the words and illustrations to tell about characters and events in stories. RL.1.3, RL.1.9

See **Routines** on pp. TR2–TR31.

Compare Characters

LESSON 6 FIRST READ

Build Understanding

SET THE PURPOSE Explain to children that as they revisit both *Stellaluna* and "Dragons and Giants," they will explore the following Enduring Understanding: *Learners understand that living things depend on one another.* Remember that characters are the people or animals in a story. Today, we are going to look at the characters in both stories we have read and find ways their experiences and adventures are alike and different. The characters in these books depend, or need, one another.

ENGAGE CHILDREN Display the cover of *Stellaluna* and "Dragons and Giants" on p. 5 of the *Text Collection.* Recall with children the basic plot of each story. Discuss what the stories have in common: they both have characters, outdoor settings, exciting events, etc. Remind children to think about the following Essential Questions as they read, talk, and write about the texts: *How do readers know what makes a good retelling? How do writers create interesting events?* Tell children: In this lesson, we are going to learn how to use details in the words or illustrations to compare and contrast characters' experiences and adventures.

READ Read "Dragons and Giants" with children. Encourage children to read along silently. Pause to allow children to turn the pages. Then page through *Stellaluna* to help children recall the events and details about the characters. As you read, use the appropriate reading routine from pp. TR8–TR19. Have children focus on details that tell about the relationship between the characters in each story.

TURN AND TALK After reading, have children turn to a partner and discuss these questions using examples from the texts: How are Frog and Toad good friends? How are Stellaluna and the birds good friends? Use the **Think-Pair-Share Routine** on pp. TR2–TR3 and make sure children are using best practices for speaking and listening outlined in the routine. (Children should share examples such as: Frog and Toad read books together, p. 6; They go on adventures together, pp. 8–12; Stellaluna and the birds teach each other things, p.14.)

FOUNDATIONAL SKILLS MINI-LESSON

Consonants *c*/k/, *p*/p/, *n*/n/

- Display the Picture Card *cat.* Let's say *cat.* Now let's say the first sound in *cat:* /k/.
- Display Sound-Spelling Card 3. Point to *c.* The letter *c* can stand for the sound /k/, which you hear at the beginning of *carrot.* Write *carrot.* What is the first sound in *carrot?* What letter can stand for the sound /k/? Write *c.*
- Repeat the procedure for *p* and *n,* using Picture Cards *pan* and *nut* and Sound-Spelling Cards 18 and 16.

For more explicit instruction, see p. FS6 in this Teacher's Guide.

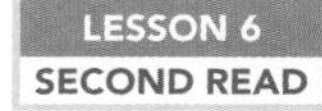

Close Read

CITE TEXT EVIDENCE Engage the class in a discussion about what you just read. Remind children that readers use details in the words and illustrations to help them understand characters. Use these questions to guide the discussion about pp. 40–45 of *Stellaluna,* and ask children to support their answers with evidence.

- The text says, "As the birds flew among the bats, Flap said, 'I feel upside down here.' So the birds hung by their feet." How are Flap's words connected to the illustration on page 41? (The illustration shows what happens in the text.) How are the bats and birds different? How are they alike? (They both have wings and can fly. Birds have feathers and beaks; bats don't.) Show me where you found the information. **DOK L3**

- What happens on pages 42–43? (The birds try to fly at night, but they can't see. Stellaluna has to save them.) Let's read what the characters say that tells this. Read aloud what each character says with expression, and then have children echo read the dialogue. How do the birds feel? (scared) Show me how you know this. Children should identify the words *yelled, howled,* and *shrieked* and the exclamation mark. **DOK L1**

- On page 44, the text says, "They perched in silence for a long time." What do you think Stellaluna and the birds were thinking about? (Possible response: how alike and different they are) Let's read the sentences that tell ways they are different. **DOK L2**

BY-THE-WAY WORDS During close reading, define the following word for children involving known concepts that can be stumbling blocks to comprehending the text.

excitedly, p. 40: Help children recognize the word part *excited*. Tell them that Stellaluna speaks in an excited way.

Scaffolded Instruction

ENGLISH LANGUAGE LEARNERS

VOCABULARY Review the meanings of *alike* and *different* with children. Point out items in the classroom that are both alike and different, such as: *A pencil and a crayon are alike because they can both be used for writing. They are different because they look different and make different kinds of lines.*

STRATEGIC SUPPORT

CLOSE READING If children have difficulty understanding why Stellaluna has to grab the birds as shown in the illustration on p. 43, reread p. 42 and remind children that the birds can't see in the dark. Ask: *What might happen if the birds keep trying to fly around the trees?*

OBJECTIVES

Determine the meaning of and use academic and domain-specific words in a text.
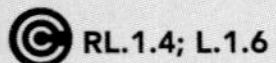 RL.1.4; L.1.6

Compare characters using details from the stories. RL.1.9

BENCHMARK VOCABULARY

- nighttime, p. 36
- crash, p. 42
- rescue, p. 42

BENCHMARK VOCABULARY

- Have children find and read sentences from *Stellaluna* with the words *nighttime, crash,* and *rescue*.
  Use the **Benchmark Vocabulary Routine for Literary Text** on pp. TR28–TR31 to teach the meanings of the words.
- Use the information on pp. 2–5 of this Teacher's Guide to discuss other words connected to each of the Benchmark Vocabulary words.

PRACTICE Have children use p. 16 in their *Reader's and Writer's Journal* to show contextual understanding of the Benchmark Vocabulary. Monitor children's vocabulary development.

Reading Analysis

TEXT TALK

COMPARE CHARACTERS

Tell children that comparing characters means telling how they are alike. Explain that when we read more than one story, we can think about each character's experiences and find ways to compare and contrast them. Provide a T-Chart on p. TR39. Write "Frog and Toad" and "Stellaluna" as headings.

Comparing Characters

Frog and Toad	Stellaluna
• animals • have an exciting adventure • help each other • learn about themselves	• bat • has an exciting adventure • helps her bird friends • learns about herself

MODEL Let's read the last paragraph on page 42 of *Stellaluna*. I read that Stellaluna needs to rescue her bird friends. She grabs them and puts them on a tree branch. I'm going to write "helps her bird friends" on the chart. Do Frog and Toad help each other? They do! Let's look in the story and find out how.

PRACTICE/APPLY Have children work as a group to complete the graphic organizer with details that tell about the appearance, traits, and events that involve the characters. Use the **Whole Class Discussion Routine** on pp. TR4–TR5. Have children complete p. 17 in their *Reader's and Writer's Journal.* They should circle the words that tell how Stellaluna, Frog, and Toad are the same. Then have them draw a picture to show how the characters are alike.

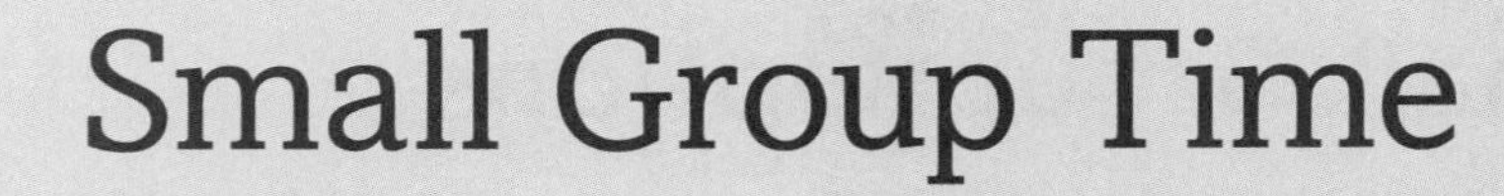

Generative Vocabulary Games
Reader's and Writer's Journal
Leveled Text Library
Independent Reading Activities
Independent Reading How-To Video

Small Group Time

STEP 1 Focused Independent Reading

BUILD ACCOUNTABILITY Prepare children to read their **self-selected texts.** Announce the two focus points to the class, and help children make a plan for their reading. Children will apply both focus points to their self-selected texts.

TODAY'S PROCESS FOCUS	
☐ Engagement and Identity	☑ Independence
☐ Stamina	

Tell children to choose a book they know well or one that has been read to them or with them before. Encourage them to read their book on their own today.

TODAY'S STRATEGY FOCUS	
☐ Vocabulary Knowledge	☐ Critical Thinking
☑ Fluency	☐ Comprehension

Guide children in improving their oral reading fluency using their self-selected texts. When we read aloud, we want listeners to be able to understand us. We should read at a speed that is not too slow or too fast. One way to get better at this is to practice reading aloud. Today as you are reading, choose one page you know well to read many times. First, whisper read it to yourself. Then read it again and again. Alternatively, have children log into Pearson Realize to find an Independent Reading Activity that is appropriate for the text they are reading.

MONITOR PROGRESS

- **Process Focus:** Have children record their reading in a daily reading log. They should write how well they know the book they chose. They can also write notes about what to remember to help them read their book more independently the next time they read it.
- **Strategy Focus:** Have children read aloud to you the page they have been practicing. Provide feedback on accuracy and rate. Alternatively, have children log into Pearson Realize and review with you the Independent Reading Activity they completed for their book.

For further guidance, see the **Independent Reading Routine** on pp. TR12–TR19.

While children are reading independently, use the Small Group Options on pp. 66–67.

INDEPENDENT LITERACY WORK

Text Club (pp. TR20–TR23)

Leveled Text Library

Center Options (pp. 10–11)

Use **Write in Response to Reading** on p. 16 of the *Reader's and Writer's Journal* to check children's opinion of *Stellaluna* and "Dragons and Giants."

Phonics: Decodable Practice Readers

GUIDED READING OPTIONS

Use the **Leveled Text Library** to choose appropriate texts based on children's needs.

Use ***ReadyUp! Intervention*** for children who require additional instruction with this lesson's reading and foundational standards or with prerequisite standards.

STEP 2 Small Group Options

Based on formative assessments of children's progress, use the following options to provide additional instruction, practice, or extension as needed.

PHONICS

For children who need support with this week's Phonics skill, use pp. FS6–FS9 in this Teacher's Guide.

UNLOCK THE TEXT

For children who need support in accessing key ideas, key language, and key structures in ***Stellaluna*** and **"Dragons and Giants,"** use **Unlock the Text** in the *Scaffolded Strategies Handbook,* pp. 8–13 and 14–19.

CONFERENCE

For independent reading accountability, **conference** each day with two or three children to discuss **self-selected texts** and support their reading.

READING ANALYSIS SUPPORT

For children who struggle with comparing characters from ***Stellaluna*** and **"Dragons and Giants,"** use this **Support Reading Analysis Mini-Lesson.**

COMPARE CHARACTERS Page through the texts and ask direct questions about the characters. Are Frog and Toad animals? What is Stellaluna? Is that an animal or a person? What do Frog and Toad do together? Are they good friends? How do you know? Who are Stellaluna's friends? Is she nice to them? What does Stellaluna experience? What do Frog and Toad experience? Add children's ideas to the T-Chart. Then model how to compare one piece of information from each column.

Invite children to find other comparisons between the columns. Use the **Think-Pair-Share Routine** on pp. TR2–TR3.

Compare characters' adventures and experiences. RL.1.9

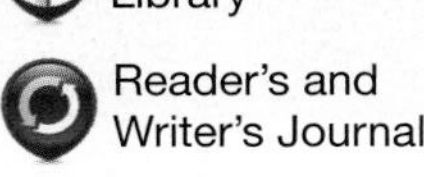

Scaffolded Strategies Handbook

Independent Reading Activities

Leveled Text Library

Reader's and Writer's Journal

Games

READING ANALYSIS EXTENSION

For children who can easily compare characters from ***Stellaluna*** and **"Dragons and Giants,"** use this **Extend Reading Analysis Mini-Lesson.**

COMPARE CHARACTERS After children compare Frog and Toad to Stellaluna, have them choose a character from another story to compare to Frog, Toad, or Stellaluna. Tell children to use a T-chart to list details about the chosen characters and then circle the things the characters have in common. Then have children share their comparisons with a partner and use the following questions to guide the discussion, comparing their characters with their partner's:

- Which of the characters are animals? Which are people?
- Which characters seem real? What details in the text tell you that?
- What kinds of experiences or adventures do the characters have?
- What do the characters learn? How do they learn it?

Compare characters' adventures and experiences. RL.1.9

FLUENCY

For fluent reading accountability, use the **Oral Reading Fluency Quick Check.** ☑ **Today assess 2–3 children.**

MODEL EXPRESSION Explain to children that reading with expression helps make a story more interesting for the listener. When we read with expression, we read with feeling. When we read what characters say, we can read to show excitement or to show fear. Turn to p. 9 of "Dragons and Giants" and read aloud the last sentence with expression: "I am not afraid!" he cried. Explain that quotation marks show the exact words a character says. Then point to the exclamation point and tell children that this punctuation mark tells readers that this sentence should be read with strong feeling. Does Toad say this loudly or quietly? (loudly) Why? (He is scared even though he says he is not.) Have children follow along as you read the sentence "Toad was shaking." Then have children say the last sentence with strong feeling and expression. Repeat with p. 42 of *Stellaluna*.

Read grade-level text with appropriate expression. RF.1.4.b

QUICK CHECK

MONITOR PROGRESS

If . . . children are struggling to read with expression,

then . . . encourage them to practice reading the sentence with different emotions to see which fits best in the situation.

If . . . children are not reading the right sections with expression,

then . . . review with them what punctuation marks can tell readers about a sentence.

OBJECTIVE

Write a narrative that recounts details about events.

 W.1.3

Narrative Writing

Event Details

SET THE PURPOSE Remind children that stories have events in the beginning, middle, and end. A story's events happen in a certain order. Tell children they will be writing details about a story event.

TEACH AND MODEL Explain to children that when writers write about events in a story, they include details to help readers better understand what is happening. Sometimes writers think about what kinds of questions readers might have as they read, so they write details that might answer those questions. Provide examples of questions writers can use to make sure their events have details to help readers, such as:

- What makes this event happen?
- Where is this event happening?
- How do the characters feel about what is happening?

Provide the following models from p. 12 of *Stellaluna* and p. 8 of "Dragons and Giants" that show details about the events:

Finally, though, the little bat could bear it no longer. She climbed into the nest, closed her eyes, and opened her mouth. *Plop!* In dropped a big green grasshopper!

The writer uses details to tell about the event when Stellaluna is so hungry that she eats the birds' food.

Frog went leaping over rocks, and Toad came puffing up behind him.

The writer uses the words *leaping* and *puffing up* to tell more about what happens when Frog and Toad climb the mountain. It is not an easy task for them.

Write About a Story Event

PREPARE TO WRITE Remind children that when they write about events in a narrative, they should include details to help readers better understand their story. Sometimes writers will write about the event and then go back to add details. Tell children that when they finish writing about an event for a narrative, they can go back and answer these questions:

- Is the event clear to readers?
- What else do readers need to know to understand what is happening?

RETELL THE EVENT Explain that you will model how to write details about an event from "Dragons and Giants." I'm going to write about when Frog and Toad meet the hawk. I'm going to use the words and the picture in the story to retell the event. Then I will go back to add details. Read aloud your writing, pointing to each word as you say it.

Frog and Toad finally get to the top of the big mountain. A hawk's shadow fell over them. The hawk was huge! It swooped so close to Frog and Toad. They jumped under a rock. The hawk flew away.

Point out that the underlined parts are details that you added to make the event more interesting and help readers understand why Frog and Toad run away from the hawk.

Scaffolded Instruction

STRATEGIC SUPPORT

EVENT DETAILS Some children may have difficulty deciding which details are relevant and necessary to be included in their writing. Tell them to ask themselves *Is this detail needed for readers to understand what is happening? Is this detail needed for readers to understand what happened before or what will happen after?* If the answer is no, children do not need to include the detail. If the answer is yes, they should look back at their writing to decide on the best place to add the detail.

OBJECTIVES

Write a narrative by telling about a story event using details.  W.1.3

With guidance, use technology to produce and publish writing and to collaborate with others. W.1.6

Spell words phonetically. L.1.2.e

Independent Writing Practice

WRITE Have children choose an event from *Stellaluna* or "Dragons and Giants." Ask them to look back at the appropriate story to recall what happened. Tell children to use details from the words and illustrations to recount the event they chose. Children should

- use details in the words and picture to write about what happened.
- include details to help readers better understand the event.

Have children use p. 18 of their *Reader's and Writer's Journal* to write about the event.

CONVENTIONS If you wish to teach children about spelling phonetically, use the Conventions Mini-Lesson on p. 71. Encourage children to use the sounds they hear in the words to spell words in their narrative writing.

DIGITAL OPTIONS If available, have children use computers or tablets to type their sentences and print them. Then, on the same sheet of paper, have them draw a picture to illustrate their sentences.

Share Writing

Ask volunteers to share their event with the class. Have the class discuss the details that were used in the writing. Ask them if there are other details that could be added that would make the writing better.

Conventions Mini-Lesson

Spell Words Phonetically

TEACH AND MODEL Remind children that sounds in a word may give writers good clues for how to spell the word. Sometimes, however, the sounds of vowels are not as easy to hear. When a vowel is a short vowel, it has a different sound than a long vowel, which says the name of the vowel. Introduce short vowel sounds to children so they can begin to listen for those sounds in words as they continue phonetic spelling.

> Flap, Flitter, and Pip ate bugs.

As children are familiar with the names of the baby birds in *Stellaluna*, point out that each name has a short vowel sound.

PRACTICE Have children work in small groups. Ask them to brainstorm a word for each of the short vowels. You may give them a model word to help them hear the sound, for example, *cat, bed, hit, got,* and *hug*. For more practice with phonetic spelling, have children answer the question on p. 18 of their *Reader's and Writer's Journal*. Remind them to use the sounds they hear in the word to best answer the question.

Scaffolded Instruction

ENGLISH LANGUAGE LEARNERS

PHONETIC SPELLING English language learners may find the short vowel sounds difficult to hear when they are saying words aloud. Continue to provide samples of words along with pictures of those words to help them practice the vowel sounds. You may even provide simple sentences to have them write, such as: *The fat cat sat.*

OBJECTIVES

Focus Understand how word choices enable an author to explain the events in a story.

 RL.1.3, RL.1.4

Use details in a story to tell about characters and events. RL.1.3

 See **Routines** on pp. TR2–TR31.

Understand That Authors Choose Words to Tell a Story

LESSON 7 FIRST READ Build Understanding

SET THE PURPOSE Focus the instruction by sharing the following Enduring Understanding: *Writers understand that details play a role in explaining the events in a story*. We are going to read parts of *Stellaluna* again and look closely at the words the author uses to tell the story. Remember that authors write the words in a story. They choose what words to use to make the story interesting for readers.

ENGAGE CHILDREN Display an illustration from the beginning, middle, or end of *Stellaluna* and have children explain what is happening. As children share minor details, point out that the author adds those details to the story to make it more interesting for readers. Remind children of the Essential Questions: *How do readers know what makes a good retelling? How do writers create interesting events?* Tell children: In this lesson we are going to learn about the words that authors choose to use in a story and how those words can make a story better.

READ Read aloud pp. 5–10 of *Stellaluna*. As you read, pause at words and phrases that children may recognize or know how to decode and have them chorally read with you. Use the appropriate reading routine from pp. TR8–TR19. In this reading, have children focus on the interesting words and phrases they read.

TURN AND TALK After reading, have children turn to a partner and discuss this question and point to the place in the text where they found the answer: What happens to Stellaluna after the owl attack? Use the **Think-Pair-Share Routine** on pp. TR2–TR3, making sure children are using best practices for speaking and listening outlined in the routine. (Children should explain that Stellaluna fell down into the forest, p. 6.)

FOUNDATIONAL SKILLS MINI-LESSON

High-Frequency Words; Consonants c/k/, p/p/, n/n/

- Display the High-Frequency Word Card *see*. Have children spell and say the word. The word *see* is spelled *s-e-e*. Have children write the word and use it in a sentence. Repeat with *I* and *the*.
- Use Sound-Spelling Cards 3, 18, and 16 to review consonants *c*, *p*, and *n*.
- Have children turn to *Decodable Practice Reader R2A* on p. 17. Ask them to read aloud the title and then read the story with a partner.

For more explicit instruction, see p. FS7 in this Teacher's Guide.

Close Read

CITE TEXT EVIDENCE Engage the class in a discussion about what you just read. Remind children that readers look closely at the words and details the author uses to tell about the events. Use these questions to guide the discussion, and ask children to support their answers with evidence.

- What does Mother Bat do with Stellaluna each night? (Mother Bat carries Stellaluna when she searches for food.) Let's read that part together. Point to each word in the last sentence on p. 5 as you read it, having children repeat after you. **DOK L1**
- On page 6 the author repeats some words. Read aloud the third sentence and point out the word *again.* Then read aloud the last sentence, pointing out the words *down* and *faster.* Why do you think the author repeats those words? (The words *again and again* make it clear the owl strikes the bats many times. The words *down, down she went* show that Stellaluna falls a long distance. *Faster and faster, into the woods below* shows that Stellaluna picks up speed as she falls.) **DOK L3**
- What words and phrases does the author use to describe the owl? *(silent wings, powerful, swooped)* How do those words make you feel about the owl? (Possible response: The owl seems big and scary.) **DOK L2**
- How does Stellaluna feel when she lands in the branches? (She is afraid and lonely.) Let's find words the author uses to support that idea. The author uses the word *clutched* to describe how tightly Stellaluna holds on to the branch. Stellaluna also *trembles* with fear. **DOK L2**

BY-THE-WAY WORDS During close reading, define the following words for children involving known concepts that can be stumbling blocks to comprehending the text.

swooped, p. 6: Tell children that *swooped* means "came down fast."

dodging, p. 6: Explain to children that *dodging* means "moving quickly to get away from someone or something."

Scaffolded Instruction

ENGLISH LANGUAGE LEARNERS

CONTEXT CLUES Guide children to use context clues to find meanings of unfamiliar words on p. 5. For *crooned,* read aloud the second paragraph, using a soft gentle voice for Mother Bat's words. For *clutched,* point out the context clue "clutched to her breast as she flew."

STRATEGIC SUPPORT

CONTEXT CLUES If children have difficulty understanding the use of action words, guide them through the text on p. 6 to find action words and list them under the name of the character. Ask clarifying questions, such as: *How does the owl get close to the bats?*

OBJECTIVES

Determine the meaning of and use academic and domain-specific words in a text. 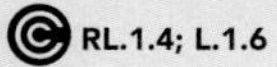

Identify words and phrases in a story that appeal to the senses. RL.1.4

BENCHMARK VOCABULARY

- clutched, p. 5
- trembling, p. 8

BENCHMARK VOCABULARY

- Have children find and read sentences from the text with the words *clutched* and *trembling.*

  Use the **Benchmark Vocabulary Routine for Literary Text** on pp. TR28–TR31 to teach the meanings of the words.

- Use the information on pp. 2–5 of this Teacher's Guide to discuss other words connected to each of the Benchmark Vocabulary words.

PRACTICE Have children use p. 19 in their *Reader's and Writer's Journal* to show contextual understanding of the Benchmark Vocabulary. Monitor children's vocabulary development.

Language Analysis

TEXT TALK

WORD CHOICE Explain to children that authors use interesting and lively words and phrases to help explain events or show characters' actions in a story. Words that tell what characters do are called action words. Provide an example about Stellaluna, such as *Stellaluna flies*. As a class, make a list of interesting words and phrases from *Stellaluna* and discuss ordinary words that mean almost the same thing. Read aloud the second sentence on p. 10.

MODEL When I read this sentence, I see the action word *clambered*. That is such an interesting word! The word *clambered* means "climbed with some difficulty." I wonder why the author chose that word. The author could have written that Stellaluna *quickly got out of the nest.* Why is *clambered* a better word than the phrase *quickly got out of?* What does *clambered* help you picture in your mind about what is happening? I think the word *clambered* clearly describes how Stelllaluna got out of the nest. I can picture that she is clumsy and startled.

PRACTICE/APPLY Have children work in small groups to identify other interesting words or phrases from pp. 5–10 of *Stellaluna,* such as *dodging, shrieking, clutched,* and *trembling.* Have children use a dictionary or context clues to determine ordinary words that mean almost the same thing as the colorful words. Have children work together to create drawings or other visuals to clarify their thoughts and ideas about each word. Ask volunteers to share with the class. Then have children complete p. 20 of their *Reader's and Writer's Journal.*

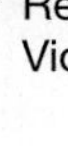

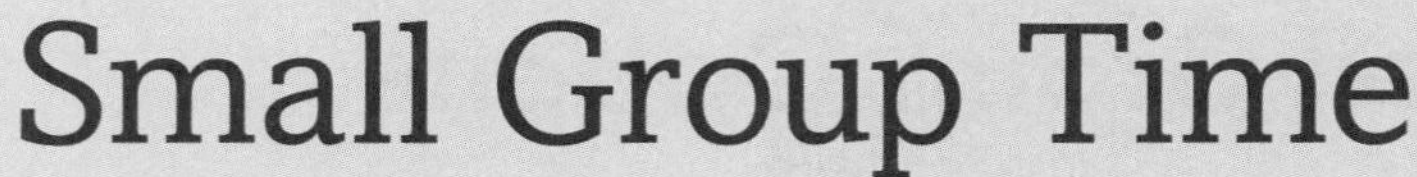

Small Group Time

STEP 1 Focused Independent Reading

BUILD ACCOUNTABILITY Prepare children to read their **self-selected texts.** Announce the two focus points to the class, and help children make a plan for their reading. Children will apply both focus points to their self-selected texts.

TODAY'S PROCESS FOCUS	
☐ Engagement and Identity	☑ Independence
☐ Stamina	

Tell children to choose a storybook that they know well enough to retell using the illustrations and whatever words they recognize or have memorized. Encourage them to read their book on their own today.

TODAY'S STRATEGY FOCUS	
☑ Vocabulary Knowledge	☐ Critical Thinking
☐ Fluency	☐ Comprehension

Guide children in applying the content of today's Language Analysis lesson to their self-selected texts. We learned that authors use interesting words such as *clambered* and *clutched* to tell about characters' actions and story events. Today as you are reading, I would like you to find interesting action or describing words. When you find a word, write it on a sheet of paper and keep reading. After you finish, you can use a dictionary or other words to figure out ordinary words that mean nearly the same thing. Alternatively, have children log into Pearson Realize to find an Independent Reading Activity that is appropriate for the text they are reading.

MONITOR PROGRESS

- **Process Focus:** Have children record their reading in a daily reading log. Have them draw pictures or write words, phrases, or sentence to retell the major events.
- **Strategy Focus:** Have children review with you their list of interesting action or describing words. Ask them to use ordinary words to tell what the words from their book mean. Alternatively, have children log into Pearson Realize and review with you the Independent Reading Activity they completed for their book.

For further guidance, see the **Independent Reading Routine** on pp. TR12–TR19.

While children are reading independently, use the Small Group Options on pp. 76–77.

INDEPENDENT LITERACY WORK

Text Club (pp. TR20–TR23)

Leveled Text Library

Center Options (pp. 10–11)

Use **Write in Response to Reading** on p. 19 of the *Reader's and Writer's Journal* to check children's understanding of key ideas in *Stellaluna.*

Phonics: Decodable Practice Readers

GUIDED READING OPTIONS

Use the **Leveled Text Library** to choose appropriate texts based on children's needs.

Use ***ReadyUp! Intervention*** for children who require additional instruction with this lesson's reading and foundational standards or with prerequisite standards.

STEP 2 Small Group Options

Based on formative assessments of children's progress, use the following options to provide additional instruction, practice, or extension as needed.

PHONICS

For children who need support with this week's Phonics skill, use pp. FS6–FS9 in this Teacher's Guide.

UNLOCK THE TEXT

For children who need support in accessing key ideas, key language, and key structures in ***Stellaluna,*** use **Unlock the Text** in the *Scaffolded Strategies Handbook*, pp. 8–13.

CONFERENCE

For independent reading accountability, **conference** each day with two or three children to discuss **self-selected texts** and support their reading.

LANGUAGE ANALYSIS SUPPORT

For children who struggle with word choice in ***Stellaluna,*** use this **Support Language Analysis Mini-Lesson.**

WORD CHOICE Help children work through p. 20 of their *Reader's and Writer's Journal* by first discussing the words from *Stellaluna.* Begin by asking questions, such as: When Mother Bat talks to her baby does she croon or yell? Is Mother Bat dodging or striking the owl? As children answer your questions, ask follow-up questions, such as: Why does Mother Bat croon? How does the owl swoop? Why is Mother Bat dodging the owl? Encourage children to think of other interesting words used on pp. 5–10 of *Stellaluna* and discuss what they mean.

Have children use the words to complete p. 20 of their *Reader's and Writer's Journal* with a partner. Use the **Think-Pair-Share Routine** on pp. TR2–TR3.

Identify words from stories that appeal to the senses. RL.1.4

LANGUAGE ANALYSIS EXTENSION

For children who can easily understand author's word choice in *Stellaluna,* use this **Extend Language Analysis Mini-Lesson.**

WORD CHOICE Have children work together to find other interesting words the author uses to tell about characters' actions or events in *Stellaluna*. Read aloud p. 42.

- The author uses different words to show how the characters speak. What words does the author use to show how Pip, Flitter, and Flap speak? (*yelled, howled, shrieked*) How are these words alike? How are they different? (They have similar meanings. They tell how the characters say things.) Let's say what the characters say using the words *yelled, howled,* and *shrieked* to guide how to say it.
- Point out the words *flew, leapt, lifted, swooped,* and *hung* on p. 42. What do these words have in common? (They tell about actions.)
- Read aloud p. 6 and p. 42. The author chose to repeat some words on these pages. What action words are on both? (*swooped, shrieking/shrieked*) Which characters swoop? (the owl, Stellaluna) Which characters shriek? (Mother Bat, Flap) Have children dictate or write sentences giving details about the events that happen that make the characters swoop and shriek.

Identify words from stories that appeal to the senses. RL.1.4

Distinguish shades of meaning among words. L.1.5.d

FLUENCY

For fluent reading accountability, use the **Oral Reading Fluency Quick Check.** ☑ **Today assess 2–3 children.**

MODEL APPROPRIATE RATE Explain that reading at an appropriate rate means reading at just the right speed—not too fast and not too slow—in order to keep the listener interested. When there are exciting events in a story, we can read those parts a little bit faster. Have children follow along as you model reading aloud p. 6 of *Stellaluna,* first very slowly and then at an appropriate rate. Review why a reader would read this exciting event of the story a little bit faster. Then choral read with children a portion of a leveled text at an appropriate rate.

Read grade-level text with appropriate rate. RF.1.4.b

QUICK CHECK

MONITOR PROGRESS

If . . . children don't know how fast or slow to read the text,

then . . . discuss when a reader would read something slow and fast. Then discuss the type of text they will be reading.

If . . . children are rushing and reading too quickly,

then . . . remind them that even though it is an exciting event of the story, the listener still needs to understand what is happening.

OBJECTIVE

Write a narrative using details about characters. W.1.3

Narrative Writing

Use Character Details

SET THE PURPOSE Remind children that characters are who or what does the action in a story. Characters can be people or animals. When we look at how writers use details in their stories to describe characters, we can use that skill when we write details about characters for our own stories. Tell children that they will be writing about a character from the story.

TEACH AND MODEL Explain to children that when writers write stories, they give details about what the characters do, what the characters say, what the characters look like, and what the characters think and feel. These details help readers better understand the characters.

Provide the following models from pp. 5, 6, and 8 of *Stellaluna* that show details about the characters:

Each night, Mother Bat would carry Stellaluna clutched to her breast as she flew out to search for food.

The writer uses a detail about what Mother Bat does to show how much Mother Bat loves Stellaluna.

Dodging and shrieking, Mother Bat tried to escape, but the owl struck again and again, knocking Stellaluna into the air.

The writer uses the words *dodging* and *shrieking* and the phrase *tried to escape* to show details about Mother Bat's actions.

Wrapping her wings around her, she clutched the thin branch, trembling with cold and fear.

The writer uses the words *clutched* and *trembling* to show how scared Stellaluna is to be away from Mother Bat.

"Mother," Stellaluna squeaked. "Where are you?"

The writer uses what Stellaluna says and how she says it to show that she is scared to be alone and not with Mother Bat.

Write About a Character

PREPARE TO WRITE Remind children that when they write about characters for their own narratives, they should include as many details as they can to make sure that readers get a good idea about who the characters are. Encourage children to answer questions about the characters before writing about them. Once they have answers, children can carefully choose words that would be best in showing readers who the characters are. Provide possible questions, such as:

- What does the character look like? What kind of clothes does the character wear? What things does the character carry?
- What does the character like to do?
- Is the character nice or mean? What can the character do to show he or she is nice or mean?

ADD CHARACTER DETAILS Explain that you will model writing about Mother Bat from *Stellaluna.* I'm going to add a few sentences to the story about Mother Bat. I'm going to think about what I already know about Mother Bat and add more details about what she can do or say. Read aloud your writing as you write it. Ask volunteers to add on. Focus children on sharing details about Mother Bat that help readers understand the character by telling her actions, her feelings, and what she says.

Mother Bat flew right beside Stellaluna as she tried out her wings in the pitch black. "I'm right here," Mother Bat said gently as they flew. She wanted to make sure Stellaluna did not get scared or lost again.

WRITE ABOUT A CHARACTER Explain to children that as they write about a character, they need to remember to think about what they want to get across to the reader about their character. They can show details by writing about what the character looks like, says, does, or feels.

Scaffolded Instruction

STRATEGIC SUPPORT

CHARACTER DETAILS If children struggle with choosing the right details to tell about characters, prompt them with questions such as: *Is the character friendly? What can the character do to show he or she is friendly?* Explain that the detail shows what the character does. Readers can now use that detail to understand if the character is friendly or not.

OBJECTIVES

Write details about a character. W.1.3

With guidance, use technology to produce and publish writing and to collaborate with others. W.1.6

Produce simple sentences. L.1.1.j

Independent Writing Practice

WRITE As a class, have children brainstorm a list of the characters from *Stellaluna* that they might write about. After the class creates a list, ask them to briefly share what they know about each character. Have children choose one of the characters from the list and add details about that character to a scene from the story. Children should

- page through *Stellaluna* and flag a scene they want to add to.
- write or dictate a sentence or two on p. 21 of their *Reader's and Writer's Journal* that tells details about a character in the scene.

CONVENTIONS If you wish to teach children about simple sentences, use the Conventions Mini-Lesson on p. 81. Encourage children to use simple sentences in their narrative writing.

DIGITAL OPTIONS If available, have children use computers or tablets to type their sentences and print them. Then, on the same sheet of paper, have them draw a picture to illustrate their sentences.

Share Writing

Have children share their writing with a partner. Have them discuss the words in the sentences that tell about the character they chose. Ask the partners to work together to think of another detail they could add about what the character could say, do, feel, or think.

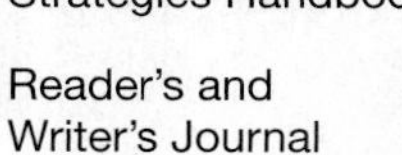

Conventions Mini-Lesson

Produce Simple Sentences

TEACH AND MODEL Remind children that a sentence is a group of words that tells a complete idea. A sentence begins with an uppercase letter and ends with a punctuation mark.

A simple sentence tells who or what the sentence is about and what that person, animal, or thing is or does.

> Stellaluna slept all night.

This is a complete simple sentence. It tells a complete idea. It begins with a capital letter and ends with a period. *Stellaluna* is who the sentence is about. *Slept all night* is what she does.

PRACTICE Write complete and incomplete simple sentences. Read each one aloud. Have children stand up when they hear a complete sentence. Then reread the sentence and ask children to tell who or what the sentence is about and what that person, animal, or thing is or does. Then have children complete the activity on p. 21 of their *Reader's and Writer's Journal.*

Scaffolded Instruction

ENGLISH LANGUAGE LEARNERS

PARTS OF SENTENCES English language learners may find it difficult to identify the subject and predicate that makes up a complete sentence. Say the complete simple sentence again. Ask: *Who or what is this sentence about? What does (subject) do?*

LESSON 8

Identify and Describe the Setting of a Story

OBJECTIVES

Focus Understand how authors use sensory details to create a story's setting. RL.1.3

Use text evidence to answer questions about a story. RL.1.1

 See **Routines** on pp. TR2–TR31.

LESSON 8 FIRST READ

Build Understanding

SET THE PURPOSE Focus the instruction by sharing the following Enduring Understanding: *Writers understand that details play a role in explaining the events in a story.* The events in a story are important. The setting of the story is also important for understanding the events and characters. The setting of a story is when and where it takes place. Authors can use details in the words and illustrations to tell more about the setting.

ENGAGE CHILDREN Display the front cover of *Stellaluna.* Have children use the details in the illustration to tell about where Stellauna is. Remind them to think about the Essential Questions as they read, talk, and write about the text: *How do readers know what makes a good retelling? How do writers create interesting events?* Tell children: In this lesson we are going to read *Stellaluna* to learn how authors tell about the setting.

READ As you read pp. 4–11 of *Stellaluna*, use the appropriate reading routine from pp. TR8–TR19. Have children follow along as you read. You may have some children who can read parts of this section aloud. Have volunteers read sentences or pages if they can. In this reading, children should focus on the details that tell about the setting.

TURN AND TALK After reading, have children turn to a partner and discuss this question using details from the text: What is the bird nest like in the illustration on page 11? Use the **Think-Pair-Share Routine** on pp. TR2–TR3. Tell children to describe the place with as many details as they can to express their ideas. (Children should identify details such as made of sticks, wrapped around a branch, big enough to fit three birds.)

FOUNDATIONAL SKILLS MINI-LESSON

Short *a*

- Display Picture Card *apple*. Let's say *apple*. *Apple* begins with /a/.
- Use Sound-Spelling Card 1 to teach short *a* spelled *Aa*. Point to *Aa*. The letter *Aa* stands for the sound /a/. Have children name the picture and its beginning sound. *Astronaut* begins with /a/. The first letter of the word *astronaut* is *Aa*.
- Write the word *can*. Model how to say the sound for each letter and then blend the sounds to read the word. Have children try it independently for the words *mat* and *pan*.

For more explicit instruction, see p. FS8 in this Teacher's Guide.

LESSON 8 SECOND READ

Close Read

CITE TEXT EVIDENCE Engage the class in a discussion about what you just read. Remind children that readers look for details about the setting in the words and illustrations. Use these questions to guide the discussion, and ask children to support their answers with evidence.

- What does the text on page 5 tell us about where the story takes place? ("In a warm and sultry forest far, far away") Let's read that sentence together. **DOK L1**
- On pages 6 and 7, what clues are given in the text about when this story begins? What clues are given in the illustration? Show me in the illustration. (The text says "one night." The illustration shows a dark sky with stars.) **DOK L2**
- In the story, Mother Bat followed the "heavy scent of ripe fruit." What is ripe fruit? (Possible response: It is ready to eat. It is soft and has a good smell.) What would a place that has "the heavy scent of ripe fruit" be like? (Possible response: The place could have lots of trees with fruit that is ready to eat. You could smell the fruit from far away.) **DOK L2**
- What details does the author use to explain how the setting changes after Stellaluna drops off the branch? (*daybreak* and *in a soft downy nest*) Let's read those sentences together. Read the last sentence on p. 8 and the first sentence on p. 10. Look at the illustration on page 11. What is different about the setting? (It is daytime. Stellaluna is in a nest with birds.) **DOK L2**

BY-THE-WAY WORDS During close reading, define the following words for children involving known concepts that can be stumbling blocks to comprehending the text.

sultry, p. 5: Tell children that *sultry* means "hot and humid, or damp."

downy, p. 10: Explain to children that *downy* is a describing word that means "covered in soft feathers."

Scaffolded Instruction

ENGLISH LANGUAGE LEARNERS

LITERARY ELEMENTS Help children understand where Stellaluna is when she falls into a "tangle of branches." Focus on the illustration on p. 9. Model first, and then have children trace the branches with a finger as they repeat the phrase. Have them draw a picture or use craft sticks to build a "tangle of branches."

STRATEGIC SUPPORT

LITERARY ELEMENTS If children have difficulty understanding when a story event happens, have them use the illustrations to answer questions about the setting, such as: *What color is the sky? What time of day do you see stars? When do you see the sun shining?*

OBJECTIVES

Determine the meaning of and use academic and domain-specific words in a text.

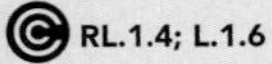

RL.1.4; L.1.6

Use details to describe the setting of a story.

RL.1.3, RL.1.7

BENCHMARK VOCABULARY

- daybreak, p. 8
- headfirst, p. 10

BENCHMARK VOCABULARY

- Have children find and read sentences from the text with the words *daybreak* and *headfirst*.

  Use the **Benchmark Vocabulary Routine for Literary Text** on pp. TR28–TR31 to teach the meanings of the words.

- Use the information on pp. 2–5 of this Teacher's Guide to discuss other words connected to each of the Benchmark Vocabulary words.

PRACTICE Have children use p. 23 in their *Reader's and Writer's Journal* to show contextual understanding of the Benchmark Vocabulary. Monitor children's vocabulary development.

Language Analysis

TEXT TALK

SENSORY DETAILS

Explain to children that sensory words are words that tell how something looks, tastes, smells, sounds, and feels. We use our senses to understand these words. Authors can use these words to describe the setting. Display a T-Chart from p. TR39 with the headings "Story Details" and "Senses."

Sensory Details Chart

Story Details	Senses
warm and sultry forest	see, feel
heavy scent of ripe fruit	smell
dark leafy tangle of branches	see, feel
soft downy nest	feel

MODEL On page 5, it says that Stellaluna and Mother Bat are in a "warm and sultry forest." I'll write that in the "Story Details" column. When I read the word *forest*, I see many trees together. When I read the words *warm* and *sultry*, I feel very hot, sweaty, and sticky. I will write *see* and *feel* in the "Senses" column.

PRACTICE/APPLY Have children work in small groups to complete the graphic organizer. Use the **Small Group Discussion Routine** on pp. TR6–TR7 to have children discuss the details on their completed chart. Remind them to ask and answer questions to clarify information they do not understand. Then have the groups share their ideas with the class. Ask children to describe what the sensory words made them see, smell, taste, hear, or feel. Encourage them to create drawings or other visual displays to clarify their descriptions.

Generative Vocabulary Games
Leveled Text Library
Independent Reading How-To Video
Reader's and Writer's Journal
Independent Reading Activities

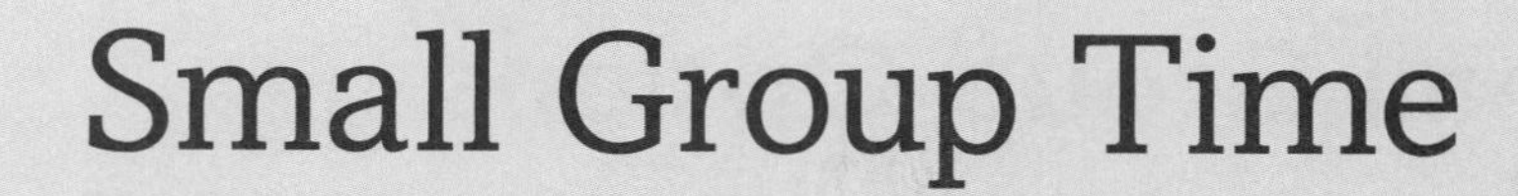

Small Group Time

STEP 1 Focused Independent Reading

BUILD ACCOUNTABILITY Prepare children to read their **self-selected texts.** Announce the two focus points to the class, and help children make a plan for their reading. Children will apply both focus points to their self-selected texts.

TODAY'S PROCESS FOCUS	
☐ Engagement and Identity ☐ Stamina	☑ Independence

Tell children to select a storybook that they can read on their own. Encourage them to consider selecting a text that they have read before. They can also take a quick look at the pages in the book to determine if it is something they will be able to read independently.

TODAY'S STRATEGY FOCUS	
☐ Vocabulary Knowledge ☐ Fluency	☑ Critical Thinking ☐ Comprehension

Guide children in applying the content of today's Language Analysis lesson to their self-selected texts. We learned that authors sometimes use words that make readers use their senses to better understand the setting. Today as you are reading, I want you to find words that make you use your senses. What do you picture in your mind? What other words can you use? Be prepared to explain your word choice. Alternatively, have children log into Pearson Realize to find an Independent Reading Activity that is appropriate for the text they are reading.

MONITOR PROGRESS

- **Process Focus:** Have children record their reading in a daily reading log. They should draw pictures and write or dictate words, phrases, or sentences to tell a short summary of the book.
- **Strategy Focus:** Have children use details in the text or illustrations to explain what they picture in their mind and why the word they thought of would fit. Alternatively, have children log into Pearson Realize and review with you the Independent Reading Activity they completed for their book.

For further guidance, see the **Independent Reading Routine** on pp. TR12–TR19.

While children are reading independently, use the Small Group Options on pp. 86–87.

INDEPENDENT LITERACY WORK

Text Club (pp. TR20–TR23)

Leveled Text Library

Center Options (pp. 10–11)

Use **Write in Response to Reading** on p. 23 of the *Reader's and Writer's Journal* to check children's understanding of a setting from *Stellaluna.*

Phonics: Decodable Practice Readers

GUIDED READING OPTIONS

Use the **Leveled Text Library** to choose appropriate texts based on children's needs.

Use ***ReadyUp! Intervention*** for children who require additional instruction with this lesson's reading and foundational standards or with prerequisite standards.

STEP 2 Small Group Options

Based on formative assessments of children's progress, use the following options to provide additional instruction, practice, or extension as needed.

PHONICS

For children who need support with this week's Phonics skills, use pp. FS6–FS9 in this Teacher's Guide.

UNLOCK THE TEXT

For children who need support in accessing key ideas, key language, and key structures in ***Stellaluna,*** use **Unlock the Text** in the *Scaffolded Strategies Handbook*, pp. 8–13.

CONFERENCE

For independent reading accountability, **conference** each day with two or three children to discuss **self-selected texts** and support their reading.

LANGUAGE ANALYSIS SUPPORT

For children who struggle with sensory details in ***Stellaluna,*** use this **Support Language Analysis Mini-Lesson.**

SENSORY DETAILS Help children work through one sensory detail together for the T-Chart by having them close their eyes and picture what they see, taste, smell, hear, and feel when you read aloud the words "the heavy scent of ripe fruit." Ask questions about how these words describe the forest setting, such as: What does the ripe fruit look like? What can you taste when you eat the ripe fruit? What does the ripe fruit smell like? Have children respond orally and then help them write the senses they use on the chart.

Invite children to work with a partner or small group to discuss the sensory details for another phrase from *Stellaluana*, such as "dark leafy tangle of branches." Remind children to ask about what they *see, smell, taste, hear,* and *feel*. Use the **Think-Pair-Share Routine** on pp. TR2–TR3.

Identify and describe words and phrases that appeal to the senses. RL.1.4

Use details to describe the setting of a story. RL.1.3

LANGUAGE ANALYSIS EXTENSION

For children who can easily describe sensory details in ***Stellaluna,*** use this **Extend Language Analysis Mini-Lesson**.

SENSORY DETAILS Read aloud the first sentence on p. 8. Have children work together to create a labeled poster picture of this tree setting. Children should look back at the text and illustrations for details. Remind them to choose words for their labels that tell what they *see, hear, feel, taste, smell,* and *touch*. Before they begin, have children discuss the following questions:

- When is Stellaluna caught in the branches? (nighttime) What might you see in the sky at night? (stars, moon) What animals might be awake? (bats, owls) How might you describe these setting details in your picture labels? (Possible responses: dark night, bright stars; glowing moon; flying bat; powerful owl)
- What will you draw to show a "dark leafy tangle of branches"? (Possible response: a lot of dark green leaves on black twisted branches)

Identify and describe words and phrases that appeal to the senses. RL.1.4

FLUENCY

For fluent reading accountability, use this **Oral Reading Fluency Quick Check.** ☑ **Today assess 2–3 children.**

MODEL APPROPRIATE RATE Remind children that reading at an appropriate rate means reading at just the right speed—not too fast and not too slow. Have children follow along as you model reading the first paragraph on p. 8 of *Stellaluna*. First, read the paragraph too fast. Point out how you rushed through the words and it was difficult to follow. Then read the paragraph slowly. Have children discuss why that was not a good rate either. Finally read at the right speed. Then have children take turns reading aloud a portion of an appropriately leveled text at an appropriate rate.

Read grade-level text with appropriate rate. RF.1.4.b

QUICK CHECK

MONITOR PROGRESS

If . . . children are reading too slowly,
then . . . have them identify the words that make them stumble or slow down. Review the words before reading the text again.

If . . . children are reading too quickly,
then . . . have them listen to you read it like them and discuss why that is not easy to listen to.

OBJECTIVE

Write a narrative that recounts details about a setting.

 W.1.3

Narrative Writing

Setting Details

SET THE PURPOSE Remind children that a narrative is a story. It has characters, setting, and events. The setting is when and where the narrative takes place. Writers use details in the words and illustrations to describe the setting. Explain to children that when they write about a setting, they can think about how other writers described the setting in their stories.

TEACH AND MODEL Explain that *Stellaluna* has several settings: the forest where Stellaluna is born and the nest where Stellaluna lives with the birds.

- On page 5, the writer uses the words *warm and sultry forest* to tell about the setting. What do these words tell you about the forest? (The word *sultry* means "hot and humid," so I think it tells us that the forest is a warm, comfortable place for bats to live.)
- Which words on page 8 help readers understand where Stellaluna lands after the owl attacks? (*dark leafy tangle of branches*) How do these words help readers picture the new place? (*A tangle of branches* makes it sound as if Stellaluna had a rough landing on an uncomfortable place.)

Provide the following models from pp. 10 and 18 of *Stellaluna* that show details about the setting:

> *Flump!* Stellaluna landed headfirst in a soft downy nest, startling the three baby birds who lived there.

The writer uses the phrase *soft downy nest* to help readers understand how Stellaluna's setting changes: from uncomfortable branches to a comfortable nest.

> All the babies grew quickly. Soon the nest became crowded.

The writer uses the word *crowded* to show how the setting in the nest is changing. The word choice makes readers imagine what it feels like in the nest now for Stellaluna and the birds.

Write About a Setting

PREPARE TO WRITE Explain to children that writers use many details to fully describe the setting of a narrative. Once writers have decided on a setting for their story or part of their story, they can begin to think about the best words to use to help readers better understand the story.

ORGANIZE DETAILS Have children use a word web or other graphic organizer to organize ideas about the settings in *Stellaluna*. Write *Setting* in the center circle and the words that describe it on the lines.

The settings changed in Stellaluna as the story went along. The places that Stellaluna ended up affected how safe she felt. When she was first born, she was in a warm place. The writer uses the words *warm and sultry forest*. She was with Mother Bat and felt safe. After the owl attacks, she falls onto a *dark leafy tangle of branches*. That place is not comfortable. Stellaluna probably feels scared. Then she lands in a *soft downy nest*. She feels comfortable and safe.

WRITE ABOUT SETTING Explain to children that when they write about the setting, they can

- choose a setting that is interesting.
- discuss words that can describe the setting with a partner.
- use a graphic organizer.
- draw a picture.
- write a sentence using the describing words.

Model the assignment: I am going to write about the forest where Stellaluna was born. I imagine that the trees are tall and crowded together. The writer described the forest as *warm* and *sultry*, so I imagine that the forest has many plants on the ground. I can use words such as *green* and *towering* to describe the forest. Here's a sentence I can write: *Stellaluna was born in a green forest with towering trees.*

Scaffolded Instruction

STRATEGIC SUPPORT

WORD CHOICE If children have difficulty using a graphic organizer or determining describing words or phrases to use for a setting, practice with a more simple setting. Use the classroom. Ask children to think about how they would tell about the classroom to a family member. *What do you see? What can you feel? Can you smell something? What sounds can you hear?*

OBJECTIVES

Write about a setting using details.
 W.1.3

With guidance, use technology to produce and publish writing and to collaborate with others. W.1.6

Use end punctuation. L.1.2.b

Independent Writing Practice

BRAINSTORM Have children work with a partner to brainstorm the settings in *Stellaluna* and possible words they might use to describe them. Then have partners discuss which setting they will write about.

WRITE Have children draw a picture of the setting they chose. Tell them to draw at least one character in their picture. Then have them write or dictate a sentence that tells details about the setting and what the character does there on p. 24 of their *Reader's and Writer's Journal*.

CONVENTIONS If you wish to teach children about end punctuation, use the Conventions Mini-Lesson on p. 91. Encourage children to check for end punctuation in their narrative writing.

DIGITAL OPTIONS If available, have children use computers or tablets to type their sentences and print them. Then, on the same sheet of paper, have them draw a picture to illustrate their sentences.

Share Writing

Ask volunteers to share their writing with a partner or small group. Have them discuss how the words in the sentence help provide more details for the illustration.

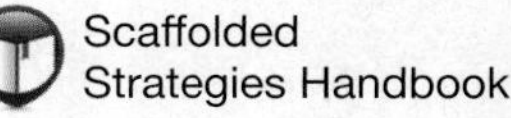
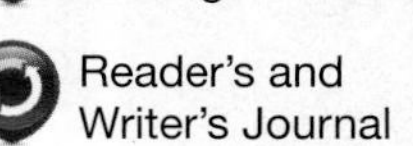

Conventions Mini-Lesson
Use End Punctuation

TEACH AND MODEL Remind children that a sentence tells a complete idea. It tells who or what the sentence is about and what that person, animal, thing is or does. A sentence begins with an uppercase letter and ends with an ending punctuation mark. Different types of sentences use different kinds of ending punctuation. One type is a telling sentence. A telling sentence tells something or makes a statement. A telling sentence ends with a period. A period is a clue to readers to stop before reading the next sentence.

Her baby wings were as limp and useless as wet paper.	This sentence ends with a period. It is a telling sentence. It tells readers that Stellaluna has limp, useless wings.
She listened to the babble of the birds.	This sentence also ends with a period. It is a telling sentence. It tells that Stellaluna listened to the birds.

PRACTICE Have children say telling sentences to the class. Write the examples, leaving off the period at the end. Then invite volunteers to add periods to each sentence as you remind them that sentences that tell something or make a statement end with a period. Have children complete the activity on p. 24 of their *Reader's and Writer's Journal*.

Scaffolded Instruction

ENGLISH LANGUAGE LEARNERS

END PUNCTUATION Help English language learners understand when they need to insert periods. Read simple telling sentences aloud, pausing at the periods. Reread each sentence and point to and name the end punctuation. Have children then read aloud simple sentences, such as *Ben sat,* and identify the periods.

OBJECTIVES

Focus Understand that illustrations can provide details to describe a story's characters, setting, and events. RL.1.3

Use text evidence to answer questions about a story. RL.1.1

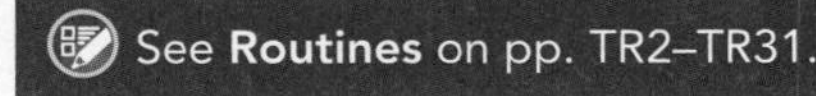
See **Routines** on pp. TR2–TR31.

Use Illustrations to Understand a Story

LESSON 9 FIRST READ Build Understanding

SET THE PURPOSE Focus the instruction by sharing the following Enduring Understanding: *Readers understand that they improve their comprehension by identifying story elements.* Remember that stories have characters, setting, and events. The details in the illustrations can help readers better understand what they are reading.

ENGAGE CHILDREN Display pp. 24–25 of *Stellaluna*. Ask children to describe the illustration. Read the sentences on p. 24. Discuss the features of the first sentence, pointing out the first and last word, the initial capitalization, and the end punctuation mark. Have volunteers identify the features of the second sentence. Remind children of the Essential Questions: *How do readers know what makes a good retelling? How do writers create interesting events?* Tell children: In this lesson we are going to focus on the details in the illustrations in *Stellaluna*.

READ Review the events of *Stellaluna* by paging through the book using the illustrations. Read aloud pp. 30–33. Use the appropriate reading routine from pp. TR8–TR19. In this reading, have children focus on the sequence of the illustrations, noting the order of events as they retell the key points of the story. Have children help you read any text as necessary to clear up any confusion.

TURN AND TALK After reading, have children turn to a partner and discuss this question using examples from the text: How does Mother Bat recognize Stellaluna? Use the **Think-Pair-Share Routine** on pp. TR2–TR3 and make sure children are using best practices for speaking and listening as outlined in the routine. (Children should recall that when Stellaluna tells her story, Mother Bat recognizes it. Then she smells Stellaluna. p. 32)

FOUNDATIONAL SKILLS MINI-LESSON

High-Frequency Words; Short *a*

- Display the High-Frequency Word Cards for *we, see, the,* and *like* one at a time. Ask children to say and spell each word.
- Distribute *Decodable Practice Reader R2B*. Ask children to preview the story. In this story, you will read words with *c, n, p,* and short *a*.
- Have pairs read the story, switching readers after each page.

For more explicit instruction, see p. FS9 in this Teacher's Guide.

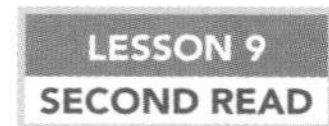

LESSON 9
SECOND READ

Close Read

CITE TEXT EVIDENCE Engage the class in a discussion about what you just read. Focus on the events in the middle of the story on pp. 30–33. Remind children that readers look for details in the words and illustrations to better understand the story. Use these questions to guide the discussion, and ask children to support their answers with evidence.

- Who is Stellaluna talking to? (other bats) What makes the first bat come talk to Stellaluna? (Stellaluna is not hanging like a bat. She is not upside down.) Let's read together what the other bat says. Why does the other bat seem so interested in Stellaluna? (Stellaluna is not acting like a bat.) **DOK L2**
- What does "wrong for a bird, maybe, but not for a bat" mean? (The other bat is explaining that the way Stellaluna acted is right for a bat.) When can something be wrong in one situation but not in another? (Possible response: You cannot yell in the library, but you can yell on the playground.) **DOK L3**
- How does the illustration on page 31 help readers understand the conversation Stellaluna has with the other bat? (It shows Stellaluna hanging by her thumbs, and the other bat hanging by its feet.) Show me in the picture which bat is Stellaluna. **DOK L2**

BY-THE-WAY WORDS During close reading, define the following words for children involving known concepts that can be stumbling blocks to comprehending the text.

stuttered, p. 32: Explain to children that when a speaker *stuttered* he or she repeated the same sound until he or she finished the word.

gasped, p. 32: Tell children that *gasped* means "breathed in suddenly and loudly."

murmured, p. 32: Explain to children that if a speaker *murmured,* he or she said something in a quiet, soft voice.

Scaffolded Instruction

ENGLISH LANGUAGE LEARNERS

SHADES OF MEANING Remind children that different English words can describe the same action but with a different shade of meaning. Demonstrate the meanings of the words *gasp, stutter,* and *murmur* by saying "how very strange" three times, one for each word. Have children tell how each way you said the sentence was different. Explain that the differences show shades of meaning.

STRATEGIC SUPPORT

KEY DETAILS If children have difficulty understanding the conversation between Stellaluna and the other bat, reread p. 30 and ask clarifying questions, such as *Why does Stellaluna see a "peculiar" face? What does the bat explain to Stellaluna? Why is Stellaluna confused?*

OBJECTIVES

Determine the meaning of and use academic and domain-specific words in a text.

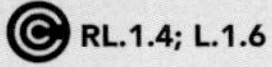 RL.1.4; L.1.6

Describe the major events in a story using details in the illustrations.

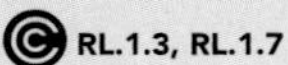 RL.1.3, RL.1.7

BENCHMARK VOCABULARY

- obey, p. 16
- rules, p. 16
- behaved, p. 16

BENCHMARK VOCABULARY

- Have children find and read sentences from the text with the words *obey, rules,* and *behaved.*

  Use the **Benchmark Vocabulary Routine for Literary Text** on pp. TR28–TR31 to teach the meanings of the words.

- Use the information on pp. 2–5 of this Teacher's Guide to discuss other words connected to each of the Benchmark Vocabulary words.

PRACTICE Have children use p. 25 in their *Reader's and Writer's Journal* to show contextual understanding of the Benchmark Vocabulary. Monitor children's vocabulary development.

Reading Analysis

TEXT TALK

STORY EVENTS Explain to children that stories have plots. A story's plot is the events that happen in the beginning, middle, and end.

Point out the small drawings at the tops of the pages with text. Explain that these drawings show Mother Bat's story. The drawings show what happens to Mother Bat while we read about what happens to Stellaluna.

MODEL Let's take a look at these drawings to help us imagine what Mother Bat is doing. Let's look at pages 8 and 9. This is when Stellaluna falls into the tangle of branches after the owl attacks her and Mother Bat. When I look at the small drawing at the top of page 8, I see that Mother Bat flies into a cave as the owl gets closer. So now I understand that after Stellaluna falls, the owl goes after Mother Bat! The only thing Mother Bat can do is fly away to safety.

PRACTICE/APPLY Have children work with a partner or in small groups to discuss what Mother Bat does when Stellaluna is living with the birds and what happens when Stellaluna and Mother Bat meet again. Use the **Small Group Discussion Routine** on pp. TR6–TR7, reminding children to build on what others say by responding to their comments. Then have children work independently to retell Mother Bat's story by drawing pictures to show what happens to her at the beginning, middle, and end of the story. Children can then use their drawings to retell the story orally.

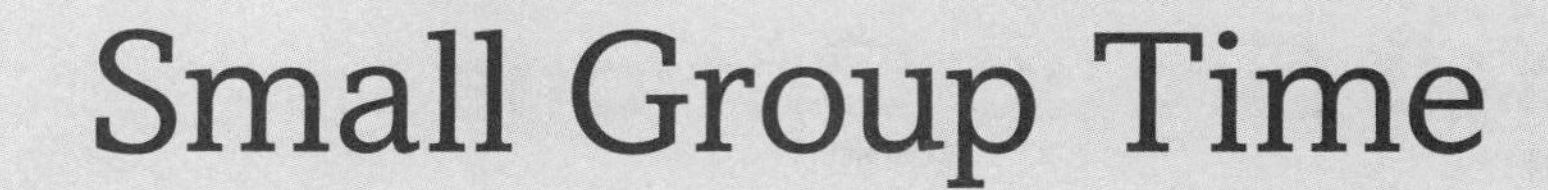

Small Group Time

STEP 1 Focused Independent Reading

BUILD ACCOUNTABILITY Prepare children to read their **self-selected texts**. Announce the two focus points to the class, and help children make a plan for their reading. Children will apply both focus points to their self-selected texts.

TODAY'S PROCESS FOCUS	
☑ Engagement and Identity	☐ Independence
☐ Stamina	

Tell children to select a book that they think they will enjoy reading. Give them time to page through a few books to look at the illustrations and choose a book that appeals to them visually.

TODAY'S STRATEGY FOCUS	
☐ Vocabulary Knowledge	☐ Critical Thinking
☑ Fluency	☐ Comprehension

Guide children in improving their oral reading fluency using their self-selected texts. When we read aloud, we want to make sure our listeners can understand what we are saying. We need to be loud and clear. We don't want to read too fast or too slow. Sometimes we need to practice reading independently before we can read aloud for others. Today as you are reading, choose a page to read many times. Decide on the correct speed. First, whisper-read the page to yourself. Then read it again and again. Alternatively, have children log into Pearson Realize to find an Independent Reading Activity that is appropriate for the text they are reading.

MONITOR PROGRESS

- **Process Focus:** Have children record their reading in a daily reading log by drawing a picture of their favorite part and labeling it with a word or phrase that tells about the part.
- **Strategy Focus:** Have children read their chosen page aloud to you. After they read it once, correct any errors. Have them read it one more time. Alternatively, have children log into Pearson Realize and review with you the Independent Reading Activity they completed for their book.

For further guidance, see the **Independent Reading Routine** on pp. TR12–TR19.

While children are reading independently, use the Small Group Options on pp. 96–97.

INDEPENDENT LITERACY WORK

Text Club (pp. TR20–TR23)

Leveled Text Library

Center Options (pp. 10–11)

Use **Write in Response to Reading** on p. 25 of the *Reader's and Writer's Journal* to check children's understanding of key ideas in *Stellaluna.*

Phonics: Decodable Practice Readers

GUIDED READING OPTIONS

Use the **Leveled Text Library** to choose appropriate texts based on children's needs.

Use ***ReadyUp! Intervention*** for children who require additional instruction with this lesson's reading and foundational standards or with prerequisite standards.

STEP 2 Small Group Options

Based on formative assessments of children's progress, use the following options to provide additional instruction, practice, or extension as needed.

PHONICS

For children who need support with this week's Phonics skill, use pp. FS6–FS9 in this Teacher's Guide.

UNLOCK THE TEXT

For children who need support in accessing key ideas, key language, and key structures in ***Stellaluna,*** use **Unlock the Text** in the *Scaffolded Strategies Handbook,* pp. 8–13.

CONFERENCE

For independent reading accountability, **conference** each day with two or three children to discuss **self-selected texts** and support their reading.

READING ANALYSIS SUPPORT

For children who struggle with story events in ***Stellaluna,*** use this **Support Reading Analysis Mini-Lesson.**

STORY EVENTS Help children retell Mother Bat's story from *Stellaluna* using the small drawings on the top of each page with text. Ask questions, such as: Which bat is shown in the small drawings? What is happening in the drawing? How do you think the bat feels? As children answer, encourage them to elaborate by asking follow-up questions, such as: Why is this drawing different from the full-color picture? How is Mother Bat's story different from Stellaluna's story? Create a list of the events by writing key words and details in order.

Invite children to choose one event from the list and draw one picture that shows what Mother Bat is doing and one picture that shows what Stellaluna is doing at that time. Use the **Think-Pair-Share Routine** on pp. TR2–TR3.

Identify and describe story events. RL.1.3

Use details in the illustrations to tell about story events. RL.1.7

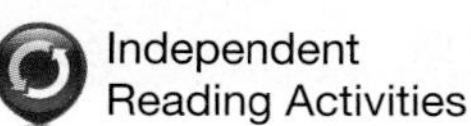

Scaffolded Strategies Handbook

Leveled Text Library

Games

Independent Reading Activities

Reader's and Writer's Journal

READING ANALYSIS EXTENSION

For children who can easily describe story events using illustrations in ***Stellaluna,*** use this **Extend Reading Analysis Mini-Lesson.**

STORY EVENTS Have partners work together to create illustrations that retell the birds' story. Children may choose to tell about the events of Mama Bird or Flap, Flitter, and Pip. Have them look back at the text to find the details about the events. Then have children work together to think about details they can add based on what they read. Have children discuss the following questions:

- When do the birds first meet Stellaluna? (when she falls into the nest)
- What happens after Mama Bird brings home many bugs for the birds? (Stellaluna eats a grasshopper.) Why is that an important event? (After this, Stellaluna acts more and more like a bird.)
- What happens when the birds and Stellaluna try to land on a branch for the first time? (The birds land gracefully. Stellaluna cannot stay on top of the branch.)
- When do the birds meet the other bats? (when Stellaluna brings the birds to the bat family)

Identify and describe story events. RL.1.3
Use details in the illustrations to tell about story events. RL.1.7

FLUENCY

For fluent reading accountability, use the **Oral Reading Fluency Quick Check.** ☑ **Today assess 2–3 children.**

MODEL APPROPRIATE RATE Remind children that reading at an appropriate rate means reading at just the right speed—not too fast and not too slow. Have children follow along as you model reading the third sentence in the first paragraph on p. 16 of *Stellaluna.* Read the sentence very slowly. Then discuss with children how your speed affects their understanding. Then read the sentence again at an appropriate rate. Have children read it with you. Then provide each child with a leveled text at his or her reading level to read at the appropriate rate.

Read grade-level text with appropriate rate. RF.1.4.b

QUICK CHECK

MONITOR PROGRESS

If . . . children are reading too slowly,
then . . . have them identify the words that cause them to stumble or slow down. Review the words before reading the text again.

If . . . children are reading too quickly,
then . . . have them listen to you read the text quickly and discuss why that is not easy to understand.

OBJECTIVE

Write a narrative that recounts details about events. W.1.3

Narrative Writing

Event Details

SET THE PURPOSE Discuss the features of a story with children: it has characters, setting, and events. Point out that the events in the story tell what happens. Writers use details to tell more about the events. Illustrations can also tell details about the events. Tell children that they will be drawing and writing about an event from a story.

TEACH AND MODEL Review the beginning, middle, and ending of *Stellaluna* with children. As children retell events, follow up their retelling by pointing out details that they include that help others follow what is happening during that event.

Reread p. 26 of *Stellaluna.* Prompt discussion about the events on this page using the following questions:

- What details are important for readers to know when they hear about this event? (that Stellaluna and the birds flew far from home; that the sun is setting; that Stellaluna had flown far ahead of the birds)
- How do those details help readers understand the importance of this event? (Without those details, readers would not understand how serious it was that Stellaluna had flown ahead of the birds. Because of those details, readers can begin to feel how worried the birds are and why.)

Provide the following models from pp. 26 and 28 of *Stellaluna* that show details about the events:

But Stellaluna had flown far ahead and was nowhere to be seen. The three anxious birds went home without her.	The writer uses the phrase *flown far ahead* to clearly state a detail about the event. The word *anxious* gives readers a clue that maybe Stellaluna has gone too far.
All alone, Stellaluna flew and flew until her wings ached and she dropped into a tree.	The detail *until her wings ached* helps readers understand just how far Stellaluna has flown away from the nest.

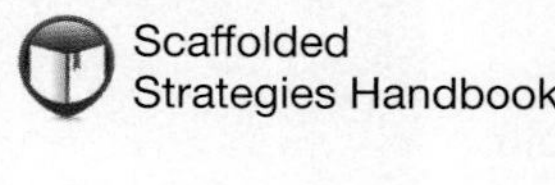

Write Event Details

PREPARE TO WRITE Review with children how details about events are essential to creating interesting stories for readers. Sometimes writers will write about an event and then go back to add or change details in order to make their writing better.

WRITING ABOUT AN EVENT Explain that children will be drawing a picture of an event from *Stellaluna* and then writing about that event. Point out steps they can use to write about the event:

- Choose an event from *Stellaluna.*
- Retell the event in your own words.
- Draw a picture of what happens.
- Write a sentence that tells about the event.
- Reread the sentence and add details about the event.

Model following the steps to write about an event from *Stellaluna:* One of my favorite parts of *Stellaluna* is when the bat finds Stellaluna hanging by her thumbs. The other bat asks her why she is hanging upside down. Stellaluna is confused until the bat explains that bats hang from their feet, so Stellaluna is upside down. I'm going to write this sentence: *Stellaluna feels silly hanging by her thumbs.*

ADD DETAILS Read aloud your sentence. Then model how to add more details to tell about the event.

When I read my sentence again, I think it needs more details. I think I can add something to it. Listen: *Stellaluna feels silly hanging by her thumbs in front of a bat.* Now that sounds better. It explains why Stellaluna feels silly.

Scaffolded Instruction

STRATEGIC SUPPORT

ADDING DETAILS If children have difficulty using or adding details in their writing, have them write to tell about the event. Then ask them to ask and answer questions about what they wrote. Encourage them to see if they can answer *who, what, where, when,* and *why* questions. If they can't, they can go back to include one detail that can better clarify the event and answer one of those questions.

OBJECTIVES

Write about an event using details. W.1.3

With guidance, use technology to produce and publish writing and to collaborate with others. W.1.6

Use end punctuation. L.1.2.b

Independent Writing Practice

BRAINSTORM Have children flip through *Stellaluna* to review in their minds the events of the story. Then have them turn and talk to a partner about the event they are going to draw.

WRITE Have children choose one of the events from *Stellaluna* to write about. Then have them draw a detailed picture of the event. Children will then use p. 26 of their *Reader's and Writer's Journal* to write or dictate a sentence that tells details about the event in their picture.

CONVENTIONS If you wish to teach children about end punctuation, use the Conventions Mini-Lesson on p. 101. Encourage children to check for end punctuation in their narrative writing.

DIGITAL OPTIONS If available, have children use computers or tablets to type their sentences and print them. Then, on the same sheet of paper, have them draw a picture to illustrate their sentences.

Share Writing

Ask volunteers to share their writing and drawing with the class. Have them identify the detail they included to tell about the event.

Writing Keystone Checklist

Writing About Events Using Details

Use this checklist to assess children's narrative writing. If children need additional support writing details about events, use the Unlock Narrative Writing beginning on p. 272 of the *Scaffolded Strategies Handbook.*

	Achieved	Notes
Identify a major event in the story.		
Write a complete sentence about the event.		
Include at least one detail that tells about the event.		

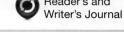

Conventions Mini-Lesson

Use End Punctuation

TEACH AND MODEL Remind children that there are different types of sentences that use different kinds of end punctuation. One type is a question. A question is an asking sentence. An asking sentence ends with a question mark. A question mark is a clue to readers to stop before reading the next sentence. It also indicates that readers' voices should rise at the end of the sentence. Write a question mark. Have children write the question mark on a sheet of paper as you write it.

Why are you hanging upside down?

This sentence ends with a question mark. It is an asking sentence. The other bat wants to know why Stellaluna is hanging by her thumbs.

An *owl* attacked you?

This sentence also ends with a question mark. It is an asking sentence. Mother Bat wants to know if an owl attacked Stellaluna when she was a baby.

PRACTICE Have children orally state questions. Point out how their voices change inflection at the end of questions. Write the questions, leaving off the question marks. Ask children to add the question mark to each sentence. Then tell them to complete the activity on p. 26 of their *Reader's and Writer's Journal.*

Scaffolded Instruction

ENGLISH LANGUAGE LEARNERS

END PUNCTUATION Help English language learners understand the difference between periods and question marks. Orally state telling sentences and asking sentences. After each sentence, ask: *Does this sentence tell something? Does this sentence want to know something?* After children have identified the type of sentences, help them choose the correct punctuation mark. Point out to native Spanish speakers that the inverted question mark at the beginning of a question in Spanish is not used in English.

OBJECTIVES

Focus Identify and understand the important details in a story's ending. RL.1.3

Use text evidence to answer questions during a close reading. RL.1.1

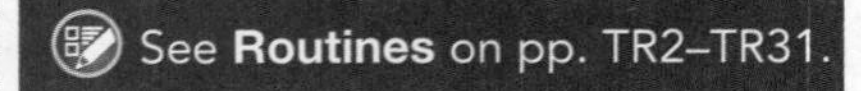

See **Routines** on pp. TR2–TR31.

Understand the Ending of a Story

LESSON 10 FIRST READ Build Understanding

SET THE PURPOSE Focus the instruction for the lesson by reading the following Enduring Understanding: *Readers understand that they improve their comprehension by identifying story elements.* An important part of any story is the ending. Authors add endings that close the action of the story. The ending can answer any questions that readers may have. It may also leave readers wondering about characters or other parts of the story. Readers often understand the point of the story once they have read the ending.

ENGAGE CHILDREN Remind children that they have read two stories: *Stellaluna* and "Dragons and Giants" from *Frog and Toad Together*. Ask them to use the illustrations to recall the beginning and middle of *Stellaluna* and "Dragons and Giants." Remind children to think about the following Essential Questions as they read, talk, and write about the texts: *How do readers know what makes a good retelling? How do writers create interesting events?* Tell children: In this lesson, we are going to learn why the ending of a story is important by looking closely at the details in the words and illustrations.

READ As you read aloud pp. 44–45 of *Stellaluna,* have children follow along and read with you when they can. Then read aloud pp. 14–15 of "Dragons and Giants" with children. Encourage children to read along silently. As you read, use the appropriate reading routine from pp. TR8–TR19. Have children focus on what they learn about the characters' friendship in each book.

TURN AND TALK After reading, have children turn to a partner and discuss this question using examples from the texts: How do the characters in each book feel about each other? Use the **Think-Pair-Share Routine** on pp. TR2–TR3. Tell children they can add drawings or other visuals to clarify their thoughts about the characters' feelings. (Children should share examples such as: Frog and Toad are happy they are friends, p. 14; Stellaluna and the birds will always be friends even though they are different, p. 44.)

FOUNDATIONAL SKILLS MINI-LESSON

Consonants *c/k/, p/p/, n/n/;* Short *a*

- Use Sound-Spelling Cards 3, 18, and 16 to review *c/k/, p/p/,* and *n/n/*. For each card, ask: What is this letter? What is the sound for this letter?
- Use Sound-Spelling Card 1 to review short *a*. Ask: What is this letter? What is the sound for this letter?
- Have children reread *Decodable Practice Readers R2A* and *R2B*. Remind them that they will read words with *c/k/, p/p/, n/n/,* and short *a*.

For more explicit instruction, see p. FS9 in this Teacher's Guide.

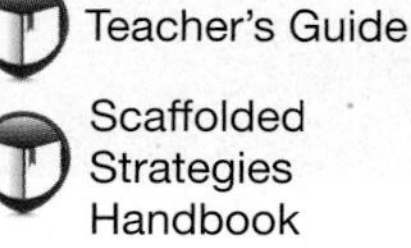

LESSON 10 SECOND READ

Close Read

CITE TEXT EVIDENCE Engage the class in a discussion about what you just read. Remind children that readers use details in the words and illustrations to help them understand the ending of a story. Use these questions to guide the discussion about pp. 44–45 of *Stellaluna* and pp. 14–15 of "Dragons and Giants." Ask children to support their answers with evidence.

- How does Stellaluna feel about the birds in the end? Let's read what she says. Read aloud the last two lines. Then have children read with you. What does Stellaluna do to show how she feels about the birds? Show me in the picture. Children should point out how they are hugging in the tree. **DOK L2**
- Would you call this a happy ending? Why? (Yes, because Stellaluna and the birds are not in danger. They are together and happy to be friends despite their differences.) Let's read what they say to each other. **DOK L2**
- Frog and Toad are scared by a snake, an avalanche, and a hawk. What does the picture show about where they are now? (Toad is under the covers in bed, and Frog is in the closet.) Let's read the part that explains this. **DOK L1**
- How do Frog and Toad feel about each other in the end? (They are happy they are friends.) Let's look for details that support this view. On page 14, Toad tells Frog he is glad to have a brave friend, and Frog tells Toad he is happy to know a brave friend. **DOK L2**
- Would you call this a happy ending? Why? (Yes, because Frog and Toad are not in danger any more. They are together and happy to be friends.) Let's find words that support our answer. **DOK L2**

Scaffolded Instruction

ENGLISH LANGUAGE LEARNERS

CONTRACTIONS The contractions *we're* and *that's* appear on p. 44 of *Stellaluna.* Explain to children that English speakers sometimes combine two words into one: *we're* means "we are" and *that's* means "that is." Use *we are* in a simple sentence and then replace it with *we're*. Do the same for *that is* and *that's*. Encourage children to provide their own example sentences.

STRATEGIC SUPPORT

LITERARY ELEMENTS If children have difficulty understanding the closure of the stories, have them study each closing illustration closely. For each illustration, ask: *Are the characters in danger? Are they happy to be with each other?*

OBJECTIVES

Determine the meaning of and use academic and domain-specific words in a text.
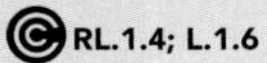 RL.1.4; L.1.6

Describe how authors end stories.
 RL.1.3

BENCHMARK VOCABULARY

- safe, p. 44

BENCHMARK VOCABULARY

- Have children find and read the sentence from *Stellaluna* with the word *safe*.

  Use the **Benchmark Vocabulary Routine for Literary Text** on pp. TR28–TR31 to teach the meaning of the word.

- Use the information on pp. 2–5 of this Teacher's Guide to discuss other words connected to the Benchmark Vocabulary word.

PRACTICE Have children use p. 27 in their *Reader's and Writer's Journal* to show contextual understanding of the Benchmark Vocabulary. Monitor children's vocabulary development.

Language Analysis

TEXT TALK

STORY ENDINGS Explain to children that sometimes authors use key words and phrases at the end of a story. These words help readers know what is important about the story. Focus children on reading key words and sentences in *Stellaluna* to better understand how the author brought the story to a close. Read aloud the final two sentences on p. 44.

MODEL The author chose to end the story with these two sentences. That makes me think they are important for us to know so we can better understand the story. Let's look closely at the words. Stellaluna says that she and the birds are friends. We know what friends are. Friends are people who like spending time together. Then Stellaluna says that is a fact. What is a fact? A fact is something that is true. Stellaluna and the birds are different in some ways but alike in other ways. That doesn't matter to Stellaluna and the birds. It is a true statement that they are friends!

Now let's look at another interesting sentence at the end of *Stellaluna*: "They perched in silence for a long time." I wonder why the author would want to end the story in this quiet, peaceful way. I think its because Stellaluna and the birds had such a scary moment before, the author wanted to have them feel safe.

PRACTICE/APPLY Reread p. 14 of "Dragons and Giants." Have children identify key words and sentences that help them better understand how the author ends the story. Use the **Small Group Discussion Routine** on pp. TR6–TR7 to have children discuss why the author would want to end the story the way he did. Remind children to ask questions to clear up any confusion about the end of the story.

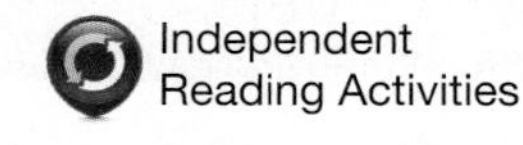

Leveled Text Library

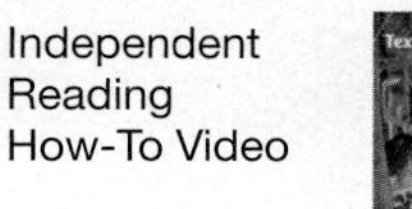

Small Group Time

STEP 1 Focused Independent Reading

BUILD ACCOUNTABILITY Prepare children to read their **self-selected texts.** Announce the two focus points to the class, and help children make a plan for their reading. Children will apply both focus points to their self-selected texts.

TODAY'S PROCESS FOCUS	
☑ Engagement and Identity	☐ Independence
☐ Stamina	

Tell children to choose a storybook they think will be interesting or fun to read. Discuss with children what they can do to decide if a book might be fun or interesting before they read it. Encourage them to think about how words or illustrations can be appealing.

TODAY'S STRATEGY FOCUS	
☐ Vocabulary Knowledge	☑ Critical Thinking
☐ Fluency	☐ Comprehension

Guide children in applying the content of today's Language Analysis lesson to analyzing their self-selected texts. We learned that authors sometimes use key words and sentences at the end of the story to help readers have closure to the events. Today as you are reading, pay attention to the words the author uses at the end. What words do you think are important for ending the story? Alternatively, have children log into Pearson Realize to find an Independent Reading Activity that is appropriate for the text they are reading.

MONITOR PROGRESS

- **Process Focus**: Have children record their reading in a daily reading log. They should draw a picture of a character, the setting, or an event and then write or dictate a phrase or sentence about the picture.
- **Strategy Focus:** Have children share what words they think are important to include in their story's ending. Alternatively, have children log into Pearson Realize and review with you the Independent Reading Activity they completed for their book.

For further guidance, see the **Independent Reading Routine** on pp. TR12–TR19.

While children are reading independently, use the Small Group Options on pp. 106–107.

INDEPENDENT LITERACY WORK

Text Club (pp. TR20–TR23)

Leveled Text Library

Center Options (pp. 10–11)

Use **Write in Response to Reading** on p. 27 of the *Reader's and Writer's Journal* to check children's understanding of key ideas in "Dragons and Giants."

Phonics: Decodable Practice Readers

GUIDED READING OPTIONS

Use the **Leveled Text Library** to choose appropriate texts based on children's needs.

Use ***ReadyUp! Intervention*** for children who require additional instruction with this lesson's reading and foundational standards or with prerequisite standards.

STEP 2 Small Group Options

Based on formative assessments of children's progress, use the following options to provide additional instruction, practice, or extension as needed.

PHONICS

For children who need support with this week's Phonics skill, use pp. FS6–FS9 in this Teacher's Guide.

UNLOCK THE TEXT

For children who need support in accessing key ideas, key language, and key structures in ***Stellaluna*** and **"Dragons and Giants,"** use **Unlock the Text** in the *Scaffolded Strategies Handbook,* pp. 8–13 and 14–19.

CONFERENCE

For independent reading accountability, **conference** each day with two or three children to discuss **self-selected texts** and support their reading.

LANGUAGE ANALYSIS SUPPORT

For children who struggle with story endings in ***Stellaluna*** and **"Dragons and Giants,"** use this **Support Language Analysis Mini-Lesson.**

STORY ENDINGS Discuss the effect of changing some words and phrases on p. 44 of *Stellaluna*. Right now, *Stellaluna* has a great ending. We know that Stellaluna and the birds are friends. What if the story ended with "'I agree,' said Stellaluna." What would that make you wonder about? Have children share their ideas about how the change would affect their understanding of the story.

Invite children to discuss another change to the text with a partner. What if the author wrote: "They perched in silence until a big owl swooped by." Would you expect the story to end? Why or why not? Use the **Think-Pair-Share Routine** on pp. TR2–TR3.

Describe how authors end stories. RL.1.3

Leveled Text Library

Reader's and Writer's Journal

Games

LANGUAGE ANALYSIS EXTENSION

For children who can easily understand the key words in the endings of *Stellaluna* and **"Dragons and Giants,"** use this **Extend Language Analysis Mini-Lesson.**

STORY ENDINGS Have children examine the closing spreads of both *Stellaluna* and "Dragons and Giants." Ask them to discuss the following questions to compare the endings:

- What sorts of problems do Stellaluna and the birds have during the story? (Possible responses: Stellaluna is separated from her mother. The birds are falling in the dark.) What sorts of problems do Frog and Toad have during the story? (They are afraid of an avalanche, a snake, and a hawk.)
- At what point in the story do Stellaluna and the birds stop having problems? (at the end) What about Frog and Toad? (at the end)
- How are Stellaluna and the birds behaving with each other at the end? (They are perched together and talking about being friends.) How are Frog and Toad behaving with each other at the end? (They are hiding together and talking about how great it is to be friends.)
- Are the endings of *Stellaluna* and "Dragons and Giants" very much alike or very much different? Why do you say so? (They are alike because the characters no longer have problems and are happy to be friends.)

Compare characters' adventures and experiences. RL.1.9

TIKATOK

For writing practice connected to the unit topic of Connecting to Our World, use **TikaTok.**

WRITE TikaTok, a digital publishing studio, allows children to write and illustrate their very own book online. Have children log in to www.tikatok.com and find the activity for this unit. Children will write in response to prompts, insert images, and illustrate their own book however they wish. Encourage children to be creative and to work through the writing process carefully before they begin creating their books.

Be sure to give children adequate time throughout the unit to log in to www.tikatok.com to work on their books.

OBJECTIVE

Plan a narrative piece of writing. W.1.3

Narrative Writing

Writing Process: Plan

SET THE PURPOSE Explain that children will have the opportunity to plan a narrative about Frog and Toad that tells about their friendship. When writers plan, they think about what they will write about. Explain that planning is the first step in the writing process. Over the next few lessons, children will work through each step of the writing process. Today they will plan their narrative.

TEACH AND MODEL Review the events that occurred in "Dragons and Giants." Have volunteers retell the story events in order.

- What is the first thing that Frog and Toad do? (They read a book together about brave people.)
- What adventures do Frog and Toad have while they try to see if they are brave? (They run into a big snake, they escape from an avalanche, and they hide from a hawk.)
- How does the author end the story? (Frog and Toad run back to Toad's house. They decide to stay inside and be brave together.)

Reread p. 6 of "Dragons and Giants." Focus on the details that help readers understand that Frog and Toad are friends. This first event of the story is essential to helping readers understand that Frog and Toad are friends.

> Frog and Toad were reading a book together. . . . "I wonder if we are brave," said Frog.

This event establishes the friendship between Frog and Toad. Readers begin to understand how the characters are together.

USE ILLUSTRATIONS Display illustrations from "Dragons and Giants." Point out that the illustrations show Frog and Toad close together.

On page 13, it looks like the characters are holding hands as they race toward Toad's home. This illustration helps me realize how strong the friendship is between Frog and Toad.

Explain to children that the writer likely thought through each of the events in the story before beginning to write. He may have sketched out the events first as well. Point out that children can take time to plan their stories by sketching the events in order first before writing.

Trade Book
Teacher's Guide
Text Collection
Scaffolded Strategies Handbook

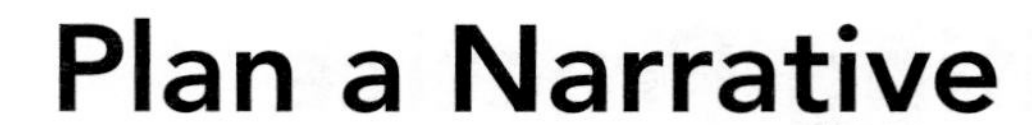

Plan a Narrative

PREPARE TO WRITE Explain to children that writers follow a process when writing. They begin by planning their writing. When planning their writing, they may organize their thoughts and make a list of characters and settings. They may even sketch out the events so they can be sure to tell what happens in an order that makes sense. Planning is just the first step in the writing process. Planning is followed by drafting, revising, editing, and publishing and presenting.

Explain that children will begin a writing project. They will be writing a narrative about Frog and Toad's friendship and how the events in the story show their friendship. First, they will begin by planning what they will write.

IDENTIFY EVENTS As a class, plan a narrative by sketching a scene from "Dragons and Giants."

I am going to write about Frog and Toad's friendship. First, I need to think about what I am going to write. I can draw my ideas. I think I'm going to tell about an event in the story and how that event shows that Frog and Toad are good friends. Let's think about the very beginning of the story. Draw a quick sketch of Frog and Toad reading a book together. Frog and Toad read a book together about brave people. This is one example of something Frog and Toad do to show they are good friends. Now let's come up with other ideas.

PLAN A NARRATIVE Work with children to brainstorm other things Frog and Toad can do that are not in "Dragons and Giants" to show they are good friends. I have an idea. I'm going to sketch a drawing of Frog sick in bed. Then I will show how Toad can be a good friend to Frog since he is sick. Toad can bring soup to Frog. Draw simple sketches.

DISCUSS THE PLAN Discuss with children how the sketches are a plan for what to write. After discussing the sketches, children should understand that the things they discussed can be written as a narrative to explain Frog and Toad's friendship.

Scaffolded Instruction

STRATEGIC SUPPORT

WRITING PROCESS Some children may have difficulty understanding or even using the planning stage of the writing process. Explain to them that sketching is not the only way to plan a piece of writing. They can make a list, use a graphic organizer, use self-stick notes to flag details in the story, or write phrases or short sentences. Encourage children to plan the way that works best for them.

OBJECTIVES

Plan a narrative piece of writing. W.1.3

With guidance, use technology to produce plans for writing and to collaborate with others. W.1.6

Use end punctuation. L.1.2.b

Independent Writing Practice

WRITE Have children go back and look at the illustrations in "Dragons and Giants" and think about the characters, Frog and Toad, and their friendship. Then have them discuss the characters' friendship in a small group, sharing reasons why they think Frog and Toad are good friends. After meeting in small groups, have children use p. 28 of their *Reader's and Writer's Journal* to

- draw two sketches of events that will take place in their own narratives about Frog and Toad and their friendship.
- number the events so they are in the correct order. Remind children that those sketches are their plans for the narrative they will write about Frog and Toad in the coming days.

CONVENTIONS If you wish to teach children about end punctuation, use the Conventions Mini-Lesson on p. 111. Encourage children to use the correct end punctuation for the sentences in their narrative writing.

DIGITAL OPTIONS If available, have children e-mail a classmate and tell about one of the sketches they've drawn.

Share Writing

Ask volunteers to share their sketches with the group. Discuss as a class how the sketches will help them write their narratives at a later time.

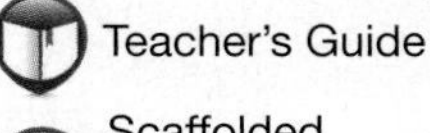

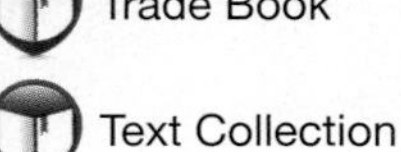
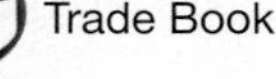

Conventions Mini-Lesson
Use End Punctuation

TEACH AND MODEL Remind children that there are different types of sentences that use different kinds of end punctuation. One type of sentence is an exclamation. An exclamation is a type of sentence that expresses strong emotions or surprise, and it ends with an exclamation mark. An exclamation mark is a clue to readers to stop before reading the next sentence. It also tells readers to add excitement or surprise to their voice as they read the sentence. Write an exclamation mark. Have children write the exclamation mark on a sheet of paper as you write it.

"They're going to crash," gasped Stellaluna. "I must rescue them!"

The last sentence ends with an exclamation mark. It shows strong emotion. Stellaluna is very worried when she states she has to rescue her friends.

PRACTICE Say the following sentences with no inflection in your voice: *I can't wait to see my grandma. What a great idea. We will have so much fun.* Then have volunteers restate those sentences with excitement. Write the sentences and have children add an exclamation mark to the end of each one. Then tell them to complete the activity on p. 28 of their *Reader's and Writer's Journal.*

Scaffolded Instruction

ENGLISH LANGUAGE LEARNERS

END PUNCTUATION Help English language learners understand when to use exclamation marks. Children may be tempted to use them more often than needed, so stress that they should be used only when there is a lot of excitement or emotion. Point out to native Spanish speakers that in English, there is no inverted exclamation mark at the beginning of a sentence.

OBJECTIVES

Focus Understand that authors use details to tell the central message of a story. RL.1.2

Use text evidence to answer questions about a story. RL.1.1

 See **Routines** on pp. TR2–TR31.

FOUNDATIONAL SKILLS MINI-LESSON

Consonants *f, ff*/f/; *b*/b/; *g*/g/

- Show the Picture Card *fan*. Let's say *fan*. Now let's say the first sound in *fan*: /f/.
- Show Sound-Spelling Card 7. Point to *f*. The letter *f* stands for the sound /f/, which you hear at the beginning of *firefighter*. Write *fad*. What is the first sound in *fad*? What letter stands for the sound /f/? *(Ff)*
- Repeat the above procedure for *b* and *g*, using the Picture Cards *bat* and *goat* and Sound-Spelling Cards 2 and 8.
- Write these words: *mat, can, tag, gap, bad*. Have children say the sound for each letter and then blend the sounds to read the word.

For more explicit instruction, see p. FS10 in this Teacher's Guide.

Identify the Central Message of a Story

LESSON 11 FIRST READ

Build Understanding

SET THE PURPOSE Focus the instruction by sharing the following Enduring Understanding: *Writers understand that details play a role in explaining the events in a story.* Remember that the events are what happen in a story. Sometimes authors use the events in a story to tell a central message. The central message is a lesson that readers can learn from the story.

ENGAGE CHILDREN Display pp. 40–41 of *Stellaluna*. Ask children to describe the illustration. Read the first sentence on p. 40. Have volunteers identify parts of the sentence, including the first word, the last word, the end punctuation mark, and uppercase letters. Remind children of the Essential Questions: *How do readers know what makes a good retelling? How do writers create interesting events?* Tell children: In this lesson we are going to focus on the details that help us identify and understand the central message, or lesson, of the story. What is the point of the story?

READ Read aloud pp. 36–45, using the appropriate reading routine from pp. TR8–TR19. Some children may be able to read along with you. Point to words as you read them so children may follow along. In this reading, have children focus on what Stellaluna and the birds learn on these pages.

TURN AND TALK After reading, have children turn to a partner and discuss this question using examples from the text: What do you learn from the last illustration? Use the **Think-Pair-Share Routine** on pp. TR2–TR3, making sure children are using best practices for speaking and listening outlined in the routine. (Children should use details such as Stellaluna and the birds hugging to explain that they are friends even though they are different, p. 45.)

LESSON 11 SECOND READ

Close Read

CITE TEXT EVIDENCE Engage the class in a discussion about what you just read, reminding them to follow the discussion rules by taking turns speaking and listening carefully to others. Tell children to focus on the details that help them identify the central message of the story. Use these questions to guide the discussion, and ask children to support their answers with evidence.

- Why do the birds follow Stellaluna when she flies at night? (Stellaluna wants to show them what it's like to fly at night.) What do they all learn? (They learn that the birds cannot see in the dark.) Let's read what the birds say to let Stellaluna know they cannot see. Read the dialogue aloud with children. Show me in the illustration how you know the birds cannot fly at night. Children should point out how Stellaluna is holding on to them. **DOK L2**
- How are the birds and Stellaluna alike? (They all can fly. They all perch in trees. They are all friends.) How are they different? (Stellaluna can see in the dark and the birds cannot. Stellaluna hangs upside down and the birds perch right-side up on a branch.) **DOK L2**
- After Stellaluna rescues the birds, why do they all sit in silence for a long time? (Possible responses: They might be feeling scared. They are relieved they are safe. They are thinking about the ways they are alike and different.) **DOK L3**
- What questions do the birds and Stellaluna have after they sit in silence? (They wonder how they can be so alike and so different at the same time.) How does the author show that the birds do not know the answers to the questions? (The writer does not answer the questions, but uses Flap to say that the answer is a mystery.) **DOK L3**
- Ask your "reading sleuths" to work with a partner to find details that support a lesson readers can learn from this story. (Friends can be alike and different at the same time.) Let's read the words that help us figure that out. **DOK L3**

Scaffolded Instruction

ENGLISH LANGUAGE LEARNERS

KEY IDEAS Review the meanings of the words *alike* and *different*. Have children think of two objects that are similar but different, such as two balls of different sizes and colors. Have children tell how the balls are alike and different. Emphasize the correct usage of the terms *alike* and *different* in the descriptions.

STRATEGIC SUPPORT

KEY IDEAS If children have difficulty listing things that the birds and Stellaluna learn, read pp. 42–44 and ask clarifying questions, such as: *Did Stellaluna know that the birds would have trouble flying at night? How did they learn this lesson?*

OBJECTIVES

Determine the meaning of and use academic and domain-specific words in a text.
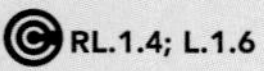 RL.1.4; L.1.6

Demonstrate understanding of the central message of a story. RL.1.2

BENCHMARK VOCABULARY

- mused, p. 44
- wondered, p. 44
- mystery, p. 44

BENCHMARK VOCABULARY

- Have children find and read sentences from the text with the words *mused, wondered,* and *mystery*.

  Use the **Benchmark Vocabulary Routine for Literary Text** on pp. TR28–TR31 to teach the meanings of the words.

- Use the information on pp. 2–5 of this Teacher's Guide to discuss other words connected to each of the Benchmark Vocabulary words.

PRACTICE Have children use p. 30 in their *Reader's and Writer's Journal* to show contextual understanding of the Benchmark Vocabulary. Monitor children's vocabulary development.

Reading Analysis

TEXT TALK

CENTRAL MESSAGE Remind children that a story often has a message or lesson. The message or lesson is what readers can learn from the story. Sometimes readers can ask themselves, "What is the point of this story?" "What does the author want me to know when I have finished reading?" Readers often have to use key details and what they already know to figure out the message or lesson. As a group, create a list of lessons the birds and Stellaluna learn in this section of the story. Discuss how Stellaluna and the birds are alike and different.

MODEL When I read this section of the story, I learn that bats can fly at night but birds cannot. Stellaluna and the birds learn this lesson too. It's good that they have something in common: they can all fly. But they cannot all fly at the same time. Now Stellaluna and the birds realize that they cannot do some things together because of this difference. But when I read that Stellaluna rescues the birds at night, I understand that she really cares about the birds. And they really care about Stellaluna because they are willing to try to fly at night with her. They are good friends even though they are different.

PRACTICE/APPLY Have children work in small groups to identify other ways Stellaluna and the birds are different and how those differences affect what they can do together. Use the **Small Group Discussion Routine** on pp. TR6–TR7 to have children discuss what they know and how they can combine that with the details in the book to determine the central message of the story. Then have them work independently to complete p. 31 of their *Reader's and Writer's Journal*. They should write or draw pictures to tell the central message of *Stellaluna*.

Generative Vocabulary Games
Reader's and Writer's Journal
Leveled Text Library
Independent Reading Activities
Independent Reading How-To Video

Small Group Time

STEP 1 Focused Independent Reading

BUILD ACCOUNTABILITY Prepare children to read their **self-selected texts**. Announce the two focus points to the class, and help children make a plan for their reading. Children will apply both focus points to their self-selected texts.

TODAY'S PROCESS FOCUS	
☑ Engagement and Identity	☐ Independence
☐ Stamina	

Tell children to select a storybook they might enjoy reading. They can ask a friend for a recommendation, take a picture walk through a book, or decide based on the cover illustration.

TODAY'S STRATEGY FOCUS	
☐ Vocabulary Knowledge	☐ Critical Thinking
☐ Fluency	☑ Comprehension

Guide children in applying the content of today's Reading Analysis lesson to their self-selected texts. We learned that readers use key details from a story and what they already know to figure out the central message, or lesson, of a story. Today as you are reading, use self-stick notes to mark interesting details that may help you figure out the lesson of your book. Once you finish reading, go back and look at the details you marked. Use the details and what you know to figure out the lesson of the story. Alternatively, have children log into Pearson Realize to find an Independent Reading Activity that is appropriate for the text they are reading.

MONITOR PROGRESS

- **Process Focus:** Have children record their reading in a daily reading log. Ask them to draw or write about what made them choose and read that book.
- **Strategy Focus:** Have children review their self-stick notes with you. Then ask them what they think the lesson of the book is. Alternatively, have children log into Pearson Realize and review with you the Independent Reading Activity they completed for their book.

For further guidance, see the **Independent Reading Routine** on pp. TR12–TR19.

While children are reading independently, use the Small Group Options on pp. 116–117.

INDEPENDENT LITERACY WORK

Text Club (pp. TR20–TR23)

Leveled Text Library

Center Options (pp. 10–11)

Use **Write in Response to Reading** on p. 30 of the *Reader's and Writer's Journal* to check children's understanding of the central message in *Stellaluna.*

Phonics: Decodable Practice Readers

GUIDED READING OPTIONS

Use the **Leveled Text Library** to choose appropriate texts based on children's needs.

Use ***ReadyUp! Intervention*** for children who require additional instruction with this lesson's reading and foundational standards or with prerequisite standards.

STEP 2 Small Group Options

Based on formative assessments of children's progress, use the following options to provide additional instruction, practice, or extension as needed.

PHONICS

For children who need support with this week's Phonics skill, use pp. FS10–FS13 in this Teacher's Guide.

UNLOCK THE TEXT

For children who need support in accessing key ideas, key language, and key structures in ***Stellaluna***, use **Unlock the Text** in the *Scaffolded Strategies Handbook*, pp. 8–13.

CONFERENCE

For independent reading accountability, **conference** each day with two or three children to discuss **self-selected texts** and support their reading.

READING ANALYSIS SUPPORT

For children who struggle with the central message of ***Stellaluna,*** use this **Support Reading Analysis Mini-Lesson**.

CENTRAL MESSAGE Help children work through p. 31 of their *Reader's and Writer's Journal*. For example, ask children to list ways Stellaluna and the birds are alike and different. Then ask them to find details that describe how the birds and Stellaluna feel at the end of the story. As children answer your questions, help them use the information to draw or write sentences to record those details.

Invite children to use their drawings or sentences to tell the central message of the story. Remind them to use what they already know and the details in the story to figure out the central message, or lesson. Tell them to think of the point of the story or what the author wants readers to understand after reading the story. Use the **Think-Pair-Share Routine** on pp. TR2–TR3.

Demonstrate an understanding of the central message of a story. RL.1.2

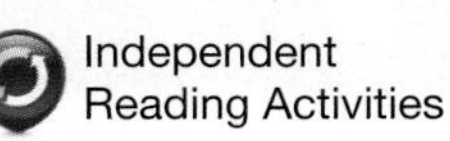

Games

Independent Reading Activities

Reader's and Writer's Journal

READING ANALYSIS EXTENSION

For children who can easily identify and understand the central message in *Stellaluna,* use this **Extend Reading Analysis Mini-Lesson**.

CENTRAL MESSAGE Have children think of a time in their own lives when they realized they were both alike and different from a friend. On a separate sheet of paper, children should write or draw pictures to show how they and their friends are alike and different and what message they want to share about this. Then have children discuss the following questions:

- In what ways are you and your friend alike? How are you different? (Possible response: My friends and I are the same age and go to the same school, but we like different games.)
- How do the differences make you feel? (Possible responses: I like that my friend and I have different favorite toys because it is fun to play with something new. I don't like it when my friend doesn't want to play the game I want to play.)
- What do you learn from your differences? (Possible response: We have to take turns.)
- How is the lesson from *Stellaluna* something you can apply in your life? (Possible response: I have met people who are like me and others who different, but they can all be my friends.)

Demonstrate an understanding of the central message of a story. RL.1.2

FLUENCY

For fluent reading accountability, use the **Oral Reading Fluency Quick Check**. ☑ **Today assess 2–3 children.**

MODEL ACCURACY Explain to children that reading with accuracy means pronouncing each word correctly and not skipping or adding words. When readers read, they try to read all the words correctly so that listeners can understand the story. Read aloud the last paragraph on p. 42 of *Stellaluna*. Read a few words incorrectly, such as *grapping* for *grabbing* and *hug* for *hung*. Discuss how reading those words incorrectly affected their comprehension of the story. Read the paragraph again with accuracy. Then provide each child with a leveled text at his or her reading level to read accurately.

Read grade-level text with accuracy. RF.1.4.b

QUICK CHECK

MONITOR PROGRESS

If . . . children are misreading words,

then . . . have them think about what word would make sense in the sentence. Then have them use that word to check comprehension.

If . . . . children cannot read a word,

then . . . have them sound out the word and reread the sentence.

OBJECTIVE
Write a narrative that recounts two events with details. W.1.3

Narrative Writing

Writing Process: Draft

SET THE PURPOSE Remind children that they are working through the writing process. In the previous lesson, they planned a narrative about Frog and Toad's friendship by drawing illustrations about two events. Explain that today they will use their plans to write about those events.

TEACH AND MODEL To help children recall details about Frog and Toad and their relationship, revisit pp. 8–9 of "Dragons and Giants" and discuss the illustrations using the following questions:

- What does the illustration on page 8 tell readers about Frog and Toad's friendship? (Frog is leading the way up the mountain, but he looks back to make sure that Toad is following him. He wants to make sure that Toad doesn't get too far behind.)
- What does the illustration on page 9 tell readers about Frog and Toad's friendship? (As the snake is scaring them, Frog and Toad are still together. That means they are staying side by side to protect each other.)

Provide the following models from pp. 8 and 9 of "Dragons and Giants" to show how the text supports the illustrations:

Frog went leaping over rocks, and Toad came puffing up behind him.

Frog looks back over his shoulder to make sure Toad is following along. The illustration on page 8 helps readers understand that Frog is waiting for Toad. He is acting like a good friend should.

Frog and Toad jumped away.

The illustration on page 9 shows Frog and Toad together. The text confirms that they stayed with each other as they escaped from the snake. Good friends stay together during scary times.

Write a Narrative

PREPARE TO WRITE Review with children that writers follow a process when writing. Remind them that they have spent time planning how and what they will write about Frog and Toad's friendship. Now they will draft, or write, their narrative. Children will use their sketches or other methods of planning to write. Tell them that during the drafting stage, they should focus on getting their ideas down on paper. There are steps later in the writing process that will allow them to review their writing and fix it before publishing and presenting it.

REVIEW WRITING PLANS Return to the sketches you created in Lesson 10. Tell children you will use the sketches to help tell your story about Frog and Toad's friendship.

The sketches I made about two events with Frog and Toad help me think about my story before I begin writing. I am going to review each sketch and write a sentence to go with each illustration. As I write, I want to make sure to include details about the characters, setting, and events. If I forget to add a detail, there will be a time to go back to my writing and fix it later.

DRAFT A NARRATIVE Discuss the steps children can use as they write their story about Frog and Toad's friendship.

- Look at the sketches and think about details that will help readers better understand what the sketches show.
- Write a sentence about the first illustration. Include details about the characters, the setting, or the event.
- Write a sentence about the second illustration. Include details about the characters, the setting, or the event.

Here's what I can write to tell about my sketches: *Frog is sick in bed. Toad makes soup for Frog.*

Scaffolded Instruction

STRATEGIC SUPPORT

WRITING NARRATIVES To help struggling writers get their thoughts on paper, have them share their ideas with you orally. Then help them break down the writing process by guiding them to write a key word about each event. Then they can return to each word to write an entire sentence.

OBJECTIVES

Write a narrative that recounts two events with details. W.1.3

With guidance, use technology to produce and publish writing and to collaborate with others. W.1.6

Capitalize sentences and names of people. L.1.2.a

Independent Writing Practice

WRITE Have children review their illustrations from Lesson 10 or p. 28 of their *Reader's and Writer's Journal*. Tell them to think about what they want to write to tell their readers a story about the two events. Some children may find it helpful to discuss the events with a partner before writing. Then have children use p. 32 of their *Reader's and Writer's Journal* to write a sentence about each picture to create a narrative about Frog and Toad's friendship.

CONVENTIONS If you wish to teach children about capitalizing the first word in sentences and names of people, use the Conventions Mini-Lesson on p. 121. Encourage children to check for correct use of capital letters in their narrative writing.

DIGITAL OPTIONS If available, have children use computers or tablets to type their sentences and print them.

Share Writing

Ask volunteers to share their narrative with a small group. Invite the group to identify the two events and discuss ideas for illustrations to accompany each event.

Conventions Mini-Lesson

Capitalize Sentences and Names of People

TEACH AND MODEL Tell children that a word that begins with a capital letter begins with an uppercase letter. When we write, we have to follow certain rules. Some rules tell about what kinds of words begin with a capital, or uppercase, letter. The first word in a sentence always begins with a capital letter. Remind children that a sentence is a group of words that tell a complete idea. The names of people always begin with a capital letter too.

"Hello lunch," said the snake when he saw Frog and Toad.

The first word in this sentence begins with a capital letter. The names of the characters are *Frog* and *Toad*, so those words begin with a capital letter.

The next day Stellaluna went to visit the birds.

The first word in this sentence begins with a capital letter. The character's name is *Stellaluna*, so it always begins with a capital letter.

PRACTICE Write short sentences that are not capitalized correctly. Be sure to include names. Point to and read each word in the sentence one at a time and ask children if the word should begin with a capital letter. If the word needs a capital letter, have a volunteer say the name of the letter that should be an uppercase letter. For more practice with capitalizing, complete the activity on p. 32 of their *Reader's and Writer's Journal*.

Scaffolded Instruction

ENGLISH LANGUAGE LEARNERS

CAPITALIZATION English language learners may need more practice writing uppercase letters. Provide a sheet of all uppercase letters for them to trace, first with their finger and then with a pencil. After children have practiced writing the uppercase letters, display pages from *Stellaluna* or "Dragons and Giants." Ask them to find words that begin with capital letters. Discuss why each word needs to begin with a capital letter.

OBJECTIVES

Focus Identify and use key details to demonstrate understanding of a story's central message or lesson.

Use text evidence to answer questions about a story. RL.1.1

See Routines on pp. TR2–TR31.

Identify the Central Message of a Story

LESSON 12 FIRST READ Build Understanding

SET THE PURPOSE Focus the instruction by sharing the following Enduring Understanding: *Learners understand that living things depend on one another.* Authors often want readers to learn something when they read their stories. The lesson that authors want them to learn is called the central message. Sometimes we can think about the characters and what they do and learn to help us figure out what the author wants us as readers to learn.

ENGAGE CHILDREN With children, take a picture walk through "Dragons and Giants" to refresh their memories about the key events of the story. Ask volunteers to tell what is happening in each picture. Remind children to think about the Essential Questions as they read, talk, and write about the story: *How do readers know what makes a good retelling? How do writers create interesting events?* Tell children: In this lesson we are going to focus on the details that help us identify and understand the central message of the story. Remember that the central message is the lesson that the author wants readers to know. Sometimes we can ask ourselves "What is the point of the story?"

READ As you read "Dragons and Giants," use the appropriate reading routine from pp. TR8–TR19. Have children read aloud sentences with you and then on their own. In this reading, have children focus on Frog and Toad and their behavior toward each other.

TURN AND TALK After reading, have children turn to a partner and discuss this question using examples from the text: Why do Frog and Toad run down the mountain? Use the **Think-Pair-Share Routine** on pp. TR2–TR3. (Children should explain that they are afraid of things on the mountain, such as an avalanche, p. 11, and a hawk, p. 12.) As you check children's understanding, make sure they are using best practices for speaking and listening as outlined in the routine.

FOUNDATIONAL SKILLS MINI-LESSON

High-Frequency Words; Consonants *f, ff/f/; b/b/; g/g/*

- Display the High-Frequency Word Card for *you*. Have children spell and say the word with you. Repeat with the words *see* and *the.*
- Ask children to use the high-frequency words in sentences.
- Have children turn to *Decodable Practice Reader R3A* on p. 33. Have children read the title and preview the story. You will be reading words with the consonants *f, b,* and *g*.
- Have partners take turns reading the story.

For more explicit instruction, see p. FS11 in this Teacher's Guide.

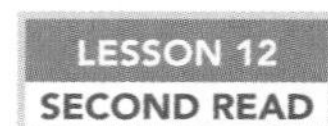
LESSON 12 SECOND READ

Close Read

CITE TEXT EVIDENCE Engage the class in a discussion about what you just read. Tell them to focus on details that help them figure out the central message of the story. Remind children that they can always ask a speaker to clarify information or provide more information if they are not understanding what is being discussed. Use these questions to guide the discussion, and ask children to support their answers with evidence.

- What does Toad do when they get to his house after running down the mountain? (He jumps into the bed and pulls the cover over his head.) Let's read that part together and then show me in the picture. **DOK L1**
- What words tell you that Frog and Toad like each other? Let's read that part. Choral read the dialogue that Frog and Toad have on p. 14. How do Frog and Toad feel about each other? (They really care about each other. They are glad they are friends.) **DOK L2**
- Are Frog and Toad really brave? How can you tell? (No, they're not brave because they are hiding from the things that scared them on the mountain.) Why do you think they call each other brave? (because they are friends and want to make each other feel good and brave) **DOK L2**
- What do you think the author is saying about the importance of friendship? (Possible response: It is more important to have friends than be like the brave people you read about in stories.) What words and details in the story support your idea? Let's find those words and details and read them aloud. **DOK L3**
- Ask your "reading sleuths" to work with a partner to find words the author uses to explain that Frog and Toad are really afraid even though they say they are not. (Children can find the words *shaking* and *cried* on p. 9, *trembling* on p. 11, and *screamed* on p. 13.)

Scaffolded Instruction

ENGLISH LANGUAGE LEARNERS

ORAL READING For certain English learners, consonant blends in English pose difficulties if children do not have those sound combinations in their home languages. Guide children to practice initial *r* blends, such as *fr* (*frog, from*) and *br* (*brave, broken*).

STRATEGIC SUPPORT

KEY IDEAS If children have difficulty understanding why Frog and Toad call each other brave, show how the two are friends and then discuss how friends do not want to hurt each other's feelings. Ask how Toad might feel if Frog said he was not brave, and vice versa.

OBJECTIVES

Determine the meaning of and use academic and domain-specific words in a text. 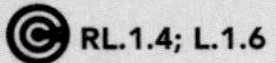 RL.1.4; L.1.6

Determine the central message of a story. RL.1.2

BENCHMARK VOCABULARY

- together, p. 6

BENCHMARK VOCABULARY

- Have children find and read the sentence from the text with the word *together*.

  Use the **Benchmark Vocabulary Routine for Literary Text** on pp. TR28–TR31 to teach the meaning of the word.
- Use the information on pp. 2–5 of this Teacher's Guide to discuss other words connected to the Benchmark Vocabulary word.

PRACTICE Have children use p. 33 in their *Reader's and Writer's Journal* to show contextual understanding of the Benchmark Vocabulary. Monitor children's vocabulary development.

Reading Analysis

TEXT TALK

CENTRAL MESSAGE Remind children that authors often want readers to learn something from their stories. This is the central message, or lesson. Readers can think about what they learn from a story or what the point of the story is. The author usually does not state the lesson in the story, but rather includes details to help the reader figure it out. Readers can use the details as well as things they already know to figure out what the author is trying to say.

MODEL In this story, Frog and Toad do many things together. One thing they do is read a book about brave people. They really like reading about those brave people. I can tell they really like reading together because they eventually try to do brave things together so they can be like the people in the book. Let's think about other ways Frog and Toad act. How do Frog and Toad talk to each other and feel about each other? List children's ideas. We can use what we know to figure out what lesson this story is teaching about friends and friendship. How does the author use details to teach the lesson?

PRACTICE/APPLY Have children work with a partner or in small groups to write or draw a picture that shows details about Frog and Toad's friendship. Use the **Think-Pair-Share Routine** on pp. TR2–TR3 to have children discuss what lesson Frog and Toad's friendship can teach readers. Check understanding by asking children to share or by circulating among children or groups.

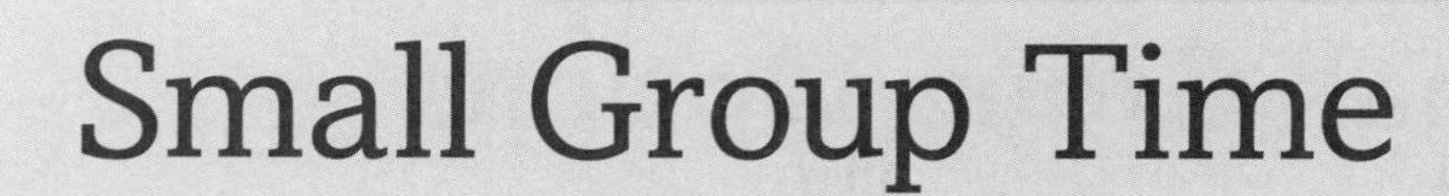

Independent Reading How-To Video

Small Group Time

STEP 1 Focused Independent Reading

BUILD ACCOUNTABILITY Prepare children to read their **self-selected texts.** Announce the two focus points to the class, and help children make a plan for their reading. Children will apply both focus points to their self-selected texts.

TODAY'S PROCESS FOCUS	
☐ Engagement and Identity ☑ Stamina	☐ Independence

Explain to children that they are going to try to read as many words as they can in their self-selected text. Have them choose a book they have read before so that many of the words will be familiar. Then give them the signal to begin reading. When time is up, have children look back at how many words they were able to read.

TODAY'S STRATEGY FOCUS	
☑ Decoding and Word Recognition ☐ Fluency	☐ Critical Thinking ☐ Comprehension

Guide children in recognizing and reading high-frequency words in their self-selected texts. Write the words *you, see, the, look, like,* and *I*. We have learned many high-frequency words. Let's read them together. As you read today, look for these words and create a list of the ones you find. Alternatively, have children log into Pearson Realize to find an Independent Reading Activity that is appropriate for the text they are reading.

MONITOR PROGRESS

- **Process Focus:** Have children record their progress in a daily reading log. Have them write how many words or how many pages they were able to read. Ask them to explain to you whether it was easy or difficult for them to continue reading during the time they were given.
- **Strategy Focus:** Have children point out places where they found the words *you, see, the, look, like,* and *I*. Ask children to read the sentences with the words. Alternatively, have children log into Pearson Realize and review with you the Independent Reading Activity they completed for their book.

For further guidance, see the **Independent Reading Routine** on pp. TR12–TR19.

While children are reading independently, use the Small Group Options on pp. 126–127.

INDEPENDENT LITERACY WORK

Text Club Club (pp. TR20–TR23)

Leveled Text Library

Center Options (pp. 10–11)

Use **Write in Response to Reading** on p. 33 of the *Reader's and Writer's Journal* to check children's understanding of "Dragons and Giants."

Phonics: Decodable Practice Readers

GUIDED READING OPTIONS

Use the **Leveled Text Library** to choose appropriate texts based on children's needs.

Use ***ReadyUp! Intervention*** for children who require additional instruction with this lesson's reading and foundational standards or with prerequisite standards.

STEP 2 Small Group Options

Based on formative assessments of children's progress, use the following options to provide additional instruction, practice, or extension as needed.

PHONICS

For children who need support with this week's Phonics skill, use pp. FS10–FS13 in this Teacher's Guide.

UNLOCK THE TEXT

For children who need support in accessing key ideas, key language, and key structures in **"Dragons and Giants,"** use **Unlock the Text** in the *Scaffolded Strategies Handbook,* pp. 14–19.

CONFERENCE

For independent reading accountability, **conference** each day with two or three children to discuss **self-selected texts** and support their reading.

READING ANALYSIS SUPPORT

For children who struggle with identifying the central message in **"Dragons and Giants,"** use this **Support Reading Analysis Mini-Lesson.**

CENTRAL MESSAGE Help children work through the details in "Dragons and Giants" to figure out the central message. In "Dragons and Giants," Frog and Toad are friends. How do we know? What do they do to show they are friends? Write children's ideas in a list. Then ask children to describe how Frog and Toad act and feel at the end of the story. Discuss what children can draw to show these details and then provide time and materials.

Invite children to use their drawings to tell the story's central message about friends and friendship to a partner. Ask them to think of the point of the story. Use the **Think-Pair-Share Routine** on pp. TR2–TR3.

Use story details to understand the central message or lesson. RL.1.2

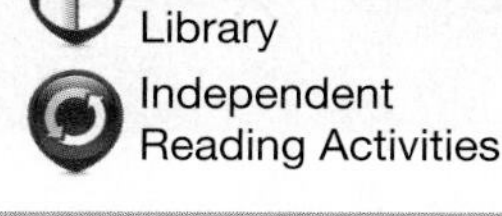

Scaffolded Strategies Handbook
Reader's and Writer's Journal
Leveled Text Library
Independent Reading Activities
Games

READING ANALYSIS EXTENSION

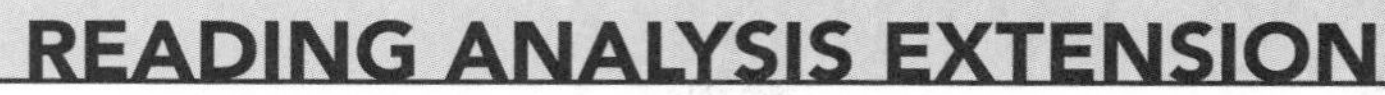

For children who can easily identify the central message in **"Dragons and Giants,"** use this **Extend Reading Analysis Mini-Lesson.**

CENTRAL MESSAGE Have children place their drawn or written central message of "Dragons and Giants" next to the central message activity for *Stellaluna* on p. 31 of their *Reader's and Writer's Journal*. Then have partners use a Venn diagram to compare the central messages of the two stories. Ask children to write *Stellaluna* on the left side and "Dragons and Giants" on the right side of the diagram. Have them use the answers from the following questions to fill in the diagram:

- What did you learn about friends and friendship from *Stellaluna?* (People can be different but still be friends.)
- What did you learn about friends and friendship from "Dragons and Giants"? (Friends feel happy when they are together.)
- How are the central messages of the stories alike? (They both tell something about what it means to be friends.)
- Do you think these messages about friends are true? Why or why not? Encourage children to use evidence from the stories to support their responses.

Use story details to understand the central message or lesson of a story. RL.1.2

FLUENCY

For fluent reading accountability, use the **Oral Reading Fluency Quick Check.** ☑ **Today assess 2–3 children.**

MODEL ACCURACY Explain that reading with accuracy means pronouncing each word correctly and not skipping or adding words. Have children follow along as you model reading aloud p. 10 from "Dragons and Giants," mispronouncing several words that children will recognize. Ask children to name the words you read incorrectly and tell how you should pronounce them. Read the text again, this time with accuracy. Then provide each child with a leveled text at his or her reading level to read accurately.

Read grade-level text with accuracy. RF.1.4.b

QUICK CHECK

MONITOR PROGRESS

If . . . children mispronounce words as they read,

then . . . have them practice reading aloud with a partner who can help them pronounce the words correctly.

If . . . children are skipping or adding words as they read,

then . . . have them point to each word as they read it aloud to ensure they do not miss or add any words.

OBJECTIVE

Revise and edit a narrative with two events. W.1.3

Narrative Writing

Writing Process: Revise and Edit

SET THE PURPOSE Review the writing process with children, reminding them that they have planned and written a story about Frog and Toad's friendship. Tell them that today they will revise and edit their writing.

Explain that after writers write their stories, they revise them. When writers revise, they reread their writing and look for ways to make their stories even better. During revising, writers may add details that they forgot to include in the first draft. They may also change details if it makes their writing better. If the writers are also the illustrators, as you are, then they will add to their illustrations as well. Then, explain that once revisions are done, writers will edit their writing. When writers edit, they go back through their writing one more time to look for errors in capitalization, punctuation, and spelling.

TEACH AND MODEL Display the illustrations on pp. 8–9 of "Dragons and Giants." Provide the following models from those pages:

Frog went leaping over rocks, and Toad came puffing up behind him.

The writer may have gone back to his writing and added details to tell how Frog went over the rocks and how Toad came up the mountain. The words ***leaping*** and ***puffing*** make the writing more interesting.

They came to a dark cave. A big snake came out of the cave.

The writer may have gone back to his writing to add adjectives to describe the cave and the snake. The words ***dark*** and ***big*** give the readers details about why Frog and Toad might be scared.

Then revisit the text on p. 12 of "Dragons and Giants." With children, revise the sentence.

The shadow of a hawk fell over them.

Discuss how the writer might add details to make this event even more exciting. Questions such as "What was the shadow like?" or "How big is the hawk?" can provide ideas for details to revise the sentence.

Revise and Edit a Narrative

PREPARE TO REVISE AND EDIT Explain to children that you will revise and edit the sentences you wrote in Lesson 11 as well as the sketches if necessary. They will add or change details and then check to make sure their capitalization and end punctuation are correct. Tell children that you will also revisit your sketches and add final details to them too.

Have children consider these steps when they revise and edit their story:

- Reread your story. Think about questions readers might wonder about as they read your story.
- Have a friend read your story and share questions he or she has.
- Add details based on your thoughts as well as your friend's questions.
- Reread your story again, focusing on capitalization at the beginning of sentences and punctuation at the end of sentences.

ASK QUESTIONS Read aloud the sentences you wrote from Lesson 11: *Frog is sick in bed. Toad makes soup for Frog.*

As I reread my story, I wonder what questions readers might have. Perhaps they might wonder about Frog's illness. I could add a detail about what is wrong with Frog. Readers might also wonder what kind of soup Toad makes and why he makes it. I can add some details to my writing to answer those questions.

ADD DETAILS Write your new, revised sentences, and then read them aloud:

Frog is sick in bed with a bad cold.

Toad makes chicken soup ~~for~~ to help Frog feel better.

I added details that tell more about Frog's illness and why Toad makes him soup. I added the word *chicken* to tell what kind of soup Toad makes. Then I looked back to make sure each sentence begins with a capital letter and ends with a punctuation mark.

Scaffolded Instruction

STRATEGIC SUPPORT

REVISING NARRATIVES Help struggling writers revise their writing by asking them questions about their original drafts. Children may not see an immediate way to add details, but with some prompts, they may find it easier to add more information or clarify what they have written.

OBJECTIVES

Revise and edit a narrative with two events. W.1.3

With guidance, use technology to edit and revise writing and to collaborate with others. W.1.6

Produce simple sentences. L.1.1.j

Independent Writing Practice

WRITE Have children review their stories and think about the questions that readers might have about their stories. Then have children share their stories with a partner. Have partners share questions they have about the story. Have children

- add details to their stories based on their own thoughts and the questions of their partners.
- reread and edit their stories, making sure they have capital letters at the beginning of sentences and the correct end punctuation.
- add final details to their illustrations.
- write one revised sentence on p. 34 of the *Reader's and Writer's Journal*.

CONVENTIONS If you wish to teach children about producing simple sentences, use the Conventions Mini-Lesson on p. 131. Encourage children to check that they write complete sentences in their narratives.

DIGITAL OPTIONS If available, have children revisit their writing on a computer or tablet to make any revisions and edits to their sentences.

Share Writing

Have volunteers share their revised narratives with their partners. Ask them to discuss how the revisions helped readers better understand their stories.

Writing Keystone Checklist

Writing a Narrative

Use this checklist to assess children's narrative writing. If children need additional support writing a narrative using the writing process, use the Unlock Narrative Writing beginning on p. 272 of the *Scaffolded Strategies Handbook.*

	Achieved	Notes
Plan a narrative.		
Write a narrative that includes two or more events.		
Revise and edit the narrative by adding details and checking capitalization and end punctuation.		

Conventions Mini-Lesson

Produce Simple Sentences

TEACH AND MODEL Remind children that a sentence is a group of words that tell a complete idea. A sentence tells who or what the sentence is about and what that person, animal, or thing is or does.

Frog and Toad were reading a book together.

This sentence tells who was doing something: *Frog and Toad.* It tells what they were doing: *reading a book together.* This sentence begins with a capital letter and ends with a punctuation mark.

A big snake came out of the cave.

This sentence tells who was doing something: *a big snake.* It tells what the snake did: *came out of the cave.* This sentence begins with a capital letter and ends with a punctuation mark.

PRACTICE Have volunteers suggest complete sentences. Write these sentences. Discuss who or what each sentence is about and what that person, animal, or thing is or does. For more practice producing simple sentences, have children complete the activity on p. 34 of their *Reader's and Writer's Journal.*

Scaffolded Instruction

ENGLISH LANGUAGE LEARNERS

PRODUCING SENTENCES Some English language learners may struggle with producing sentences. Provide a subject, such as *The cat* or *Frog and Toad*. Then prompt them to answer the question, "What do (does) _____ do?" Write their suggestions and then help children use those words to create sentences, such as *The cat plays. Frog and Toad climb.*

OBJECTIVES

Focus Understand that authors can use facts to create characters and settings in literary text. RL.1.5

Use text evidence to answer questions about a text. RL.1.1

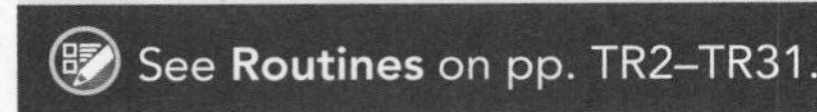
See **Routines** on pp. TR2–TR31.

Discuss Informational and Literary Texts

LESSON 13 FIRST READ

Build Understanding

SET THE PURPOSE Explain that today children will listen to an informational text about bats. They will add the new information they learn about real bats to their understanding of the character Stellaluna. Focus the instruction by sharing the following Enduring Understanding: *Writers understand that details play a role in explaining the events in a story.* Remember that *Stellaluna* is a story about a make-believe bat that does many things that real bats do. Sometimes writers use facts about real people or animals to help explain the events in a story.

ENGAGE CHILDREN Display the last two pages of *Stellaluna.* Read the heading, "BAT NOTES." Explain to children that the text and illustrations on these pages give facts about real bats. Tell them that this part of *Stellaluna* is scientific nonfiction. What do you think each illustration shows? Have volunteers identify the features of sentences, pointing out the first word, the capital letter, and the end punctuation. Remind children of the Essential Questions: *How do readers know what makes a good retelling? How do writers create interesting events?* Tell children: We are going to learn how the writer uses interesting facts about bats to create the characters and settings in *Stellaluna.*

READ Have children read the title, "BAT NOTES" with you. Then read aloud the section, having children read the word *bats* with you. Use the appropriate reading routine from pp. TR8–TR19. As you read, ask them to think about how Stellaluna is like a real bat.

TURN AND TALK After reading, have children turn to a partner and discuss this question using examples from the text: What interesting facts did you learn about bats? Use the **Think-Pair-Share Routine** on pp. TR2–TR3 and make sure children are using best practices for speaking and listening as outlined in the routine. (Children should share examples such as: Many bats eat insects, while others catch fish, amphibians, and reptiles, p. 46; Fruit bats are often called flying foxes, p. 47.)

FOUNDATIONAL SKILLS MINI-LESSON

Short *i*: /i/

- Show the Picture Card *insect*. Let's say *insect.* Now let's say the first sound in *insect:* /i/. Show the Picture card *pig*. Let's say *pig.* Now let's say the middle sound in *pig:* /i/.
- Display Sound-Spelling Card 11. Point to *i.* The letter *i* stands for the sound /i/, which you hear at the beginning of *insects*. It also stands for the middle sound in *pig*, /p/ /i/ /g/. Let's write *i* and say its sound.
- Write the words *fin, it, big,* and *it.* Have children say the sound for each letter and then blend the sounds to read the words.

For more explicit instruction, see p. FS12 in this Teacher's Guide.

LESSON 13 SECOND READ

Close Read

CITE TEXT EVIDENCE Engage the class in a discussion about what you just read. Remind children that an informational text tells facts and details about real people or animals, real places, and real events. Use these questions to lead the discussion. Ask children to support their answers with evidence to confirm understanding.

- Why is the scientific name for bats Chiroptera, meaning "hand-wing"? (because the skeleton in their wings is made of their finger bones) Show me how the illustration explains this. **DOK L2**
- The text says fruit bats are sometimes called flying foxes. Look at the illustration on page 47. How does the illustration help you understand the text? (It shows a bat and a fox so we can see how they are alike.) In what ways are the fox and the fruit bat alike? (The text says they both have long muzzles, large eyes, pointy ears, and furry bodies.) **DOK L2**
- How do fruit bats find their way? (Fruit bats have great vision and sense of smell.) Let's find where it says that. **DOK L1**
- Ask your "reading sleuths" to work with a partner to find details in the illustrations of Stellaluna that show she is like a real fruit bat. (Stellaluna has "hand-wings," big eyes, pointy ears, and a furry body in the illustrations.) **DOK L3**

BY-THE-WAY WORDS During close reading, define the following words for children involving known concepts that can be stumbling blocks to comprehending the text.

species, p. 46: Tell children that a species is a group of animals or plants that are alike in some ways.

navigate, p. 47: *Navigate* means "to find the way to get to a place".

Scaffolded Instruction

ENGLISH LANGUAGE LEARNERS

MAIN IDEA The high-level vocabulary may present a challenge to many English language learners. Summarize and simplify the text so that children can understand the main ideas, focusing on p. 47 and the information about fruit bats.

STRATEGIC SUPPORT

KEY DETAILS If children have difficulty understanding the characteristics of fruit bats, read p. 47 and ask direct questions after every key piece of information, such as: *Is a fruit bat big or small? What does a fruit bat look like? What helps a fruit bat get from place to place? What do fruit bats eat?*

OBJECTIVES

Determine the meaning of and use academic and domain-specific words in a text.

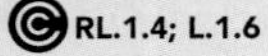

Compare literary and informational texts.

BENCHMARK VOCABULARY

- wingspan, p. 47
- tropical, p. 47

BENCHMARK VOCABULARY

- Have children find and read sentences from the text with the words *wingspan* and *tropical.*

  Use the **Benchmark Vocabulary Routine for Literary Text** on pp. TR28–TR31 to teach the meanings of the words.

- Use the information on pp. 2–5 of this Teacher's Guide to discuss other words connected to each of the Benchmark Vocabulary words.

PRACTICE Have children use p. 36 in their *Reader's and Writer's Journal* to show contextual understanding of the Benchmark Vocabulary. Monitor children's vocabulary development.

Language Analysis

TEXT TALK

FICTION AND NONFICTION

Remind children that a literary text tells a made-up story. It can have made-up characters, setting, and events. An informational text gives facts and information about real people, places, and events. Discuss other features of literary and informational texts, creating a list. Provide the T-chart graphic organizer on p. TR39.

Comparing Chart

Literary Text	Informational Text
Stellaluna is a made-up story. The characters are animals that can talk.	"BAT NOTES" is an informational text. It tells information about real bats.

MODEL Let's think about the features of literary and informational texts. I know that *Stellaluna* is a literary text because the characters are animals that can talk. Animals cannot talk in real life. I'll write this on my chart. I know that "BAT NOTES" is an informational text because it tells facts about real bats. I'll write that information on my chart too.

PRACTICE/APPLY Have children work independently or in small groups to complete the graphic organizer about features of literary and informational texts using examples from *Stellaluna* and "BAT NOTES." Use the **Small Group Discussion Routine** on pp. TR6–TR7 to have children compare and contrast literary and informational texts. Remind them to use the T-chart for examples to support their analysis.

Leveled Text Library

Independent Reading Activities

Independent Reading How-To Video

PEARSON realize.

Small Group Time

STEP 1 Focused Independent Reading

BUILD ACCOUNTABILITY Prepare children to read their **self-selected texts.** Announce the two focus points to the class, and help children make a plan for their reading. Children will apply both focus points to their self-selected text.

TODAY'S PROCESS FOCUS	
☐ Engagement and Identity	☐ Independence
☑ Stamina	

Explain to children that they are going to try to read as many words as they can in their self-selected text. Have them choose a book they have read before. Then give them the signal to begin reading. When time is up, have children look back at how many words they were able to read.

TODAY'S STRATEGY FOCUS	
☑ Decoding and Word Recognition	☐ Critical Thinking
☐ Fluency	☐ Comprehension

Guide children in recognizing and reading words with short *i* in their self-selected texts. Write the words *in* and *big.* We learned that the letter *i* can stand for the short *i* sound /i/. The short *i* sound can come at the beginning of a word, as in the word *in.* It can be in the middle of a word, such as in *big.* As you go through your book today, look for words with short *i* and count how many you read. Alternatively, have children log into Pearson Realize to find an Independent Reading Activity that is appropriate for the text they are reading.

MONITOR PROGRESS

- **Process Focus:** Have children record their progress in a daily reading log. Have them write how many words or how many pages they were able to read. Then have them make notes about words that caused them to slow down or stop.
- **Strategy Focus:** Have children share how many short *i* words they found. Read the sentences with the words and have children repeat. Alternatively, have children log into Pearson Realize and review with you the Independent Reading Activity they completed for their book.

For further guidance, see the **Independent Reading Routine** on pp. TR12–TR19.

While children are reading independently, use the Small Group Options on pp. 136–137.

INDEPENDENT LITERACY WORK

Text Club (pp. TR20–TR23)

Leveled Text Library

Center Options (pp. 10–11)

Use **Write in Response to Reading** on p. 36 of the *Reader's and Writer's Journal* to check children's understanding of key ideas in *Stellaluna.*

Phonics: Decodable Practice Reader

GUIDED READING OPTIONS

Use the **Leveled Text Library** to choose appropriate texts based on children's needs.

Use ***ReadyUp! Intervention*** for children who require additional instruction with this lesson's reading and foundational standards or with prerequisite standards.

STEP 2 Small Group Options

Based on formative assessments of children's progress, use the following options to provide additional instruction, practice, or extension as needed.

PHONICS

For children who need support with this week's Phonics skill, use pp. FS10–FS13 in this Teacher's Guide.

UNLOCK THE TEXT

For children who need support in accessing key ideas, key language, and key structures in ***Stellaluna,*** use **Unlock the Text** in the *Scaffolded Strategies Handbook,* pp. 8–13.

CONFERENCE

For independent reading accountability, **conference** each day with two or three children to discuss **self-selected texts** and support their reading.

CLOSE READING SUPPORT

For children who struggle with close reading, use this **Support Mini-Lesson for *Sleuth.***

SLEUTH WORK Read aloud "A New Family" on pp. 10–11 of *Sleuth*. Then discuss the following questions with the group. Have children use text evidence to support their answers.

LOOK FOR CLUES Explain how the pictures match the words. Ask children to match the picture to the words in the story.

ASK QUESTIONS Imagine that Ben tells his friend about the birds. What would they want to know? Have children dictate questions.

MAKE YOUR CASE Tell about the things you learned from the words and things you learned from the pictures. Which helped you learn more? Have children cite examples from the text.

PROVE IT! Have children work in groups to find details about the nest and present them to the class.

Ask and answer questions about key details in a text. RL.1.1

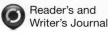

CLOSE READING EXTENSION

For children who are adept or excel at close reading, use this **Extend Mini-Lesson for *Sleuth.***

SLEUTH WORK Help children read "A New Family" on pp. 10–11 of *Sleuth.* Then discuss the following questions with the group. Have children use text evidence to support their answers.

LOOK FOR CLUES Who are the characters in "A New Family"? (Ben and Dad) How are the characters in "A New Family" and *Stellaluna* different? (The characters in "A New Family" are people. The characters in *Stellaluna* are animals.)

ASK QUESTIONS Imagine you are telling a family member how the two stories are alike and different. What questions might they have about the stories? Have children dictate questions.

MAKE YOUR CASE How is "A New Family" like *Stellaluna?* (Both stories have nests of birds.) Ask children to read sentences or point to pictures in the stories that help them answer the question.

PROVE IT! Is "A New Family" a literary or informational text? How do you know? Arrange children into groups. Tell them to find sentences in the text to help them answer the question.

After children discuss the *Sleuth* work, direct them to pp. 37–38 of their *Reader's and Writer's Journal* to further explore "A New Family."

Ask and answer questions about key details in a text. RL.1.1

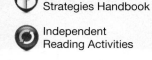

OBJECTIVE

Publish a narrative with reasons.

 W.1.3, W.1.6

Narrative Writing

Writing Process: Publish

SET THE PURPOSE Remind children that in the previous lesson they revised their narratives about Frog and Toad and their friendship. Today they will publish a final copy of their narrative. Publishing is a way to share the final copy of your writing with other people. You can use a computer or tablet to publish an electronic copy, or you can use your best handwriting to publish a final copy.

After writers publish their writing, they can present it to others. Remind children that when they present, they should express their thoughts and ideas clearly. Explain that they should use the drawings they added to their writing to provide additional details. Tell children they can present their writing in different ways:

- They can read their writing aloud.
- They can explain what their pictures show.
- They can display their writing for others to see.

TEACH AND MODEL Display *Stellaluna.* Explain that the author published her writing in a book. Point out how the book has a cover with a title and the author's name. It also has an illustration that supports the text.

Display pages 4–5 of *Stellaluna*. In this published book, all of the sentences have been typed on a computer and have no errors. The sentences begin with a capital letter and have an ending punctuation mark. Explain that on page 4, the illustration goes along with and adds detail to the text on page 5.

Make sure children understand that there are many different ways to publish their writing. Books, posters, and blog posts are just a few ways writers share their work with others.

Publish a Narrative

PREPARE TO PUBLISH Explain to children that now they will publish the stories they revised in Lesson 12.

Have children consider the kind of format they want to publish their writing in by asking: What is the best way to share this writing? Create a list of children's suggestions.

MODEL Tell children that once they have determined the best way to share their writing, they can start publishing their stories.

Model the publishing process with children: I have revised and edited my story about Frog and Toad and their friendship. Now I am ready to publish my writing so I can add it to our classroom library. I want my story to be in a book format.

PUBLISH Have children work together as a class to publish the story about Frog and Toad.

- Create a cover for your story. Be sure to add the writer's and illustrator's names.
- Write your sentences with your best handwriting on a clean piece of paper or type an error-free copy on a computer.
- Add your drawings to your writing.
- Present your published story to the class.

Scaffolded Instruction

STRATEGIC SUPPORT

PUBLISHING NARRATIVES For children who struggle with the physical act of writing, it may be helpful to have them type their final sentences on a computer or tablet and then print them out to add to their illustrations.

OBJECTIVES

Publish a narrative that recounts two events. W.1.3

With guidance, use technology to produce and publish writing and to collaborate with others. W.1.6

Use capitalization and punctuation.

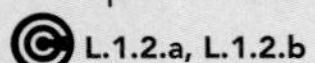

Independent Writing Practice

WRITE Have children publish their Frog and Toad stories using p. 39 of their *Reader's and Writer's Journal.* Provide time to complete the publishing process. Have children think of a title and write it on the page. Then have them draw a picture for their cover on the page. Then, on a separate sheet of paper, create a clean copy of their story by using their best handwriting. Remind them to use letter formation, lines, and spaces to create a readable document.

CONVENTIONS If you wish to review capitalization and punctuation with children, use the Conventions Mini-Lesson on p. 141. Encourage children to review their writing one last time to make sure that it includes capital letters where needed and correct end punctuation marks.

DIGITAL OPTIONS If available, have children use computers or tablets to publish their writing via a classroom blog or Web site, or to e-mail to a classmate.

Share Writing

Have volunteers share the published pieces with the group. Encourage others to respond with positive feedback. Remind the class to listen attentively and ask any questions after the presentation.

Conventions Mini-Lesson

Capitalization and Punctuation

TEACH AND MODEL Remind children of the capitalization and punctuation rules they have learned. Review that names begin with capital letters, such as *Stellaluna* and *Grace.* Also, review that a sentence begins with a capital letter and ends with an end mark. Telling sentences end with a period. Questions end with a question mark. Sentences that show excitement or strong feelings end with an exclamation point.

Oh no! The bird cannot see at night.	The first word of each sentence has a capital letter. The first sentence ends with an exclamation point. The second sentence ends with a period.
What is Tom's favorite part of the book?	The first word begins with a capital letter. The word *Tom's* begins with a capital letter because it is a name. The sentence ends with a question mark.

PRACTICE Write several simple sentences that are missing capital letters and end punctuation and include names. Read the sentences aloud with the class. Then have volunteers revise the sentences so that they have correct capitalization and end punctuation. For more practice with capitalization and punctuation, have children complete the activity on p. 39 of their *Reader's and Writer's Journal.*

Scaffolded Instruction

ENGLISH LANGUAGE LEARNERS

CAPITALIZATION AND PUNCTUATION English language learners may still need additional practice using capital letters and end punctuation. Revisit *Stellaluna* or "Dragons and Giants" and go on a capital letter or punctuation scavenger hunt. Ask children to find a capital letter or to identify various end punctuation marks used in these texts.

OBJECTIVE
Write a narrative, recounting two sequenced events with details. W.1.3

Performance-Based Assessment

NARRATIVE TASK

WRITE ABOUT FRIENDSHIP

Children will think about the friendship between the birds and Stellaluna. Then they will illustrate and write sentences about how the characters showed their friendship when they first met and then later in the story. **DOK L2**

Children will

- illustrate two events in the order in which they occurred in the story.
- write a sentence to tell about each event and how the birds and Stellaluna showed their friendship.

See p. 146 for reproducible page for student distribution.

TEACHER NOTE You may wish to administer this assessment over multiple lessons.

Use the *Scaffolded Strategies Handbook* to provide additional support for the diverse learners in your class. The Performance-Based Assessment lesson in the handbook provides guidance with unlocking the task, breaking down the writing process, and examining conventions and craft.

Prepare

REVIEW Discuss the Essential Questions: *How do readers know what makes a good retelling?* and *How do writers create interesting events?* Then introduce the Performance-Based Assessment to children.

REVISIT THE TEXT Remind children that at one point in the story, Stellaluna wanted to save her friends Pip, Flitter, and Flap from danger. Model a good retelling of this section of the text by recounting the events that show how Stellaluna saved her friends.

> When night came Stellauna flew away. Pip, Flitter, and Flap leapt from the tree to follow her.
> "I can't see a thing!" yelled Pip.
> "Neither can I," howled Flitter.
> "Aaeee!" shrieked Flap.
> "They're going to crash," gasped Stellaluna. "I must rescue them!"
> Stellaluna swooped about, grabbing her friends in the air. She lifted them to a tree, and the birds grasped a branch.
> – *Stellaluna,* p. 42

Tell children that before they draw their pictures and write their sentences, they should think about what they learned about friendship in *Stellaluna*.

Create

MATERIALS

- Notebooks or paper
- Pencils, crayons, or markers
- Text: *Stellaluna*

WRITE

Have children work independently on their writing tasks, but circulate to assist children if they are unsure about how to proceed.

DIGITAL OPTION If desired, you may incorporate technology into the Performance-Based Assessment. Once children have completed their pictures and sentences, scan their work into a computer. You may then project their work when they share their writing with the class.

BEST PRACTICES

- Encourage children to ask questions before they begin the writing task.
- Suggest that children refer to the text *Stellaluna* for help with remembering the events in the story and for spelling and vocabulary support.
- If children are unsure of word spellings, suggest that they write a word the way it sounds.

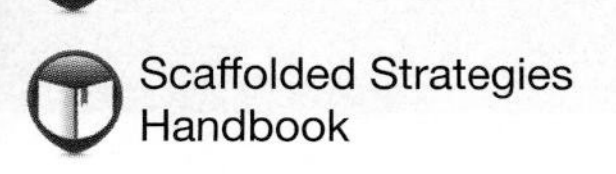

Teacher's Guide

Trade Book

Scaffolded Strategies Handbook

Scaffolded Support

In order for all children to access the Performance-Based Assessment, additional supports can be provided as necessary.

CHECKLIST Provide a checklist or a graphic, such as the one on p. 192 of the *Scaffolded Strategies Handbook,* that details expectations for this project. It will clarify for children what is being assessed.

GRAPHIC ORGANIZER Work with small groups to complete a Story Sequence A chart. Have children cross out the Middle box. Guide them to fill in the Beginning box to show when Stellaluna and the birds first met. Then guide them to complete the End box to show the characters later in the story.

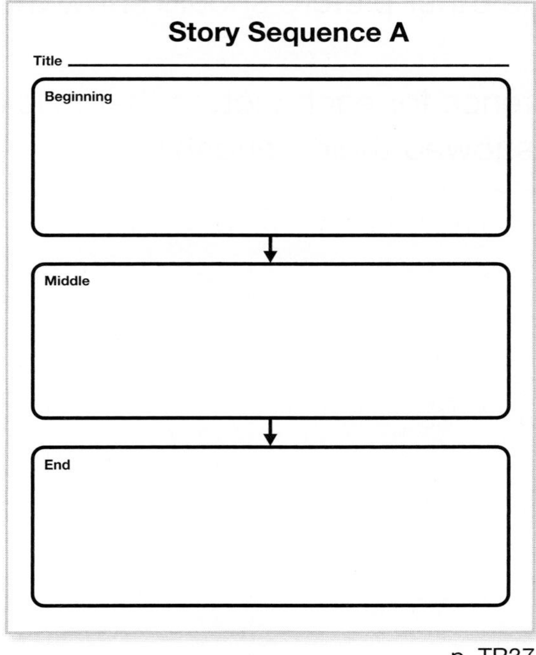

Story Sequence A

Title ______________________

Beginning

Middle

End

p. TR37

WRITING TASKS Writing tasks can be previewed and broken down into smaller steps for clarity. For example, have conferences with children about their ideas before they begin to write.

EDITING TASKS Post examples of complete sentences with highlighted capitalization and punctuation.

Performance-Based Assessment
Grade 1 • Unit 1 • Module A

NARRATIVE TASK

WRITE ABOUT FRIENDSHIP

Think about the friendship between the birds and Stellaluna.

- Draw pictures of two events from the story. One picture should show when Stellaluna and the birds first met. The other picture should show them later in the story.
- Write a sentence for each picture that tells how the characters showed their friendship.

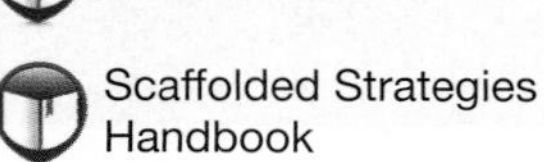

Narrative Writing Rubric

Score	Focus	Organization	Development	Language and Vocabulary	Conventions
4	Narrative is clearly focused on the friendship between Stellaluna and the birds using details from the text.	Narrative recounts two sequenced events. Sentences and pictures correspond.	Narrative effectively shows the theme of friendship through pictures and sentences.	Narrative includes two or more details that clearly describe characters, settings, or events.	Narrative includes two complete sentences with end punctuation; untaught words are spelled phonetically.
3	Narrative is about the friendship between Stellaluna and the birds.	Narrative recounts two events. Sentences and pictures correspond.	Narrative shows some evidence of the theme of friendship through pictures and sentences.	Narrative includes one or more details that describe characters, settings, or events.	Narrative includes two sentences without end punctuation; untaught words are spelled phonetically.
2	Narrative is about friendship or Stellaluna and the birds.	Narrative recounts one event. Sentence and picture correspond.	Narrative shows limited evidence of a theme of friendship or other theme through pictures or sentences.	Narrative includes one detail that tells the characters, settings, or events.	Narrative includes one sentence without end punctuation; untaught words are spelled phonetically.
1	Narrative is not about friendship or Stellaluna and the birds.	Narrative recounts one event. Sentence and picture do not correspond.	Narrative shows no evidence of a theme through pictures or sentences.	Narrative includes no details that tell the characters, settings, or events.	Narrative includes one fragment; untaught words are unintelligible.
0	Possible characteristics that would warrant a 0: • Child does not write a narrative. • Narrative does not recount an event. • Narrative lacks any sense of organization.				

Present

AUTHOR CELEBRATION Children share their writing with the class.

Children have worked hard writing about friendship. They may be curious to hear what their classmates had to say about the theme. Have children share their work with the class.

- Organize the classroom: Find one big chair to be the author's chair.
- Have children take turns sitting in the author's chair and reading what they have written.
- As children read, encourage them to speak clearly and slowly.
- Post children's work in the library corner or in another prominent place in the classroom. Title the display with wording from the selection, such as: "We're friends. And that's a fact."
- **DIGITAL OPTION** If you chose to incorporate technology into the Performance-Based Assessment, then use a computer, projector, and screen to display the scanned versions of children's work. As authors share their writing with the class, project their pictures and sentences on a screen for the audience to see.

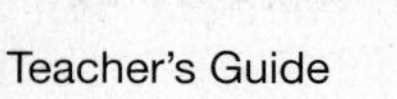
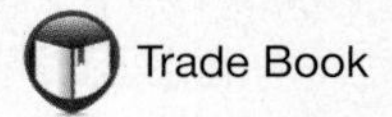

Reflect and Respond

LOOKING AHEAD For children who received a score of 0, 1, or 2 on the rubric, use the following suggestions to support them with specific elements of the Performance-Based Assessment. Graphic organizers and other means of support will help guide children to success as they complete other Performance-Based Assessments throughout the school year.

If . . . children struggle with writing events in sequence,

then . . . provide them with a story sequence graphic organizer to help them visualize the order of the events.

If . . . children need extra support with focusing on the friendship theme,

then . . . give them other examples of acts of friendship to help them better understand the theme.

If . . . children have trouble adding details about characters,

then . . . share and discuss books with strong character development to help children transfer their understandings to their own writing.

If . . . children need extra support with providing details about settings or events,

then . . . point out details of settings and events during read-alouds to help children transfer this understanding to their own writing.

Path to College and Career Readiness

Dig Deeply into Complex Text

Connecting to Our World

TEXT SET

PEARSON realize™

ANCHOR TEXT

Time to Sleep
Lexile 140L
Informational Text

SUPPORTING TEXT

What Do You Do With a Tail Like This?
Lexile 620L
Informational Text

SLEUTH

"A Happy Ending"
Lexile 360L

Leveled Text Library
Lexile BR–370L

Enduring Understandings

- **Readers** understand that informational texts have features that help them determine main topics.
- **Writers** understand that informational texts can have a variety of features.
- **Learners** understand that living things have certain behaviors that shape them and allow them to survive.

"Knows"

ESSENTIAL QUESTIONS

How do features in informational texts help **readers** understand the main topic?

How does the organizational structure of a text help **writers** explain information?

"Dos"

MODULE GOALS

Readers will use features of informational texts to better comprehend what they read.

Writers will write questions and answers about animals.

EXPLORE CONTENT **Learners** will identify behaviors and relationships that help animals survive.

PERFORMANCE-BASED ASSESSMENT

INFORMATIVE/EXPLANATORY: WRITE QUESTIONS AND ANSWERS

Children will use facts from *Time to Sleep* and *What Do You Do With a Tail Like This?* to write questions and answers about animals.

Vocabulary to Unlock Text

Generative Vocabulary

ReadyGEN provides systems for understanding how words work. Teach **generative vocabulary** as children dig deeply into complex texts. Focus on sets of rare Tier II and Tier III words that unlock meaning, build knowledge of critical content domains, and help children internalize word-learning strategies. Go to www.PearsonSchool.com/ReadyGEN to read more about generative vocabulary instruction in *ReadyGEN.*

BENCHMARK VOCABULARY Benchmark Vocabulary words are important for understanding concepts within a text. These can be defined as

- words needed to deeply comprehend a text.
- words from other disciplines.
- words that are part of a thematic, semantic, and/or morphological network.
- words central to unlocking the Enduring Understanding of the text.

BY-THE-WAY WORDS By-the-Way Words are sophisticated or unusual Tier II and Tier III words for known concepts that can be stumbling blocks to comprehending a text. They should be defined quickly during reading, but instruction should not interfere with the fluent reading of the text. These are addressed during Close Reading and can be defined as

- words that don't require lengthy discussion within a particular text.
- words supported by the text for meaning.
- words that are more concrete.

Generative Vocabulary in Speaking and Writing Children should demonstrate a deep understanding of vocabulary by using those words and words generated from them in conversation, writing practice, and the Performance-Based Assessments.

Additional Vocabulary Support

For Spanish cognates, see the *Scaffolded Strategies Handbook*.

ANCHOR TEXT *Time to Sleep*

Informational Text Use this chart as a starting point for your class to generate related words. There may be more words in each cluster than those listed here.

Benchmark Vocabulary	Possible Morphological Links	Possible Semantic Links	Informational Links
time	timely	moment	*Topic*
sleep	sleeping, sleepy	nap, bedtime	*Unit Theme*
animals		duck, horse, bat	*Unit Theme*
sorts		kinds	*Topic*
upside down		flipped	*Topic*
scared	scary	frightened, afraid	*Topic*
lock	locked	stiff	*Topic*
danger	dangerous	harm	*Unit Theme*
tuck	tucking, tucked	fold	*Topic*
day	Monday, daytime	light	*Topic*
high	higher	up, above	*Topic*
anywhere		anyplace	*Unit Theme*
hang	hanging	dangle	*Topic*

Vocabulary to Unlock Text

SUPPORTING TEXT *What Do You Do With a Tail Like This?*

Informational Text Use this chart as a starting point for your class to generate related words. There may be more words in each cluster than those listed here.

Benchmark Vocabulary	Possible Morphological Links	Possible Semantic Links	Informational Links
underground		tunnel, burrow, cave	*Unit Theme*
breathe	breath	living, air, lungs	*Topic*
pesky	pest, pester	annoy, bother, irritate	*Topic*
warn	warning	advise, alert, urge, signal, inform	*Topic*
spot (verb)		see, spy, locate	*Topic*
squirt	squirting	shoot, spray, splash, spout, fountain	*Topic*
sticky		gummy, tricky	*Topic*
scoop	scooping	spoon, bucket, shovel	*Topic*
swallow	swallowing	eat, drink, consume	*Topic*
eyes	eyeball, eyesight	vision, seeing	*Topic*
feet	foot	paws, toes	*Topic*

Additional Vocabulary Support

For Spanish cognates, see the *Scaffolded Strategies Handbook*.

UNIT 1 • MODULE B Overview

Readers understand that informational texts have features that help them determine main topics.

READYGEN LESSONS	READING INSTRUCTIONAL FOCUS Text Talk / Close Read / Text Analysis	INDEPENDENT READING Process and Strategy
LESSONS 1–7 *Time to Sleep* 	Identify Main Topic Using Text Features	**P** Engagement and Identity **S** Vocabulary Knowledge
	Use Text Features to Locate Key Information	**P** Engagement and Identity **S** Comprehension
	Identify Main Topic and Key Details	**P** Engagement and Identity **S** Comprehension
	Ask and Answer Questions about Key Details	**P** Engagement and Identity **S** Critical Thinking
	Identify Information from Pictures and Words	**P** Engagement and Identity **S** Decoding and Word Recognition
	Identify How Information Is Connected	**P** Independence **S** Critical Thinking
	Answer Questions Using Text Features	**P** Independence **S** Decoding and Word Recognition
LESSON 8 *What Do You Do With a Tail Like This?* 	Use Structure and Organization to Understand a Text	**P** Independence **S** Fluency
LESSON 9 *Time to Sleep* and *What Do You Do With a Tail Like This?*	Compare and Contrast Texts	**P** Engagement and Identity **S** Comprehension
LESSONS 10–12 *What Do You Do With a Tail Like This?*	Identify Elements of Informational Texts	**P** Engagement and Identity **S** Vocabulary Knowledge
	Ask and Answer Questions	**P** Engagement and Identity **S** Comprehension
	Use Illustrations to Understand Details	**P** Stamina **S** Critical Thinking

P = Process Focus **S** = Strategy Focus

Connecting to Our World

Writers understand that informational texts can have a variety of features.

WRITING INSTRUCTIONAL FOCUS	INDEPENDENT WRITING
Write Facts About a Topic	Write a Fact About a Text
Write a Heading	Write About a Photograph
Structure of Informative Writing	Write a Question and an Answer
Use Facts	Write a Fact
Write About a Main Topic	Use a Graphic Organizer
Question-and-Answer Text Structure	Write an Answer to a Question
Question-and-Answer Text Structure	Write a Question and an Answer
Question-and-Answer Text Structure	Write a Question and an Answer
Write Facts About a Topic	Write a Fact
Writing Process: Plan	Plan a Question and an Answer
Writing Process: Draft	Write a Question and an Answer
Writing Process: Revise, Edit, Publish	Revise, Edit, and Publish a Question and an Answer

PERFORMANCE-BASED ASSESSMENT

Children will use facts from *Time to Sleep* and *What Do You Do With a Tail Like This?* to write questions and answers about animals.

Planner

Suggested Pacing

READING
30–40 minutes

- Build Understanding
- Close Read
- Benchmark Vocabulary
- Text Analysis

SMALL GROUP TIME
30–40 minutes

- Focused Independent Reading
- Small Group Options

WRITING
30–40 minutes

- Informative/Explanatory Writing
- Independent Writing Practice

LESSON 1

Teacher's Guide, pp. 162–171

READ Trade Book Read the entire book.
Time to Sleep

BENCHMARK VOCABULARY
time, sleep

LANGUAGE ANALYSIS Ask and Answer Questions

WRITING Write a Fact About a Text

LESSON 2

Teacher's Guide, pp. 172–181

READ Trade Book Read the entire book.
Time to Sleep

BENCHMARK VOCABULARY
animals

READING ANALYSIS Text Features

WRITING Write About a Photograph

LESSON 6

Teacher's Guide, pp. 212–221

READ Trade Book pp. 8–11
Time to Sleep

BENCHMARK VOCABULARY
danger, tuck

READING ANALYSIS Describe Connections

WRITING Write an Answer to a Question

LESSON 7

Teacher's Guide, pp. 222–231

READ Trade Book pp. 12–16
Time to Sleep

BENCHMARK VOCABULARY
day, high, anywhere

READING ANALYSIS Text Features

WRITING Write a Question and an Answer

LESSON 11

Teacher's Guide, pp. 262–271

READ *Text Collection* pp. 24–35
What Do You Do With a Tail Like This?

BENCHMARK VOCABULARY
spot, squirt

READING ANALYSIS Ask and Answer Questions

WRITING Write a Question and an Answer

LESSON 12

Teacher's Guide, pp. 272–281

READ *Text Collection* pp. 36–43
What Do You Do With a Tail Like This?

BENCHMARK VOCABULARY
sticky, scoop, swallow

READING ANALYSIS Illustrations and Text

WRITING Revise, Edit, and Publish a Question and an Answer

LESSON 3
Teacher's Guide, pp. 182–191
READ Trade Book pp. 2–3
Time to Sleep
BENCHMARK VOCABULARY
sorts
READING ANALYSIS Main Topic
WRITING Write a Question and an Answer

LESSON 4
Teacher's Guide, pp. 192–201
READ Trade Book pp. 4–5
Time to Sleep
BENCHMARK VOCABULARY
upside down, scared
READING ANALYSIS Ask and Answer Questions
WRITING Write a Fact

LESSON 5
Teacher's Guide, pp. 202–211
READ Trade Book pp. 6–7
Time to Sleep
BENCHMARK VOCABULARY
lock
READING ANALYSIS Distinguish Information in Text and Pictures
WRITING Use a Graphic Organizer

LESSON 8
Teacher's Guide, pp. 232–241
READ *Text Collection* Read the entire book.
What Do You Do With a Tail Like This?
BENCHMARK VOCABULARY
underground, breathe
LANGUAGE ANALYSIS Text Structure
WRITING Write a Question and an Answer

LESSON 9
Teacher's Guide, pp. 242–251
COMPARE
- *Time to Sleep*
- *What Do You Do With a Tail Like This?*

BENCHMARK VOCABULARY
hang, high, feet, eyes
READING ANALYSIS Compare and Contrast
WRITING Write a Fact

LESSON 10
Teacher's Guide, pp. 252–261
READ *Text Collection* pp. 24–31
What Do You Do With a Tail Like This?
BENCHMARK VOCABULARY
pesky, warn
READING ANALYSIS Main Topic and Key Details
WRITING Plan a Question and an Answer

LANGUAGE AND FOUNDATIONAL SKILLS IN THIS MODULE
Conventions Nouns and Verbs; Common and Proper Nouns; Plural Nouns; Question Marks; Capitalization and Punctuation; Verbs *is* and *are* **Phonics** Consonants *d*/d/, *l*, *ll*/l/, *h*/h/, *r*/r/, *w*/w/, *j*/j/, *k*/k/, *v*/v/, *y*/y/, *z*, *zz*/z/, *qu*/kw/; Short *o*: *o*/o/; Short *e*: *e*/e/

PERFORMANCE-BASED ASSESSMENT
Teacher's Guide, pp. 282–289
INFORMATIVE/EXPLANATORY TASK: WRITE QUESTIONS AND ANSWERS
Children will use facts from *Time to Sleep* and *What Do You Do With a Tail Like This?* to write questions and answers about animals.

Center Options

During Small Group Time, children can use independent center activities to practice and apply standards while you work with individuals or groups. Options for activities focusing on both concepts and learning objectives for this unit are included here.

READING CENTER

- Have children tell a partner how text features from an independent reading book helped them locate information.
- Have children share with a partner the main topic and two key details from an independent reading book.
- Log into Pearson Realize and use the instruction in the Comprehension Focus and Vocabulary Focus sections of the Reading Mat activity for this module. Then have children read EnVision Math Problem-Solving Mat for Topic 7, *How many legs?*, and complete the accompanying graphic organizer.

DOK L2

WRITING CENTER

- Have children draw a picture of something they learned from reading an informational text. Then have them write a fact that they learned and write a question and an answer based on the facts they read.

Write in Response to Reading

Have children complete the appropriate Write in Response to Reading prompts, found within pp. 40–75 of their *Reader's and Writer's Journal.*

- Have children log into TikaTok and write their own informational book about an interesting animal they choose. Explain that they will tell about the animal using questions and answers. Have children go to www.tikatok.com

DOK L2

DIGITAL CENTERPIECES

STUDENTS AS AUTHORS
Powered by TikaTok

Children write their own books connected to the unit topic. They log into **www.tikatok.com**, respond to prompts, insert images, and produce a book to keep.

STUDENTS AS THINKERS

Children use EnVision Math Problem-Solving Mats to practice comprehension and vocabulary. They apply what they learn as they complete a unique online activity.

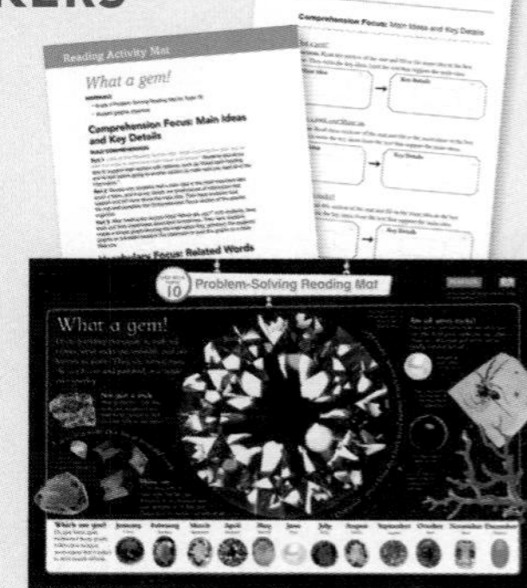

Connecting to Our World

MODULE GOALS

Readers will use features of informational texts to better comprehend what they read.

Writers will write questions and answers about animals.

Learners will identify behaviors and relationships that help animals survive.

WORD WORK CENTER

- Have children write new headings for sections in an informational text they have read.
- Have children create a list of words used at the beginning of questions, such as *who* and *what.* Have children look for these words when used in independent reading texts.
- Have children make a list of words that describe one of the animals they have read about. As they read books during independent reading, they may find other interesting words to describe the animal they chose.

DOK L2

RESEARCH CENTER

- Have children brainstorm a list of animals that they know. Have them choose an animal and find out how that animal sleeps. Children may look on the Internet or use other resources.
- Have children choose an animal and research what it does to survive. Have children share one interesting survival fact with a partner.
- Have children draw an animal that has interesting features. Have them label the features on the animal, for example, a duck's webbed feet. The pictures could be collected and placed in a class book.

DOK L2

STUDENTS AS WORD WORKERS

Children play online foundational skills and generative vocabulary games to strengthen their word analysis skills and build their vocabulary.

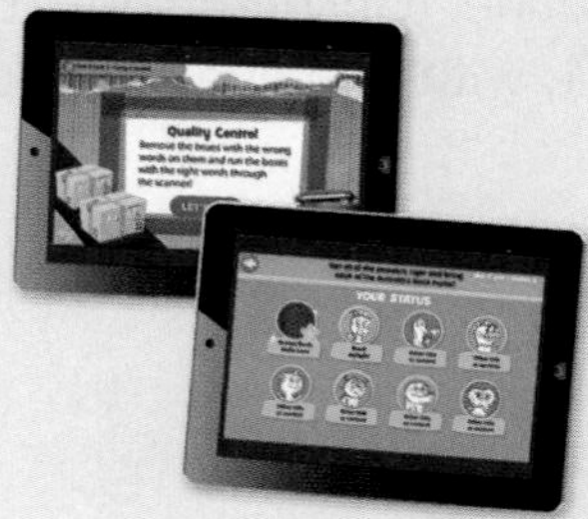

STUDENTS AS READERS

Children use online leveled texts to practice reading at their independent levels. Texts are related to the unit topic and offer a range of levels to meet every child's needs.

OBJECTIVES

Focus Identify the main topic of a text. RI.1.2

Use text features to locate key information in a text. RI.1.5

Text Complexity Rubrics pp. TR48–TR54.

See **Routines** on pp. TR2–TR31.

FOUNDATIONAL SKILLS MINI-LESSON

Consonants *d*/d/; *l*, *ll*/l/; *h*/h/

- Show the *duck* Picture Card. Let's say this word: *duck*. Now let's say the first sound in *duck:* /d/.
- Show Sound-Spelling Card 5. Point to *d*. The letter *d* stands for the sound /d/. Write *dot.* What is the first sound in *dot?* What letter stands for the sound /d/? (*d*)
- Repeat the procedure for *l*, *ll* and *h* using the *lamp* and *hen* Picture Cards and Sound-Spelling Cards 10 and 14.
- Say these words: *let, hop, dip, him, lit, den.* Have children say the letter that spells the beginning sound for each word.

For more explicit instruction, see p. FS14 in this Teacher's Guide.

Identify Main Topic Using Text Features

LESSON 1 FIRST READ Build Understanding

SET THE PURPOSE Focus the instruction for the unit by sharing the following Enduring Understanding: *Readers understand that informational texts have features that help them determine main topics.* We are going to read several texts to see how different authors use text features to share information about a topic.

ENGAGE CHILDREN Introduce the book *Time to Sleep.* Display the front and back covers and have children identify them and tell what they see. Point to the title and the author's and illustrator's names as you read them aloud. Point out the headings and other text features in the book, and explain the purpose of each feature. Share the following Essential Questions with children and tell them that they should think about the questions as the class reads, talks, and writes about the texts in this module: *How do features in informational texts help readers understand the main topic? How does the organizational structure of a text help writers explain information?* Tell children: In this lesson we are going to learn how readers can use features and words in a text to better understand the topic.

READ As you introduce this selection, use the appropriate reading routine from pp. TR8–TR19. Have children follow along as you read. In this first reading, children should be reading for an understanding of what the text is mainly about.

TURN AND TALK After reading, have children turn to a partner and discuss this question using examples from the text: What different ways of sleeping are described in the text? Use the **Think-Pair-Share Routine** on pp. TR2–TR3 and make sure children are using best practices for speaking and listening as outlined in the routine. (Children should share examples such as: upside down, p. 4; with one eye open, p. 8; in a tree, p. 12.)

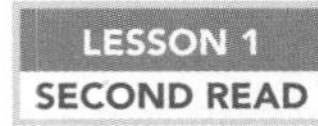

LESSON 1 SECOND READD

Close Read

CITE TEXT EVIDENCE Engage the class in a discussion about what you just read. Remind children that readers can use features to identify main topics and important details in a text. Use these questions to guide the discussion, and ask children to support their answers with evidence.

- What are pages 6 and 7 mostly about? (how horses sleep standing up) Which parts of the pages help you identify the topic? (the big words "Standing Up" at the top of page 6 and the photograph of a sleeping horse with the label "ZZZZZZZZZZ" next to it) When we want to know what a part of a book is mostly about, we can look at the pictures and find key words. **DOK L2**
- How are the way horses sleep and the way ducks sleep similar and different? (Both sleep standing up. Horses stand on all of their legs, and ducks stand on just one leg.) Show me where the text says so. **DOK L2**
- Why do dolphins sleep with one eye open? Let's read those sentences together. Have children choral read the final two sentences on p. 8 together. **DOK L2**
- What are pages 12 and 13 mostly about? (sleeping in a tree) Let's look at the details that helped us figure that out. The heading, or the big words on the top of page 12, says *In a Tree.* The pictures show a koala sleeping in a tree and the boy sleeping in a tree. Let's read together why koalas like to sleep in trees. **DOK L2**

Scaffolded Instruction

ENGLISH LANGUAGE LEARNERS

MULTIPLE-MEANING WORD Explain to English language learners that the word *lock* has more than one meaning. In this text, the phrase *lock their legs* on p. 6 means that horses make their legs so that they cannot move. Remind children that they can use surrounding words and pictures to help them figure out the correct meaning of a word or phrase.

STRATEGIC SUPPORT

COMPARE AND CONTRAST Help children compare and contrast how horses and ducks sleep using a Venn diagram. List details in the text that are the same for both animals in the overlapping part of the circles and details that are different in the outer parts of the circles.

OBJECTIVES

Determine the meaning of and use academic and domain-specific words in a text.

Ask and answer questions about words in a text.

BENCHMARK VOCABULARY

- time, p. 2
- sleep, p. 2

Keystones Reading and Writing Keystones are a quick check to

- assess children's understanding of key language, key text structures, and key ideas.
- indicate children's progress toward the Performance-Based Assessment.
- inform your Small Group Time decisions.

BENCHMARK VOCABULARY

- Have children find and read sentences from the text with the words *time* and *sleep*.

  Use the **Benchmark Vocabulary Routine for Informational Text** on pp. TR24–TR27 to teach the meanings of the words.

- Use the information on pp. 152–155 of this Teacher's Guide to discuss other words connected to each of the Benchmark Vocabulary words.

PRACTICE Have children use p. 41 in the *Reader's and Writer's Journal* to show contextual understanding of the Benchmark Vocabulary. Monitor children's vocabulary development.

Language Analysis

TEXT TALK

ASK AND ANSWER QUESTIONS Tell children that readers can ask and answer questions to find out more about the words in a text. Provide the K-W-L Chart on p. TR35.

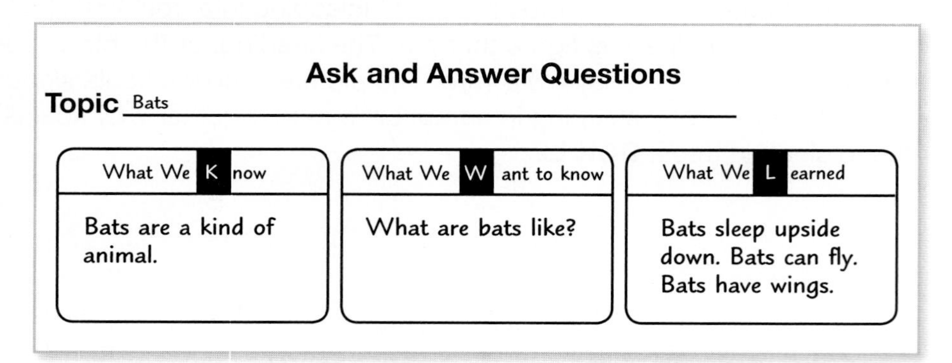

MODEL I see the word *bats* on page 4. I know that bats are a kind of animal, so I will write that in the first column of the chart. I want to know what bats are like, so I will write "What are bats like?" in the second column. Then I look for details to answer my question about this word. The text says that bats sleep upside down. They can fly. The picture shows that they have wings. I will write these details in the third column.

PRACTICE/APPLY Have children work independently or in small groups to complete the graphic organizer with what they know, want to know, and learn about the word *ducks* on p. 10. Have them share their ideas with the class. For more practice answering questions about words in the text, have children complete the activity on p. 42 in the *Reader's and Writer's Journal*.

Generative Vocabulary Games
Reader's and Writer's Journal
Leveled Text Library
Independent Reading Activities
Independent Reading How-To Video

Small Group Time

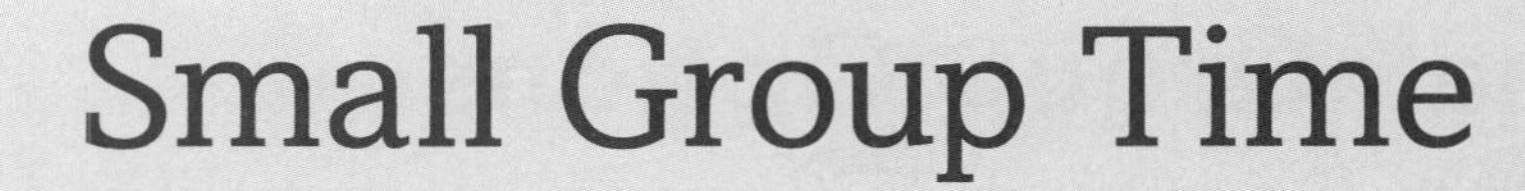

STEP 1 Focused Independent Reading

BUILD ACCOUNTABILITY Prepare children to read their **self-selected texts.** Announce the two focus points to the class, and help children make a plan for their reading. Children will apply both focus points to their self-selected text.

TODAY'S PROCESS FOCUS	
☑ Engagement and Identity	☐ Independence
☐ Stamina	

Tell children to select a book they think they will enjoy reading. Have them preview several books by reading the title and glancing at the pictures. Ask children to choose the book on the topic that interests them the most.

TODAY'S STRATEGY FOCUS	
☑ Vocabulary Knowledge	☐ Critical Thinking
☐ Fluency	☐ Comprehension

Guide children in applying the content of today's Language Analysis lesson to their self-selected texts. We learned that readers can ask and answer questions about words in a text to better understand the words. Today as you are reading, I want you to find words that you can ask and answer questions about. Record what you learn about the meanings of the words from the details in the text. Alternatively, have children log into Pearson Realize to find an Independent Reading Activity that is appropriate for the text they are reading.

MONITOR PROGRESS

- **Process Focus:** Have children record their reading in a daily reading log. They should write the most interesting fact or detail they learned from their reading.
- **Strategy Focus:** Have children review the words they found in the book. Ask them to share the details they learned about each word and how they figured out the meanings of the words. Alternatively, have children log into Pearson Realize and review with you the Independent Reading Activity they completed for their book.

For further guidance, see the **Independent Reading Routine** on pp. TR12–TR19.

While children are reading independently, use the Small Group Options on pp. 166–167.

INDEPENDENT LITERACY WORK

Text Club (pp. TR20–TR23)

Leveled Text Library

Center Options (pp. 160–161)

Use **Write in Response to Reading** on p. 41 of the *Reader's and Writer's Journal* to check children's understanding of key ideas in *Time to Sleep.*

Phonics: Decodable Practice Reader

GUIDED READING OPTIONS

Use the **Leveled Text Library** to choose appropriate texts based on children's needs.

Use ***ReadyUp! Intervention*** for children who require additional instruction with this lesson's reading and foundational standards or with prerequisite standards.

STEP 2

Small Group Options

Based on formative assessments of children's progress, use the following options to provide additional instruction, practice, or extension as needed.

PHONICS

For children who need support with this week's Phonics skill, use pp. FS14–FS17 in this Teacher's Guide.

UNLOCK THE TEXT

For children who need support in accessing key ideas, key language, and key structures in ***Time to Sleep,*** use **Unlock the Text** in the *Scaffolded Strategies Handbook,* pp. 22–27.

CONFERENCE

For independent reading accountability, **conference** each day with two or three children to discuss **self-selected texts** and support their reading.

LANGUAGE ANALYSIS SUPPORT

For children who struggle to ask and answer questions about ***Time to Sleep,*** use this **Support Language Analysis Mini-Lesson.**

ASK AND ANSWER QUESTIONS Help children fill in the first two columns in the K-W-L Chart. First, point to the word *ducks* on p. 10 and ask guiding questions, such as: What are ducks? Where do ducks live? As children answer the questions, have them draw or write the details about ducks that they know in the first column of the chart. Then help children think of a question to write in the second column. Use guiding questions to help them think of what they want to know about ducks, such as: What is this book all about? What would you like to learn about ducks? Have children write a question in the second column of their chart, such as "What do ducks do when they sleep?"

Invite children to look at the words and photograph on p. 10 to find details that will help them answer their question. Have them share the details they find with the class. Use the **Think-Pair-Share Routine** on pp. TR2–TR3.

Ask and answer questions about words in a text. RI.1.4

LANGUAGE ANALYSIS EXTENSION

For children who can easily ask and answer questions about words in *Time to Sleep,* use this **Extend Language Analysis Mini-Lesson.**

ASK AND ANSWER QUESTIONS Have children turn to the Picture Index on p. 16 and ask and answer questions about the remaining words. Then have them discuss the following questions to make connections between the words:

- Which words name animals that sleep in a tree? (*bat* and *koala*) How is the way bats sleep in a tree different from the way koalas sleep in a tree? (Bats sleep upside down by hanging onto a branch with their feet. Koalas do not sleep upside down.)
- The words *dolphins* and *ducks* name two different animals. What is one way these animals are alike, according to the text? (They both have ways of looking out for danger while they sleep.) What is different about the way these animals look out for danger? (Dolphins keep one eye open when they sleep so they can watch for danger. One duck looks out for danger while the other ducks sleep.)
- Think about the details you learned about the words *bats* and *horses.* What do these animals do when they are scared? Are their reactions similar or different? (Their reactions are different. Bats fly away, and horses run away.)

Ask and answer questions about words in a text. RI.1.4

FLUENCY

For fluent reading accountability, use the Oral Reading **Fluency Quick Check.** ☑ **Today assess 2–3 children.**

MODEL ACCURACY Explain that reading with accuracy means pronouncing each word correctly and not skipping or adding words. Have children follow along as you model reading aloud p. 14 from *Time to Sleep,* mispronouncing several words that children will recognize. Ask children to name the words you read incorrectly and tell how you should pronounce them. Read the text again, this time with accuracy. Then have children read the page chorally with accuracy.

Read grade-level text with accuracy. RF.1.4.b

QUICK CHECK

MONITOR PROGRESS

If . . . children mispronounce words as they read,

then . . . have them practice reading aloud with a partner who can help them pronounce the words correctly.

If . . . children are skipping or adding words as they read,

then . . . have them point to each word as they read it aloud to ensure they do not miss or add any words.

OBJECTIVE

Supply facts about a topic. W.1.2

Informative/Explanatory Writing

Write Facts About a Topic

SET THE PURPOSE Explain that informative writing tells readers about a topic. Point out that informative writing may explain how to do something. It may answer questions or give information. The writer of an informative text wants readers to understand more about the topic he or she is writing about. The writer tells facts, or pieces of true information, about the topic.

Display p. 2 in *Time to Sleep.* Talk about what makes this text informative writing. Distinguish statements that tell a fact from statements that do not tell a fact. Guide the discussion with the following questions.

- What is this text about? (the different ways that animals can sleep)
- Is this text true or make believe? (true) How do you know this? (The writer tells true things about how animals sleep.)
- Does the heading "How Do You Sleep?" tell a fact? How do you know? (No, it does not tell a fact because it does not give any information.)
- Point to the third and fourth sentences. Which of these sentences is a fact? What information does the fact tell? (The sentence "No, but some animals do" is a fact. It tells that some animals sleep on one leg.)

TEACH AND MODEL Help children notice how the writer includes facts about the topic of each section of the text. Provide the following model from p. 8 of *Time to Sleep* to show how to write interesting facts about a topic.

One Eye Open	The heading lets readers know the topic of this section. All the facts in the section will be about this topic.
Dolphins sleep with one eye open.	This fact tells a piece of true information about the topic of the section: animals that sleep with one eye open.
They can see where they are going while they are sleeping. They can look out for danger.	Readers might wonder why dolphins sleep with one eye open, so the writer tells more facts that answer this question.

Write a Fact About a Text

PREPARE TO WRITE Explain to children that when writers write informative text, they often must do research first.

When writers write informative books, they must make sure that what they write is true. In order to make sure the information they write about is true, writers sometimes have to look at other books or on the Internet to find information about their topic.

MODEL RESEARCH Explain that you will model researching facts about how an animal sleeps. Point out that you will look at *Time to Sleep* to find something to write about. Also point out that when writers research facts in other books, they must not copy what the authors of those books said. Instead, writers must learn to write information in a different way.

On page 12 in *Time to Sleep,* the writer talks about how koalas sleep in trees. She said, "They sleep for most of the day. They feel safe when they are up high." I think these facts are interesting. I did not know this information about koalas.

MODEL WRITING FACTS Explain to children that you will model rewriting the facts you learned about koalas in your own words.

I can rewrite this information using my own words to tell others these interesting facts about koalas. My writing will tell the same facts, just in different words.

Being up high makes koalas feel safe. They spend a lot of time each day sleeping in trees.

Compare your modeled sentences with the information in the book. Have children tell how the sentences are alike and different. Point out that your new sentences still tell facts about how koalas sleep.

Scaffolded Instruction

STRATEGIC SUPPORT

WRITE FACTS Work with children who are struggling with the concept of writing a fact without copying the fact from the book. Have children orally state the fact they want to write about. If they use the same wording as the book, prompt with: *How else might you say that?* Then prompt with: *Yes, you can write it like this: "Koalas like to sleep high up in trees where they feel safe."*

OBJECTIVES

Supply facts about a topic. W.1.2

With guidance, use technology to produce and publish writing and to collaborate with others. W.1.6

Use singular and plural nouns that match the verb.

Independent Writing Practice

WRITE Have children review the text in *Time to Sleep,* flagging pages that tell information they found especially interesting. Then have children work with a partner to orally tell two things they learned by reading this text. Children will then

- draw an illustration that explains what they learned. They will draw their picture on a separate sheet of paper.
- write a sentence about their illustration. They will write their sentence on p. 43 in the *Reader's and Writer's Journal.*
- review the use of capital letters and punctuation marks.

CONVENTIONS If you wish to teach children about using singular and plural nouns with matching verbs, use the Conventions Mini-Lesson on p. 171. Encourage children to underline the nouns they use in their writing.

DIGITAL OPTIONS If available, have children use computers or tablets to type their sentence. Then print out their writing and have children attach it to their illustration.

Share Writing

Have volunteers share their sentences with a partner. Have each partner identify why the sentence is considered informative writing.

Conventions Mini-Lesson
Matching Nouns and Verbs

TEACH AND MODEL Explain to children that a word in a sentence that names a person, place, animal, or thing is a noun. The word that tells the action in a sentence is a verb. Explain that the verb in a sentence needs to match the noun it tells about. A singular noun matches a verb with an *-s* at the end. A plural noun matches a verb without an *-s* at the end.

Bats sleep upside down.

The word *bats* is a plural noun. It names more than one animal. The word *sleep* tells the action. It is the verb. The verb *sleep* matches the plural noun *bats* because *sleep* does not have an *-s* at the end.

One duck looks out for danger.

The word *duck* names one animal. It is a singular noun. The word *looks* tells the action, so it is the verb. The verb *looks* matches the singular noun *duck* because it has an *-s* at the end.

PRACTICE Say these sentences one at a time: *The koala feels safe. The horses run away.* Have children name the noun and verb in each sentence. For more practice identifying nouns and verbs, have children complete the activity on p. 43 of their *Reader's and Writer's Journal.*

Scaffolded Instruction

ENGLISH LANGUAGE LEARNERS

IDENTIFY NOUNS AND VERBS English language learners may have difficulty understanding how to make sure nouns and verbs match. Review singular and plural nouns. Write simple sentences and read them aloud. Prompt children to identify the noun by asking: *Which word names a person, place, animal, or thing?* Then have them identify the verb. Prompt: *Which word tells what the noun does/did?* Review how the nouns and verbs match.

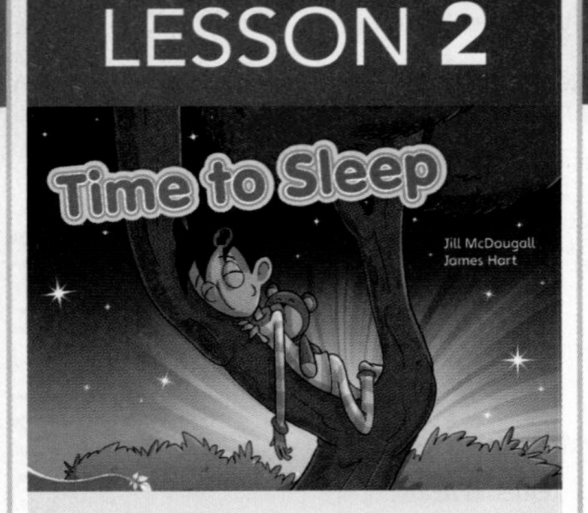

OBJECTIVES

Focus Use various text features to locate key facts or information in a text. RI.1.5

Distinguish between information provided by pictures or other illustrations and information provided by words in a text.

 RI.1.6

See **Routines** on pp. TR2–TR31.

FOUNDATIONAL SKILLS MINI-LESSON

High-Frequency Words; Consonants *d*/d/; *l*, *ll*/l/; *h*/h/

- Display the High-Frequency Word Cards *was*, *look*, and *I*. Have children say and spell each word. Then have them use the words in sentences.
- Have children turn to *Decodable Practice Reader R4A* on p. 49. Ask them to read the title and words. You will read words with consonants *d*/d/, *l*/l/, and *h*/h/.
- Have partners read the story together, switching readers after each page.

For more explicit instruction, see p. FS15 in this Teacher's Guide.

Use Text Features to Locate Key Information

LESSON 2 FIRST READ Build Understanding

SET THE PURPOSE Focus the instruction by sharing the following Enduring Understanding: *Writers understand that informational texts can have a variety of features.* Informational texts tell information about a topic. Some writers include text features in their books to help readers find information quickly.

ENGAGE CHILDREN Display the table of contents of *Time to Sleep.* Explain that a table of contents is a type of text feature. The table of contents shows the chapter titles and on what page number each chapter begins. Ask children to look for words that are capitalized in the table of contents. Explain that the words in the table of contents are capitalized because they are chapter titles. Share the following Essential Questions with children and tell them that they should think about the questions as the class reads, talks, and writes about the text: *How do features in informational texts help readers understand the main topic? How does the organizational structure of a text help writers explain information?* Tell children: In this lesson, we are going to use text features to find information in the book.

READ As you read *Time to Sleep*, use the appropriate reading routine from pp. TR8–TR19. Have children follow along as you read. Encourage them to read aloud sentences with you and then on their own. In this reading, have children focus on the chapter titles and illustrations.

TURN AND TALK After reading, have children turn to a partner and discuss these questions using examples from the text: How many sections are in this book? How can you find that out? Use the **Think-Pair-Share Routine** on pp. TR2–TR3, making sure children are following the best practices for speaking and listening. (Children should explain that the table of contents shows that there are 8 sections in this book.)

LESSON 2 SECOND READ

Close Read

CITE TEXT EVIDENCE Engage the class in a discussion about what you just read. Remind children that readers can use features to find information. Use these questions to guide the discussion, and ask children to support their answers with evidence.

- Display the table of contents. This is a table of contents. What do you notice about it? (It shows short phrases and page numbers.) What kind of information can we learn from this page? (the chapter titles and on what page they begin) Read a line from the table of contents and have children repeat after you. What can we read about starting on page 4? (animals that sleep upside down) Let's read other chapter titles together. **DOK L2**
- Display the illustration on p. 3. Where is the boy? (in his bedroom) How can you tell? Point to the details in the illustration that tell this. Children should point to the bed as a clue. What is the boy doing? (yawning) What does this mean? (He is tired.) Why is this important in this book? (This book is about sleep.) How will the boy sleep? (lying down in his bed) **DOK L3**
- Display the illustration on p. 7. What is the boy doing? (He is sleeping standing up.) Let's read the question on the page together. Could you sleep standing up? How can we answer this question? When I look at the illustration, I see that the boy is slumped over. It looks like he might fall over! That does not look comfortable. Think about standing and sleeping. Could you do it? **DOK L2**

Scaffolded Instruction

ENGLISH LANGUAGE LEARNERS

CONVENTIONS In many languages, pronoun usage is very different from English, so children may have difficulty understanding the use of *they*. Use the photographs and illustrations in the book to show that *they* is referring to more than one animal.

STRATEGIC SUPPORT

VOCABULARY If children have difficulty understanding the definition of *sleep* and the connection between *sleep* and *sleeping,* act out the words by pantomiming being asleep. Then ask children to pantomime with you.

OBJECTIVES

Determine or clarify the meanings of words and phrases in a text. RI.1.4; L.1.6

Know and use various text features. RI.1.5

BENCHMARK VOCABULARY

- animals, p. 2

BENCHMARK VOCABULARY

- Have children find and read the sentence from the text with the word *animals*.

  Use the **Benchmark Vocabulary Routine for Informational Text** on pp. TR24–TR27 to teach the meaning of the word.

- Use the information on pp. 152–155 of this Teacher's Guide to discuss other words connected to the Benchmark Vocabulary word.

PRACTICE Have children use p. 44 in the *Reader's and Writer's Journal* to show contextual understanding of the Benchmark Vocabulary. Monitor children's vocabulary development.

Reading Analysis

TEXT TALK

TEXT FEATURES Explain that text features are parts of a text that help readers find and understand information.

TABLE OF CONTENTS Display the table of contents. We use the table of contents to tell us what is in the book. It also tells us where to find each part of the book. Find the entry "On One Leg." On what page number will we find "On One Leg"? (10) Let's turn to page 10. Does this match the table of contents? (yes)

CHAPTER HEADINGS Chapter headings help us figure out which chapter has information we want. The headings match the titles in the table of contents. A heading is usually in bigger print or different color print at the top of a page. Look the heading for page 10. What is this chapter about? (sleeping on one leg)

INDEX Display the picture index. This kind of page is called a picture index. What do you see in this picture index? (pictures of animals from the book) What are the numbers in the index for? (page numbers to find the animals in the book) Look at the words in the picture index. What order are the words in? (alphabetical) How can we use the index? (If we want to know about ducks sleeping, we can find the word *duck* in the picture index and then turn to that page.)

PRACTICE/APPLY Have children work independently or in small groups to use the features to find the page number of a particular chapter or animal. Use the **Small Group Discussion Routine** on pp. TR6–TR7 to have children discuss how the table of contents, chapter headings, and picture index are useful for finding information.

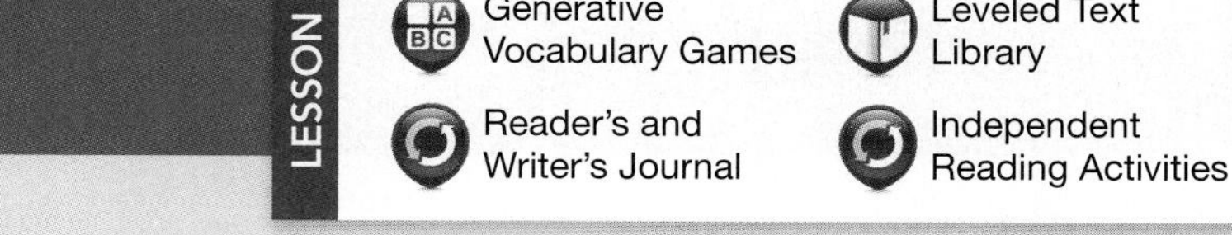

Small Group Time

STEP 1 Focused Independent Reading

BUILD ACCOUNTABILITY Prepare children to read their **self-selected texts.** Announce the two focus points to the class, and help children make a plan for their reading. Children will apply both focus points to their self-selected texts.

TODAY'S PROCESS FOCUS	
☑ Engagement and Identity ☐ Stamina	☐ Independence

Tell children to select an informational book they like to read. Encourage them to consider selecting a text by a favorite author, about a topic that interests them, or in a genre they have enjoyed in the past.

TODAY'S STRATEGY FOCUS	
☐ Vocabulary Knowledge ☐ Fluency	☐ Critical Thinking ☑ Comprehension

Guide children in applying the content of today's Language Analysis lesson to their self-selected texts. We learned that writers use text features, such as chapter headings and indexes, to organize information in a book. Today as you are reading, I would like you to find the table of contents, chapter headings, or indexes. If they're in your book, use them to help you find information. If your book does not have these features, think about what might be included if your book did have a table of contents or an index. Alternatively, have children log into Pearson Realize to find an Independent Reading Activity that is appropriate for the text they are reading.

MONITOR PROGRESS

- **Process Focus:** Have children identify their favorite part of their book by copying the chapter heading and/or the book title in their reading log.
- **Strategy Focus:** Have children review with you the text features from their book or what they might include in a text feature for their book. Alternatively, have children log into Pearson Realize and review with you the Independent Reading Activity they completed for their book.

For further guidance, see the **Independent Reading Routine** on pp. TR12–TR19.

While children are reading independently, use the Small Group Options on pp. 176–177.

INDEPENDENT LITERACY WORK

Text Club (pp. TR20–TR23)

Leveled Text Library

Center Options (pp. 160–161)

Use **Write in Response to Reading** on p. 44 of the *Reader's and Writer's Journal* to check children's understanding of key ideas in *Time to Sleep*.

Phonics: Decodable Practice Reader

GUIDED READING OPTIONS

Use the **Leveled Text Library** to choose appropriate texts based on children's needs.

Use ***ReadyUp! Intervention*** for children who require additional instruction with this lesson's reading and foundational standards or with prerequisite standards.

STEP 2 Small Group Options

Based on formative assessments of children's progress, use the following options to provide additional instruction, practice, or extension as needed.

PHONICS

For children who need support with this week's Phonics skill, use pp. FS14–FS17 in this Teacher's Guide.

UNLOCK THE TEXT

For children who need support in accessing key ideas, key language, and key structures in ***Time to Sleep,*** use **Unlock the Text** in the *Scaffolded Strategies Handbook,* pp. 22–27.

CONFERENCE

For independent reading accountability, **conference** each day with two or three children to discuss **self-selected texts** and support their reading.

READING ANALYSIS SUPPORT

For children who struggle with identifying and using text features in ***Time to Sleep,*** use this **Support Reading Analysis Mini-Lesson.**

TEXT FEATURES Model how to connect the table of contents and chapter headings to each other. Display the table of contents on page 1. Explain that the first entry is "How Do You Sleep?" and point to the number 2 next to the title. Show children that the 2 stands for the page number for this chapter and go to page 2. On page 2, point to the chapter heading "How Do You Sleep?" Explain to children that each chapter heading is also a line from the table of contents. Repeat the procedure to show that the next line in the table of contents is "Upside Down" and is on page 4. Page 4 has a chapter heading with the words "Upside Down" at the top.

Invite children to match the remaining entries on the table of contents with the pages that show the chapter headings. Use the **Think-Pair-Share Routine** on pp. TR2–TR3.

Know and use various text features to locate key facts or information in a text. RI.1.5

READING ANALYSIS EXTENSION

For children who can easily identify and use text features in ***Time to Sleep,*** use this **Extend Reading Analysis Mini-Lesson.**

TEXT FEATURES Use the following discussion questions to have children explain how the table of contents, chapter headings, and picture index help them understand the text.

- What is the chapter heading for the page about koalas? ("In a Tree") Why do you think that is? (because koalas sleep in trees)
- If there were a chapter about how people sleep, what might be the chapter heading? Why? (Possible response: "In a Bed" or "Lying Down" because people usually sleep in beds lying down)
- What is true of all the pictures in the index? (They are all pictures of the animals in the book.)
- If the author added another page about how elephants sleep, between which two animals would the elephant appear in the index? (between the duck and the horse) How do you know? (because *e* comes after *d* and before *h*)

Know and use various text features to locate key facts or information in a text. RI.1.5

FLUENCY

For fluent reading accountability, use the **Oral Reading Fluency Quick Check.** ☑ **Today assess 2–3 children.**

MODEL ACCURACY Explain that reading with accuracy means reading and pronouncing each word correctly without missing words, substituting words, or adding words. Reading accurately avoids confusion for the reader and the listener. Have children follow along as you model reading aloud p. 4 from *Time to Sleep* by pronouncing each word carefully. Review what would happen if a reader mispronounced or skipped a word while reading. Then have children take turns accurately reading aloud a portion of an appropriately leveled text.

Read on-level text orally with accuracy. RF.1.4.b

QUICK CHECK

MONITOR PROGRESS

If . . . children are mispronouncing words,

then . . . encourage them to use context to determine the correct word.

If . . . children are guessing the words incorrectly,

then . . . remind them to break each word down into its sounds.

OBJECTIVE
Write an informative/explanatory text that names a topic.
 W.1.2

Informative/Explanatory Writing

Write a Heading

SET THE PURPOSE Remind children that informative writing tells facts and details about a topic. Explain to children that a chapter heading is a title that summarizes, or tells the most important idea of the information in the chapter. The heading should be short and descriptive. There are many different options a writer can choose when writing a chapter heading. We can rewrite the chapter headings in *Time to Sleep* to practice.

Share with children the features of strong headings:

- have capital letters
- are short, only a couple of words
- describe the main topic

TEACH AND MODEL Remind children that the chapter heading sums up the most important idea for the chapter. Provide the following models from pp. 4, 6, and 8 of *Time to Sleep,* pointing out how the details from the text support the headings.

Upside Down
Bats sleep upside down.

The heading describes the way some animals sleep in just two words. Both words begin with an uppercase letter.

Standing Up
Horses can sleep standing up.

The heading describes the way some animals sleep. The chapter is about how horses sleep standing on their legs. Each word in the heading begins with an uppercase letter.

One Eye Open
Dolphins sleep with one eye open.

The heading describes the main topic of the chapter: animals that sleep with one eye open. Each word in the heading begins with an uppercase letter.

Write About a Photograph

PREPARE TO WRITE Tell children they are going to choose a part of the book and write or rewrite a new heading for it. Explain to children that before they begin writing their headings, they should develop a plan.

Have children consider these guiding questions as they prepare to write:

- Which part of the text is the most interesting to write about?
- How can I describe the text and pictures in a few words?
- What are some key details?
- What is the most important part of the chapter?

CHOOSE IMPORTANT DETAILS Explain that a heading does not tell all the information of a chapter or section. It only provides a simple summary of the main topic or idea of the chapter.

Model how to determine the important details from pp. 10–11: These pages tell about how ducks sleep. The picture on page 10 shows sleeping ducks standing on one leg. The ducks' heads are turned around. The picture on page 11 shows the boy sleeping while standing on one leg. The boy's head is also to the side. I know that this chapter is about sleeping on one leg.

WRITE A HEADING Tell children that once writers have determined the information they think is important, they can begin writing their headings. Explain that several different headings can be used to tell about a chapter.

I looked for important details about the ducks on page 10. I read the information on the page, and I looked at the picture. I know ducks sleep standing on one leg at a time. But I also see that the ducks have their heads turned around. The boy on page 11 is also on one leg with his head turned. I'm going to write something short that tells the main idea and uses capital letters. My heading could be "One Leg Only" or "Turned Head."

Scaffolded Instruction

STRATEGIC SUPPORT

HEADINGS If children have difficulty determining the main topic or key details of a picture or information, have them begin a conversation about it. Ask them to tell you about what they see and read. Capture words and phrases that they share. Discuss what children said and help them turn those words and phrases into headings.

OBJECTIVES

Write an informative/explanatory text that names a topic.
 W.1.2

With guidance, use technology to produce and publish writing and to collaborate with others.  W.1.6

Use common nouns. L.1.1.b

Independent Writing Practice

WRITE Have children choose one photograph from *Time to Sleep* they find interesting and write a sentence that tells about it. Then have them write a short heading about the photograph. Remind children to first think about the important details of the photograph and what information they want readers to understand about it. Have children write about the photograph on p. 45 of their *Reader's and Writer's Journal.*

CONVENTIONS If you wish to teach children how to identify nouns, use the Conventions Mini-Lesson on p. 181. Encourage children to use correct nouns in their informative/explanatory writing.

DIGITAL OPTIONS If available, have children use computers or tablets to type their sentences and headings and print them.

Share Writing

Ask volunteers to share their writing with the class. Ask the class to identify the nouns used in each sentence. Discuss how children who chose to write about the same photos have different sentences and headings.

Conventions Mini-Lesson

Identify Common Nouns

TEACH AND MODEL A noun is a word that names a person, place, animal, or thing. Nouns are all around us. Ask children to name things they see in the room. Start a list of nouns based on children's suggestions. Use the example sentences below to practice identifying nouns in sentences.

Bats sleep upside down.

The word *bats* names an animal. The other words in the sentence do not describe a person, place, animal, or thing. Therefore, *bats* is the only noun in the sentence.

The koalas at the zoo sleep differently than people.

The words *koalas, zoo,* and *people* are all nouns. The word *koalas* names a kind of animal, the word *zoo* names a place, and the word *people* names a group of people.

PRACTICE Have children identify nouns around the classroom or school. To help children determine if the word is a noun, ask questions such as Does that word name a person, place, animal, or thing? Write different common nouns that children frequently use. Then have them practice identifying nouns on p. 45 of their *Reader's and Writer's Journal.*

Scaffolded Instruction

ENGLISH LANGUAGE LEARNERS

NOUNS English language learners may not understand where nouns fall in sentences. Provide them with many examples of simple sentences that provide opportunities to identify nouns. For examples, write *Dolphins swim. Cats purr. Dogs bark. Bats fly*. Help children identify the nouns *Dolphins, Cats, Dogs,* and *Bats*.

OBJECTIVES

Focus Identify the main topic and retell key details of a text. RI.1.2

Use text evidence to answer questions about a text. RI.1.1

See **Routines** on pp. TR2–TR31.

Identify Main Topic and Key Details

LESSON 3 FIRST READ

Build Understanding

SET THE PURPOSE Focus the instruction by sharing the following Enduring Understanding: *Learners understand that living things have certain behaviors that shape them and allow them to survive.* Remember that the book *Time to Sleep* is about different animals and how they sleep. Sleep is an important behavior that living things need to do. We can learn about how animals sleep by looking for details that tell more about the book's main topic.

ENGAGE CHILDREN Review the book *Time to Sleep*. Display the Contents page and ask children to tell how readers can use it to find information about animals that sleep in a tree. Discuss the other text features they learned about in Lesson 2: the Picture Index and chapter headings. Remind children that informational texts often have these features. Share the following Essential Questions with children and tell them that they should think about the questions as the class reads, talks, and writes about the texts in this module: *How do features in informational texts help readers understand the main topic? How does the organizational structure of a text help writers explain information?* Tell children: In this lesson, we are going to learn how to identify the main topic and key details of a book.

READ Read aloud pp. 2–3 of *Time to Sleep* and invite children to chorally read with you. Use the appropriate reading routine from pp. TR8–TR19. In this reading, have children focus on details in the words and pictures.

TURN AND TALK After reading, have children turn to a partner and discuss this question using examples from the text: How do some animals sleep? Use the **Think-Pair-Share Routine** on pp. TR2–TR3. (Children should identify that some animals sleep on one leg or in a tree.) As you check children's understanding, encourage them to ask and answer questions about what the speaker says to clarify when something is not understood.

FOUNDATIONAL SKILLS MINI-LESSON

Short *o*: *o*/o/

- Show the Picture Card *ox*. Let's say *ox*. Now let's say the first sound in *ox*: /o/.
- Show Sound-Spelling Card 17. Point to *o*. The letter *o* stands for the sound /o/, which you hear at the beginning of *octopus*. It also stands for the middle sound in *dot*, /d/ /o/ /t/. Let's write *o* and say its sound.
- Display p. 14 of *Time to Sleep*. Ask children to read the last word in the first sentence. (*lot*)

For more explicit instruction, see p. FS16 in this Teacher's Guide.

LESSON 3 SECOND READ

Close Read

CITE TEXT EVIDENCE Engage the class in a discussion about what you just read. Remind children that readers look for details to help them identify the main topic of a book. Use these questions to guide the discussion, and ask children to support their answers with evidence.

- What is the title of the chapter that begins on page 2? (How Do You Sleep?) Why do you think the chapter is called that? (because the chapter asks about how you sleep) Let's find details in the words and picture that support our answer. **DOK L2**
- Ask children to identify the questions on p. 2. Have them identify the features of each sentence, pointing out the initial capital letter and the question mark. Who are these questions for? (the reader) Who is asking these questions? (the author) Explain how you know. Guide children to understand that "you" refers to the reader. **DOK L2**
- What do you notice in the picture on page 3? (The boy is in a bedroom wearing pajamas. He is yawning.) Why is this picture in this book? On page 2, the author asks, "How do you sleep?" This book is about sleep. So this picture shows one way to sleep: in a bed. **DOK L2**
- The book says that people do not sleep standing on one leg or in a tree. How would you describe how people sleep? (Possible responses: in a bed, lying down, at night, in the dark) **DOK L3**
- What can you figure out about how animals sleep from reading page 2? (Some animals sleep on one leg. Some animals sleep in a tree.) Let's read those sentences together. Read aloud the question and answer, pointing to each word as you say it. Then have children echo read. **DOK L3**

Scaffolded Instruction

ENGLISH LANGUAGE LEARNERS

CONVENTIONS English language learners may not notice that three different types of sentences are used on p. 2. Review the types of sentences. Read the first sentence and identify its features. This is a statement. It begins with a capital letter. It ends with a period. Read aloud a question and an exclamation, identifying the features of each. Then read each sentence type again, showing children how your voice changes depending on the ending punctuation mark.

STRATEGIC SUPPORT

USE ILLUSTRATIONS Help children use the illustrations to better understand the text. Have them reread the first sentence on p. 2 and look at the picture on p. 3 to identify what is described in the sentence. (The boy is ready to sleep. It is time to sleep.)

OBJECTIVES

Ask and answer questions to help determine or clarify the meanings of words and phrases in a text.  RI.1.4; L.1.6

Identify the main topic and retell key details of a text. RI.1.2

BENCHMARK VOCABULARY

- sorts, p. 2

BENCHMARK VOCABULARY

- Have children find and read the sentence from the text with the word *sorts*.

  Use the **Benchmark Vocabulary Routine for Informational Text** on pp. TR24–TR27 to teach the meaning of the word.

- Use the information on pp. 152–155 of this Teacher's Guide to discuss other words connected to the Benchmark Vocabulary word.

PRACTICE Have children use p. 47 in the *Reader's and Writer's Journal* to show contextual understanding of the Benchmark Vocabulary. Monitor children's vocabulary development.

Reading Analysis

TEXT TALK

MAIN TOPIC Remind children that the main topic is what the text is all about. Sometimes the main topic is stated in the text. Other times, readers can use details to figure out the main topic. Provide the Main Idea graphic organizer on p. TR36.

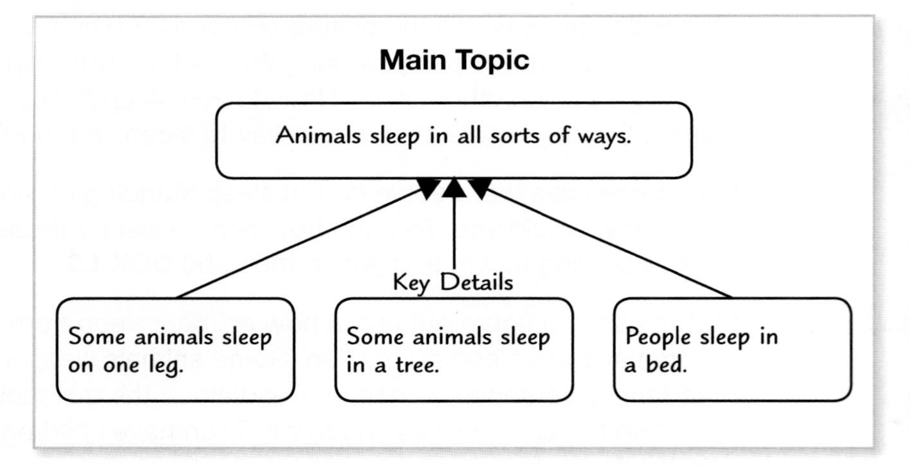

MODEL On page 2, the author is asking questions about sleep. When I get to the end of the page, I read the sentence "Animals sleep in all sorts of ways!" I think this is what the author wants readers to know. This is what the book is all about. I'll write this statement in the "Main Idea" box.

PRACTICE/APPLY Have children work independently or in small groups to complete the graphic organizer by finding details on pp. 2–3 that support the main topic. Use the **Small Group Discussion Routine** on pp. TR6–TR7 to have children discuss the details from the text that support their ideas. Check understanding by asking children to share or by circulating among children or groups. Have children complete the activity on p. 48 in the *Reader's and Writer's Journal*.

Independent Reading How-To Video

Small Group Time

STEP 1 Focused Independent Reading

BUILD ACCOUNTABILITY Prepare children to read their **self-selected texts.** Announce the two focus points to the class, and help children make a plan for their reading. Children will apply both focus points to their self-selected texts.

TODAY'S PROCESS FOCUS	
☑ Engagement and Identity	☐ Independence
☐ Stamina	

Tell children to select an informational book that they would enjoy reading. Encourage them to consider selecting a text by a favorite author, about a topic that interests them, or in a genre they have enjoyed in the past.

TODAY'S STRATEGY FOCUS	
☐ Vocabulary Knowledge	☐ Critical Thinking
☐ Fluency	☑ Comprehension

Guide children in applying the content of today's Reading Analysis lesson to their self-selected texts. We learned that a main topic can be stated directly in a book or we can use key details to figure out the main topic. Today as you are reading, pay attention to the key details. They can help you determine the main topic of what you are reading. Make a note of the key details that you believe support the main topic. Then write a main topic that is supported by the key details. Alternatively, have children log into Pearson Realize to find an Independent Reading Activity that is appropriate for the text they are reading.

MONITOR PROGRESS

- **Process Focus:** Have children record their reading in a daily reading log. They should write whether they are enjoying their book, describe why, and note the title, author, and pages they read.
- **Strategy Focus:** Have children review with you the main topic they determined for their book. Ask them to explain how the key details helped them figure out the main topic or how the main topic was directly stated in the book. Alternatively, have children log into Pearson Realize and review with you the Independent Reading Activity they completed for their book.

For further guidance, see the **Independent Reading Routine** on pp. TR12–TR19.

While children are reading independently, use the Small Group Options on pp. 186–187.

INDEPENDENT LITERACY WORK

Text Club (pp. TR20–TR23)

Leveled Text Library

Center Options (pp. 160–161)

Use **Write in Response to Reading** on p. 47 of the *Reader's and Writer's Journal* to check children's understanding of key ideas in *Time to Sleep*.

Phonics: Decodable Practice Readers

GUIDED READING OPTIONS

Use the **Leveled Text Library** to choose appropriate texts based on children's needs.

Use ***ReadyUp! Intervention*** for children who require additional instruction with this lesson's reading and foundational standards or with prerequisite standards.

STEP 2 Small Group Options

Based on formative assessments of children's progress, use the following options to provide additional instruction, practice, or extension as needed.

PHONICS

For children who need support with this week's Phonics skill, use pp. FS14–FS17 in this Teacher's Guide.

UNLOCK THE TEXT

For children who need support in accessing key ideas, key language, and key structures in ***Time to Sleep,*** use **Unlock the Text** in the *Scaffolded Strategies Handbook,* pp. 22–27.

CONFERENCE

For independent reading accountability, **conference** each day with two or three children to discuss **self-selected texts** and support their reading.

READING ANALYSIS SUPPORT

For children who struggle with identifying the main topic and key details in ***Time to Sleep,*** use this **Support Reading Analysis Mini-Lesson.**

MAIN TOPIC Model how to identify a detail on p. 2 that supports the main topic. Reread the first four lines. The main topic is that animals sleep in all sorts of ways. Key details that support this topic might tell about different ways that animals sleep. I see that the text says, "Do you sleep on one leg? No, but some animals do." These lines tell a key detail about the main topic. They tell one way that some animals sleep: on one leg. Reread the rest of p. 2 and ask children to identify the key detail. Ask a guiding question, such as: How does the author say some animals sleep? Have children record the key detail on their graphic organizer.

Invite children to look at the illustration on p. 3 and identify what it shows about how people sleep. Ask them to explain the key detail they find. Use the **Think-Pair-Share Routine** on pp. TR2–TR3.

Identify the main topic and retell key details of a text. RI.1.2

READING ANALYSIS EXTENSION

For children who can easily identify the main topic and key details in *Time to Sleep,* use this **Extend Reading Analysis Mini-Lesson.**

MAIN TOPIC Use the following discussion questions to have children explain how the key details on pp. 2–3 support the main topic.

- What is the chapter heading on page 2? (How Do You Sleep?) How does the heading relate to the text and the illustration? (The text and illustration both have to do with sleeping.)
- What details in the illustration support the main topic that animals sleep in all sorts of ways? (Possible responses: The boy is in pajamas; There's a bed; The boy has a stuffed toy; The light is turned off; The boy is yawning; The illustration shows how people sleep.)
- Why do you think the author asks if the reader sleeps on one leg or in a tree? (to tell details about how animals sleep)
- Now that you know the main topic of the book, what kind of information do you expect to read about? (I expect to read about many different ways that animals sleep. I expect to learn which animals sleep in certain ways.)

Identify the main topic and retell key details of a text. RI.1.2

FLUENCY

For fluent reading accountability, use the **Oral Reading Fluency Quick Check.** ☑ **Today assess 2–3 children.**

MODEL APPROPRIATE EXPRESSION Explain that reading with expression means changing your voice as you read. Reading with expression helps the listener to identify questions, statements, and exclamations. Have children follow along as you model reading aloud p. 2 from *Time to Sleep,* first with no expression and then with expression. Review how your voice rises when you come to the end of a question and how it shows excitement when reading an exclamation. Then choral read with children a portion of a leveled text, practicing appropriate expression.

Read grade-level text with expression. RF.1.4.b

QUICK CHECK

MONITOR PROGRESS

If . . . children are reading without expression,

then . . . point out punctuation such as question marks and exclamation points and model how their expression should change.

OBJECTIVE

Identify text structure in informative writing. W.1.2

Informative/Explanatory Writing

Structure of Informative Writing

SET THE PURPOSE Explain to children that writers carefully choose the order of their sentences and how they organize their ideas. When writers write informative texts, they sometimes use questions and answers to share facts and information about a topic.

Display p. 2 of *Time to Sleep*. Talk about the types of sentences.

- The first two lines of text are grouped together. The writer uses two types of sentences: a question and a statement. Which type of sentence does the writer use first? (The author uses a statement first.) The second sentence is a question. How are these two sentences related? (The writer says that it is time to sleep and then asks how the reader sleeps.)
- Look at the third and fourth sentences. First, the writer asks if the reader sleeps on one leg. Then what does the writer do? (The writer answers the question by stating, "No, but some animals do.")

Explain that the writer uses this same question-and-answer format for the next two lines. A writer can ask and answer questions in a text. This structure encourages the reader to think about the question. After the reader has thought about the question, the writer gives the answer.

TEACH AND MODEL Explain that writers sometimes use this question-and-answer structure in informative texts. Good writers use thought-provoking questions that will keep the reader interested and thinking about the topic. Review this structure on p. 2 of *Time to Sleep*.

It is time to sleep. How do you sleep?	The writer begins with a statement and then asks a question. This helps the reader think about how he or she sleeps.
Do you sleep in a tree? No, but some animals do.	The writer asks if the reader sleeps in a tree. Then the writer answers the question for the reader. The writer also points out that some animals do sleep in a tree. This helps show the reader that the book is about how animals sleep.

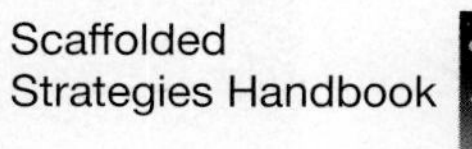

Write a Question and Answer

PREPARE TO WRITE Explain that you will write about how animals sleep. You will use a question-and-answer structure to share facts and details about the topic with your readers.

BRAINSTORM QUESTIONS Tell children that before you begin writing, you are going to brainstorm several questions you have about how animals sleep that you might want to answer in your writing.

I've always wondered how dolphins sleep. I can ask questions about dolphins that I might want to answer in my writing. What do dolphins do when they sleep? How long do they sleep? How do they protect themselves from danger while they are sleeping? These are all questions I have about how dolphins sleep.

MODEL A QUESTION AND ANSWER Read p. 8 in *Time to Sleep* and talk about which facts on this page answer some of your questions. Then model how to choose and answer a question.

I want to inform my readers about how dolphins sleep, so I think the most important question I have asked is "What do dolphins do when they sleep?" I will answer this question using facts from *Time to Sleep*.

MODEL WRITING
What do dolphins do when they sleep?
Dolphins keep one eye open when they sleep.

Remind children that when they use a source, such as *Time to Sleep,* it is important to write facts in their own words. Explain that children will now write about how animals sleep. Remind them to think carefully about the kinds of questions they can ask and answer about this topic.

Scaffolded Instruction

STRATEGIC SUPPORT

WRITING QUESTIONS Review with children the features of questions. Questions are sentences that ask something. They often begin with a question word, such as *who, what, where, when, why,* or *how*. They always end with a question mark. Invite volunteers to ask questions, and write their ideas on the board. Circle any question word at the beginning and the question mark at the end of each question.

OBJECTIVES

Write a question and answer that tells information. W.1.2

With guidance, use technology to produce and publish writing and to collaborate with others. W.1.6

Use proper nouns. L.1.1.b

Independent Writing Practice

WRITE Have children orally brainstorm several questions about *Time to Sleep* with a partner. Have children choose one question they want to answer and write it on p. 49 of their *Reader's and Writer's Journal*. Then have them write a sentence to answer that question or draw a picture on a separate sheet of paper. Remind children to begin their question with a capital letter and end it with a question mark.

CONVENTIONS If you wish to teach children about proper nouns, use the Conventions Mini-Lesson on p. 191. Have children circle any proper nouns they use in their writing.

DIGITAL OPTIONS If available, have children use computers or tablets to type their question and answer. Then, on the same sheet of paper, have them draw a picture to illustrate their answer.

Share Writing

Have children share their answer sentences or drawings with the group. Have volunteers ask the question they think each sentence or drawing answers.

Conventions Mini-Lesson

Use Proper Nouns

TEACH AND MODEL Remind children that a noun is a word that names a person, animal, place, or thing. Explain that when a word names a specific person, animal, place, or thing, it is a proper noun. *Dog* is a noun. It names an animal. *Fido* is a proper noun because it tells the name of a specific dog. Explain that proper nouns begin with a capital letter.

My cat Fluffy sleeps on a large pillow.

The first noun in this sentence is *cat*. It does not name a specific animal, so it does not begin with a capital letter. The next noun is *Fluffy*. This is a proper noun because it names a specific cat. Fluffy begins with a capital letter.

Todd and Max sleep on bunk beds in their room.

Names of people are proper nouns and always begin with a capital letter.

I can see animals sleeping at City Zoo.

City Zoo names a specific place, so each word in the name begins with a capital letter.

PRACTICE Have children identify proper nouns they see and use every day. Ask questions such as, What are the names of people in your family? What stores or other places do you go to? Write the proper nouns that children identify. Have volunteers point to the capital letters. Then have children practice identifying proper nouns on p. 49 of their *Reader's and Writer's Journal*.

Scaffolded Instruction

ENGLISH LANGUAGE LEARNERS

PROPER NOUNS Help English language learners understand the difference between common nouns and proper nouns. For example, say, *You are a girl. The word* girl *is a noun. It starts with a lowercase letter. Your name is Mai.* Mai *is a proper noun. It starts with a capital letter.* Continue with other examples.

LESSON 4

OBJECTIVES

Focus Ask and answer questions about key details in a text. RI.1.1

Use text evidence to answer questions about a text. RI.1.1

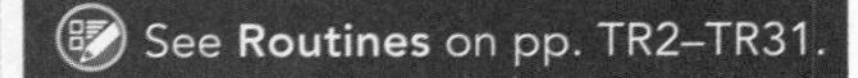

Ask and Answer Questions about Key Details

LESSON 4 FIRST READ Build Understanding

SET THE PURPOSE Focus the instruction for the unit by sharing the following Enduring Understanding: *Learners understand that living things have certain behaviors that shape them and allow them to survive.* Plants and animals are living things. Animals adapt and change to stay safe. We can learn about how animals stay safe and the things they do by asking and answering questions about details in this book.

ENGAGE CHILDREN Review the book *Time to Sleep*. Point to sentences in the book and ask children to identify their features, such as the capital letter at the beginning and the punctuation mark at the end. Share the following Essential Questions with children and tell them that they should think about the questions as the class reads, talks, and writes about the texts in this module: *How do features in informational texts help readers understand the main topic? How does the organizational structure of a text help writers explain information?* Tell children: In this lesson we are going to learn how readers can ask and answer questions about key details in a text.

READ Read aloud pp. 4–5 of *Time to Sleep* and have children chorally read with you. Use the appropriate reading routine from pp. TR8–TR19. In this reading, have children focus on understanding how bats sleep.

TURN AND TALK After reading, have children turn to a partner and discuss this question using examples from the text: How do bats sleep? Use the **Think-Pair-Share Routine** on pp. TR2–TR3 and make sure children are using best practices for speaking and listening as outlined in the routine. (Children should share details such as: Bats sleep upside down.)

FOUNDATIONAL SKILLS MINI-LESSON

High-Frequency Words; Short *o*

- Display the High-Frequency Word Cards for the words *you* and *we*. Have children spell each word and then say it. Then ask them to use the words in a sentence.
- Have children turn to *Decodable Practice Reader R4B*, p. 57. Tell them to read the title and then practice reading the story with a partner. Ask children to reread the words in the story with short *o*.

For more explicit instruction, see p. FS17 in this Teacher's Guide.

LESSON 4 SECOND READ

Close Read

CITE TEXT EVIDENCE Engage the class in a discussion about what they just read. Remind children that readers ask and answer questions about key details in a text. Use these questions to guide the discussion, and ask children to support their answers with evidence.

- According to the text, why do bats sleep upside down? (so they can fly away if they're scared) Show me how you figured that out. **DOK L2**
- Direct children's attention to the text and pictures on pp. 4–5. Ask children to explain how the photograph and illustration support the information in the text. What are the bats and the boy doing in the pictures? (They are hanging upside down.) How do the pictures help you better understand the description in the text? (Possible response: The chapter is called "Upside Down" and the pictures show how bats and the boy would sleep upside down.) **DOK L2**
- Why don't people sleep the same way as bats? (People cannot fly and do not need to be high up to avoid danger.) Have children discuss their answers with partners before sharing with the group. **DOK L3**
- What questions do you have about these pages? Write children's questions. Discuss how they can find the answers to their questions. **DOK L1**

BY-THE-WAY WORDS During close reading, define the following words for children involving known concepts that can be stumbling blocks to comprehending the text.

bats, p. 4: In this context, *bats* refers to animals that hang upside down and can fly.

branches, p. 4: *Branches* are parts of trees that stick out from the trunk.

Scaffolded Instruction

ENGLISH LANGUAGE LEARNERS

MULTIPLE-MEANING WORD Explain to English language learners that the word *bats* has more than one meaning. In this text, *bats* refers to the flying animals that hang upside down. The word *bat* could also refer to a baseball bat or to the action of hitting something away. Remind children to use surrounding words to help them figure out the correct meaning.

STRATEGIC SUPPORT

USE PICTURES Help children use the visuals to better understand the text. Have them describe what they see in the photograph and compare their description to the words on the page. Encourage children to recognize that pictures are used in books to reinforce or demonstrate the words.

OBJECTIVES

Determine the meaning of an unknown word or phrase. RI.1.4; L.1.4

Ask and answer questions about key details in a text. RI.1.1

BENCHMARK VOCABULARY

- upside down, p. 4
- scared, p. 4

BENCHMARK VOCABULARY

- Have children find and read the sentences from the text with the words *upside down* and *scared*.

  Use the **Benchmark Vocabulary Routine for Informational Text** on pp. TR24–TR27 to teach the meanings of the words.

- Use the information on pp. 152–155 of this Teacher's Guide to discuss other words connected to each of the Benchmark Vocabulary words.

PRACTICE Have children use p. 50 in the *Reader's and Writer's Journal* to show contextual understanding of the Benchmark Vocabulary. Monitor children's vocabulary development.

Reading Analysis

TEXT TALK

ASK AND ANSWER QUESTIONS Explain to children that when we read, we can ask and answer questions about what we read to better understand what we are reading. Use the T-Chart graphic organizer on p. TR39 to model asking and answering questions about key details. Write "Questions" and "Answers" as the column headings.

Ask and Answer Questions

Questions	Answers
• What kind of animal is hanging in the tree?	• They are bats.

MODEL Let's look at pages 4 and 5 of *Time to Sleep*. The picture shows animals hanging from a tree. I ask myself, "What kind of animal is hanging in the tree?" Write the question on the chart. Then reread the first sentence on p. 4. The text says that bats sleep upside down. These animals must be bats. Record the answer on the chart.

PRACTICE/APPLY Have children work independently or in small groups to complete the graphic organizer by asking questions about the pictures on pp. 4–5 and then answering the questions using details in the text. Use the **Small Group Discussion Routine** on pp. TR6–TR7 to have children discuss the details and examples from the text that support their ideas. Check understanding by asking children to share or by circulating among children or groups.

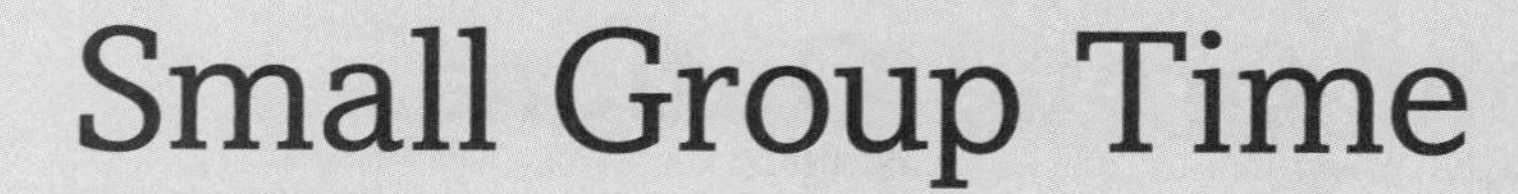

Small Group Time

STEP 1 Focused Independent Reading

BUILD ACCOUNTABILITY Prepare children to read their **self-selected texts.** Announce the two focus points to the class, and help children make a plan for their reading. Children will apply both focus points to their self-selected texts.

TODAY'S PROCESS FOCUS	
☑ Engagement and Identity	☐ Independence
☐ Stamina	

Tell children to select a book that they will take pleasure in reading. Encourage them to consider selecting a text they have enjoyed reading in the past or a book about one of their favorite topics.

TODAY'S STRATEGY FOCUS	
☐ Vocabulary Knowledge	☑ Critical Thinking
☐ Fluency	☐ Comprehension

Guide children in using the content of today's Reading Analysis lesson to analyze their self-selected texts. We learned that good readers ask and answer questions about key details in a text. How can asking and answering questions help you understand your book? Think about this question and be prepared to discuss your answer with examples. Alternatively, have children log into Pearson Realize to find an Independent Reading Activity that is appropriate for the text they are reading.

MONITOR PROGRESS

- **Process Focus:** Have children record their reading in a daily reading log. They should write whether they are enjoying their book, describe why, and note the title, author, and pages they read.
- **Strategy Focus:** Have children answer the question, explaining how asking and answer questions about details helped them understand the book. Alternatively, have children log into Pearson Realize and review with you the Independent Reading Activity they completed for their book.

For further guidance, see the **Independent Reading Routine** on pp. TR12–TR19.

While children are reading independently, use the Small Group Options on pp. 196–197.

INDEPENDENT LITERACY WORK

Text Club (pp. TR20–TR23)

Leveled Text Library

Center Options (pp. 160–161)

Use **Write in Response to Reading** on p. 50 of the *Reader's and Writer's Journal* to check children's understanding of key ideas in *Time to Sleep*.

Phonics: Decodable Practice Readers

GUIDED READING OPTIONS

Use the **Leveled Text Library** to choose appropriate texts based on student's needs.

Use ***ReadyUp! Intervention*** for children who require additional instruction with this lesson's reading and foundational standards or with prerequisite standards.

STEP 2 Small Group Options

Based on formative assessments of children's progress, use the following options to provide additional instruction, practice, or extension as needed.

PHONICS

For children who need support with this week's Phonics skill, use pp. FS14–FS17 in this Teacher's Guide.

UNLOCK THE TEXT

For children who need support in accessing key ideas, key language, and key structures in ***Time to Sleep,*** use **Unlock the Text** in the *Scaffolded Strategies Handbook*, pp. 22–27.

CONFERENCE

For independent reading accountability, **conference** each day with two or three children to discuss **self-selected texts** and support their reading.

READING ANALYSIS SUPPORT

For children who struggle with asking and answering questions in ***Time to Sleep,*** use this **Support Reading Analysis Mini-Lesson.**

ASK AND ANSWER QUESTIONS Help children ask and answer questions about key details in the text. Ask children to look at the pictures on pp. 4–5 of *Time to Sleep*. Model asking questions, such as: How do the animals hang from the tree? Why do they sleep upside down? Is the boy really sleeping like that? Explain that some of the questions you come up with may not be answered in the text. Then read the text and note when a detail from the text answers one of your questions.

Invite children to continue to ask and answer questions about details on these pages. Have children share their questions and answers with the class. Use the **Think-Pair-Share Routine** on pp. TR2–TR3.

Ask and answer questions about key details in a text. RI.1.1

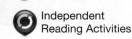

READING ANALYSIS EXTENSION

For children who can easily ask and answer questions in ***Time to Sleep,*** use this **Extend Reading Analysis Mini-Lesson.**

ASK AND ANSWER QUESTIONS Use the following discussion questions to strengthen children's abilities to ask and answer questions about a text.

- Does the text answer everything there is to know about how bats sleep? (no) Are there any questions you can think of that are not answered in the text? (Possible responses: Do bats sleep during the day? Do bats only sleep in trees? Do bats hang upside down when they are not sleeping? How long can bats hang for? What are bats scared of?)
- What are some details you would like to know that are not shown in the pictures? (Possible responses: what the bats' feet look like, what bats look like when they're not sleeping)
- What is the answer to the question the author asks on page 5? (Possible response: No, I could not sleep upside down; I would fall.)
- What general questions can we ask about any page in this book? (Possible responses: What kind of animal is that? How does that animal sleep? Why does the animal sleep like that?)

Ask and answer questions about key details in a text. RI.1.1

FLUENCY

For fluent reading accountability, use the **Oral Reading Fluency Quick Check.** ☑ **Today assess 2–3 children.**

MODEL APPROPRIATE PHRASING Explain that words go together to form phrases and that phrases should be read together. Model phrasing by reading the first line of the text on p. 4 and grouping the words incorrectly. For example, group "sleep upside" instead of "upside down": "Bats / sleep upside / down." Ask children if it sounds better or worse than when "upside down" is grouped together: "Bats sleep / upside down." Group the following line of text with pauses between phrases. For example, "They hang / from branches / by their feet." Explain that only two or three words should be grouped at a time. Continue practicing phrasing with the remaining sentence on page 4.

Read grade-level text with appropriate phrasing. RF.1.4.b

QUICK CHECK

MONITOR PROGRESS

If . . . children are reading without phrasing,

then . . . model for children how to read two or three words at a time. Encourage them to not begin reading until they know the next group of words.

If . . . children are phrasing words incorrectly,

then . . . underline appropriate phrases for children and have them read each line twice, focusing on the phrases in the second reading.

OBJECTIVE
Understand that writers use facts in informative writing.
W.1.2

Informative/Explanatory Writing

Use Facts

SET THE PURPOSE Remind children that facts are pieces of true information. When writing informative text, writers give facts about the topic. Writers use these facts to tell readers about the topic. In *Time to Sleep*, the writer gives facts about how animals sleep.

Display pp. 4–5 of *Time to Sleep*. Talk about the facts the writer uses.

- A fact is a true statement. Let's read the first line together and tell if it is a fact. "Bats sleep upside down." Is this a fact? (yes) I can see in the picture that it is true that bats sleep upside down. This is a fact.
- The next line says that bats hang from branches by their feet. Is this a fact? (yes) How can you tell? (The picture shows bats hanging upside down from the branches of a tree.) The picture shows that this is a true statement, so it is a fact.
- The last line on page 4 says that bats can fly away if they're scared. This also sounds like a fact. It tells a piece of information about bats.
- The line on page 5 asks if the reader could sleep upside down. Is this a fact? Why? (No, it does not tell any information.)

TEACH AND MODEL Explain that writers use facts to tell readers true information about a topic. Writers answer questions that readers might have about the topic using facts. Each fact answers a question. Provide the following models from p. 4 of *Time to Sleep:*

Bats sleep upside down.

The book is about how animals sleep. Readers might wonder, "How do bats sleep?" The first sentence answers this question.

They hang from branches by their feet.

When readers learn that bats sleep upside down, they might ask, "How do bats hang upside down?" The next sentence answers this question.

They can fly away if they are scared.

Readers might also wonder, "Why do bats sleep upside down?" The writer answers this question with her last sentence.

Write a Fact

PREPARE TO WRITE Tell children that writers should always have a purpose for writing. Explain that a writer's purpose for writing an informative text is to inform readers about a topic. A writer does this by giving facts about the topic.

BRAINSTORM FACTS Model brainstorming facts you can use to write about the topic of how animals sleep. Review pp. 2–3 of *Time to Sleep*.

I know that this book is all about how animals sleep. On these pages, I learn that animals sleep in many different ways. I can write notes or draw pictures about the information I learn to help me think of facts I can write about this topic.

Draw simple pictures to illustrate these facts: *some animals sleep on one leg, some animals sleep in a tree, people sleep in a bed.*

These pictures show what I learned from this section of the text. Each picture shows a fact I can write about the topic.

WRITE A FACT Model choosing a picture to write a sentence about. Explain that this sentence should tell a fact about the topic of how animals sleep.

I like this drawing that shows a tree with some animals sleeping in it. Now I will write a sentence that describes this picture. The purpose of this sentence is to inform my readers about the topic of how animals sleep.

MODEL WRITING
Some animals sleep high up in trees.

Remind children that when they use a source, such as *Time to Sleep*, it is important to write facts in their own words.

Scaffolded Instruction

STRATEGIC SUPPORT

FACTS AND OPINIONS Children may have difficulty understanding when they are writing a fact and when they are writing an opinion. Review that a fact is a true statement about something. Explain that an opinion tells how a writer feels about something. One at a time, say sentences, such as *Birds sleep in trees* and *I think beds are comfortable.* Help children tell which are statements of fact and which are statements of opinion.

OBJECTIVES

Write informative text. W.1.2

With guidance, use technology to produce and publish writing and to collaborate with others. W.1.6

Use verbs. 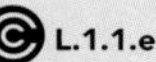

Independent Writing Practice

WRITE Have children review what they learned about how animals sleep on pp. 4–5 of *Time to Sleep*. Have them work with a partner to illustrate two things they learned. Then have children choose one illustration and write a sentence about it on p. 51 in their *Reader's and Writer's Journal*. Each partner can choose an illustration and write a sentence.

CONVENTIONS If you wish to teach children about using verbs, use the Conventions Mini-Lesson on p. 201. Have children circle the verbs they use in their informative/explanatory writing.

DIGITAL OPTIONS If available, have children use computers or tablets to type their sentences and print them. Have them attach their sentences to the drawings they describe.

Share Writing

Have children work in small groups to share their sentences and illustrations. Have children discuss how drawing helped them think carefully about the key details they wanted to write about.

Writing Keystone Checklist

Writing a Fact About a Topic

Use this checklist to assess children's informative/explanatory writing. If children need additional support writing a fact about a topic, use the Unlock Informative/Explanatory Writing beginning on p. 266 of the *Scaffolded Strategies Handbook*.

	Achieved	Notes
Identify the topic.		
Write a fact as a sentence.		

Conventions Mini-Lesson

Use Verbs

TEACH AND MODEL Explain that a verb often tells an action that someone or something does. *Bats sleep upside down* is a sentence with the verb *sleeps*. *Sleeps* tells what the bats do.

Bats hang from branches.	The word *hang* is a verb. It tells what bats do. They hang from branches.
Bats fly away when they are scared.	The word *fly* is a verb. It tells what bats do. They fly away when they are scared.
The children see the bats.	The word *see* is a verb. It tells what the children do. They see the bats.

PRACTICE Have children suggest sentences that tell what animals do. Ask questions such as, What do snakes do? What do birds do? Write the sentences and have children identify the verbs. Then have children practice identifying verbs on p. 51 of their *Reader's and Writer's Journal*.

Scaffolded Instruction

ENGLISH LANGUAGE LEARNERS

VERBS Help English language learners understand the meanings of basic verbs that they may use in sentences, such as *run, walk, play, drink,* and *eat*. Write a verb and then act it out with children. Ask more advanced learners to use the word in an oral sentence.

OBJECTIVES

Focus Distinguish between information provided by pictures and information provided by words in a text. RI.1.6

Use the illustrations and details in a text to describe its key ideas.

 RI.1.7

See **Routines** on pp. TR2–TR31.

Identify Information from Pictures and Words

LESSON 5 FIRST READ

Build Understanding

SET THE PURPOSE Focus the instruction for the unit by sharing the following Enduring Understanding: *Readers understand that informational texts have features that help them determine main topics.* Authors and illustrators communicate information using words and pictures. Some information is given by the words. Some information is given in the pictures.

ENGAGE CHILDREN Return to *Time to Sleep* and call attention to the photo on p. 6 and the illustration on p. 7. Have children compare the photo and illustration. Have children focus on what the horse and the boy are doing. Model how to use the details in the pictures to determine that these pages are about sleeping while standing up. Share the following Essential Questions with children and tell them that they should think about the questions as the class reads, talks, and writes about the texts in this module: *How do features in informational texts help readers understand the main topic? How does the organizational structure of a text help writers explain information?* In this lesson we will discuss information we can learn from the pictures and the words of an informational text.

READ As you read pp. 6–7 of *Time to Sleep,* use the appropriate reading routine from pp. TR8–TR19. Have children follow along and read with you when they can. In this reading, children should be reading to determine how the text supports the pictures and how the pictures support the text.

TURN AND TALK After reading, have children turn to a partner and discuss this question using support from the text: Why do you think horses sleep standing up? Use the **Think-Pair-Share Routine** on pp. TR2–TR3. (Children should understand that horses sleep standing up so they can easily run away if they get scared.) Remind children to speak one at a time and to listen carefully when their partner is speaking.

FOUNDATIONAL SKILLS MINI-LESSON

Consonants *d*/d/; *l*, *ll*/l/; *h*/h/; Short *o*

- Review /d/ spelled *Dd,* /l/ spelled *Ll,* and /h/ spelled *Hh* using Sound-Spelling Cards 15, 21, and 23. Then write these words: *lob, dot, hop.* Ask the class to blend the sounds and read each word.
- Review short *o* using Sound-Spelling Card 17. Have children use letter tiles to build the following words as you say them: *dot, hot, lot.*

For more explicit instruction, see p. FS17 in this Teacher's Guide.

Close Read

CITE TEXT EVIDENCE Engage the class in a discussion about what they just read. Remind children that readers use the illustrations and details in a text to describe its key ideas. Use these questions to guide the discussion, and ask children to support their answers with evidence.

- According to the text, how do horses sleep? (Horses sleep standing up.) Show me where the text says so. **DOK L1**
- Why doesn't the horse fall over when it is sleeping? (The horse doesn't fall over because it locks its legs.) Let's read the sentence that tells us this together. **DOK L1**
- How does the picture on page 6 help you better understand the description in the text? (Possible response: I can see a sleeping horse that is standing up. The text talks about how horses sleep.) **DOK L2**
- What advantages are there to sleeping while standing up? (Possible responses: stay out of the mud, can run away quickly) Tell me how you determined your answer. **DOK L3**
- How does the illustrator help you see that these pages are about sleeping? (The horse and boy have their eyes closed; there is a line of *Z*s that are used to indicate sleeping noises.) **DOK L2**
- What is the purpose of the illustration on page 7? (Possible response: to show what it would look like if a person tried sleeping while standing up) **DOK L2**
- Why do you think the author chose to write about how horses sleep? (Possible response: because sleeping standing up is different from how people sleep.) **DOK L3**

Scaffolded Instruction

ENGLISH LANGUAGE LEARNERS

VOCABULARY Demonstrate the meaning of the phrase *standing up* by having one child stand up and another child sit down. Point to the child that is standing up and say: *He/She is standing up*. Have children practice sitting down and standing up until both phrases make sense. Then have them use the phrase to describe the horse in the photo on p. 6.

STRATEGIC SUPPORT

USE PICTURES Help children use the pictures to support their understanding of the text. For example, ask children to point to the horse in the photograph on p. 6. Then have them point to the horse's legs, and guide them to notice that the horse's eyes are closed. Help them connect this picture to the concept that horses can sleep standing up.

OBJECTIVES

Determine or clarify the meanings of words and phrases in a text. RI.1.4; L.1.6

Distinguish between information provided by pictures and information provided by words in a text. RI.1.6

BENCHMARK VOCABULARY

- lock, p. 6

BENCHMARK VOCABULARY

- Have children find and read the sentence from the text with the word *lock.* Use the **Benchmark Vocabulary Routine for Informational Text** on pp. TR24–TR27 to teach the meaning of the word.
- Use the information on pp. 152–155 of this Teacher's Guide to discuss other words connected to the Benchmark Vocabulary word.

PRACTICE Have children use p. 52 in the *Reader's and Writer's Journal* to show contextual understanding of the Benchmark Vocabulary. Monitor children's vocabulary development.

Reading Analysis

TEXT TALK

DISTINGUISH INFORMATION IN TEXT AND PICTURES Tell children that readers can compare and contrast the information they see in pictures and information they learn from words in a text. Provide the Venn diagram on p. TR43. Review with children how to complete a Venn diagram.

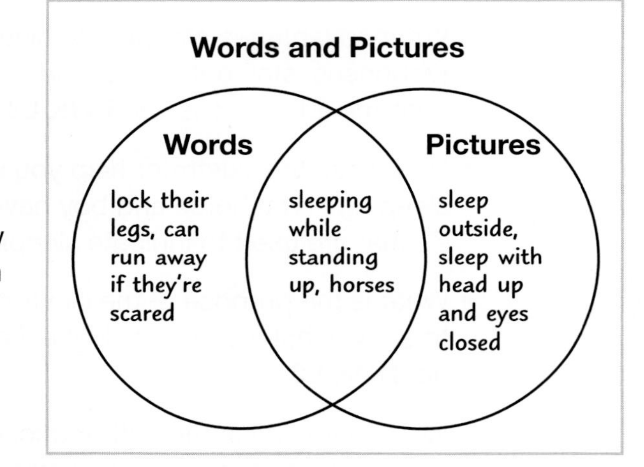

MODEL Let's look at pages 6 and 7 and compare and contrast the information in the words and pictures. I see from both the words and pictures that these pages are about sleeping while standing up. I also see that the pages are about horses. I will write these ideas in the middle section of the diagram.

PRACTICE/APPLY Have children work independently or in small groups to complete the graphic organizer with the information they find in the words and pictures on pp. 6–7. Use the **Small Group Discussion Routine** on pp. TR6–TR7 to have children discuss the details and examples from the text that support their ideas. Check understanding by asking children to share or by circulating among children or groups.

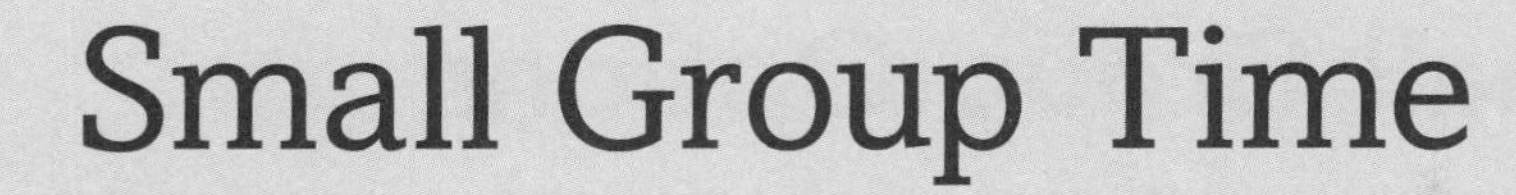

Small Group Time

STEP 1 Focused Independent Reading

BUILD ACCOUNTABILITY Prepare children to read their **self-selected texts.** Announce the two focus points to the class, and help children make a plan for their reading. Children will apply both focus points to their self-selected texts.

TODAY'S PROCESS FOCUS	
☑ Engagement and Identity	☐ Independence
☐ Stamina	

Display a variety of informational texts about animals. Ask children to page through several of the books and choose one that appeals to them. It may be a familiar book or a new book.

TODAY'S STRATEGY FOCUS	
☑ Decoding and Word Recognition	☐ Critical Thinking
☐ Fluency	☐ Comprehension

Guide children in recognizing and reading high-frequency words in their self-selected texts. Write the words *was* and *look.* This week we learned the words *was* and *look.* As you go through your book today, look for these words and mark them with self-stick notes. Alternatively, have children log into Pearson Realize to find an Independent Reading Activity that is appropriate for the text they are reading.

MONITOR PROGRESS

- **Process Focus:** Have children record their reading in a daily reading log. They should write whether they are enjoying their book, describe why, and note the title, author, and pages they read.
- **Strategy Focus:** Have children point out places where they marked the words *was* and *look.* Read the sentences with the words and have children repeat after you. Alternatively, have children log into Pearson Realize and review with you the Independent Reading Activity they completed for their book.

 For further guidance, see the **Independent Reading Routine** on pp. TR12–TR19.

While children are reading independently, use the Small Group Options on pp. 206–207.

INDEPENDENT LITERACY WORK

Text Club (pp. TR20–TR23)

Leveled Text Library

Center Options (pp. 160–161)

Use **Write in Response to Reading** on p. 52 of the *Reader's and Writer's Journal* to check children's understanding of key ideas in *Time to Sleep.*

Phonics: Decodable Practice Readers

GUIDED READING OPTIONS

Use the **Leveled Text Library** to choose appropriate texts based on children's needs.

Use ***ReadyUp! Intervention*** for children who require additional instruction with this lesson's reading and foundational standards or with prerequisite standards.

STEP 2 Small Group Options

Based on formative assessments of children's progress, use the following options to provide additional instruction, practice, or extension as needed.

PHONICS

For children who need support with this week's Phonics skill, use pp. FS14–FS17 in this Teacher's Guide.

UNLOCK THE TEXT

For children who need support in accessing key ideas, key language, and key structures in ***Time to Sleep,*** use **Unlock the Text** in the *Scaffolded Strategies Handbook,* pp. 22–27.

CONFERENCE

For independent reading accountability, **conference** each day with two or three children to discuss **self-selected texts** and support their reading.

READING ANALYSIS SUPPORT

For children who struggle with identifying information provided by pictures and information provided by words in ***Time to Sleep,*** use this **Support Reading Analysis Mini-Lesson.**

DISTINGUISH INFORMATION IN TEXT AND PICTURES

Point to the photograph on p. 6. Ask children to tell what they see in the picture (a horse standing outside with its head up and eyes closed). We can figure out that the horse is sleeping from the *Zs* the illustrator added. The words on the page confirm that this is a picture of a sleeping horse. This is information that we learn from both the words and the picture. The words do not tell us that horses sleep outside or that they keep their head up and their eyes closed. This is information that we learn from just the picture.

Read the text on p. 6 aloud to children. Have them identify the information they learn from the words that they do not learn from the picture. Have them record the information on their Venn diagram and then share it with the class.

Identify information from pictures and from words in a text. RI.1.6

READING ANALYSIS EXTENSION

For children who can easily distinguish between information provided by pictures and information provided by words in ***Time to Sleep,*** use this **Extend Reading Analysis Mini-Lesson.**

DISTINGUISH INFORMATION IN TEXT AND PICTURES

Have children review the text and pictures on pp. 4–5 in *Time to Sleep.* Use the following discussion questions.

- What is a detail from the picture on page 4 that is not described in the text? (Possible response: Bats fold their wings around them when they sleep.)
- What are some details in the words that are not shown in the picture? (Possible response: Bats fly away if they are scared.)
- How are the pictures and words both important to the reader? (Responses will vary.)
- The question on page 5 asks if you could sleep upside down. Do you think you could sleep upside down? Why or why not? (Possible response: No, because I cannot hang by my feet and would fall down.)

Distinguish between information provided by pictures and information provided by words in a text. RI.1.6

READING ACTIVITY MATS

For comprehension and vocabulary practice, use the **Reading Activity Mat** Graphic Organizer on Pearson Realize.

COMPREHENSION FOCUS Work with children in small groups to build comprehension skills by using the EnVision Math Problem-Solving Reading Mat *How many legs?* Follow the teaching plan on the instruction page that accompanies the student graphic organizer on Pearson Realize.

VOCABULARY FOCUS Work with children in small groups to build their vocabulary skills by using the EnVision Math Problem-Solving Reading Mat *How many legs?* Follow the teaching plan that accompanies the graphic organizer.

If children need more time to complete the activity, have them log in to Pearson Realize during Small Group Time in subsequent lessons throughout the module.

OBJECTIVE

Understand that writers focus on a main topic in their informative writing.

 W.1.2

Informative/Explanatory Writing

Write About a Main Topic

SET THE PURPOSE Explain that writers of informative text choose a topic to write about and then they stick to that topic. It is important for writers to make sure that the details they add to their writing support the main topic of their writing.

Display *Time to Sleep.* The writer of this book wrote about how animals sleep. All the details she includes in this book focus on ways different animals sleep. She does not give information about things animals eat or sounds animals make. She only tells facts about how animals sleep.

Read pp. 6–7 in *Time to Sleep* to children. Talk about the key details and how these details support the topic of how animals sleep.

- What detail does the heading give? (The heading "Standing Up" tells us that some animals sleep standing up.) How does this detail support the main topic of the book? (It tells about one way that animals can sleep.)
- What detail tells what horses do when they are scared? (The sentence "They can run away if they are scared" tells us what they do.) How does this detail support the main topic of the book? (It gives a reason why one kind of animal sleeps the way it does.)

TEACH AND MODEL Remind children that the main topic of this book is how animals sleep. Point out that the writer tells facts or details about how horses sleep on these pages. All these facts help to support the main topic. Provide the following models from pp. 6–7:

Horses can sleep standing up.	This sentence tells us one fact about how animals sleep: Horses sleep standing up.
They lock their legs so they do not fall over.	This sentence tells another fact about how animals sleep: Horses lock their legs when they sleep. This fact explains how horses keep from falling over while they are sleeping.

Use a Graphic Organizer

PREPARE TO WRITE Explain to children that writers plan their writing before they begin in order to make sure that what they write supports and focuses on the main topic. Using the Main Idea graphic organizer on p. TR36, put yourself in the shoes of the writer of *Time to Sleep.* Tell children that you will organize your thoughts using this graphic organizer just as if you were the writer of this book.

If I were the writer of this book, I would have organized my thoughts on a graphic organizer like this one before I began writing. Let's take a look at how I would have organized the chapter called "Upside Down."

MODEL For this chapter, the main focus is how bats sleep. I will write that in the Main Idea box. Now I will look for details in the sentences to write in the Key Details boxes. One detail is that bats sleep upside down. Another detail is that they hang from branches by their feet. Finally, we learn that bats can fly away when they are scared.

Explain to children that you do not want to copy sentences from the book. Instead, you want to use the most important words from a sentence. For example, the text reads "They hang from branches by their feet." You can write this as "hang from branches."

Explain that this graphic organizer can provide you with a map for your writing. A writer can return to a main idea/key details chart to make sure that he or she is writing details that support the main idea.

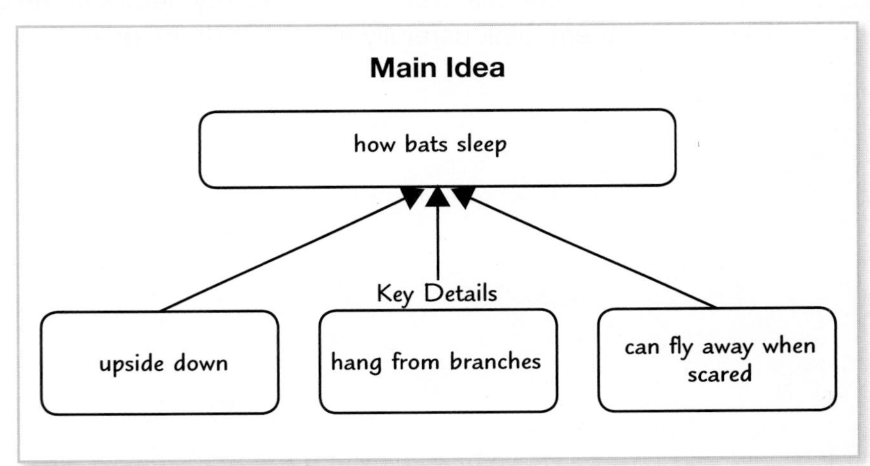

Scaffolded Instruction

STRATEGIC SUPPORT

MAIN TOPIC Children may have difficulty determining the main topic and key details. Tell them to look for clues in the text features, such as headings, to help them determine the main topic. The heading often tells the main topic, and the sentences below tell the details supporting the main topic. Use "Upside Down" as an example.

OBJECTIVES

Write informative text. W.1.2

With guidance, use technology to produce and publish writing and to collaborate with others. W.1.6

Use plural nouns. L.1.1.c

Independent Writing Practice

WRITE Have children work with a partner to complete a Main Idea graphic organizer about the chapter "Standing Up" on pp. 6–7 of *Time to Sleep.* Tell them that they should first determine the main topic of this chapter. Then they can look for details that support the main topic. Have children record the main topic and key details on p. 53 of their *Reader's and Writer's Journal* or they can create the graphic organizer on a separate sheet of paper.

CONVENTIONS If you wish to teach children about plural nouns, use the Conventions Mini-Lesson on p. 211. Have children circle plural nouns they use in their informative/explanatory writing.

DIGITAL OPTIONS If available, have children use computers or tablets to type their main topic and key details and print them. Children can draw their own Main Idea graphic organizer and cut and paste the main topic and key details onto the paper.

Share Writing

Have children work in small groups to share their graphic organizers. Have children discuss how writing key details in the graphic organizers helped them think carefully about the main topic.

Conventions Mini-Lesson

Use Plural Nouns

TEACH AND MODEL Review that a noun names a person, place, animal, or thing. Explain that singular nouns name one and plural nouns name more than one. Many times you can add -*s* to a singular noun to make it plural. Write: *A zebra sleeps standing up*. The word *zebra* names one animal. I can add -*s* to *zebra* to make it plural, or to name more than one animal. Write: *Zebras sleep standing up*. The word *zebras* names more than one animal.

Bats hang from trees.	Add -*s* to many nouns to make the noun plural, or to name more than one. The nouns *bat* and *tree* can be made plural by adding -*s* to the end.
Horses lock their legs when they sleep.	The nouns *horse* and *leg* can be made plural by adding -*s* to the end.
Animals sleep in different ways.	The nouns *animal* and *way* can be made plural by adding -*s* to the end.

PRACTICE Have children page through *Time to Sleep* to find three examples of plural nouns that are formed by adding -*s* to a singular noun, such as *dolphins, ducks,* and *koalas.* Write the plural nouns that children find on the board. Ask questions such as, What would you say if there were only one of this animal? Then have children practice making nouns plural on p. 53 of their *Reader's and Writer's Journal.*

Scaffolded Instruction

ENGLISH LANGUAGE LEARNERS

PLURAL NOUNS Some languages, including Chinese, Hmong, and Vietnamese, do not have the plural noun form. Instead, the plural is indicated with an adjective. Help children practice forming plural nouns by adding -*s*. Make word cards featuring basic nouns and letter *s* cards. The hands-on experience of using these cards to build plural nouns may help children solidify their understanding of this concept.

OBJECTIVES

Focus Describe the connection between two pieces of information in a text. RI.1.3

Use text evidence to answer questions about a text. RI.1.1

See **Routines** on pp. TR2–TR31.

Identify How Information Is Connected

LESSON 6 FIRST READ

Build Understanding

SET THE PURPOSE Focus the instruction by sharing the following Enduring Understanding: *Learners understand that living things have certain behaviors that shape them and allow them to survive.* We are going to read to learn about the behaviors of two different animals and how these behaviors are similar and different.

EXPLORE POETRY Read the poem "The Elephant" in the *Text Collection*, p. 45, and discuss it with children. How does the poet describe the elephant? What words in the poem rhyme?

ENGAGE CHILDREN Display the Contents page in *Time to Sleep*. Point out the sections titled "One Eye Open" and "On One Leg." Ask children what they think each section will be about. Remind them to think about the Essential Questions as they read, talk, and write about the text: *How do features in informational texts help readers understand the main topic? How does the organizational structure of a text help writers explain information?* Tell children: In this lesson we are going to learn how to identify and describe ways that pieces of information are connected.

READ As you read pp. 8–11 of *Time to Sleep,* use the appropriate reading routine from pp. TR8–TR19. Encourage children to read along silently, following the words from left to right and top to bottom. In this reading, children should focus on the details that tell about the behaviors of these animals.

TURN AND TALK After reading, have children turn to a partner and discuss this question using examples from the text: What behaviors do these animals have? Use the **Think-Pair-Share Routine** on pp. TR2–TR3. (Children should identify details such as sleep with one eye open, watch where they are going, sleep on one leg, tuck the other leg under their feathers, and look out for danger.)

FOUNDATIONAL SKILLS MINI-LESSON

Consonants /r/, /w/, /j/, /k/

- Show the Picture Card *red.* Let's say this word: *red.* Now let's say the first sound in *red:* /r/.
- Show Sound-Spelling Card 20. Point to *r.* The letter *r* stands for the sound /r/. Write *rip.* What is the first sound in *rip?* What letter stands for the sound /r/? *(r)*
- Repeat the procedure for *w, j,* and *k* using the *wig, jet,* and *kitten* Picture Cards and Sound-Spelling Cards 12, 13, and 26.
- Say these words: *job, kid, rig, wet, rod, win, jog, kit.* Have children say the letter that spells the beginning sound for each word.

For more explicit instruction, see p. FS18 in this Teacher's Guide.

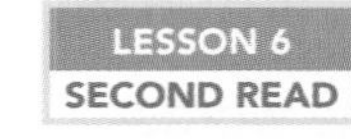

Close Read

CITE TEXT EVIDENCE Engage the class in a discussion about what you just read. Remind children that readers can learn about animals by looking for details about their behaviors and making connections between the pieces of information. Use these questions to guide the discussion, and ask children to support their answers with evidence.

- How do dolphins sleep? (with one eye open) Let's read the sentence that tells us this together. Why do you think it is important for dolphins to see while they sleep? (Possible response: They are in the water when they sleep, so maybe they need to make sure they do not run into anything or come across dangerous plants or animals.) **DOK L2**
- How do ducks sleep? (on one leg) What do they do with their other leg? (They tuck it under their feathers.) Point to the part of the text that tells you that. Why do you think ducks change legs when they sleep? (Possible response: Maybe one leg gets tired, so they need to stand on the other leg.) **DOK L2**
- Ask your "reading sleuths" to work with a partner to explain why they think the illustrator draws the boy and his teddy bear sleeping in different ways. (The illustrator shows the boy and his teddy bear sleeping just like the animals. People do not sleep in those ways, so maybe the illustrator wanted to show how silly that would look.) **DOK L3**

BY-THE-WAY WORDS During close reading, define the following words for children involving known concepts that can be stumbling blocks to comprehending the text.

dolphins, p. 8: Tell children that *dolphins* are a kind of animal that lives in the water.

feathers, p. 10: Explain to children that *feathers* are a kind of body covering that birds have.

Scaffolded Instruction

ENGLISH LANGUAGE LEARNERS

IDIOM Explain to English language learners that the expression *look out for* means "to watch for something." Tell them that dolphins and ducks watch for danger when they sleep. To reinforce the meaning of the expression, invite volunteers to use it in sentences, such as "I look out for cars when I cross the street."

STRATEGIC SUPPORT

USE PICTURES If children have difficulty understanding or inferring details about what dolphins and ducks do and why, point out that they can study the pictures for clues about the animals' behaviors. Ask questions about the pictures, such as: *Where do dolphins live? What is the dolphin doing as it sleeps?*

OBJECTIVES

Determine the meaning of and use academic and domain-specific words in a text.

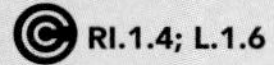 RI.1.4; L.1.6

Describe the connection between two pieces of information in a text.

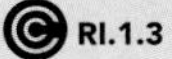 RI.1.3

BENCHMARK VOCABULARY

- danger, p. 8
- tuck, p. 10

BENCHMARK VOCABULARY

- Have children find and read the sentences from the text with the words *danger* and *tuck*.

  Use the **Benchmark Vocabulary Routine for Informational Text** on pp. TR24–TR27 to teach the meanings of the words.
- Use the information on pp. 152–155 of this Teacher's Guide to discuss other words connected to each of the Benchmark Vocabulary words.

PRACTICE Have children use p. 55 in their *Reader's and Writer's Journal* to show contextual understanding of the Benchmark Vocabulary. Monitor children's vocabulary development.

Reading Analysis

TEXT TALK

DESCRIBE CONNECTIONS Explain to children that when they read an informational text, they can tell how pieces of information in the text are connected. One way to connect pieces of information is to tell how they are alike and different. Provide the Compare and Contrast graphic organizer on p. TR33.

Describe Connections

Topics: Dolphins and Ducks

Alike:
both animals sleep

Different:
Dolphins sleep with one eye open, and ducks sleep on one leg.

MODEL I see on page 8 that dolphins sleep with one eye open. I see on page 10 that ducks sleep on one leg. Both animals sleep, but they sleep in different ways. I will write these details on the chart.

PRACTICE/APPLY Have children work independently or in small groups to complete the graphic organizer with more details about how dolphins and ducks are similar and different. Then have them share their ideas with the class. Ask them to tell how the pieces of information in "One Eye Open" and "On One Leg" are alike and different.

Small Group Time

STEP 1 Focused Independent Reading

BUILD ACCOUNTABILITY Prepare children to read their **self-selected texts.** Announce the two focus points to the class, and help children make a plan for their reading. Children will apply both focus points to their self-selected texts.

TODAY'S PROCESS FOCUS	
☐ Engagement and Identity	☑ Independence
☐ Stamina	

Tell children to select an informational book that they can read on their own. Encourage them to consider selecting a text that they have read before. They can also take a quick look at the pages in the book to determine if it is something they will be able to read independently.

TODAY'S STRATEGY FOCUS	
☐ Vocabulary Knowledge	☑ Critical Thinking
☐ Fluency	☐ Comprehension

Guide children in using the content of today's Reading Analysis lesson to analyze their self-selected texts. We learned that we can look at pieces of information in a text and find ways that they are connected. How can finding connections between details or pieces of information help you understand your book? Be prepared to answer the question with examples. Alternatively, have children log into Pearson Realize to find an Independent Reading Activity that is appropriate for the text they are reading.

MONITOR PROGRESS

- **Process Focus:** Have children record their reading in a daily reading log. Children should write a short summary of the book using words and pictures. They should also note any parts of the reading that they found difficult and why.
- **Strategy Focus:** Have children answer the question, pointing out connections between details or pieces of information and explaining how these connections helped them understand the book. Alternatively, have children log into Pearson Realize and review with you the Independent Reading Activity they completed for their book.

For further guidance, see the **Independent Reading Routine** on pp. TR12–TR19.

While children are reading independently, use the Small Group Options on pp. 216–217.

INDEPENDENT LITERACY WORK

Text Club (pp. TR20–TR23)

Leveled Text Library

Center Options (pp. 160–161)

Use **Write in Response to Reading** on p. 55 of the *Reader's and Writer's Journal* to check children's understanding of key ideas in *Time to Sleep.*

Phonics: Decodable Practice Readers

GUIDED READING OPTIONS

Use the **Leveled Text Library** to choose appropriate texts based on children's needs.

Use ***ReadyUp! Intervention*** for children who require additional instruction with this lesson's reading and foundational standards or with prerequisite standards.

STEP 2 Small Group Options

Based on formative assessments of children's progress, use the following options to provide additional instruction, practice, or extension as needed.

PHONICS

For children who need support with this week's Phonics skill, use pp. FS18–FS21 in this Teacher's Guide.

UNLOCK THE TEXT

For children who need support in accessing key ideas, key language, and key structures in ***Time to Sleep,*** use **Unlock the Text** in the *Scaffolded Strategies Handbook*, pp. 22–27.

CONFERENCE

For independent reading accountability, **conference** each day with two or three children to discuss **self-selected texts** and support their reading.

READING ANALYSIS SUPPORT

For children who struggle with describing connections in ***Time to Sleep,*** use this **Support Reading Analysis Mini-Lesson.**

DESCRIBE CONNECTIONS Help children make a connection between two pieces of information in the text. Read aloud pp. 8 and 10. Point out the final sentences on these pages. Help children make connections by asking guiding questions, such as: How are the behaviors of dolphins and ducks similar? How is the way they look out for danger different? As they answer the questions, have children record the connections in the appropriate boxes on their Compare and Contrast graphic organizer.

Invite children to work with a partner or small group to discuss other connections between dolphins and ducks in the words and pictures in *Time to Sleep*. Use the **Think-Pair-Share Routine** on pp. TR2–TR3.

Describe the connection between two pieces of information in a text.
RI.1.3

READING ANALYSIS EXTENSION

For children who can easily describe connections in ***Time to Sleep,*** use this **Extend Reading Analysis Mini-Lesson**.

DESCRIBE CONNECTIONS Read aloud the text on p. 6. Have children make connections between the information about horses on this page and the information about ducks on p. 10. Remind them to look for details in the words and pictures to tell how horses and ducks are similar and different. Then have them discuss the following questions:

- How are the way horses sleep and the way ducks sleep similar? (They both sleep standing up.) How are the ways that they sleep different? (Horses use all of their legs when they are sleeping, and ducks use only one leg.)
- How are the ways horses and ducks use their legs when they sleep similar and different? (Both animals do something special with their legs when they sleep. Horses lock their legs. Ducks tuck one leg under their feathers and change legs while they sleep.)
- In what other ways are the behaviors of horses and ducks similar and different? (Both animals have things they are afraid of. Horses are ready to run away if they get scared. One duck watches for danger while the other ducks sleep.)

Describe the connection between two pieces of information in a text. RI.1.3

FLUENCY

For fluent reading accountability, use the **Oral Reading Fluency Quick Check.** ☑ **Today assess 2–3 children.**

MODEL ACCURACY Explain that reading with accuracy means pronouncing each word correctly and not skipping or adding words. Have children follow along as you read aloud p. 10 from *Time to Sleep*, mispronouncing several words that children will recognize. Ask children to name the words you read incorrectly and tell how you should pronounce them. Model reading the text again, this time with accuracy. Then have children read the page chorally with accuracy.

Read grade-level text with accuracy. RF.1.4.b

QUICK CHECK

MONITOR PROGRESS

If . . . children mispronounce words as they read,

then . . . have them practice reading aloud with a partner who can help them pronounce the words correctly.

If . . . children are skipping or adding words as they read,

then . . . have them point to each word as they read it aloud to ensure they do not miss or add any words.

OBJECTIVE
Understand text structure in informative writing.
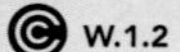 W.1.2

Informative/Explanatory Writing

Question-and-Answer Text Structure

SET THE PURPOSE Remind children that text structure is how an author organizes a text. Review the text structure used in *Time to Sleep*.

In *Time to Sleep*, the author tells about how different animals sleep. This is the main topic. She describes how and where the animals sleep and why they sleep the way they do. She writes descriptions to share facts about her main topic.

Explain that sometimes writers share facts about a topic in a question-and-answer format. They ask a question and then answer it. Explain that sometimes a writer will also ask a question without giving an answer. This can help readers think more about the topic.

TEACH AND MODEL Review the question-and-answer format on p. 2 in *Time to Sleep*. Then point out the questions on pp. 9 and 11.

- Look at pages 9 and 11. Why do you think the writer asks these questions? (Possible response: The writer wants readers to imagine what it would be like to sleep like these animals.) If the writer wanted to write a section about how people sleep, she could ask questions like these to help her begin thinking about what to write. She could look for answers to these questions and then use the facts to write about ways that people sleep.

Provide the following model from p. 8 of *Time to Sleep* that describes how dolphins sleep:

Dolphins sleep with one eye open.
They can see where they are going while they are sleeping.
They can look out for danger.

The writer uses facts and details to describe how dolphins sleep. What questions might the writer have asked as she prepared to write this section? The writer might have asked: *How do dolphins sleep? How does sleeping this way help them?*

Write an Answer to a Question

PREPARE TO WRITE Explain to children that writers often brainstorm to think of ideas before they begin writing. When writing an informative text, writers can brainstorm by asking questions about a topic.

We have been reading about how some animals sleep. If we want to write an informative text about how other animals sleep, we can begin by asking questions about the topic.

BRAINSTORM With children, brainstorm questions about how animals sleep. Encourage them to think of questions about animals that are not in *Time to Sleep*. List their questions. Then explain why brainstorming questions before they begin writing is helpful.

It is important for writers to think about what they are going to write before they begin writing an informative text. Brainstorming questions like we did about how animals sleep is a good way to begin thinking about what to write. The questions we asked might be helpful to us as writers to guide us in our research about the topic. The questions we asked might also give structure to our writing. We might write about our topic in a question-and-answer format.

ORGANIZE DETAILS Choose two questions asked by the class. Model briefly how you can look up the answers to these questions in a book or on the Internet. Share the findings with children by reading the sources aloud to them. Then take time to write a short informative text in a question-and-answer format.

MODEL

How do elephants sleep? Elephants can sleep standing up or lying down. Where do bears sleep? Bears often sleep in dens.

Scaffolded Instruction

STRATEGIC SUPPORT

ASKING QUESTIONS If children have difficulty thinking of questions, suggest that they first narrow the topic. Prompt them with questions, such as: *What animals do you like? What animals would you like to know more about?* Tell children that once they have narrowed the topic by thinking of several animals, they can begin to ask questions. Remind them that their questions should be about the animals' sleeping behaviors. Help them think of questions, such as: *Where do chipmunks sleep? How long do chipmunks sleep each night?*

OBJECTIVES

Write informative text. W.1.2

With guidance, use technology to produce and publish writing and to collaborate with others. W.1.6

Use singular and plural nouns and verbs that match.
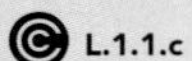

Independent Writing Practice

WRITE Have children practice the concept of brainstorming questions to guide their research before they write informative text. With a partner, have them discuss the kinds of questions they might ask each other if they wanted to write an informative text about their partner. Have children orally discuss the kinds of questions they might ask.

After partners have had a few minutes to brainstorm questions orally, have them share their questions with the whole group. Write the questions on separate sheets of paper. Then hand out the questions to children and have them write the answer to the question they were assigned on p. 56 of their *Reader's and Writer's Journal.* Have partners share their answers with each other.

CONVENTIONS If you wish to teach children about matching nouns and verbs, use the Conventions Mini-Lesson on p. 221. Encourage children to check their writing to make sure nouns and verbs match.

DIGITAL OPTIONS If available, have children use computers or tablets to type their questions and answers and print them. Children can draw a picture to illustrate their answer on the same sheet of paper.

Share Writing

Gather children together and have each child share his or her partner's response to the assigned question. Then have volunteers share their own answer to the question.

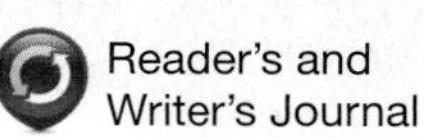

Conventions Mini-Lesson

Matching Nouns and Verbs

TEACH AND MODEL Explain that verbs should match the nouns in a sentence. If a noun names one person, animal, place, or thing, the verb should be singular to match the singular noun. If a noun names more than one person, animal, place, or thing, the verb should be plural to match the plural noun. To simplify the concept of singular and plural nouns and verbs, help children understand that singular nouns often do not have an *-s* at the end but singular verbs do. The opposite often holds true for plural nouns and verbs—plural nouns have an *-s* at the end but plural verbs do not.

Singular: A dolphin sleeps with one eye open.
Plural: Dolphins sleep with one eye open.

The singular noun (*dolphin*) matches the singular verb (*sleeps*). The plural noun (*dolphins*) matches the plural verb (*sleep*).

Singular: The duck stands on one leg.
Plural: The ducks stand on one leg.

The singular noun (*duck*) matches the singular verb (*stands*). The plural noun (*ducks*) matches the plural verb (*stand*).

PRACTICE Write several simple sentences, leaving out the verb for each sentence. Have volunteers fill in the verbs so that they match the nouns. For example: *The bat (hangs) upside down/The bats (hang) upside down. A duck (swims) in the pond/Ducks (swim) in the pond.* Then have children complete the activity on p. 56 of their *Reader's and Writer's Journal*.

Scaffolded Instruction

ENGLISH LANGUAGE LEARNERS

MATCHING NOUNS AND VERBS Not all languages match nouns and verbs with the simple "add *-s*" or "don't add *-s*" rules. Depending on their language backgrounds, children may need additional practice matching nouns and verbs. Provide examples of both singular and plural nouns. Then provide examples of both singular and plural verbs that use regular spelling. Have children match the nouns and verbs accordingly and state a sentence orally using those matches.

Answer Questions Using Text Features

LESSON 7 FIRST READ

Build Understanding

SET THE PURPOSE Focus the instruction by sharing the following Enduring Understanding: *Writers understand that informational texts can have a variety of features*. We are going to read to see how the author of *Time to Sleep* uses text features to share information about the topic.

ENGAGE CHILDREN Display *Time to Sleep*. Display headings, photographs, illustrations, labels, and the Picture Index and explain the purpose of each. Share the following Essential Questions with children and tell them that they should think about the questions as the class reads, talks, and writes about the text: *How do features in informational texts help readers understand the main topic? How does the organizational structure of a text help writers explain information?* Tell children: In this lesson we are going to learn how to use text features to find information and answer questions about a topic.

READ As you read pp. 12–16 of *Time to Sleep,* use the appropriate reading routine from pp. TR8–TR19. Have children follow along as you read. Encourage them to read the headings and other sentences that they know. In this reading, children should focus on the details and information they find in the features of the text.

TURN AND TALK After reading, have children turn to a partner and discuss this question using examples from the text: What topics did you read about in this section of the text? Use the **Think-Pair-Share Routine** on pp. TR2–TR3 and make sure children are using best practices for speaking and listening as outlined in the routine. (Children should identify these topics: animals that sleep in a tree, p. 12; animals that sleep anywhere, p. 14.)

OBJECTIVES

Use text features to locate key information in a text. RI.1.5

Answer questions about key details in a text. RI.1.1

See Routines on pp. TR2–TR31.

FOUNDATIONAL SKILLS MINI-LESSON

High-Frequency Words; Consonants *r*/r/, *w*/w/, *j*/j/, *k*/k/

- Display the High-Frequency Word Card *the*. Have children say and spell the word. The word *the* is spelled *t-h-e*. Have children write the word and use it in a sentence. Repeat with *do, you,* and *see*.
- Use Sound-Spelling Cards 12, 13, 20, and 26 to review consonants *r, w, j,* and *k*.
- Have children turn to *Decodable Practice Reader R5A* on p. 65. Ask them to read aloud the title and then read the story with a partner.

For more explicit instruction, see p. FS19 in this Teacher's Guide.

Close Read

CITE TEXT EVIDENCE Engage the class in a discussion about what you just read. Remind children that readers can use features to answer questions about the topic of a text. Use these questions to guide the discussion, and ask children to support their answers with evidence.

- Display p. 12. How do koalas keep from falling out of the tree while they are sleeping? (They hold on to the tree with their claws.) When I reread the page, the words do not tell me this information. So I will look at the photograph to see if it has any details to help me answer the question. I see the koala's claw is spread out and gripping the tree. That must be how it stays in the tree. **DOK L2**
- Why do you think people do not sleep in trees? How are people different from koalas? (People do not have claws like koalas, so they might fall out of the tree.) Point to the parts of the book that helped you answer these questions. **DOK L2**
- Where can cats sleep? Let's find and read the answer together. Have children choral read the final sentence on p. 14. What is one place that cats might sleep? (in a flowerbox) How do you know this? (The photograph shows a cat sleeping in a flowerbox.) **DOK L2**
- Ask your "reading sleuths" to work with a partner to find details in the words and picture about koalas and how they sleep. (The text uses the words and phrases *trees, most of the day,* and *up high.* The picture shows the koala hugging the tree while it sleeps.) **DOK L2**

Scaffolded Instruction

ENGLISH LANGUAGE LEARNERS

MULTIPLE-MEANING WORD Explain to English language learners that the word *sort* has more than one meaning. In this text, the phrase *all sorts of* means "many different." Cats sleep in many different ways and in many different places. Remind children that they can use surrounding words to help them figure out the correct meaning of a word or phrase.

STRATEGIC SUPPORT

USE PHOTOGRAPHS If children have difficulty identifying details in photographs to help them answer the questions, guide them by first pointing out a photograph and then asking a question about it. For example: *Look at this photograph on page 12. Do koalas like to sleep alone or with other koalas?* Discuss with children the details in the photograph that can help them answer the question.

OBJECTIVES

Determine the meaning of and use academic and domain-specific words in a text.  RI.1.4; L.1.6

Use text features to locate key information in a text.  RI.1.5

Answer questions about key details in a text. RI.1.1

BENCHMARK VOCABULARY

- day, p. 12
- high, p. 12
- anywhere, p. 14

BENCHMARK VOCABULARY

- Have children find and read sentences from the text with the words *day, high,* and *anywhere.*
  Use the **Benchmark Vocabulary Routine for Informational Text** on pp. TR24–TR27 to teach the meanings of the words.
- Use the information on pp. 152–155 of this Teacher's Guide to discuss other words connected to each of the Benchmark Vocabulary words.

PRACTICE Have children use p. 57 in the *Reader's and Writer's Journal* to show contextual understanding of the Benchmark Vocabulary. Monitor children's vocabulary development.

Reading Analysis

TEXT TALK

TEXT FEATURES Tell children that they can use the information they find in text features, such as headings and the Picture Index, to answer questions about the text. Remind children that a heading is the title of a section of a text. It can be found at the beginning of the section and tells what the section is all about. Remind them that an index is a list of words or topics found in a text and the pages on which those words or topics can be found. A picture index also includes a picture of each word or topic.

MODEL When I turn to page 12, I see a heading at the top of the page. The heading lets me know that this page begins a new section of the text. I ask myself, "What is this section all about?" The heading tells me that this section is all about a type of animal that sleeps in a tree. Now I will turn to the Picture Index on page 16. I ask myself, "Where can I find information about how horses sleep?" I look for the picture of a horse. Next to the picture is the number 6. Now I know that I can find information about how horses sleep on page 6.

PRACTICE/APPLY Have children work independently or in small groups to use text features to answer these questions: *What are pages 14 and 15 all about? Where can we find information about how ducks sleep?* Have children write or draw their answers on a sheet of paper. Invite volunteers to share their answers with the class.

Generative Vocabulary Games
Reader's and Writer's Journal
Leveled Text Library
Independent Reading Activities
Independent Reading How-To Video

PEARSON realize

Small Group Time

STEP 1 Focused Independent Reading

BUILD ACCOUNTABILITY Prepare children to read their **self-selected texts.** Announce the two focus points to the class, and help children make a plan for their reading. Children will apply both focus points to their self-selected text.

TODAY'S PROCESS FOCUS	
☐ Engagement and Identity	☑ Independence
☐ Stamina	

Have children choose a book that they know well or have heard read aloud several times before. Encourage them to read the book on their own today. Afterwards, have children explain why they chose that book.

TODAY'S STRATEGY FOCUS	
☑ Decoding and Word Recognition	☐ Critical Thinking
☐ Fluency	☐ Comprehension

Guide children in recognizing and reading high-frequency words in their self-selected texts. Write the words *the, do, you,* and *see*. We learned the high-frequency words *the, do, you,* and *see*. As you go through your book today, look for these words and create a list to include in your daily reading log. Alternatively, have children log into Pearson Realize to find an Independent Reading Activity that is appropriate for the text they are reading.

MONITOR PROGRESS

- **Process Focus:** Have children record their reading in a daily reading log. They can draw or write about their favorite part of the book. Suggest that they copy the title of their book into their reading log.
- **Strategy Focus:** Have children look back to where they found the high-frequency words *the, do, you,* and *see*. Read the sentences with the words and have children repeat. Alternatively, have children log into Pearson Realize and review with you the Independent Reading Activity they completed for their book.

For further guidance, see the **Independent Reading Routine** on pp. TR12–TR19.

While children are reading independently, use the Small Group Options on pp. 226–227.

INDEPENDENT LITERACY WORK

Text Club (pp. TR20–TR23)

Leveled Text Library

Center Options (pp. 160–161)

Use **Write in Response to Reading** on p. 57 of the *Reader's and Writer's Journal* to check children's understanding of key ideas in *Time to Sleep*.

Phonics: Decodable Practice Readers

GUIDED READING OPTIONS

Use the **Leveled Text Library** to choose appropriate texts based on children's needs.

Use ***ReadyUp! Intervention*** for children who require additional instruction with this lesson's reading and foundational standards or with prerequisite standards.

STEP 2 Small Group Options

Based on formative assessments of children's progress, use the following options to provide additional instruction, practice, or extension as needed.

PHONICS

For children who need support with this week's Phonics skill, use pp. FS18–FS21 in this Teacher's Guide.

UNLOCK THE TEXT

For children who need support in accessing key ideas, key language, and key structures in ***Time to Sleep,*** use **Unlock the Text** in the *Scaffolded Strategies Handbook,* pp. 22–27.

CONFERENCE

For independent reading accountability, **conference** each day with two or three children to discuss **self-selected texts** and support their reading.

READING ANALYSIS SUPPORT

For children who struggle using text features to answer questions about ***Time to Sleep,*** use this **Support Reading Analysis Mini-Lesson.**

TEXT FEATURES Help children use the heading on p. 14 to answer the question, *What are pages 14 and 15 all about?* Remind children that the main topic of the book is the different ways that animals sleep. Then read the heading aloud. Have children look at the photograph. Ask guiding questions, such as: What kind of animal does the photograph show? What does the heading tell about this section? Invite children to draw or write what the section is all about on a sheet of paper.

Invite children to turn to the Picture Index on p. 16 and work with a partner or small group to discuss the answer to the question, *Where can we find information about how ducks sleep?* Use the **Think-Pair-Share Routine** on pp. TR2–TR3.

Use text features to locate key information in a text. RI.1.5

Answer questions about key details in a text. RI.1.1

READING ANALYSIS EXTENSION

For children who can easily use text features to answer questions about *Time to Sleep,* use this **Extend Reading Analysis Mini-Lesson.**

TEXT FEATURES Invite children to think of questions they have about *Time to Sleep.* When children have thought of at least two questions, ask them to share the questions with a partner and then work together to use text features to locate information to answer their questions. Provide a model for children.

- As I think about the different ways animals sleep, I ask myself, "Do animals and people sleep the same way?" To answer my question, I look at the captions for the illustrations in the book. The captions help me understand that people and animals do not sleep the same way. People do not sleep upside down, standing up, or in the other ways these animals sleep.

Use text features to locate key information in a text. RI.1.5
Answer questions about key details in a text. RI.1.1

FLUENCY

For fluent reading accountability, use the **Oral Reading Fluency Quick Check.** ☑ **Today assess 2–3 children.**

MODEL APPROPRIATE RATE Explain that reading at an appropriate rate means reading at just the right speed—not too fast and not too slow. Have children follow along as you model reading aloud p. 12 from *Time to Sleep,* first very quickly and then very slowly. Review why a reader would not want to read too slowly or too quickly. Then have children choral read p. 14 at an appropriate rate.

Read grade-level text at an appropriate rate. RF.1.4.b

QUICK CHECK

MONITOR PROGRESS

If . . . children are reading too slowly,
then . . . have them practice reading aloud with a partner who can provide cues for the reader to speed up.

If . . . children are reading too quickly,
then . . . remind them to slow down in order to make it easier for listeners to understand what they are saying.

OBJECTIVE
Understand text structure in informative writing.
W.1.2

Informative/Explanatory Writing

Question-and-Answer Text Structure

SET THE PURPOSE Review the questions that children brainstormed together as a class during Lesson 6. After you read the questions aloud, have children name the main topic: how animals sleep. Talk about how the main topic can be broken down into smaller topics that still support the main topic.

We asked questions about how bears sleep, where bears sleep, and how long bears sleep. Those questions could all be grouped into one small topic: bears. We also asked questions about how and where elephants sleep. We can group those questions into another small topic: elephants. Both of these small topics still relate to the main topic: how animals sleep.

Display pp. 12–15 in *Time to Sleep*. Talk about how the writer organized the smaller topics in this book.

- What is the smaller topic of the first section? (sleeping in a tree) What do the details in this section all tell about? (The details all tell about a kind of animal that sleeps in a tree: a koala.)
- What is the smaller topic of the second section? (sleeping anywhere) What do the details in this section all tell about? (The details all tell about a kind of animal that can sleep anywhere: a cat.)

TEACH AND MODEL Review the Contents page in *Time to Sleep*. Talk about how the writer organized the smaller topics in this book.

Contents

How Do You Sleep?	2
Upside Down	4
Standing Up	6
One Eye Open	8

The Contents page helps readers understand how the writer organized her thoughts about the main topic. Each line names one of the smaller topics in the book.

Write a Question and an Answer

PREPARE TO WRITE Revisit the questions the class brainstormed about how animals sleep. Remind children that they can put these questions into groups to break the main topic down into smaller topics. Then they can research the answers to the questions and write an informational text to tell about the topic.

MODEL GROUPING QUESTIONS Model for children how you can group questions into a smaller topic.

I see that we have asked some questions about giraffes. We asked, "What do giraffes do when they sleep?" and "How long do giraffes sleep?" I can group these questions into one smaller topic: how giraffes sleep.

MODEL RESEARCH Explain that the next step is to research the answers to these questions. Tell children that you can look for information about how giraffes sleep in a book or on the Internet.

When I look on the Internet, I discover that giraffes do not lie down when they sleep. They sit or stand. They also curl their necks. I also discover that giraffes sleep for only about 5 minutes at a time and do not sleep more than 30 minutes each day.

MODEL WRITING FACTS Explain to children that you will model using your research to write a short informational text about how giraffes sleep.

I will write an informative piece of writing based on our questions and the facts I uncovered in my research. When I write, I am going to use a question-and-answer structure to help me tell the facts to my readers.

MODEL

What do giraffes do when they sleep?
They curl their necks. They stand or sit.

How long do giraffes sleep?
They sleep for 5 minutes at a time. They sleep less than 30 minutes a day.

Scaffolded Instruction

STRATEGIC SUPPORT

QUESTIONS AND ANSWERS If children find themselves giving answers that are not directly related to the questions, discuss the questions and model how to give simple answers. Role-play asking and answering questions to help children become more proficient with questions and answers.

OBJECTIVES

Write informative text. W.1.2

With guidance, use technology to produce and publish writing and to collaborate with others. W.1.6

Use singular and plural nouns and verbs that match.
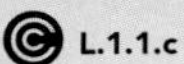

Independent Writing Practice

WRITE Have children work in small groups to review the questions the class asked about how different animals sleep. Have each group choose one question they want to find the answer to. Although children may find it difficult to read sources on the Internet or books from the library, they may look at the photos to try to find answers to their questions. You might also pair groups of children with older students to help them do research for their question.

After groups have had time to research their question, have them draw a poster that shows the answer to their question. Be sure children write their question at the top of their poster. You can gather posters to place on the wall of the classroom, making an area of the classroom into a science exhibit of sorts.

Individually, have children write a sentence that tells the answer to their group's question on p. 58 in their *Reader's and Writer's Journal*.

CONVENTIONS If you wish to teach children about using singular and plural nouns and matching verbs, use the Conventions Mini-Lesson on p. 231. Encourage children to check their writing to make sure nouns and verbs match.

DIGITAL OPTIONS If available, have children use computers or tablets to type their sentence and print it out. Children can display their sentence by their group's poster.

Share Writing

Gather children together and have each group share their poster. Talk about the research the group did and the answers they discovered.

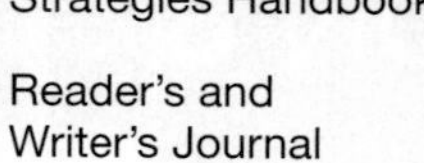

Conventions Mini-Lesson

Matching Nouns and Verbs

TEACH AND MODEL Remind children that nouns should match the verbs in a sentence. Remind them that many singular nouns, or nouns that name one person, place, animal, or thing, match with verbs that have an *-s* at the end. Review that many plural nouns, or nouns that name more than one person, animal, place, or thing, match verbs with no *-s* at the end.

Singular: The koala feels safe.
Plural: The koalas feel safe.

The singular noun *koala* matches the singular verb *feels*. The plural noun *koalas* matches the plural verb *feel*.

Singular: A cat sleeps in the flowerbox.
Plural: Cats sleep in the flowerbox.

The singular noun *cat* matches the singular verb *sleeps*. The plural noun *cats* matches the plural verb *sleep*.

PRACTICE Have a volunteer orally state a sentence with a singular noun and verb. Provide a noun, such as *dog*. Write the sentence. Then have another volunteer orally state the sentence using a plural noun and verb. Write the new sentence, and then compare the two sentences. If children use irregular nouns and verbs, help them understand how the pattern of adding *-s* or not adding *-s* changes. For more practice matching nouns and verbs, have children complete the activity on p. 58 of their *Reader's and Writer's Journal.*

Scaffolded Instruction

ENGLISH LANGUAGE LEARNERS

MATCHING NOUNS AND VERBS English language learners may need additional practice with matching nouns and verbs. Have children find examples of singular or plural nouns in *Time to Sleep* or in other familiar books in the classroom library. Prompt them by asking: *Which word names one or more than one person, animal, place, or thing?* Then have them identify the verb. Prompt them by asking: *Which word tells what the noun does/did?* Invite volunteers to explain why the nouns and the verbs match.

LESSON 8

OBJECTIVES

Focus Understand how the structure and organization of informational text helps readers understand the topic. RI.1.5

Use text evidence to answer questions during a close reading. RI.1.1

Text Complexity Rubrics
pp. TR48–TR54.

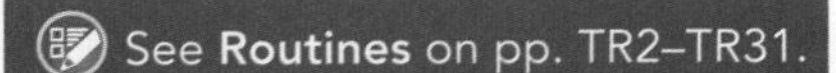

FOUNDATIONAL SKILLS MINI-LESSON

Initial and Medial /e/; Short *e*

- Say the word *edge* and ask children to listen to the beginning sound. Let's make that sound: /e/. Say *red*. What sound do you hear in the middle? Yes, the /e/ sound.
- Display Sound-Spelling Card 6. Point to *e*. The letter *e* stands for the sound /e/. Display the *pen* Picture Card. Let's say the sounds in the word: /p/ /e/ /n/. Let's spell the word: *p-e-n*.
- Say the following words: *pet, leg, men*. Have children write the letters that spell each word.

For more explicit instruction, see p. FS20 in this Teacher's Guide.

Use Structure and Organization to Understand a Text

LESSON 8 FIRST READ Build Understanding

SET THE PURPOSE Today children will begin reading *What Do You Do With a Tail Like This?* Focus the instruction by sharing the following Enduring Understanding: *Writers understand that informational texts can have a variety of features.* We are going to explore how a book can be organized and structured.

ENGAGE CHILDREN Introduce the book *What Do You Do With a Tail Like This?* on p. 16 of the *Text Collection*. Ask children to identify the punctuation mark in the title. Point out that the title is a question. Then page through the text and point out the question-and-answer structure. Remind children of the following Essential Questions and tell them that they should think about the questions as the class reads, talks, and writes about the texts in this module: *How do features in informational texts help readers understand the main topic? How does the organizational structure of a text help writers explain information?* In this lesson we are going to learn how writers use structure and organization in a text to explain information.

READ As you introduce this text, use the appropriate reading routine from pp. TR8–TR19. Have children follow along as you read. In this first reading, children should be reading for an understanding of what the text is mainly about.

TURN AND TALK After reading, have children turn to a partner and discuss this question using examples from the text: What did you learn about how animals use their body parts? Use the **Think-Pair-Share Routine** on pp. TR2–TR3. (Children should share ideas such as: Different animals use the same body parts in different ways.) Encourage children to ask and answer questions about what their partner says in order to gather additional information or clarify something that is not understood.

Close Read

LESSON 8 SECOND READ

CITE TEXT EVIDENCE Engage the class in a discussion about what they just read. Have children focus on key details in the section about noses on pp. 20–23. Remind children that authors organize texts in ways to help readers understand information. Use these questions to guide the discussion, and ask children to support their answers with evidence.

- What can you tell about the way this text is organized? (Each section tells about a different body part and explains how different animals use that body part.) What repetition do you notice? (Each section starts with a question and then gives answers to the question. Each section starts with pictures of certain body parts and then shows the whole animal that goes with that part.) Show me where you see this. **DOK L2**
- Why do you think the author set up the text this way? (Possible responses: It's fun; it makes it interesting to try to guess what the pictures show; it makes the reader think more about the body parts.) **DOK L2**

BY-THE-WAY WORDS During close reading, define the following words for children involving known concepts that can be stumbling blocks to comprehending the text.

platypus, p. 22: Tell children that a platypus is a small animal with a bill like a duck, webbed feet, and a wide flat tail.

hyena, p. 22: Tell children that a hyena is a large dog-like animal from Asia and Africa.

mole, p. 23: Tell children that a mole is a small animal with very small eyes and soft fur that digs tunnels in the ground.

alligator, p. 23: Tell children that an alligator is a large reptile with a long body, thick skin, and sharp teeth.

Scaffolded Instruction

ENGLISH LANGUAGE LEARNERS

VOCABULARY Use the pictures in the book to reinforce the English names for body parts. Point to the nose of each animal and say, "nose." Then point to each nose again as children say "nose." Do the same with tails, legs, eyes, and feet.

STRATEGIC SUPPORT

KEY IDEAS If children don't understand the connection between the pictures of noses on pp. 20–21 and the animals on pp. 22–23, point to the picture of a nose and then turn the page and point to the nose on the animal. Then have children match each nose to its animal.

OBJECTIVES

Determine the meanings of words in a text. 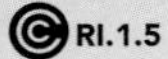 RI.1.4; L.1.6

Understand how the structure and organization of informational text helps readers understand the topic. RI.1.5

BENCHMARK VOCABULARY

- underground, p. 23
- breathe, p. 23

BENCHMARK VOCABULARY

- Find and read aloud the sentences from the text with the words *underground* and *breathe*.

  Use the **Benchmark Vocabulary Routine for Informational Text** on pp. TR24–TR27 to teach the meanings of the words.

- Use the information on pp. 152–155 of this Teacher's Guide to discuss other words connected to each of the Benchmark Vocabulary words.

PRACTICE Have children use p. 60 in the *Reader's and Writer's Journal* to show contextual understanding of the Benchmark Vocabulary. Monitor children's vocabulary development.

Language Analysis

TEXT TALK

TEXT STRUCTURE Tell children that readers can look at the structure and organization of a text to help them better understand what they are reading. Readers can look at the types of sentences the author uses and the order of the sentences. Readers can also look at where illustrations are on the page and how they are connected to the text.

MODEL When I read a text, I like to look at how the text is organized. This helps me understand more about what I am reading. As I page through the text, I notice that there are questions. For example, I see the question "What do you do with a nose like this?" on pages 20 and 21. When I turn the page, I see that the author answers the question by telling about different animals' noses. I know that this text has a question-and-answer structure. Each section begins with a new question about a body part.

- How does each question begin? ("What do you do with . . .")
- What words begin each answer? ("If you're a/an . . .")

PRACTICE/APPLY Have children work together to discuss the illustrations in the book. What do the illustrations show? How are the illustrations related to the text? How are they related to each other? Then use the **Small Group Discussion Routine** on pp. TR6–TR7 to have small groups discuss one of the noses on pp. 20–21 and decide which animal it belongs to on pp. 22–23. Check understanding by asking children to share or by circulating among groups.

Generative Vocabulary Games | Leveled Text Library | Independent Reading How-To Video
Reader's and Writer's Journal | Independent Reading Activities

Small Group Time

STEP 1 Focused Independent Reading

BUILD ACCOUNTABILITY Prepare children to read their **self-selected texts**. Announce the two focus points to the class, and help children make a plan for their reading. Children will apply both focus points to their self-selected texts.

TODAY'S PROCESS FOCUS	
☐ Engagement and Identity	☑ Independence
☐ Stamina	

Have children choose a book that they know well or have heard read aloud several times before. Encourage them to read the book on their own today. Afterwards, have children explain why they chose that book.

TODAY'S STRATEGY FOCUS	
☐ Vocabulary Knowledge	☐ Critical Thinking
☑ Fluency	☐ Comprehension

Guide children in acquiring oral fluency using their self-selected texts. To practice reading aloud, choose a page in your book that you know well and read it in a whisper voice. Then read it again and again. As you reread your text, try to memorize the words. Alternatively, have children log into Pearson Realize to find an Independent Reading Activity that is appropriate for the text they are reading.

MONITOR PROGRESS

- **Process Focus:** Have children record their reading in a daily reading log. They can draw a picture or write a word, phrase, or sentence about their favorite part of the book. Suggest that they copy the title of their book into their reading log.
- **Strategy Focus:** Have children read aloud to you the page they have been practicing on their own, speaking audibly and clearly. Alternatively, have children log into Pearson Realize and review with you the Independent Reading Activity they completed for their book.

For further guidance, see the **Independent Reading Routine** on pp. TR12–TR19.

While children are reading independently, use the Small Group Options on pp. 236–237.

INDEPENDENT LITERACY WORK

Text Club (pp. TR20–TR23)

Leveled Text Library

Center Options (pp. 160–161)

Use **Write in Response to Reading** on p. 60 of the *Reader's and Writer's Journal* to check children's understanding of key ideas in *What Do You Do With a Tail Like This?*

Phonics: Decodable Practice Readers

GUIDED READING OPTIONS

Use the **Leveled Text Library** to choose appropriate texts based on children's needs.

Use ***ReadyUp! Intervention*** for children who require additional instruction with this lesson's reading and foundational standards or with prerequisite standards.

STEP 2 Small Group Options

Based on formative assessments of children's progress, use the following options to provide additional instruction, practice, or extension as needed.

PHONICS

For children who need support with this week's Phonics skill, use pp. FS18–FS21 in this Teacher's Guide.

UNLOCK THE TEXT

For children who need support in accessing key ideas, key language, and key structures in ***What Do You Do With a Tail Like This?***, use **Unlock the Text** in the *Scaffolded Strategies Handbook*, pp. 28–33.

CONFERENCE

For independent reading accountability, **conference** each day with two or three children to discuss **self-selected texts** and support their reading.

CLOSE READING SUPPORT

For children who struggle with close reading, use this **Support Mini-Lesson for *Sleuth***.

SLEUTH WORK Read aloud "A Happy Ending" on pp. 12–13 of *Sleuth*. Then discuss the following questions with the group. Have children use text evidence to support their answers.

LOOK FOR CLUES Look at the pictures. What are two differences you see between ducks and swans? (Possible responses: Ducks and swans are different colors; ducks are smaller than swans; ducks have shorter necks.)

ASK QUESTIONS What question would you like to ask the author about how ducks and swans are alike and different? (Possible responses: Where do ducks and swans live? Do they eat the same kinds of food? Do they like each other?)

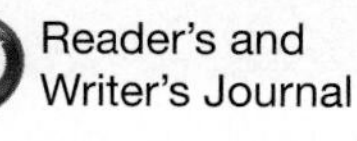

Games

Sleuth

MAKE YOUR CASE Think about how the ducks treated the swan in the story about the ugly duckling. Do you think it was right for their feelings to change when the swan's looks changed? How do you think the ducks should have acted? (Possible responses: I don't think it was right because he was still the same swan, only his looks changed. I think they should have been kind to the swan from the beginning.)

PROVE IT! What is the main idea of the text? (Possible response: Baby swans change as they grow.) Point to a supporting detail.

Ask and answer questions about key details in a text.  RI.1.1

CLOSE READING EXTENSION

For children who excel at close reading, use this **Extend Mini-Lesson for *Sleuth*.**

SLEUTH WORK Have children read "A Happy Ending" on pp. 12–13 of *Sleuth*. Then discuss the following questions with the group. Have children use text evidence to support their answers.

LOOK FOR CLUES What body part does this text tell about? (neck) What body parts does *What Do You Do With a Tail Like This?* tell about? (nose, ears, tail, eyes, feet, mouth)

ASK QUESTIONS What questions might you ask to compare swans and ducks to the animals in *What Do You Do With a Tail Like This?* (Responses will vary.)

MAKE YOUR CASE How are swans similar to platypuses? Think about what you learned from each text. (They both have long, flat noses. They both live by water.) Find the information in each text that helps you answer the question.

PROVE IT! How is the main idea of this text similar to the main idea of *What Do You Do With a Tail Like This?* (Possible responses: Both tell how animals are alike and different.) Point to sentences in each text that tell you this.

After children discuss the *Sleuth* work, direct them to pp. 61–62 of their *Reader's and Writer's Journal* to further explore "A Happy Ending."

Ask and answer questions about key details in a text. RI.1.1

OBJECTIVE

Understand text structure in informative writing.

W.1.2

Informative/Explanatory Writing

Question-and-Answer Text Structure

SET THE PURPOSE You have talked about informative text structure with children, focusing on descriptive and question-and-answer structures, as seen in *Time to Sleep*.

Review words often used to begin questions, such as *who, what, where, when, why*, or *how*. Have volunteers ask questions that begin with those words. Talk about the importance of choosing the appropriate beginning word for a question. For example, if you want to know the location of a place, you will likely begin the question with the word *where*. If you want to know the steps for making something, you will likely begin the question with the word *how*.

TEACH AND MODEL In *What Do You Do With a Tail Like This?,* each question asked throughout the text begins with the word *what*. Point out that each question asks about a body part, and the answers tell what different animals do with that part.

Through discussion, help children understand that the writers answer each question as though the reader were the animal. Provide the following model from pp. 20–22 of *What Do You Do With a Tail Like This?* to show how to write questions and answers in a text.

What do you do with a nose like this?

Each question asked in this text begins with the word *what* and ends with a question mark.

If you're a platypus, you use your nose to dig in the mud.

The answers to the questions in the text are addressed to the reader. In this example, the writers answer the question as if the reader were a platypus.

Write a Question and an Answer

PREPARE TO WRITE Tell children that you are going to write a question-and-answer informative text based on the information in *What Do You Do With a Tail Like This?* Review pp. 22–23. Explain that you will think about the information given about each of the animals. Then you will write a question and answer based on the information.

CHOOSE A TOPIC Explain that first you will choose a piece of information to write about.

I found the information about the alligator to be interesting. I can write a question that asks about the alligator and its nose.

WRITE A QUESTION Model how to write a question based on the information you learned about alligators.

I will think about the information I have learned about alligators and write a question based on that information. The information tells how alligators breathe through their nose while they are in the water, so I will ask, "How does an alligator breathe while hiding under the water?"

WRITE AN ANSWER Model how to write an answer to your question.

To answer my question, I will use the information from the text. I will write the answer using my own words. When I write my answer, I will make sure it tells only the information needed to answer the question. I will not tell how long an alligator remains under the water or what it is looking for while under the water. My answer will tell just enough information to answer the question, which is about how alligators breathe. I will write, "When they are hiding underwater, alligators use their noses to breathe."

MODEL

How does an alligator breathe while hiding under the water?
When they are hiding underwater, alligators use their noses to breathe.

Scaffolded Instruction

STRATEGIC SUPPORT

QUESTIONS AND ANSWERS If children are unsure how writing a question is different from writing an answer, focus their attention on the features of questions and statements. Remind them that a question often begins with a question word, such as *who, what, where, when, why,* or *how,* and always ends with a question mark. A statement ends with a period. Write questions and statements on the board, and help children identify the features of each.

OBJECTIVES

Write informative text. W.1.2

With guidance, use technology to produce and publish writing and to collaborate with others. W.1.6

Use end punctuation for sentences.
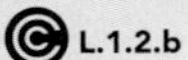

Independent Writing Practice

WRITE Have children work with a partner to review the questions asked in *What Do You Do With a Tail Like This?* Together, have them discuss one of the questions and practice answering that question with information about each of the animals mentioned on those pages. Then have children draw a picture of one of the animals in the book. On p. 63 in their *Reader's and Writer's Journal,* have them write a question based on the information given about that animal. Then have them write an answer to their question.

CONVENTIONS If you wish to teach children about using question marks, use the Conventions Mini-Lesson on p. 241. Help children check their writing to make sure they include question marks where needed.

DIGITAL OPTIONS If available, have children use computers or tablets to type their questions and answers and print them. Then, on the same sheet of paper, have them draw a picture to illustrate their sentences.

Share Writing

Ask volunteers to share their illustration, the question they asked, and the answer to their question. Talk with children about how we raise our voices at the end of a question. Remind children that this is a good way to tell if a speaker is telling something or asking something.

Writing Keystone Checklist

Writing a Question and an Answer

Use this checklist to assess children's informative/explanatory writing. If children need additional support writing a question and answer, use the Unlock Informative/Explanatory Writing beginning on p. 266 of the *Scaffolded Strategies Handbook*.

	Achieved	Notes
Choose a topic.		
Write a question.		
Use the text to write an answer to the question.		

Conventions Mini-Lesson

Use Question Marks

TEACH AND MODEL Review that a question is an asking sentence. Just like a telling sentence, a question tells a complete idea. Remind children that a question begins with a capital letter and ends with a question mark. *What do you do with a nose like this?* is an example of a question. It tells a complete idea. It begins with a capital letter and ends with a question mark.

What do you do with ears like these?

Questions always begin with a capital letter. They always end with a question mark.

What do you do with feet like these?

This question begins with a capital letter and ends with a question mark.

PRACTICE Have partners look through *What Do You Do With a Tail Like This?* to find examples of questions. Have them point to the capital letter that begins each asking sentence and the question mark that ends each asking sentence. Then have them practice writing question words and question marks to complete the sentences on p. 63 of their *Reader's and Writer's Journal.*

Scaffolded Instruction

ENGLISH LANGUAGE LEARNERS

QUESTIONS AND ANSWERS Help English language learners review the format of a question. Children may be confused that the question mark only appears at the end of the question rather than at the beginning and end as it does in other languages. Write simple sentences, read them aloud, and ask children to identify which sentences are questions.

LESSON 9

OBJECTIVES

Focus Compare and contrast two texts on similar topics. RI.1.9

Answer questions about key details in a text. RI.1.1

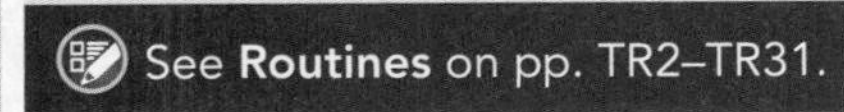
See **Routines** on pp. TR2–TR31.

Compare and Contrast Texts

LESSON 9 FIRST READ

Build Understanding

SET THE PURPOSE Tell children that today they will compare and contrast what they learn about animals in *Time to Sleep* and *What Do You Do With a Tail Like This?* Have children focus on the following Enduring Understanding: *Learners understand that living things have certain behaviors that shape them and allow them to survive.* We are going to learn about the abilities and behaviors of animals using two different texts.

ENGAGE CHILDREN Display the texts *Time to Sleep* and *What Do You Do With a Tail Like This?* on p. 16 of the *Text Collection*. Share the following Essential Questions with children and tell them that they should think about the questions as the class reads, talks, and writes about the texts in this module: *How do features in informational texts help readers understand the main topic? How does the organizational structure of a text help writers explain information?* In this lesson, we are going to use the information in both texts to compare and contrast animals' behaviors.

READ Read aloud *Time to Sleep*, choosing the appropriate reading routine from pp. TR8–TR19. Have children follow along and read with you when they can. In this reading, children should focus on the behaviors of the different animals. Then have children page through *What Do You Do With a Tail Like This?* to help them recall the different ways animals use their body parts.

TURN AND TALK After reading, have children turn to a partner and discuss this question using examples from the texts: What kinds of things can animals do? Use the **Think-Pair-Share Routine** on pp. TR2–TR3. (Children should share examples such as: some animals can sleep standing up, some animals can "see" with their ears.) Encourage children to ask and answer questions about key details in the text or to clarify something they do not understand.

FOUNDATIONAL SKILLS MINI-LESSON

High-Frequency Words; Short *e*

- Display the high-frequency words *with, is, the, do, a,* and *we.* Have children say and spell each word. Then have children write the words and use them in sentences.
- Use Sound-Spelling Card 6 to review short *e.*
- Have children turn to *Decodable Practice Reader R5B* on p. 73. Ask them to read aloud the title and then read the story with a partner.

For more explicit instruction, see p. FS21 in this Teacher's Guide.

LESSON 9
SECOND READ

Close Read

CITE TEXT EVIDENCE Engage the class in a discussion about the texts. Have children compare and contrast the details the authors use to describe how animals use their abilities to stay safe. Use these questions to guide the discussion, and ask children to support their answers with evidence.

- On page 8 in *Time to Sleep*, what do we learn about how dolphins stay safe? (They sleep with one eye open.) Yes, we learn that dolphins sleep with one eye open to look out for danger. Why do you think dolphins need to look out for danger? (There are lots of other animals that live in the water.) **DOK L3**
- Now let's look at page 6 in *Time to Sleep*. What do horses do to stay safe? (sleep standing up) How do you know? (The text says they can run away if they are scared.) **DOK L2**
- Now let's look at page 30 of *What Do You Do With a Tail Like This?* What does this book tell us about skunks? (They lift their tails to warn about a stinky spray.) How do you think a stinky spray keeps skunks safe? (Other animals will run away from the stinky spray and not attack the skunk.) **DOK L2**
- Why do you think animals need special abilities to stay safe? Use examples from the books you read. (Possible response: When animals sleep, they are not aware of what is around them. Some animals, like scorpions, are small and need a way to protect themselves.) **DOK L3**

BY-THE-WAY WORDS During close reading, define the following word for children involving known concepts that can be stumbling blocks to comprehending the text.

koalas, p. 12 of *Time to Sleep*: Tell children that koalas are an Australian animal that has thick gray fur, large ears, sharp claws for climbing, and no tail.

Scaffolded Instruction

ENGLISH LANGUAGE LEARNERS

KEY DETAILS Use the photos on pp. 6 and 8 of *Time to Sleep* and on p. 30 of *What Do You Do With a Tail Like This?* to help English language learners answer the questions. Ask: How does the photo help you understand how sleeping standing up helps a horse stay safe? (The horse looks like it is ready to run away if it sees danger.)

STRATEGIC SUPPORT

KEY DETAILS If children have difficulty finding information about how animals stay safe, guide them to scan the texts one at a time for clue words such as *danger, safe, warn*, and *get away.*

OBJECTIVES

Determine the meanings of words in a text. 

Compare and contrast two texts on similar topics. RI.1.9

BENCHMARK VOCABULARY

- hang, p. 4 *Time to Sleep*
- high, p. 12 *Time to Sleep*
- eyes, p. 33 *What Do You Do With a Tail Like This?*
- feet, p. 37 *What Do You Do With a Tail Like This?*

BENCHMARK VOCABULARY

- Have children find and read the sentences from the texts with the words *hang, high, eyes,* and *feet.*

  Use the **Benchmark Vocabulary Routine for Informational Text** on pp. TR24–TR27 to review the meanings of the words.

- Use the information on pp. 152–155 of this Teacher's Guide to discuss other words connected to each of the Benchmark Vocabulary words.

PRACTICE Have children use p. 64 in the *Reader's and Writer's Journal* to show contextual understanding of the Benchmark Vocabulary. Monitor children's vocabulary development.

Reading Analysis

TEXT TALK

COMPARE AND CONTRAST Explain that when readers have two texts that cover similar topics, they often look for details that are alike and different. Display the Venn diagram on p. TR43. Turn to p. 8 in *Time to Sleep* and to pp. 34–35 in *What Do You Do With a Tail Like This?*

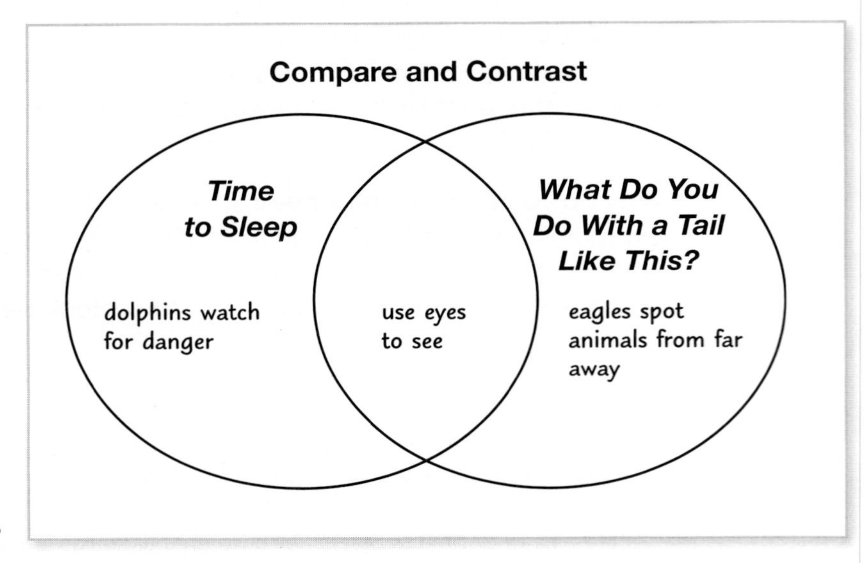

MODEL Let's look at what the texts tell us about how animals use their eyes. I notice that all of these animals use their eyes to see. That is how they are similar. I learn that some animals, such as dolphins, use their eyes to watch for danger. Other animals, such as eagles, use their eyes to spot animals from far away. That is one way they are different.

PRACTICE/APPLY Have children work in small groups to complete the graphic organizer by comparing and contrasting how animals use their feet. Have them focus on p. 4 of *Time to Sleep* and on pp. 38–39 of *What Do You Do With a Tail Like This?* Use the **Small Group Discussion Routine** on pp. TR6–TR7 to have children discuss the similarities and differences.

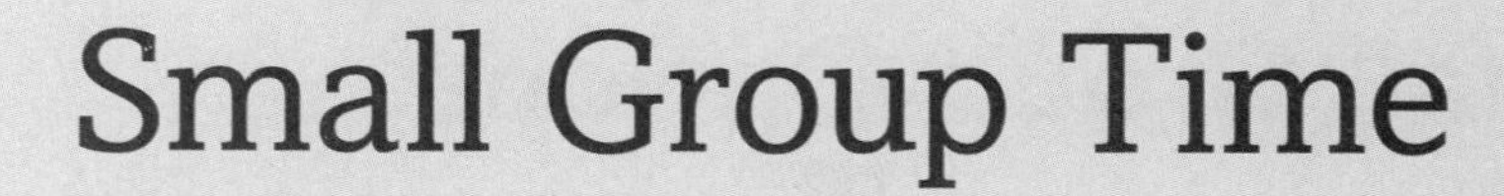

Small Group Time

STEP 1 Focused Independent Reading

BUILD ACCOUNTABILITY Prepare children to read their **self-selected texts.** Announce the two focus points to the class, and help children make a plan for their reading. Children will apply both focus points to their self-selected texts.

TODAY'S PROCESS FOCUS	
☑ Engagement and Identity ☐ Stamina	☐ Independence

Tell children to select a book they think they will enjoy reading. Encourage children to choose an informational book about an animal they would take pleasure in learning more about.

TODAY'S STRATEGY FOCUS	
☐ Vocabulary Knowledge ☐ Fluency	☐ Critical Thinking ☑ Comprehension

Guide children in applying the content of today's Reading Analysis lesson to their self-selected texts. We learned that animals have different abilities that allow them to do special things. As you go through your book, use self-stick notes to mark parts of the book that tell things an animal is able to do. Compare and contrast this animal with another animal you have read about. Alternatively, have children log into Pearson Realize to find an Independent Reading Activity that is appropriate for the text they are reading.

MONITOR PROGRESS

- **Process Focus:** Have children record their reading in a daily reading log by drawing a picture of the animal they read about and writing a word, phrase, or sentence about their book.
- **Strategy Focus:** Have children review with you the self-stick notes they placed in their book. Ask them to explain how the animal in their book uses its special abilities. Alternatively, have children log into Pearson Realize and review with you the Independent Reading Activity they completed for their book.

For further guidance, see the **Independent Reading Routine** on pp. TR12–TR19.

While children are reading independently, use the Small Group Options on pp. 246–247.

INDEPENDENT LITERACY WORK

Text Club (pp. TR20–TR23)

Leveled Text Library

Center Options (pp. 160–161)

Use **Write in Response to Reading** on p. 64 of the *Reader's and Writer's Journal* to check children's understanding of key ideas in the texts.

Phonics: Decodable Practice Readers

GUIDED READING OPTIONS

Use the **Leveled Text Library** to choose appropriate texts based on children's needs.

Use ***ReadyUp! Intervention*** for children who require additional instruction with this lesson's reading and foundational standards or with prerequisite standards.

STEP 2 Small Group Options

Based on formative assessments of children's progress, use the following options to provide additional instruction, practice, or extension as needed.

PHONICS

For children who need support with this week's Phonics skill, use pp. FS18–FS21 in this Teacher's Guide.

UNLOCK THE TEXT

For children who need support in accessing key ideas, key language, and key structures in ***Time to Sleep*** and ***What Do You Do With a Tail Like This?***, use **Unlock the Text** in the *Scaffolded Strategies Handbook*, pp. 22–33.

CONFERENCE

For independent reading accountability, **conference** each day with two or three children to discuss **self-selected texts** and support their reading.

READING ANALYSIS SUPPORT

For children who struggle with comparing and contrasting information about animals in the two texts, use this **Support Reading Analysis Mini-Lesson**.

COMPARE AND CONTRAST Help children compare the information about how animals use their feet on p. 4 of *Time to Sleep* and on pp. 38–39 of *What Do You Do With a Tail Like This?* Ask: How are the ways bats and geckos use their feet similar? (Both use their feet to be upside down.) Have children add the information to the center section on their Venn diagram.

Have small groups of children work together to answer these questions: *How are the ways bats and geckos use their feet different? What other ways do animals use their feet?* Have them record the information in the appropriate sections on their Venn diagram. Use the **Think-Pair-Share Routine** on pp. TR2–TR3.

Compare and contrast two texts on similar topics. RI.1.9

READING ANALYSIS EXTENSION

For children who can easily compare and contrast information about animals in ***What Do You Do With a Tail Like This?*** and ***Time to Sleep,*** use this **Extend Reading Analysis Mini-Lesson.**

COMPARE AND CONTRAST Have partners choose an informational text about animals from the classroom library and use self-stick notes to mark places in the text that tell about what animals can do. Then have them discuss the following questions:

- Did your text give information about any of the animals in *Time to Sleep* or *What Do You Do With a Tail Like This?* How is the information similar and different? (Responses will vary.)
- Did your text give information about how animals sleep? How are the ways the animals sleep similar to or different from the ways animals in *Time to Sleep* sleep? (Responses will vary.) Reread those sentences.
- Did your text give information about how animals use their body parts? How is this similar to or different from how the animals in *What Do You Do With a Tail Like This?* use their body parts? (Responses will vary.) Point to the sentences that tell you that.

Compare and contrast texts on similar topics. RI.1.9

FLUENCY

For fluent reading accountability, use the **Oral Reading Fluency Quick Check.** ☑ **Today assess 2–3 children.**

MODEL APPROPRIATE RATE Explain that reading at an appropriate rate means not reading too fast or too slow. Have children follow along as you model reading aloud p. 4 from *Time to Sleep* and p. 19 from *What Do You Do With a Tail Like This?* at an appropriate rate. Review why a reader would not want to read too slowly or too quickly. Then have children choral read the passages or a portion of a leveled text at an appropriate rate.

Read grade-level text at an appropriate rate. RF.1.4.b

QUICK CHECK

MONITOR PROGRESS

If . . . children are reading too slowly,

then . . . encourage them to practice the passage several times to become more confident with the words.

If . . . children are reading too quickly,

then . . . remind them that the listener needs time to think about what the reader is describing.

OBJECTIVE

Supply facts about a topic in informative/explanatory writing.

W.1.2

Informative/Explanatory Writing

Write Facts About a Topic

SET THE PURPOSE Remind children that informative writing tells readers about a topic. The writer of an informative text wants readers to understand more about the topic he or she is writing about.

The writer tells facts, or pieces of true information, to help readers learn about a topic. Often, the writer uses facts to answer questions the reader may have about the topic.

TEACH AND MODEL Review p. 2 in *Time to Sleep*. Talk about the questions and answers on this page. Guide discussion with the following questions.

- Why do you think the writers ask these questions? (to get readers to think about how they sleep)
- Look at the answers the writers give to the second and third questions. What is the purpose of these answers? (to tell facts about how animals sleep)
- What do you learn about the topic of how different animals sleep from these questions and answers? (Some animals sleep on one leg. Some animals sleep in a tree.)

Through discussion, help children understand how the writers of *What Do You Do With a Tail Like This?* use facts to answer questions about how different animals use their body parts. Provide the following models from pp. 28–31 of the text.

What do you do with a tail like this?

The main topic of this text is how animals use their body parts. The writers ask a question that readers might have about how animals use their tails.

If you're a giraffe, you brush off pesky flies with your tail.

The writers use facts to answer the question. One fact the writers give is that giraffes use their tails to get rid of flies.

If you're a monkey, you hang from a tree by your tail.

The writers give another fact to answer the question of how animals use their tails. The writers tell readers that monkeys use their tails to hang from trees.

Write a Fact

PREPARE TO WRITE Explain to children that when writers write informative texts, they often look for information about their topics in books or on the Internet. Tell children that you can look for facts in *Time to Sleep* and *What Do You Do With a Tail Like This?* to help you answer a question about animals and their behaviors.

GATHER INFORMATION Write this question on the board: *What do animals do when they are in danger?* Explain that you can look for facts in the texts to help you answer this question. Page through *Time to Sleep*.

I learn on page 4 in *Time to Sleep* that bats can fly away when they are scared. If they are scared, it is probably because they are in danger. I will place a self-stick note on this page to help me remember this fact. Now I will look through *What Do You Do With a Tail Like This?* I see on page 31 that scorpions can use their tails to sting things. This is something they do to protect themselves from danger. I will place a self-stick note on this page.

WRITE FACTS Explain to children that you will model writing the facts you learned from the texts in your own words to answer the question, *What do animals do when they are in danger?*

I can rewrite the facts I learned in my own words to answer this question. My writing will tell the same facts, just in different words.

MODEL

Bats fly away when they are in danger.
Scorpions sting things with their tails when they are in danger.

Compare your modeled sentences with the information in the texts. Have children tell how the sentences are alike and different. Then have them tell how your sentences answer the question.

Scaffolded Instruction

STRATEGIC SUPPORT

WRITING ANSWERS Help children understand that when they are writing facts to answer a question, they should begin their sentences with a capital letter and end with a period. Have children ask and answer simple questions, such as "What day is it?" "It is Friday." Write the answers on the board without capitalization or end punctuation. Have volunteers correct the sentences.

OBJECTIVES

Write informative text. W.1.2

With guidance, use technology to produce and publish writing and to collaborate with others. W.1.6

Use capitalization and end punctuation.

L.1.2.a, L.1.2.b

Independent Writing Practice

WRITE Have children work with a partner to review the information in *Time to Sleep* and *What Do You Do With a Tail Like This?*, flagging pages that tell information they find especially interesting. Then have children choose one fact from each text to answer this question: *How do animals use their body parts?* Have children write sentences to share their facts on p. 65 of their *Reader's and Writer's Journal*. Remind them to include the name of the animal and what the animal can do in their sentences.

CONVENTIONS If you wish to teach children about capitalization and punctuation, use the Conventions Mini-Lesson on p. 251. Have children check their sentences to make sure they begin with a capital letter and end with an appropriate punctuation mark.

DIGITAL OPTIONS If available, have children use computers or tablets to type their sentences and print them on separate sheets of paper. Have children draw a picture on each sheet of paper to illustrate the sentence.

Share Writing

Ask volunteers to share their writing with the class. They may wish to use drawings to help clarify their ideas. Have children identify ways the animals are similar or different.

Conventions Mini-Lesson

Use Capitalization and Punctuation

TEACH AND MODEL Remind children that a sentence is a group of words that tells a complete idea. Review that a sentence begins with a capital letter and ends with a punctuation mark, such as a period, question mark, or exclamation point. *If you're a chimpanzee, you feed yourself with your feet.* This is a sentence. It tells a complete idea. It begins with a capital letter and ends with a period.

What do you do with ears like these?	This sentence tells a complete idea. It begins with a capital letter and ends with a question mark.
Cats like to sleep a lot.	This sentence tells a complete idea. It begins with a capital letter and ends with a period.
They sleep in all sorts of places!	This sentence tells a complete idea. It begins with a capital letter and ends with an exclamation point.

APPLY Remind children that they should begin each sentence with a capital letter and finish it with an end punctuation mark. Write a statement, a question, and an exclamation. Make the beginning letters lowercase and leave off the end punctuation marks. Read aloud the sentences and have volunteers add capital letters and correct end punctuation. Talk about how all the sentences are alike: they all start with a capital letter. Talk about how the sentences are different: they end with different punctuation marks. Then have children complete the activity on p. 65 of their *Reader's and Writer's Journal.*

Scaffolded Instruction

ENGLISH LANGUAGE LEARNERS

END PUNCTUATION Some English language learners may be confused by the question mark and exclamation point only appearing at the end of a sentence, rather than at the beginning and end as it does in other languages. Help them practice using punctuation correctly. Provide word cards and punctuation cards for children to organize into sentences. If children place a punctuation mark at the beginning of a sentence, remind them that it should appear only at the end.

OBJECTIVES

Focus Understand that informational text has a main topic and key details. RI.1.2

Use text evidence to answer questions about key details in a text. RI.1.1

 See **Routines** on pp. TR2–TR31.

FOUNDATIONAL SKILLS MINI-LESSON

Consonants *r*/r/, *w*/w/, *j*/j/, *k*/k/; Short *e*

- Use Sound-Spelling Cards 20, 26, 12, and 13 to review *r*/r/, *w*/w/, *j*/j/, and *k*/k/. Have children identify each letter and the sound it stands for.
- Write these words: *ran, wig, jog, kit*. Have children say the sound for each letter and then blend the sounds to read the words.
- Use Sound-Spelling Card 6 to review short *e*. Have children identify the letter and the sound it stands for.
- Write *fed* and *pet*. Ask children to say the sound for each letter and then blend the sounds to read the words.
- Have children reread *Decodable Practice Readers R5A and R5B.*

For more explicit instruction, see p. FS21 in this Teacher's Guide.

Identify Elements of Informational Texts

LESSON 10 FIRST READ Build Understanding

SET THE PURPOSE Focus the instruction by sharing the following Enduring Understanding: *Readers understand that informational texts have features that help them determine main topics.* An informational text tells facts about a topic. Remember that a topic is what a book is all about. Many informational texts have features that readers can use to help them figure out the main topic.

ENGAGE CHILDREN Return to the text *What Do You Do With a Tail Like This?* in the *Text Collection* and have children page through pp. 24–31. Ask: What do you notice about the pictures? Are they photographs or drawings? Are texts with drawings of animals always made-up stories? Lead children to understand that some informational texts use illustrations and that *What Do You Do With a Tail Like This?* is informational. Display p. 24 and discuss the features of the sentence. Ask children to name the end punctuation mark. Remind children to think about the Essential Questions: *How do features in informational texts help readers understand the main topic? How does the organizational structure of a text help writers explain information?* In this lesson we are going to learn how readers can use details from the text and illustrations to understand the main topic.

READ As you reread pp. 24–31 of *What Do You Do With a Tail Like This?,* use the appropriate reading routine from pp. TR8–TR19. Have children follow along as you read. Tell them to read p. 28 with you and then on their own. In this reading, children should focus on what the animals' ears and tails do.

TURN AND TALK After reading, have children turn to a partner and discuss this question using examples from the text: What did you learn about animal ears? Use the **Think-Pair-Share Routine** on pp. TR2–TR3. Remind children that they can ask questions to clarify something they do not understand. (Children should share examples such as: Bats "see" with their ears, p. 26; jackrabbits keep cool with their ears, p. 26; crickets hear with their ears that are on their knees, p. 27.)

Close Read

CITE TEXT EVIDENCE Engage the class in a discussion about what you just read. Remind children that readers identify key details in a text to identify the main topic. Use these questions to guide the discussion, and ask children to support their answers with evidence.

- The text says that the bat "sees" with its ears. Why is that an interesting fact about bats? (Most living things hear with their ears and see with their eyes.) Explain that bats make chirping sounds that echo off objects so they know where things are. **DOK L2**
- Look at the jackrabbit and describe its ears. (They are long and thin.) Let's read together what a jackrabbit uses its ears for. When would a jackrabbit need its ears to keep cool? (when the weather is hot) **DOK L3**
- What do the text and illustrations tell us about how a hippopotamus and a humpback whale are alike? (They both live and swim in water.) Show me how you know this. Children should point to the words *under water* and to the blue water by the whale. What does the text tell us about how these animals are different? (The hippopotamus closes its ears under water, but the humpback whale uses its ears to hear sounds hundreds of miles away.) **DOK L2**
- What makes a lizard's tail the body part that another animal might catch? (It is long, so it is easier for other animals to grab it.) **DOK L3**

BY-THE-WAY WORDS During close reading, define the following word for children involving known concepts that can be stumbling blocks to comprehending the text.

scorpion, p. 31: Tell children that a scorpion has two front claws and a curved tail with a poisonous stinger at the end.

Scaffolded Instruction

ENGLISH LANGUAGE LEARNERS

FLUENCY The sentences on the answer pages all begin with an *If*-clause. Children may have difficulty reading sentences with such a clause. Demonstrate the function of commas at the ends of *if*-clauses by reading a few sentences from pp. 26–27 aloud, pausing briefly after each comma. Invite children to repeat those sentences after you.

STRATEGIC SUPPORT

KEY IDEAS If children have difficulty understanding the ways different animals use their ears or tails, ask clarifying questions, such as: Why might a hippopotamus close its ears under water? Why might a scorpion use its tail to sting something?

OBJECTIVES

Determine the meaning of and use academic and domain-specific words in a text. RI.1.4; L.1.6

Identify the main topic and retell key details. RI.1.2

BENCHMARK VOCABULARY

- pesky, p. 30
- warn, p. 30

BENCHMARK VOCABULARY

- Have children find and read sentences from the text with the words *pesky* and *warn*.

  Use the **Benchmark Vocabulary Routine for Informational Text** on pp. TR24–TR27 to teach the meanings of the words.

- Use the information on pp. 152–155 of this Teacher's Guide to discuss other words connected to each of the Benchmark Vocabulary words.

PRACTICE Have children use p. 66 in their *Reader's and Writer's Journal* to show contextual understanding of the Benchmark Vocabulary. Monitor children's vocabulary development.

Reading Analysis

TEXT TALK

MAIN TOPIC AND KEY DETAILS Remind children that the main topic is what a text is mostly about, or the most important idea. Key details are smaller pieces of information that tell more about the main topic. Provide the Main Idea graphic organizer on p. TR36.

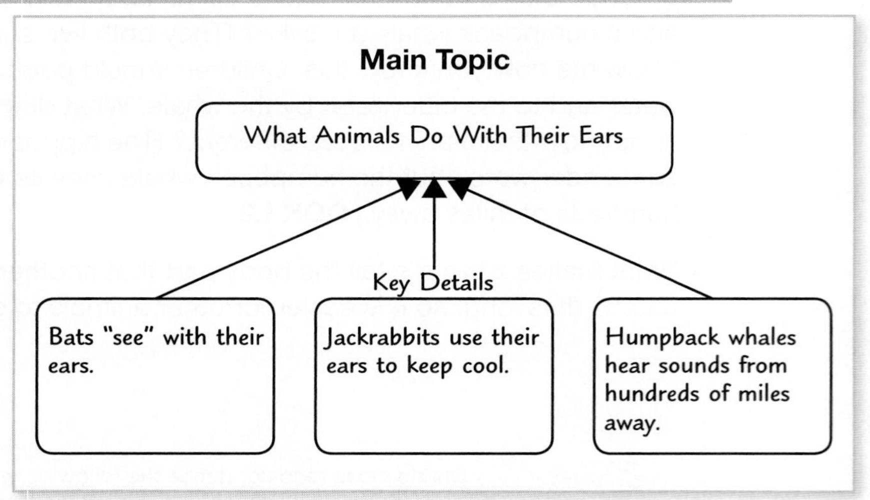

Main Topic
What Animals Do With Their Ears
Key Details
Bats "see" with their ears.
Jackrabbits use their ears to keep cool.
Humpback whales hear sounds from hundreds of miles away.

MODEL Let's look at pages 24 through 27 and figure out the main topic. When I read these pages, I see details about what animals do with their ears. I will write these details in the Key Details boxes. The details help me understand what these pages are all about. What animals do with their ears is the main topic. I'm going to write that in the Main Idea box.

PRACTICE/APPLY Have small groups complete a graphic organizer to find the main topic and key details for pp. 28–31. Have them write or draw key details that tell about at least three different animals. Use the **Small Group Discussion Routine** on pp. TR6–TR7. Check understanding by asking children to share or by circulating among groups. Ask them to use complete sentences when they share their ideas.

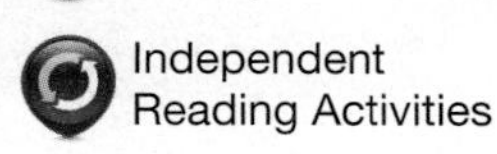

Independent Reading How-To Video

Small Group Time

STEP 1 Focused Independent Reading

BUILD ACCOUNTABILITY Prepare children to read their **self-selected texts.** Announce the two focus points to the class, and help children make a plan for their reading. Children will apply both focus points to their self-selected texts.

TODAY'S PROCESS FOCUS	
☑ Engagement and Identity	☐ Independence
☐ Stamina	

Tell children to select a book they think they will enjoy reading. Have them flip through a few books to look at the pictures and determine if the book might interest them.

TODAY'S STRATEGY FOCUS	
☑ Vocabulary Knowledge	☐ Critical Thinking
☐ Fluency	☐ Comprehension

Guide children in applying the content of today's Benchmark Vocabulary lesson to their self-selected texts. We learned the meaning of the word *pesky*. It is a describing word. As you go through your book, look for things that could be described as *pesky* and mark them with self-stick notes. Alternatively, have children log into Pearson Realize to find an Independent Reading Activity that is appropriate for the text they are reading.

MONITOR PROGRESS

- **Process Focus:** Have children tell why they chose their book. Then have them record their reading in a daily reading log by drawing or writing a short summary of the book and whether they liked it.
- **Strategy Focus:** Have children review the self-stick notes they placed in their book. Discuss why they think each thing can be pesky. Alternatively, have children log into Pearson Realize and review with you the Independent Reading Activity they completed for their book.

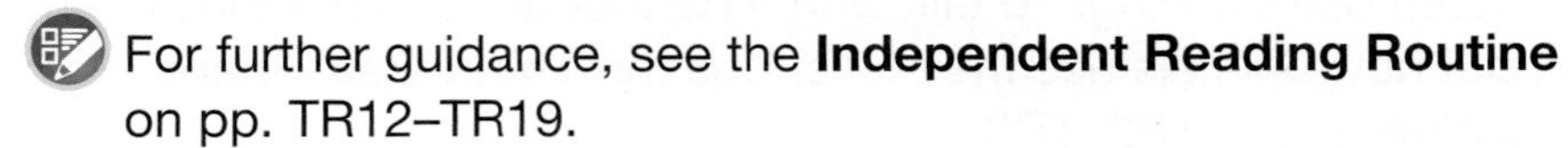
For further guidance, see the **Independent Reading Routine** on pp. TR12–TR19.

While children are reading independently, use the Small Group Options on pp. 256–257.

INDEPENDENT LITERACY WORK

Text Club (pp. TR20–TR23)

Leveled Text Library

Center Options (pp. 160–161)

Use **Write in Response to Reading** on p. 66 of the *Reader's and Writer's Journal* to check children's understanding of the main topic and key details in the text.

Phonics: Decodable Practice Readers

GUIDED READING OPTIONS

Use the **Leveled Text Library** to choose appropriate texts based on children's needs.

Use ***ReadyUp! Intervention*** for children who require additional instruction with this lesson's reading and foundational standards or with prerequisite standards.

STEP 2 Small Group Options

Based on formative assessments of children's progress, use the following options to provide additional instruction, practice, or extension as needed.

PHONICS

For children who need support with this week's Phonics skill, use pp. FS18–FS21 in this Teacher's Guide.

UNLOCK THE TEXT

For children who need support in accessing key ideas, key language, and key structures in ***What Do You Do With a Tail Like This?,*** use **Unlock the Text** in the *Scaffolded Strategies Handbook*, pp. 28–33.

CONFERENCE

For independent reading accountability, **conference** each day with two or three children to discuss **self-selected texts** and support their reading.

READING ANALYSIS SUPPORT

For children who struggle with identifying the main topic and key details in ***What Do You Do With a Tail Like This?,*** use this **Support Reading Analysis Mini-Lesson**.

MAIN TOPIC AND KEY DETAILS Help children find the main topic and key details on pp. 28–31. Ask: Which body part are these pages about? What do we learn about tails? Encourage children to elaborate by asking follow-up questions: What does the giraffe do with its tail? How do the scorpion and the skunk protect themselves with their tails? Have children find the words in the text that tell that information.

After the discussion, invite children to dictate the main topic and key details from pp. 28–31 for their graphic organizer. Have children use drawings to talk with a partner about what they learned about how animals use their tails. Use the **Think-Pair-Share Routine** on pp. TR2–TR3.

Identify the main topic and retell key details. RI.1.2

Scaffolded Strategies Handbook
Leveled Text Library
Games
Independent Reading Activities
Reader's and Writer's Journal

READING ANALYSIS EXTENSION

For children who can easily identify the main topic and key details of ***What Do You Do With a Tail Like This?***, use this **Extend Reading Analysis Mini-Lesson**.

MAIN TOPIC AND KEY DETAILS Have children draw pictures and write sentences that give key details from the parts of the book on noses (pp. 20–23) and eyes (pp. 32–35). Discuss these questions:

- What is the main topic of pages 20–23? (What Animals Do With Their Noses)
- What are the key details that helped you learn about how these animals use their noses? (A hyena finds food with it; a platypus digs in the mud with it; an elephant sprays water from it to give itself a bath; a mole finds its way underground with it; and an alligator uses it to breathe while hiding in the water.)
- What is the main topic of pages 32 through 35? (What Animals Do With Their Eyes)
- What are the key details about the main topic on these pages? (An eagle uses its eyes to spot animals; a chameleon can look two ways at once; a four-eyed fish can look above and below the water at the same time; a bush baby can see well at night; and a horned lizard can squirt blood from its eyes.)

Identify the main topic and retell key details. RI.1.2

TIKATOK

For writing practice connected to the unit topic of Connecting to Our World, use **TikaTok**.

WRITE TikaTok, a digital publishing studio, allows children to write and illustrate an online book. Have children log in to www.tikatok.com and find the activity for this unit. Children will write in response to prompts, insert images, and illustrate their own book however they wish. Encourage children to be creative and to work through the writing process carefully before they begin creating their books.

Be sure to give children adequate time throughout the unit to log in to www.tikatok.com to work on their books.

OBJECTIVE
Plan an informative piece of writing.
 W.1.2

Informative/Explanatory Writing

Writing Process: Plan

SET THE PURPOSE Review the writing process with children: plan, write, revise, edit, and publish. Remind them that this process allows writers to be proud of the writing they publish because they have planned their writing carefully, gotten their thoughts down on paper, revised their writing to make it stronger, and edited their writing for capitalization, punctuation, and spelling so it is clear for readers.

Talk about the many ways writers plan their writing before they begin actually writing.

> Writers often brainstorm their ideas before they begin writing. They think about what kind of writing they are asked to create, and then they begin to plan. They write everything that comes to mind about the topic they want to write about. Sometimes writers draw pictures to plan what they will write. Writers can ask questions they have about the topic. Then they can do research to answer their questions and find more information about the topic. When a writer researches, he or she looks for facts in books or encyclopedias or on the Internet.

Have volunteers share ideas for planning their writing, such as brainstorming, talking it out with a partner, and doing research. Then tell children that today they are going to plan an informative/explanatory piece of writing. They will write a question and an answer.

TEACH AND MODEL Review pp. 28–31 in *What Do You Do With a Tail Like This?* Have children identify the question. (What do you do with a tail like this?) Discuss the features of the question. (It begins with a question word and ends with a question mark.) Talk about how this question leads readers to continue reading on to discover the answer.

What do you do with a tail like this?	This question prompts readers to continue reading in order to discover the answers.
If you're a monkey, you hang from a tree by your tail.	This provides an answer to the question. The answer tells what monkeys do with their tails.

Plan a Question and an Answer

PREPARE TO WRITE Tell children that you are going to plan a question-and-answer piece of informative writing. Then they will get an opportunity to plan their own piece of informative writing. Explain to children that they can use the questions in books they read as examples for writing their own questions.

FEATURES OF A QUESTION Explain to children that a question is a sentence that asks something. It begins with an uppercase letter and ends with a question mark. The first word of a question is often a question word, such as *who, what, where, when, why,* or *how*. Write the following: *What day is it? Today is Wednesday.* Read the sentences aloud. Ask children to identify the question. Discuss the features of the question.

MODEL WRITING A QUESTION Tell children that you will model writing your own question.

I want to write a question and answer about one of the animals we read about in *What Do You Do With a Tail Like This?* I found one of the facts about the chameleon to be interesting, so I want to focus my question and answer on the topic of chameleons. A question I have is: *What do chameleons eat?* I will write that question.

Then explain that you will do some research to find an answer to that question. Remind children that there are many ways to do research, including using books and the Internet. Discuss research and how children can research when they plan their writing.

Review the steps below with children to show them how they can begin to plan their informative/explanatory writing:

Plan: Choose an animal to ask a question about.

Question: What do chameleons eat?

Research: Go to the library to find a book about chameleons.

Scaffolded Instruction

STRATEGIC SUPPORT

BRAINSTORMING Children may have trouble brainstorming ideas. To guide them in brainstorming, use a word web with the word *Animals* in the middle. Model how to think of different animals and write them on the web. Next, encourage children to think of questions they have about the animals on the web.

OBJECTIVES

Plan an informative piece of writing.  W.1.2

With guidance, use technology to research information to use for writing and to collaborate with others. W.1.7

Identify and use common and proper nouns. L.1.1.b

Independent Writing Practice

BRAINSTORM As a class, brainstorm and record a list of animals children read about in the unit texts. They may refer to this list as they plan their writing. Remind children to follow the classroom rules for discussions.

PLAN Have children plan their writing. Tell them to choose an animal they want to write about and draw a picture of it. Then have children think about what they want to know about the animal and write a question on p. 67 of their *Reader's and Writer's Journal*.

RESEARCH Provide child-friendly informational texts about animals for children to use to look for an answer to their question. Give them sticky notes to use to mark places in the text that provide an answer to their question. If children have difficulty finding an answer in an informational text, help them use a child-friendly site on the Internet. Print out their answer. Remind children that research is an important step of writing informative pieces.

CONVENTIONS If you wish to teach children about common and proper nouns, use the Conventions Mini-Lesson on p. 261. Encourage children to capitalize nouns correctly in their informative/explanatory writing.

DIGITAL OPTIONS If available, have children use computers or tablets to research the animal they chose. Remind children that search engines are a good way to find many sources.

Share Writing

Have partners share their questions with the whole group. Discuss sources that children may refer to in order to find answers to their questions.

Conventions Mini-Lesson

Common and Proper Nouns

TEACH AND MODEL Explain that a noun names a person, animal, place, or thing. A common noun names a general person, animal, place, or thing. A proper noun names a specific person, animal, place, or thing. Proper nouns always begin with an uppercase letter. Common nouns are not capitalized unless they are the first word of a sentence.

The dog wags his tail when he sees Jim.

The words *dog* and *tail* are common nouns. They name a general animal and thing. *Jim* is a proper noun. It is capitalized because it names a specific person.

Rex wags his tail when he sees the boy.

The words *tail* and *boy* are common nouns. They name a general thing and person. *Rex* is a proper noun. It is capitalized because it names a specific animal.

PRACTICE Write the following words: *cat, house, Pam, Grand Canyon, shoe*. Have children identify the common and proper nouns. Together with children, brainstorm a list of common and proper nouns. Then have children dictate sentences using the nouns. Have them identify if the noun they use is common or proper. For more practice with common and proper nouns, have children complete p. 67 of their *Reader's and Writer's Journal*.

Scaffolded Instruction

ENGLISH LANGUAGE LEARNERS

COMMON AND PROPER NOUNS English language learners may struggle to understand when a noun should be capitalized. Explain that proper nouns name specific people, animals, places, or things. For example, write the words *state* and *Florida*. Ask children which word names a specific place. Then provide a list of proper nouns. Help children determine which letter of each word should be capitalized.

OBJECTIVES

Focus Ask and answer questions to understand informational text.

 RI.1.1

Use illustrations and details in a text to describe its key ideas.

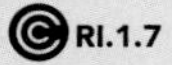 RI.1.7

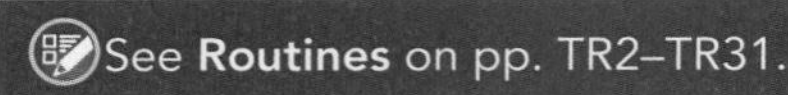
See **Routines** on pp. TR2–TR31.

FOUNDATIONAL SKILLS MINI-LESSON

Consonants v/v/; y/y/; z, zz/z/; qu/kw/

- Show the Picture Card *vase*. Let's say *vase*. Now let's say the first sound in *vase*: /v/.
- Show Sound-Spelling Card 25. Point to *v*. The letter *v* stands for the sound /v/, which you hear at the beginning of *volcano*. Write *vet*. What is the first sound in *vet*? What letter stands for the sound /v/? Let's write the letter *v*.
- Repeat the above procedure for *y*, *z*, and *qu*, using the Picture Cards *yellow*, *zebra*, and *quarter* and Sound-Spelling Cards 28, 29, and 19.
- Write and read the word *zap*. Have children change the initial consonant to make the words *yap*, *tap*, and *map*.

For more explicit instruction, see p. FS22 in this Teacher's Guide.

Ask and Answer Questions

LESSON 11 FIRST READ Build Understanding

SET THE PURPOSE Focus the instruction by reading the following Enduring Understanding: *Readers understand that informational texts have features that help them determine main topics.* Remember that informational texts tell facts and details about a topic. As you read an informational text, you can ask questions to figure out the main topic or to better understand or clarify what you read. The features in the text can help you find the answers to your questions.

ENGAGE CHILDREN Reread the title, *What Do You Do With a Tail Like This?,* to children. Discuss the ending punctuation mark. Ask: What is this end punctuation mark called? Does this sentence tell something or ask something? Display pp. 32–35 of the text. Ask: Which animals do you recognize? What are the names of the animals? Remind children to think about the Essential Questions: *How do features in informational texts help readers understand the main topic? How does the organizational structure of a text help writers explain information?* Tell children: In this lesson, we are going to learn how asking and answering questions can help us understand informational texts.

READ Read aloud pp. 24–35 of *What Do You Do With a Tail Like This?* Have children read the question on p. 33 with you. Many children can read the beginnings of the answers with you, using the illustrations to help identify the animal. As you read, use the appropriate reading routine from pp. TR8–TR19. Have children focus on what they learn about how animals use their eyes.

TURN AND TALK After reading, have children turn to a partner and discuss this question using examples from the text: What did you learn about animals' eyes? Use the **Think-Pair-Share Routine** on pp. TR2–TR3 and make sure children are using best practices for speaking and listening as outlined in the routine. (Children should share examples such as: An eagle spots tiny animals from high in the air, p. 34; a chameleon looks two ways at once, p. 34; a horned lizard squirts blood out of its eyes, p. 35.)

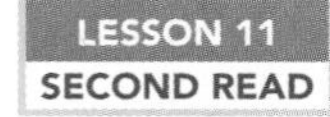

Close Read

CITE TEXT EVIDENCE Engage the class in a discussion about what you just read. Remind them to ask questions to clear up any confusion. Tell children to focus on the details about the animals. Use these questions to guide the discussion, and ask children to support their answers with evidence.

- How does an eagle use its eyes? (to spot tiny animals) Why would an eagle need its eyes to do that? Let's think about what we learn from the picture and the words. An eagle "flies high in the air" so it would have to look a long way to see something on the ground. An eagle would need to have great eyesight to do that. **DOK L2**
- How are the chameleon's eyes and the four-eyed fish's eyes alike? (Both animals can use their eyes to look more than one direction at the same time.) **DOK L3**
- Look at the chameleon and the horned lizard. How are they alike? (They are both small lizards. They have tails. They have some spikes on their bodies.) Point to their similarities in the illustrations. How does each lizard use its eyes? (Chameleons can look two ways at the same time. Horned lizards can shoot blood from their eyes.) **DOK L2**
- How can you describe a bush baby? Point to the details in the illustration as you tell about it. (Possible response: It has big eyes, claws, and a long tail. It can climb trees.) **DOK L2**

BY-THE-WAY WORDS During close reading, define the following words for children involving known concepts that can be stumbling blocks to comprehending the text.

chameleon, p. 34: Explain that a chameleon is a lizard that can change the color of its skin to look like the colors that are around it.

bush baby, p. 35: Tell children that a bush baby lives in Africa and is related to the lemur and the monkey. Explorers thought that its cries sounded like a lost child. That is how the bush baby got its name.

Scaffolded Instruction

ENGLISH LANGUAGE LEARNERS

IDIOM Explain that the phrase *at once* means "at the same time." Tell children that both the chameleon and the four-eyed fish are able to see things happening in different directions at the same time. Humans mostly see only in one direction at a time.

STRATEGIC SUPPORT

KEY DETAILS If children have difficulty understanding how one of the animals uses its eyes, reread the information about that animal. Ask questions, such as: Why would an eagle need to see food from the air? What would you think if you saw blood coming from an animal's eyes?

OBJECTIVES

Determine the meaning of and use academic and domain-specific words in a text.

RI.1.4, L.1.6

Ask and answer questions about key details in an informational text.

RI.1.1

BENCHMARK VOCABULARY

- spot, p. 34
- squirt, p. 35

BENCHMARK VOCABULARY

- Have children find and read sentences from the text with the words *spot* and *squirt*.

  Use the **Benchmark Vocabulary Routine for Informational Text** on pp. TR24–TR27 to teach the meanings of the words.

- Use the information on pp. 152–155 of this Teacher's Guide to discuss other words connected to each of the Benchmark Vocabulary words.

PRACTICE Have children use p. 69 in the *Reader's and Writer's Journal* to show contextual understanding of the Benchmark Vocabulary. Monitor children's vocabulary development.

Reading Analysis

TEXT TALK

ASK AND ANSWER QUESTIONS Explain to children that readers ask questions about a text as they read. Then they find the answers directly in the text or they think about the details to figure out the answers. Provide the T-chart graphic organizer on p. TR39.

Ask and Answer Questions

Questions	Answers
How are a cricket's ears different from other animals' ears?	its ears are on its knees
When does a hippopotamus close its ears?	when it's under water

MODEL Let's ask and answer questions about how animals use their ears. On page 27, I read about a cricket's ears. How are a cricket's ears different from other animals' ears? Let me write that question on my chart. When I read about other animals' ears, I learn that crickets' ears are different because they are on their knees, not their heads. I'll write that in the Answers column.

PRACTICE/APPLY Have children work independently to ask and answer questions and record them in the chart. Ask volunteers to share their questions and answers with the class. Then have children complete p. 70 of their *Reader's* and *Writer's Journal*.

Generative Vocabulary Games

Reader's and Writer's Journal

Leveled Text Library

Independent Reading Activities

Independent Reading How-To Video

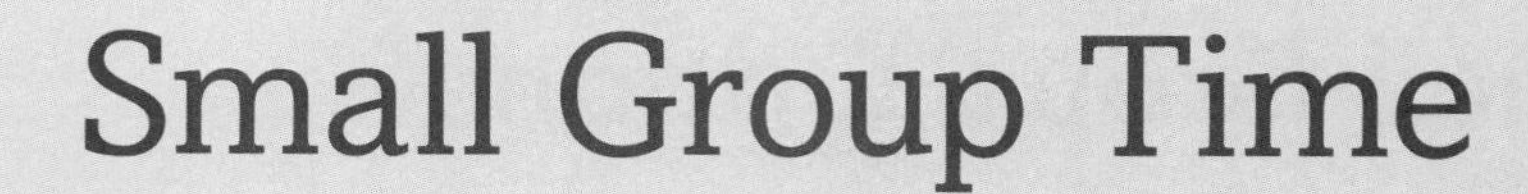

Small Group Time

STEP 1 Focused Independent Reading

BUILD ACCOUNTABILITY Prepare children to read their **self-selected texts.** Announce the two focus points to the class, and help children make a plan for their reading. Children will apply both focus points to their self-selected texts.

TODAY'S PROCESS FOCUS	
☑ Engagement and Identity	☐ Independence
☐ Stamina	

Display a variety of informational texts about animals. Ask children to page through several of the books and choose one that appeals to them. It may be a familiar book or a new book.

TODAY'S STRATEGY FOCUS	
☐ Vocabulary Knowledge	☐ Critical Thinking
☐ Fluency	☑ Comprehension

Guide children in applying the content of today's Reading Analysis lesson to their self-selected texts. We learned that readers can ask and answer questions to help them better understand what they read. Today as you are reading, think of some questions you have about the book. Write each question on a self-stick note and place it on the page that helps you answer your question. Alternatively, have children log into Pearson Realize to find an Independent Reading Activity that is appropriate for the text they are reading.

MONITOR PROGRESS

- **Process Focus:** Have children record their reading in a daily reading log. They should draw a picture of the most interesting information they read about.
- **Strategy Focus:** Have children share a question they had while reading and how they found the answer. Have them explain how their self-stick note helped them recall the place in the book that helped them answer the question. Alternatively, have children log into Pearson Realize and review with you the Independent Reading Activity they completed for their book.

For further guidance, see the **Independent Reading Routine** on pp. TR12–TR19.

While children are reading independently, use the Small Group Options on pp. 266–267.

INDEPENDENT LITERACY WORK

Text Club (pp. TR20–TR23)

Leveled Text Library

Center Options (pp. 160–161)

Use **Write in Response to Reading** on p. 69 of the *Reader's and Writer's Journal* to check children's understanding of key ideas in the text.

Phonics: Decodable Practice Readers

GUIDED READING OPTIONS

Use the **Leveled Text Library** to choose appropriate texts based on children's needs.

Use ***ReadyUp! Intervention*** for children who require additional instruction with this lesson's reading and foundational standards or with prerequisite standards.

STEP 2 Small Group Options

Based on formative assessments of children's progress, use the following options to provide additional instruction, practice, or extension as needed.

PHONICS

For children who need support with this week's Phonics skill, use pp. FS22–FS25 in this Teacher's Guide.

UNLOCK THE TEXT

For children who need support in accessing key ideas, key language, and key structures in ***What Do You Do With a Tail Like This?,*** use **Unlock the Text** in the *Scaffolded Strategies Handbook,* pp. 28–33.

CONFERENCE

For independent reading accountability, **conference** each day with two or three children to discuss **self-selected texts** and support their reading.

READING ANALYSIS SUPPORT

For children who struggle with asking and answering questions about ***What Do You Do With a Tail Like This?,*** use this **Support Language Reading Analysis Mini-Lesson.**

ASK AND ANSWER QUESTIONS Help children practice answering questions using details in *What Do You Do With a Tail Like This?* by asking questions, such as: Which animals have tails? What are some different ways that animals use their ears? As children answer your questions, encourage them to elaborate by asking follow-up questions, such as: Which animals live on land? Which could use their tails to brush away flies? Why would an animal use its ears to see?

Have children work with a partner to complete p. 70 of their *Reader's and Writer's Journal.* Then ask volunteers to share their answers and discuss where they found them. Use the **Think-Pair-Share Routine** on pp. TR2–TR3.

Ask and answer questions about key details in a text. RI.1.1

Scaffolded Strategies Handbook

Leveled Text Library

Games

Independent Reading Activities

Reader's and Writer's Journal

READING ANALYSIS EXTENSION

For children who can easily ask and answer questions about ***What Do You Do With a Tail Like This?,*** use this **Extend Reading Analysis Mini-Lesson.**

ASK AND ANSWER QUESTIONS Have children write at least two additional questions about *What Do You Do With a Tail Like This?* Encourage children to write one question that takes more thought than just looking up the answer in the text. Have children trade questions with a partner and then answer their partner's questions. Tell them to look back at the text to make sure the answers are correct. Then discuss the following questions:

- What kind of question is easier to answer: a question with an answer in the book or a question that needs to be thought about? Why? (A question with an answer in the book is easier to answer because you can look up the answer.)
- Look at the thinking question you wrote. Which part of the text helped you answer that question? (Responses will vary.)
- When can readers ask questions? (Possible responses: They can ask questions before, during, or after reading. They can ask questions when they don't understand something.)

Ask and answer questions about key details in a text. RI.1.1

FLUENCY

For fluent reading accountability, use the **Oral Reading Fluency Quick Check.** ☑ **Today assess 2–3 children.**

MODEL APPROPRIATE PHRASING Explain to children that when we read, we should pay attention to the punctuation marks, such as commas. When we see a comma, we should pause before continuing. Have children follow along as you model reading aloud p. 34 from *What Do You Do With a Tail Like This?,* first without pausing at the commas and then pausing appropriately. Review why a reader would want to be sure to pause for punctuation. Then choral read with children a portion of a leveled text with appropriate phrasing.

Read grade-level text with appropriate phrasing. RF.1.4.b

QUICK CHECK

MONITOR PROGRESS

If . . . children are not pausing at commas,

then . . . have them practice reading aloud with a partner who can provide cues for the reader to pause.

If . . . children are not phrasing chunks of text correctly,

then . . . remind them to pause when they come to the end of a chunk of text before going on.

OBJECTIVE

Write an informative piece of writing.

W.1.2

Informative/Explanatory Writing

Writing Process: Draft

SET THE PURPOSE Review the writing process with children: plan, write, revise, edit, and publish. Remind them that in the previous lesson they completed the first step of writing: planning. Have volunteers share their thoughts about how they feel planning will help them write today. Today you will be using the plans you made to write an informative piece of text. It will be in a question-and-answer format.

Informative texts use facts to tell about a topic. The facts in an informative text often give key details to readers about the main topic. Writers use text and pictures to explain facts about topics.

TEACH AND MODEL Review p. 34 in *What Do You Do With a Tail Like This?* Prompt discussion about facts with these questions:

- What fact do we learn about eagles? (Eagles use their eyes to spot tiny animals from high in the air.)
- What fact do we learn about chameleons? (Chameleons use their eyes to look two ways at once.)
- What fact do we learn about four-eyed fish? (Four-eyed fish use their eyes to look above and below the water at the same time.)

Use pp. 33 and 35 of *What Do You Do With a Tail Like This?* to help children understand that the writers use a question-and-answer format to share facts about animals. Point to the illustration of the horned lizard on p. 35.

What do you do with eyes like these?	The writer uses a question to let readers know what they will learn about as they keep reading. This helps readers know what to look for as they read: an answer to the question.
If you're a horned lizard, you squirt blood out of your eyes.	The writer answers the question from page 33. This is what the horned lizard does with its eyes.

Write a Question and an Answer

PREPARE TO WRITE Tell children that you will use the plans and research from Lesson 10 to write an informative piece of writing in a question-and-answer format. You will review the information to write the question and its answer. Remind children that the question will be answered using facts, not opinions.

REVIEW THE QUESTION Write the question from Lesson 10: *What do chameleons eat?* Review the features of the question and how you looked for the answer. Remind children that when you research information to answer your questions, you look in books or on the Internet for facts. Display the book you used to find the answer.

The question I wrote is *What do chameleons eat?* I went to the library and found an informational book about chameleons. I read so many interesting things about them. When I was reading, I found information about what they eat. I know that they eat insects. I found the answer to my question.

WRITE AN ANSWER Model how to write the answer to your question. Remind children that this is the time to use the facts from your research to answer the question.

I will write my answer under the question. Write *They eat insects* under *What do chameleons eat?* I will be able to add details later if necessary.

Review the steps for writing from Lesson 10 and add the step you completed today.

Plan: Choose an animal to ask a question about.

Question: What do chameleons eat?

Research: Go to the library to find a book about chameleons.

Answer: They eat insects.

Scaffolded Instruction

STRATEGIC SUPPORT

QUESTIONS AND ANSWERS Children may have difficulty finding answers to their questions. Help them use the index of a children's informational book to find the right pages to use. Read aloud the appropriate information and discuss what children learn about their animal. Then ask children to decide if they can use the information to answer their question.

OBJECTIVES

Write an informative piece of writing. 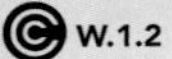 W.1.2

With guidance, use technology to produce and publish writing and to collaborate with others. W.1.6

Match singular nouns and verbs by adding *-s* or *-es* to the verbs. L.1.1.c

Independent Writing Practice

WRITE Have children review their question from Lesson 10 as well as their research. Then have them turn to p. 71 of their *Reader's and Writer's Journal* and write their question and answer. On a separate sheet of paper, ask them to draw a picture or create another kind of visual to help clarify their idea.

CONVENTIONS If you wish to teach children about adding *-s* or *-es* to action verbs to match nouns, use the Conventions Mini-Lesson on p. 271. Encourage children to match nouns and verbs in their writing.

DIGITAL OPTIONS If available, have children use computers or tablets to type their question and answer. Then print out their writing for children to illustrate.

Share Writing

Have volunteers share their question and answer with the group. Remind them to speak loudly and clearly. Tell the class to listen attentively.

Writing Keystone Checklist

Writing a Question and an Answer

Use this checklist to assess children's informative/explanatory writing. If children need additional support writing a question and answer, use the Unlock Informative/Explanatory Writing beginning on p. 266 of the *Scaffolded Strategies Handbook.*

	Achieved	Notes
Plan a question to write.		
Research the answer to the question.		
Use the research to write an answer to the question.		

Conventions Mini-Lesson

Match Nouns and Verbs

TEACH AND MODEL Remind children that nouns and verbs should match in sentences. This means that nouns that name one should have a singular verb and nouns that name more than one should have a plural verb.

If a noun names one person, animal, place, or thing, the verb usually ends in *-s* or *-es*. We add *-s* to the ends of most action verbs to make them singular. For example, *The eagle looks for tiny animals. The eagle spots animals from up high*. We add *-es* to the ends of action verbs that end in *ch*, *sh*, *s*, *ss*, or *x*. For example, *The eagle watches for fish.*

The chameleon looks two ways at once.

The noun, *chameleon*, is singular. The verb, *look*, does not end in *ch, sh, s, ss,* or *x*. That means we add *-s* to make it match the singular noun.

The giraffe brushes flies off with its tail.

The noun, *giraffe*, is singular. The verb, *brush*, ends in *sh*. That means we add *-es* to make it match the singular noun.

PRACTICE Provide children with additional examples of sentences with singular nouns. Have them identify the noun and the verb. Then ask them to tell you whether an *-s* or *-es* is needed at the end of the verb. For example: *A mole find(s) a home. An elephant splash(es) in the water*. Then provide this list of nouns and verbs: *dog, lizard, snake; watch, need, pass*. Ask children to use a noun and a matching verb in a complete sentence. For more practice with adding *-s* or *-es* to action verbs, have children complete the activity on p. 71 of their *Reader's and Writer's Journal*.

Scaffolded Instruction

ENGLISH LANGUAGE LEARNERS

MATCHING NOUNS AND VERBS If children have difficulty understanding when to add *-s* or *-es* to an action verb, have them first identify the noun. Ask: How many are there? If the noun names one person, animal, place, or thing, the verb needs an *-s* or *-es*. Review the rules for adding *-es*.

OBJECTIVES

Focus Use the illustrations and text to understand key ideas. RI.1.7

Ask and answer questions about key details in a text. RI.1.1

Identify and use words in a text. RI.1.4

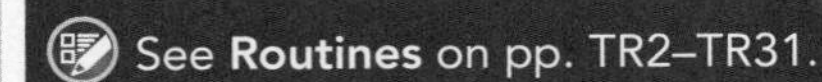
See **Routines** on pp. TR2–TR31.

FOUNDATIONAL SKILLS MINI-LESSON

High-Frequency Words; Consonants *v/v/; y/y/; z, zz/z/; qu/kw/*

- Display the High-Frequency Word Card for *the*. Have children read the word. The word *the* has three letters: *t, h, e*. Have children write the word and use it in a sentence. Repeat with the words *for, a,* and *do*.
- Have children turn to *Decodable Practice Reader R6A* on p. 81. Tell them to read the title and the lists of words. In this story, you will read words with *v, y, z,* and *qu*. Let's make the sounds for those letters: /v/, /y/, /z/, /kw/.
- Have children read the story with a partner, switching readers after each page.

For more explicit instruction, see p. FS23 in this Teacher's Guide.

Use Illustrations to Understand Details

LESSON 12 FIRST READ

Build Understanding

SET THE PURPOSE Focus the instruction by sharing the following Enduring Understanding: *Learners understand that living things have certain behaviors that shape them and allow them to survive.* The details in the illustrations can help readers better understand what they are reading. We can look at the illustrations in *What Do You Do With a Tail Like This?* to help us understand some special things that animals do to survive.

ENGAGE CHILDREN Have children describe how the author organizes the information in *What Do You Do With a Tail Like This?* What do you notice about how the author tells the reader information? Point out that the author identifies the topic of each section in a question. The key details about that topic are found in the answers to the question. By using this question-and-answer structure, the author has a conversation with the reader, rather than just telling facts about the animals. Display pp. 36–39 of *What Do You Do With a Tail Like This?* in the *Text Collection.* Ask children to identify the animals they see. Remind children to think about the Essential Questions: *How do features in informational texts help readers understand the main topic? How does the organizational structure of a text help writers explain information?* Tell children: In this lesson we are going to focus on the details in the illustrations.

READ As you reread pp. 36–43 of *What Do You Do With a Tail Like This?*, use the appropriate reading routine from pp. TR8–TR19. Have children follow along as you read. Tell them to read the question on pp. 36–37 with you and then on their own. Children should focus on what the animals do with their feet and mouths.

TURN AND TALK After reading, have children turn to a partner and discuss this question using examples from the text: What did you learn about animal feet? Use the **Think-Pair-Share Routine** on pp. TR2–TR3. (Children should share examples such as: Chimpanzees feed themselves with their feet, p. 38; water striders walk on water with their feet, p. 38; mountain goats leap from ledge to ledge, p. 39.)

LESSON 12 FIRST READ

Close Read

CITE TEXT EVIDENCE Engage the class in a discussion about what you just read. Focus on key details about the animals on pp. 36–43. Remind children that readers look for details in the words and illustrations. Use these questions to guide the discussion, and ask children to support their answers with evidence.

- Look at the pictures of feet on pages 36–37. Describe some of the differences you see. (One foot is hoofed; one is webbed. One foot is very long and slender, others are fatter. One foot looks like a hand.) Point to each foot as you describe it. **DOK L2**
- One foot looks like a hand. Whose foot is that? (The chimpanzee's foot looks like a hand.) What can the chimpanzee do with its feet? (It can feed itself.) Why do you think it is easy for a chimpanzee to eat with its feet? (because it can use its feet like hands to hold things) Explain that a chimpanzee, like humans, has an "opposable thumb." **DOK L3**
- Look at the text about the egg-eating snake on page 42. What is unique about the eggs it likes to eat? (The eggs are bigger than its head.) Let's read that part together. Now look at the illustration. How is the snake able to eat the egg? (It can open its mouth very big.) **DOK L2**
- Look at the illustration of the archerfish on page 43. What does the archerfish do to catch an insect? (It shoots water at the insect.) Let's read again to find out how the archerfish catches insects. **DOK L2**

BY-THE-WAY WORDS During close reading, define the following words for children involving known concepts that can be stumbling blocks to comprehending the text.

gecko, p. 39: Explain to children that a gecko is a small lizard. Geckos have sticky pads on their feet that help them walk on almost any surface.

anteater, p. 43: Tell children that an anteater is an animal with a long narrow snout and a long tongue. It eats ants and termites.

Scaffolded Instruction

ENGLISH LANGUAGE LEARNERS

VOCABULARY Encourage children to use the illustrations to help determine the meanings of unfamiliar words. For example, children could learn the meaning of *scoop* from the illustration of a pelican, which shows its mouth picking up a fish.

STRATEGIC SUPPORT

KEY DETAILS If children have difficulty understanding how an animal uses its feet or mouth, ask clarifying questions, such as: *What do you notice about the animal's feet? How is that animal's mouth different from your mouth?*

OBJECTIVES

Identify and use words in texts.
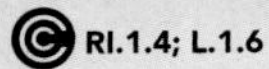
RI.1.4; L.1.6

Use the illustrations and text to understand key ideas. RI.1.7

BENCHMARK VOCABULARY

- sticky, p. 39
- scoop, p. 42
- swallow, p. 42

BENCHMARK VOCABULARY

- Have children find and read sentences from the text with the words *sticky*, *scoop*, and *swallow*.
  Use the **Benchmark Vocabulary Routine for Informational Text** on pp. TR24–TR27 to teach the meanings of the words.
- Use the information on pp. 152–155 of this Teacher's Guide to discuss other words connected to each of the Benchmark Vocabulary words.

PRACTICE Have children use p. 72 in their *Reader's and Writer's Journal* to show contextual understanding of the Benchmark Vocabulary. Monitor children's vocabulary development.

Reading Analysis

TEXT TALK

ILLUSTRATIONS AND TEXT Discuss how the text and illustrations in *What Do You Do With a Tail Like This?* work together to develop the key ideas in the text. Focus on pages 40–43. Provide the Web A graphic organizer on p. TR44. Write *egg-eating snake* in the center circle.

Illustrations and Text Web

Egg-eating snake

eats a very large egg bigger than its head

mouth is open wide, so its jaws must be big

mouth is smaller than the pelican's mouth but bigger than the mosquito's mouth

MODEL Let's take a look at an illustration on page 42 to help us understand the text. I see a snake eating an egg that looks bigger than the snake's head! I'll write that detail on one line of the web. The snake's mouth is open wide, so its jaws must be big. I'll write that on a line too. Now I can see how the snake's mouth is bigger than the mosquito's but smaller than the pelican's. But the snake's mouth looks like it can fit as much as the pelican's!

PRACTICE/APPLY Have children work in small groups to complete a web for another animal. Use the **Small Group Discussion Routine** on pp. TR6–TR7 to have children discuss their webs. Check understanding by asking children to share or by circulating among children or groups. Then have children complete the activity on p. 73 of their *Reader's and Writer's Journal*.

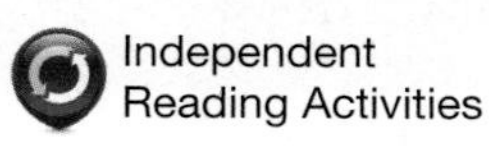

PEARSON realize™

Small Group Time

STEP 1 Focused Independent Reading

BUILD ACCOUNTABILITY Prepare children to read their **self-selected texts.** Announce the two focus points to the class, and help children make a plan for their reading. Children will apply both focus points to their self-selected texts.

TODAY'S PROCESS FOCUS	
☐ Engagement and Identity ☑ Stamina	☐ Independence

Explain to children that they are going to see how many words they can read in one minute. Have children choose a book with illustrations that they have read before. Tell them to place a self-stick note on the first word they will read. Then tell them to begin reading. When time is up, have children place a self-stick note on the word where they stopped.

TODAY'S STRATEGY FOCUS	
☐ Vocabulary Knowledge ☐ Fluency	☑ Critical Thinking ☐ Comprehension

Guide children in using the content of today's Reading Analysis lesson to analyze their self-selected texts. We learned that illustrations help us understand a text. How do the illustrations help you understand your book? Be prepared to answer this question with examples. Alternatively, have children log into Pearson Realize to find an Independent Reading Activity that is appropriate for the text they are reading.

MONITOR PROGRESS

- **Process Focus:** Have children record their reading in a daily reading log by writing how many words they read during the time frame. Children can also dictate or write if they thought it was easy or hard to read during a time limit.
- **Strategy Focus:** Have children answer the question, pointing out pictures and explaining how they helped them understand the text. Alternatively, have children log into Pearson Realize and review with you the Independent Reading Activity they completed for their book.

For further guidance, see the **Independent Reading Routine** on pp. TR12–TR19.

While children are reading independently, use the Small Group Options on pp. 276–277.

INDEPENDENT LITERACY WORK

Text Club (pp. TR20–TR23)

Leveled Text Library

Center Options (pp. 160–161)

Use **Write in Response to Reading** on p. 72 of the *Reader's and Writer's Journal* to check children's understanding of the text.

Phonics: Decodable Practice Readers

GUIDED READING OPTIONS

Use the **Leveled Text Library** to choose appropriate texts based on children's needs.

Use ***ReadyUp! Intervention*** for children who require additional instruction with this lesson's reading and foundational standards or with prerequisite standards.

STEP 2 Small Group Options

Based on formative assessments of children's progress, use the following options to provide additional instruction, practice, or extension as needed.

PHONICS

For children who need support with this week's Phonics skill, use pp. FS22–FS25 in this Teacher's Guide.

UNLOCK THE TEXT

For children who need support in accessing key ideas, key language, and key structures in ***What Do You Do With a Tail Like This?***, use **Unlock the Text** in the *Scaffolded Strategies Handbook*, pp. 28–33.

CONFERENCE

For independent reading accountability, conference each day with two or three children to discuss **self-selected texts** and support their reading.

READING ANALYSIS SUPPORT

For children who struggle using illustrations and text to understand key ideas in ***What Do You Do With a Tail Like This?,*** use this **Support Reading Analysis Mini-Lesson.**

USE ILLUSTRATIONS AND TEXT Help children complete their *Reader's and Writer's Journal* activity on p. 73 about pelicans using details from *What Do You Do With a Tail Like This?* Ask them guiding questions, such as: What do pelicans eat? Why is it useful to have a big mouth to catch fish? As children answer, encourage them to elaborate by asking follow-up questions, such as: How else can you describe the pelican's mouth? Create a list of children's ideas for them to refer to as they work on the page.

Invite children to work with a partner to draw pictures of the pelican and write words and labels to explain their drawings. Use the **Think-Pair-Share Routine** on pp. TR2–TR3.

Use illustrations and text to understand key ideas. RI.1.7

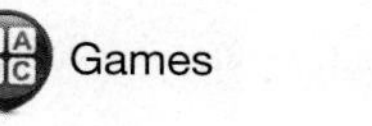

READING ANALYSIS EXTENSION

For children who can easily use illustrations and text to understand key ideas in ***What Do You Do With a Tail Like This?,*** use this **Extend Reading Analysis Mini-Lesson.**

ILLUSTRATIONS AND TEXT Have children explain their drawings of a pelican's mouth to a partner. Then have children choose another animal from pp. 36–43. Children should use a web to organize details about the animal they choose. They will draw a picture to demonstrate to the reader how the animal's body part works. Then have them write words or sentences to tell about their picture. Discuss the following questions:

- How does the drawing help a reader understand details? (Readers can understand a drawing, even if they don't know how to read the words.)
- Why is text important, even when there is a picture? (The picture might be confusing to the reader, so the text can clear up confusion.)
- What type of text needs pictures? (Responses will vary.)
- What other information would you like to know about the animal you chose? (Responses should vary.)

Use illustrations to answer questions about a text. RI.1.7

FLUENCY

For fluent reading accountability, use the **Oral Reading Fluency Quick Check.** ☑ **Today assess 2–3 children.**

MODEL APPROPRIATE RATE Explain that reading at an appropriate rate means reading words at a speed that is not too slow and not too fast. Have children follow along as you read aloud p. 38 of *What Do You Do With a Tail Like This?*, reading at a rate that is either too fast or too slow. Read the same section again, this time at an appropriate rate. Have children compare the readings, focusing on the rate that was easier for them to follow along and understand. Then provide each child with a leveled text at his or her reading level to read at an appropriate rate.

Read grade-level text with appropriate rate. RF.1.4.b

QUICK CHECK

MONITOR PROGRESS

If . . . children are reading too slowly,

then . . . have them identify and review the words that cause them to stumble. Then read the text again.

If . . . children are reading too quickly,

then . . . have them listen to you read the text quickly and discuss why that is not easy to understand.

OBJECTIVE
Revise, edit, and publish an informative piece of writing. W.1.2

Informative/Explanatory Writing

Writing Process: Revise, Edit, Publish

SET THE PURPOSE Review the writing process with children: plan, write, revise, edit, and publish. Remind them that in the previous lesson they completed the second step of the writing process by writing their first draft. Today they will revise, edit, and publish.

TEACH AND MODEL Explain to children the final steps of the writing process. Tell them the purpose of revising, editing, and publishing.

- When you revise, you reread your writing to look for places where you forgot to add a detail. You can also change a detail in order to make your writing better. Sometimes you may need to delete a detail completely because it just doesn't make sense.
- When you edit, you reread your writing again. This time you look for mistakes with capital letters, punctuation marks, and spelling.
- When you publish, you rewrite your writing neatly with no errors. You must use your best handwriting. Other times you can use a computer, tablet, or other digital tool to type your final copy.

Through discussion, help children see how the authors of *What Do You Do With a Tail Like This?* might revise the text. Read the original sentences and then discuss the possible revised sentences.

If you're a lizard, you break off your tail to get away.

The writer can add more details about the lizard. These extra details can help readers better understand the text.

Revised: If you're a lizard, you break off your long tail to escape from enemies.

If you're a water strider, you walk on water.

The writer can add more details about the water strider. These extra details can help readers better understand the text.

Revised: If you're a brown water strider, you walk softly on water.

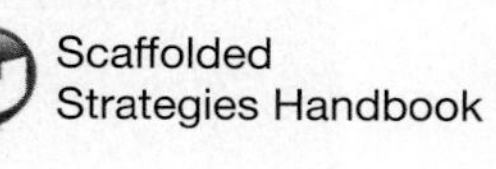

Revise, Edit, and Publish a Question and an Answer

PREPARE TO REVISE, EDIT, AND PUBLISH Review the steps and purpose of revising, editing, and publishing. Tell children that their published pieces will be put together into a class question-and-answer book for all to read.

MODEL REVISING Remind children about the question and answer you modeled in Lesson 11:

Question: What do chameleons eat?

Answer: They eat insects.

When I read the question, I think about ways I could revise it to make it more interesting. For example, I think I will change it to: *What kinds of things do chameleons eat?* I can look back at my research to see if I noted what kinds of things chameleons eat. If not, I can do additional research to find out. I think this added information will be helpful to readers.

Revised Question: What *kinds of things* do chameleons eat?

Revised Answer: They eat insects *such as grasshoppers and crickets.*

MODEL EDITING Now that we have revised our first draft, we can edit our writing. Make sure to check for punctuation, grammar, and spelling errors. Because we are writing a question and an answer, I know that I need to make sure that the question begins with a capital letter and ends with a question mark. The answer should begin with a capital letter and end with a period.

MODEL PUBLISHING After we make sure our work has no errors, we can publish it. We can put all of our writing together to make a class book.

Scaffolded Instruction

STRATEGIC SUPPORT

REVISING Some children will struggle with revising their original writing, feeling that they have completed the assignment and do not need to do anything else to their writing. In this case, have children read their writing to you. Spend a few moments prompting them, and then point out how their answers to your prompts can provide readers with additional details.

OBJECTIVES

Revise, edit, and publish an informative piece of writing. W.1.2

With guidance, use technology to produce and publish writing and to collaborate with others. W.1.6

Use the verbs *is* and *are* in complete sentences. L.1.1

Independent Writing Practice

REVISE, EDIT, PUBLISH Remind children of the steps needed for revising, editing, and publishing their piece of informative writing. Have them follow the steps in order:

- Reread your writing. Add, change, or delete details to make your writing better.
- Reread your writing again. Look for errors in capitalization, punctuation, and spelling.
- Create a final copy using your best handwriting. Remind children to use letter formation, lines, and spaces to create a readable document.

Have children review the questions and answers they wrote with a partner. Invite partners to ask questions that might lead children to realize they need to add details to their answers. Tell children to revise and edit their writing and then create a final copy of their question and answer on p. 74 of their *Reader's and Writer's Journal*.

CONVENTIONS If you wish to teach children about using the verbs *is* and *are*, use the Conventions Mini-Lesson on p. 281. Encourage children to check for the correct use of *is* and *are* in their informative/explanatory writing.

DIGITAL OPTIONS If available, have children use computers or tablets to type and print their writing. Encourage children to create drawings or other visuals to clarify their ideas and thoughts.

Share Writing

Have children celebrate their published pieces by having them read aloud their questions and answers from the "author's chair." Then gather children's writing and make a question-and-answer book for the class.

Conventions Mini-Lesson

Verbs *is* and *are*

TEACH AND MODEL Explain that *is* and *are* are forms of the verb *to be*, and that *be* follows its own rules. We use the verb *is* after a singular noun, and we use the verb *are* after a plural noun. Remember that singular nouns tell about one person, animal, place, or thing. Plural nouns tell about more than one person, animal, place, or thing. Provide the following examples:

A gecko is a small lizard.

The word *gecko* is a singular noun, so the verb *is* is used.

Geckos are small lizards.

The word *geckos* is a plural noun, so the verb *are* is used.

PRACTICE Write several simple sentences, leaving a blank where *is* and *are* need to be inserted. Read aloud the sentences. Ask children to identify the noun and if it is singular or plural. Then have volunteers write in the correct verb. For example: *My parents (are) painting the house. Her sister (is) cooking. The baby (is) crying. The dogs (are) barking.* Then tell children to complete the activity on p. 74 of their *Reader's and Writer's Journal*.

Scaffolded Instruction

ENGLISH LANGUAGE LEARNERS

VERBS *IS* AND *ARE* In some languages, including Chinese, Hmong, and Haitian Creole, the verb *to be* can be left out of a sentence. If children say, "The pelican bird" instead of "The pelican is a bird," provide extra practice with the verbs *is* and *are*.

OBJECTIVE
Write an informative piece of writing in a question-and-answer format. W.1.2

Performance-Based Assessment

INFORMATIVE/EXPLANATORY TASK

WRITE QUESTIONS AND ANSWERS

Children will use facts from *Time to Sleep* and *What Do You Do With a Tail Like This?* to write questions and answers about animals. **DOK L2**

Children will

- write two questions of their own about one or two animals they read about.
- find the answers to their questions in the books and write them.
- use correct end punctuation.

See p. 286 for reproducible page for distribution.

TEACHER NOTE You may wish to administer this assessment over multiple lessons.

Use the *Scaffolded Strategies Handbook* to provide additional support for diverse learners in your class. The Performance-Based Assessment lesson in the handbook provides guidance with unlocking the task, breaking down the writing process, and examining conventions and craft.

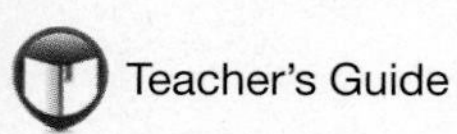

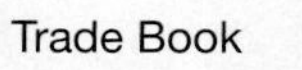

Prepare

REVIEW Discuss the Essential Questions: *How do features in informational texts help readers understand the main topic? How does the organizational structure of a text help writers explain information?* Then introduce the Performance-Based Assessment to children.

REVISIT THE TEXTS Remind children that *Time to Sleep* and *What Do You Do With a Tail Like This?* include facts about animals. Display pp. 20–23 of *What Do You Do With a Tail Like This?* to show a model of a question and answer in an informational text.

> What do you do with a nose like this?
>
> If you're an alligator, you breathe through your nose while hiding in the water.
>
> —*What Do You Do With a Tail Like This?* pp. 20–23

Display p. 2 of *Time to Sleep* to show a different question and answer about animals.

> Do you sleep on one leg?
> No, but some animals do.
> Do you sleep in a tree?
> No, but some animals do.
> — *Time to Sleep,* p. 2

Explain that children will use facts they learned in *Time to Sleep* and *What Do You Do With a Tail Like This?* to write their questions and answers.

Create

MATERIALS

- Paper
- Pencils
- Texts: *Time to Sleep* and *What Do You Do With a Tail Like This?*

WRITE

Guide children to understand that in addition to using the Module B selections, they may refer to the writing they did during the module. These writing activity products can serve as resources for children's question-and-answer writing.

Then have children work independently to write their questions and answers for the task. Circulate to assist them if necessary.

DIGITAL OPTION If desired, you may incorporate technology into the Performance-Based Assessment. Children may type their questions and answers on a computer or tablet or dictate them to you to type.

BEST PRACTICES

- Encourage children to ask questions before they begin writing.
- Tell children to refer to *Time to Sleep* and *What Do You Do With a Tail Like This?* for spelling, vocabulary, and writing conventions for questions and statements.

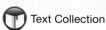

Scaffolded Support

In order for all students to access the Performance-Based Assessment, additional supports can be provided as necessary.

CHECKLIST Provide a checklist or a graphic, such as the one on p. 198 of the *Scaffolded Strategies Handbook,* that details expectations for this project. It will clarify for children what is being assessed.

GRAPHIC ORGANIZER Show children how to use a T-chart graphic organizer to list their questions and answers as they plan their writing. Tell them to label the left column *Questions* and the right column *Answers*. Explain how their questions and answers should line up.

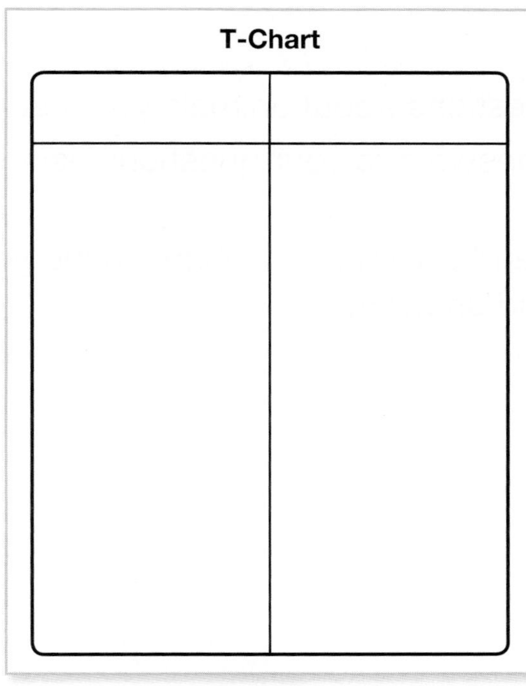

p. TR39

WRITING TASKS Have conferences with children to review their ideas before they begin to write. Show them how to use the animal facts they have written previously as resources, and discuss how this material can be incorporated into their question-and-answer writing.

EDITING TASKS Post examples of questions and answers with correct ending punctuation marks. Highlight or underline the ending punctuation.

Performance-Based Assessment
Grade 1 • Unit 1 • Module B

INFORMATIVE/EXPLANATORY TASK

WRITE QUESTIONS AND ANSWERS

Use facts from *Time to Sleep* and *What Do You Do With a Tail Like This?* to write two questions and answers about animals.

Remember to

- write two questions about animals you read about.
- find factual answers to your questions using the books.
- use correct end punctuation when writing your questions and answers.

Informative/Explanatory Writing Rubric

Score	Focus	Organization	Development	Language and Vocabulary	Conventions
4	Questions and answers focus on animals from the texts.	Writing contains two examples of a question-and-answer format.	The answers provide clear facts and details that completely answer the questions.	Writing uses complete, clear sentences with descriptive words.	All sentences are correctly punctuated.
3	Questions and answers somewhat focus on animals from the texts.	Writing contains one example of a question-and-answer format.	The answers provide sufficient facts and details to answer the questions.	Writing uses complete sentences.	Most sentences are correctly punctuated.
2	One question and answer does not focus on animals from the texts.	Writing does not consistently follow a question-and-answer format.	The answers only partially answer the questions.	Some sentences are incomplete or unclear.	Sentences are not correctly punctuated.
1	Questions and answers do not focus on animals from the texts.	Writing does not follow a question-and-answer format.	The answers do not provide facts and details to answer the questions.	Writing is unclear or uses sentence fragments.	There is no punctuation.
0	Possible characteristics that would warrant a 0: • No response is given. • Child does not demonstrate command of writing questions and answers. • Response is unintelligible or illegible.				

Present

AUTHOR CELEBRATION Children share their question-and-answer writing with another class.

Give children an opportunity to share what they wrote with an audience that shares their curiosity about animals. Arrange for a final presentation of children's work to a kindergarten or another first-grade class.

- Have children practice their question-and-answer presentations with partners before children present to another class.
- Review the best practices for speaking and listening, such as answering questions that the audience may have about something they do not understand or if they want more information.
- If equipment is available, make a video recording of children reading their writing.
- Have children share their question-and-answer writing with another class. If a video was made of their presentations, you may post that on the class Web site for parents or show it at a parents' night.
- **DIGITAL OPTION** If you chose to incorporate technology into the Performance-Based Assessment, then have children use email or a digital sharing tool to share their questions with other children and discuss the answers.

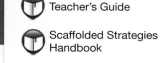

Reflect and Respond

LOOKING AHEAD For children who received a score of 0, 1, or 2 on the rubric, use the following suggestions to support them with specific elements of the Performance-Based Assessment. Graphic organizers and other means of support will help guide children to success as they complete other Performance-Based Assessments throughout the school year.

If . . . children struggle with writing facts about animals,
then . . . review with children what facts are and how to identify them in an informational text.

If . . . children struggle with writing in a question-and-answer format,
then . . . review the conventions of questions and statements to help children master this format.

If . . . children need extra support using informational texts to ask and answer questions,
then . . . model how to read a page from an informational book and use the information to ask and then answer a question.

If . . . children need extra support with writing conventions,
then . . . review the features of questions and statements, focusing on the end punctuation mark for each kind of sentence. Children can also practice writing questions and answers with a partner to help them master these conventions.

FOUNDATIONAL SKILLS

- Phonics and Word Analysis Lessons
- Check Progress Unit Assessments

Contents

LESSONS 1–5

SKILLS
- consonants *m*/m/, *s*/s/, *t*/t/
- short *a*: *a*/a/

OBJECTIVES
- Decode and read words with consonants *m, s,* and *t.*
- Recognize and read high-frequency words.
- Decode and read words with short *a.*

Lesson 1

Phonemic Awareness

Distinguish /m/, /s/, /t/

INTRODUCE Show the Picture Card *moon.* What do you see? (the moon) Say *moon* with me and listen to the sound at the beginning of the word: *m-oon.* Let's say the sound at the beginning of the word: /m/ /m/ /m/. Now let's say the picture name: *moon.* Repeat this procedure for /s/ with the Picture Card *sun* and for /t/ with the Picture Card *ten*.

PRACTICE Listen to the beginning sound in *moon:* /m/. Say the sound with me: /m/. Listen to these words. If you hear /m/ at the beginning of a word, raise your hands. Say these words: *man, cat, mouse, mop, rock.*

Continue the activity for /s/ with these words: *six, seal, wolf, soap, book.* Use the following words for /t/: *taxi, game, tent, table, monkey.*

Phonics

Consonants *m, s, t*

INTRODUCE Display Sound-Spelling Card 15. Point to *m.* The letter *m* stands for the sound /m/, which you hear at the beginning of *mountain.* Have children say /m/ several times as you point to *m.* Continue with Sound-Spelling Card 21 for the letter *s* and the word *submarine* and with Sound-Spelling Card 23 for the letter *t* and the word *tomato.*

PRACTICE Write *mat.* Say this word with me: *mat.* What is the first sound in *mat?* (/m/) What letter stands for the sound /m/? Let's all write the letter *m.* Follow this procedure with *mad* and *map.* Then repeat with the words *sat, sad,* and *Sam* for the letter *s* and the words *tab, tan,* and *tag* for the letter *t.* Have children complete p. 1 in the *Reader's and Writer's Journal.*

APPLY Write and read these words: *tag, mat, tap, sad, sat, man, mad, tan.* Ask children to write *m* if the first sound in the word is /m/, *s* if the first sound is /s/, and *t* if the first sound is /t/. Then have children use the Letter Tiles to make their own words with *m, s,* and *t.*

COMMON CORE STATE STANDARDS

RF.1.2 Demonstrate understanding of spoken words, syllables, and sounds (phonemes).

RF.1.2.c Isolate and pronounce initial, medial vowel, and final sounds (phonemes) in spoken single-syllable words.

RF.1.3 Know and apply grade-level phonics and word analysis skills in decoding words.

Decodable Practice Readers
Letter Tile Drag and Drop
Foundational Skills Games
Sound-Spelling Cards

PEARSON realize

Lesson 2

High-Frequency Words

HIGH-FREQUENCY WORDS

I

SAY AND SPELL Display the High-Frequency Word Card for the word at the right. Some words we learn by remembering the letters. Point to *I*. This word is *I*. The word *I* has just one letter, *I*. Have children say the word, first with you and then without you.

DEMONSTRATE MEANING Have children write *I* and then say sentences using the word.

Decoding

Consonants *m, s, t*

REVIEW Use Sound-Spelling Cards 15, 21, and 23 to review consonants *m, s,* and *t.* To begin, point to *m* on Sound-Spelling Card 15. This is the letter *m.* It stands for the sound /m/. Have children repeat the sound after you. This is a picture of a mountain. What sound do you hear at the beginning of *mountain?* (/m/) Point to the letter *m.* What is this letter? What sound does it stand for? Continue with Sound-Spelling Card 21 (letter *s* and word *submarine*) and Sound-Spelling Card 23 (letter *t* and word *tomato*).

DECODING WORDS Write the words below. Read the word *mat* and have children repeat after you. Ask children to identify the letter *m.* What sound does the letter *m* stand for? (/m/) Ask children to identify the letter *t.* What sound does the letter *t* stand for? (/t/) Continue with the letters *m, s,* and *t* in other words.

mat **sat** **Sam** **Tam**

COMMON CORE STATE STANDARDS

RF.1.2 Demonstrate understanding of spoken words, syllables, and sounds (phonemes).

RF.1.2.c Isolate and pronounce initial, medial vowel, and final sounds (phonemes) in spoken single-syllable words.

RF.1.3 Know and apply grade-level phonics and word analysis skills in decoding words.

RF1.3.g Recognize and read grade-appropriate irregularly spelled words.

Lesson 3

Phonemic Awareness

Short *a*: *a*/a/

INTRODUCE Show the Picture Card *ant.* What do you see in the picture? (an ant) Say *ant* with me and listen to the sound at the beginning of the word: *a-nt.* Let's say the sound at the beginning of the word: /a/ /a/ /a/. Now let's say the picture name: *ant.*

PRACTICE Listen as I say the beginning sound of the word *ant:* /a/. Say the sound with me: /a/ /a/ /a/. I am going to say some words. If you hear the /a/ sound at the beginning of a word, raise your hands. Say these words: *and, insect, apple, alligator, egg, astronaut, umbrella, ox, ax.*

Phonics

Short *a*: *a*/a/

INTRODUCE Display Sound-Spelling Card 1. Point to *a.* The letter *a* stands for the sound /a/, which you hear at the beginning of *astronaut.* Have children say /a/ several times as you point to *a.*

PRACTICE Write *ant.* In this word, the letter *a* stands for the sound /a/. Write the word *mat.* This is the word *mat.* The letter *a* is in the middle of the word. Listen as I say the sounds in the word: /m/ /a/ /t/. Say the sounds with me: /m/ /a/ /t/. Follow this procedure with *sat, tap,* and *map.* Then have children complete p. 6 in the *Reader's and Writer's Journal.*

APPLY Write these words: *tam, Sam, mat, sat.* Ask children to say the sounds in each word and then blend the sounds with you to read the word.

COMMON CORE STATE STANDARDS

RF.1.1 Demonstrate understanding of the organization and basic features of print.

RF.1.2 Demonstrate understanding of spoken words, syllables, and sounds (phonemes).

RF.1.2.b Orally produce single-syllable words by blending sounds (phonemes), including consonant blends.

RF.1.2.c Isolate and pronounce initial, medial vowel, and final sounds (phonemes) in spoken single-syllable words.

RF.1.3 Know and apply grade-level phonics and word analysis skills in decoding words.

RF.1.3.b Decode regularly spelled one-syllable words.

RF1.3.g Recognize and read grade-appropriate irregularly spelled words.

RF1.4 Read with sufficient accuracy and fluency to support comprehension.

Lesson 4

High-Frequency Words

HIGH-FREQUENCY WORDS

I

see

a

SAY AND SPELL Display the High-Frequency Word Cards for the words at the right. Some words we learn by remembering the letters. Have children say and spell each word, first with you and then without you.

IDENTIFY FAMILIAR LETTER-SOUNDS Point to the *s* in *see.* What is this letter and what is its sound? (s/s/)

DEMONSTRATE MEANING Have children write the words and then say sentences using them.

Decoding

Consonants *m, s, t;* Short *a: a/a/*

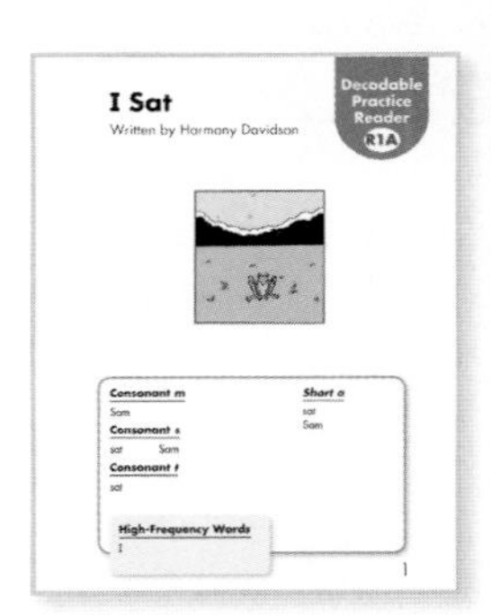
Decodable Practice Reader R1A

PREVIEW Distribute *Decodable Practice Reader R1A.* Point out the title and the author's name. Review the proper way to hold the book. Ask children to read the words on p. 1. Then have children preview the story. Remind them that they will read words with consonants *m, s,* and *t* and the short *a* vowel sound.

DECODING IN CONTEXT Have pairs of children read the story, switching readers after each page. Monitor as they decode.

FLUENCY Have children reread *Decodable Practice Reader R1A* to develop automaticity decoding words with consonants and short *a.*

Lesson 5

Review and More Practice

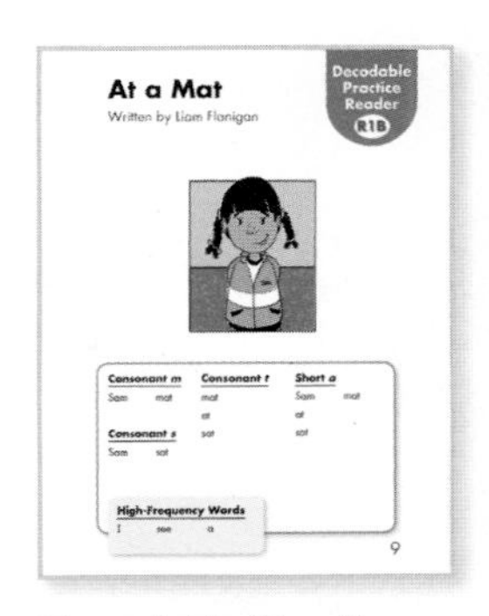
Decodable Practice Reader R1B

CONSONANTS *m, s, t* Write these words: *mat, sat, tam.* Read each word with children. Ask them to name the word's initial letter and its sound.

SHORT *a* Write these words: *am, at, Sam, sat, Tam, mat.* Have children blend the sounds and read each word.

FLUENCY Have children reread *Decodable Practice Readers R1A* and *R1B.*

SKILLS

- consonants *c*/k/, *p*/p/, *n*/n/
- short *a*: *a*/a/

OBJECTIVES

- Isolate and pronounce /k/, /p/, and /n/ in spoken words.
- Isolate initial and medial /a/ in spoken words.
- Decode and read words with consonants *c*/k/, *p*/p/, and *n*/n/.
- Decode and read words with short *a*.
- Read and spell high-frequency words.

Lesson 6

Phonemic Awareness

Distinguish /k/, /p/, /n/

INTRODUCE Show the Picture Card *can*. Say the picture name with me and listen to the sound at the beginning of the word: /k/ *-an*. Let's make the sound at the beginning of the word: /k/ /k/ /k/. Repeat for /p/ using the Picture Card *pan* and /n/ using the Picture Card *net*.

PRACTICE Listen as I say two words: *mat, car.* Say the words with me: *mat, car.* Tell me which word has the same beginning sound as the word *can*. Yes, the word *car* begins with the same sound as the word *can*. Continue with the following word pairs: *cap/dog, cat/man, top/cut.* Continue the activity for /p/ using *pan* and these word pairs: *pig/car, net/pen, pail/rug.* Use the word *net* and the following words for /n/: *six/nut, nest/rabbit, nose/seal.*

Phonics

Consonants *c*/k/, *p*/p/, *n*/n/

INTRODUCE Display Sound-Spelling Card 3. Point to *c*. The letter *c* stands for the sound, /k/, that you hear at the beginning of *carrot*. Have children say /k/ several times as you point to *c*.

PRACTICE Write *cat*. In this word, the letter *c* stands for the sound /k/. Segment and blend *cat* and then have children blend with you: /k/ /a/ /t/. Continue with Sound-Spelling Card 18 (letter *p* and the word *pat*) and Sound-Spelling Card 16 (letter *n* and the word *nap*). Have children complete p. 15 in the *Reader's and Writer's Journal.*

APPLY Write the word pattern *_at*. I will say a word. Listen to the beginning sound. Raise your hand if you know the letter that spells the beginning sound in the word. Say the word *cat*. Call on someone to name the letter that spells the beginning sound. Repeat with the word *pat*. Continue with these word patterns: *_an (pan, can)*, *_ap (cap, nap)*.

COMMON CORE STATE STANDARDS

RF.1.2.c Isolate and pronounce initial, medial vowel, and final sounds (phonemes) in spoken single-syllable words.

RF.1.3 Know and apply grade-level phonics and word analysis skills in decoding words.

Lesson 7

High-Frequency Words

SAY AND SPELL Display the High-Frequency Word Cards for the words at the right. Some words we learn by remembering the letters. Have children say and spell each word, first with you and then without you.

IDENTIFY FAMILIAR LETTER-SOUNDS Point to the *s* in *see.* What is this letter and what is its sound? (*s*/s/)

DEMONSTRATE MEANING Have children write the words and then say sentences using them.

HIGH-FREQUENCY WORDS

I **see**
the

Decoding

Consonants *c*/k/, *p*/p/, *n*/n/

PREVIEW Distribute *Decodable Practice Reader R2A.* Ask children to identify the title and author's name. Read them aloud. Then have children read the words on p. 17. Then have children preview the story. Remind them that they will read words with consonants *c*/k/, *p*/p/, and *n*/n/. Ask children to identify the first word of each sentence on each page.

DECODING IN CONTEXT Have pairs of children read the story, switching readers after each page. Monitor as they decode.

FLUENCY Have children reread *Decodable Practice Reader R2A* to develop automaticity decoding words with consonants *c, p,* and *n.*

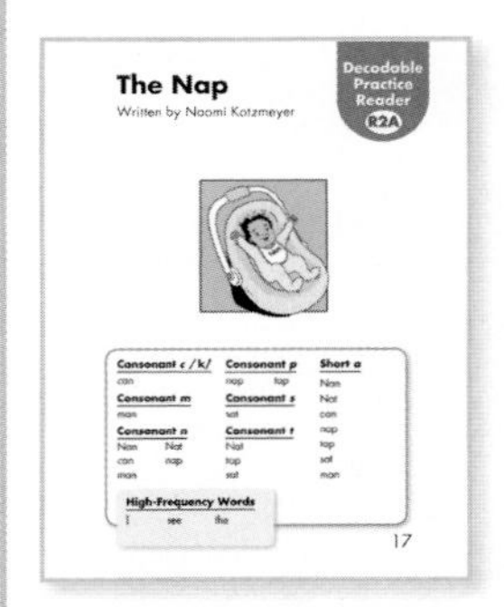

Decodable Practice Reader R2A

COMMON CORE STATE STANDARDS

RF.1.1 Demonstrate understanding of the organization and basic features of print.
RF.1.1.a Recognize the distinguishing features of a sentence (e.g., first word, capitalization, ending punctuation).
RF.1.3 Know and apply grade-level phonics and word analysis skills in decoding words.
RF.1.3.b Decode regularly spelled one-syllable words.
RF.1.3.g Recognize and read grade-appropriate irregularly spelled words.
RF.1.4.a Read grade-level text with purpose and understanding.

Lesson 8

Phonemic Awareness

Initial and Medial /a/

INTRODUCE Say the word *am.* The beginning sound of the word *am* is the short *a* sound. Now listen to this word: *can.* What sound do you hear in the middle? Segment the word: /k/ /a/ /n/. This word has the short *a* sound in the middle. The short *a* sound can be the beginning sound or the middle sound of a word.

PRACTICE Listen as I say a word. Then say the word with me. Listen for the short *a* sound. Raise your hand if you know whether the /a/ sound is at the beginning or in the middle of the word. Call on a volunteer to tell whether the sound is at the beginning or in the middle of the word. Use the following words: *cap, ant, ax, map, and, can, tan, at, sat, an, pat, tap.*

Phonics

Short *a: a/a/*

INTRODUCE Display the Picture Card *pan.* This is a pan. Let's say the sounds in the word: /p/ /a/ /n/. Who can write the letters? Have volunteers write the letters. Let's spell the word together: *p-a-n.* Now let's read the word: *pan.* The letter *a* stands for the sound, /a/, that you hear in the middle of the word *pan.*

PRACTICE Display the following Picture Cards: *can, cap, cat, pan.* Have children name the pictures with you. Then have them write the letters that spell each word. Have children complete p. 22 in the *Reader's and Writer's Journal.*

APPLY Say the following words one at a time: *nap, man, tap, pat.* Have children write the letters that spell each word on a sheet of paper.

COMMON CORE STATE STANDARDS

RF.1.1 Demonstrate understanding of the organization and basic features of print.

RF.1.2.c Isolate and pronounce initial, medial vowel, and final sounds (phonemes) in spoken single-syllable words.

RF.1.3 Know and apply grade-level phonics and word analysis skills in decoding words.

RF.1.3.b Decode regularly spelled one-syllable words.

RF.1.3.g Recognize and read grade-appropriate irregularly spelled words.

RF.1.4.a Read grade-level text with purpose and understanding.

Lesson 9

High-Frequency Words

SAY AND SPELL Display the High-Frequency Word Cards for the words at the right. Some words we learn by remembering the letters. Have children say and spell each word, first with you and then without you.

HIGH-FREQUENCY WORDS	
we	see
the	like

IDENTIFY FAMILIAR LETTER-SOUNDS Point to the *s* in *see.* What is this letter and what is its sound? (s/s/)

DEMONSTRATE MEANING Have children write the words and then say sentences using them.

Decoding

Short *a: a*/a/

PREVIEW Distribute *Decodable Practice Reader R2B.* Ask children to read the title and words on p. 25. Then have children preview the story. Remind them that they will read words with *c, n, p,* and *a.* Ask children to turn to p. 31 and review how to read the sentences from left to right and top to bottom.

Decodable Practice Reader R2B

DECODING IN CONTEXT Have pairs of children read the story, switching readers after each page. Monitor as they decode.

FLUENCY Have children reread *Decodable Practice Reader R2B* to develop automaticity decoding words with consonants and short *a.*

Lesson 10

Review and More Practice

CONSONANTS *c*/k/, *p*/p/, *n*/n/ Use Sound-Spelling Cards 3, 18, and 16 to review /k/ spelled *Cc,* /p/ spelled *Pp,* and /n/ spelled *Nn.* Then write these words: *cap, can, nap.* Ask the class to blend the sounds to read each word.

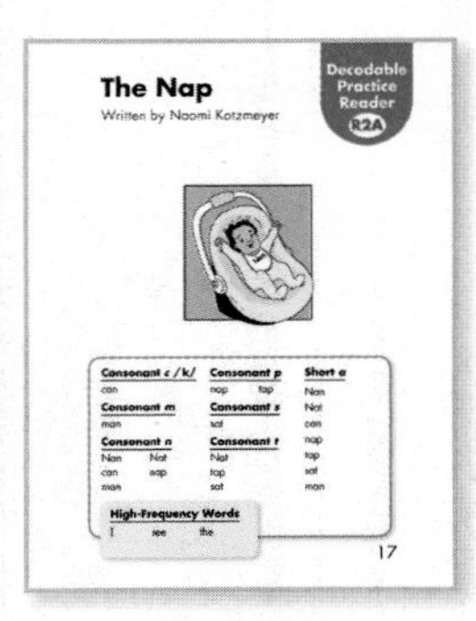

Decodable Practice Reader R2A

SHORT *a* Use Sound-Spelling Card 1 to review short *a.* Have partners use the Letter Tiles to spell the words *pat, cat, man, can,* and *tan.*

FLUENCY Have children reread *Decodable Practice Readers R2A* and *R2B.*

SKILLS
- consonants *f, ff*/f/; *b*/b/; *g*/g/
- short *i*: *i*/i/

OBJECTIVES
- Isolate and pronounce /f/, /b/, and /g/ in spoken words.
- Isolate initial and medial /i/ in spoken words.
- Decode and read words with consonants *f, ff*/f/; *b*/b/; and *g*/g/.
- Decode and read words with short *i*.
- Read and spell high-frequency words.

Performance-Based Assessment Time

After Lesson 13, your class will be working on the Performance-Based Assessment. You should plan your Foundational Skills instruction accordingly.

Lesson 11

Phonemic Awareness

Distinguish /f/, /b/, /g/

INTRODUCE Show the Picture Card *fan*. Say the picture name with me and listen to the sound at the beginning of the word: /f/ *-an*. Let's make the sound at the beginning of the word: /f/ /f/ /f/. Now let's say the picture name: *fan*. Repeat this procedure for /b/ with the Picture Card *bag* and for /g/ with the Picture Card *goat*.

PRACTICE Listen as I say three words: *fast, fun, car.* Say the words with me. Which two words begin like the word *fan?* Let's say the words together: *fan, fast, fun.* Continue with other sets of three words: *top/farm/food, face/moon/fox, five/feet/dog, rose/fire/fish.* Continue the activity for /b/ using these words with the word *bag: leaf/bug/bat, kite/boat/box, bus/nest/boot, baby/barn/rake.* Use the following words for /g/ with the word *goat: tape/garden/goose, gate/yarn/gold, game/goal/bed, gone/gas/sun.*

Phonics

Consonants *f, ff*/f/; *b*/b/; *g*/g/

INTRODUCE Display Sound-Spelling Card 7. Point to *f.* The letter *f* stands for the sound /f/ that you hear at the beginning of *firefighter.* Have children say /f/ several times as you point to *f*.

PRACTICE Write *fan.* In this word, the letter *f stands for the sound /f/.* Segment and blend *fan* and then have children blend with you: /f/ /a/ /n/. Continue with Sound-Spelling Card 2 for the letter *b* and the word *bat.* Repeat with Sound-Spelling Card 8 for the letter *g* and the word *gas.* Have children complete p. 29 in the *Reader's and Writer's Journal.*

APPLY Write the following words: *mat, tab, bat, can, tag, sat, man, bag, bad, fat, mad, fan, gap, pan, nap, gas.* Have children work with a partner to blend the sounds to read each word.

COMMON CORE STATE STANDARDS

RF.1.2.c Isolate and pronounce initial, medial vowel, and final sounds (phonemes) in spoken single-syllable words.

RF.1.3 Know and apply grade-level phonics and word analysis skills in decoding words.

RF.1.3.b Decode regularly spelled one-syllable words.

PEARSON realize

Decodable Practice Readers

Letter Tile Drag and Drop

Foundational Skills Games

Sound-Spelling Cards

High-Frequency Words

SAY AND SPELL Display the High-Frequency Word Cards for the words at the right. Some words we learn by remembering the letters. Have children say and spell each word, first with you and then without you.

IDENTIFY FAMILIAR LETTER-SOUNDS Point to the *s* in *see.* What is this letter and what is its sound? (*s*/s/)

DEMONSTRATE MEANING Have children write the words and then say sentences using them.

HIGH-FREQUENCY WORDS

you	see
the	

Decoding

Consonants *f, ff*/f/; *b*/b/; *g*/g/

PREVIEW Distribute *Decodable Practice Reader R3A.* Ask children to read the title and words on p. 33. Then have children preview the story. Remind them that they will read words with consonants *f, ff*/f/; *b*/b/; and *g*/g/.

DECODING IN CONTEXT Have pairs of children read the story, switching readers after each page. Monitor as they decode.

FLUENCY Have children reread *Decodable Practice Reader R3A* to develop automaticity decoding words with consonants *b, c, f, g, n,* and *p.*

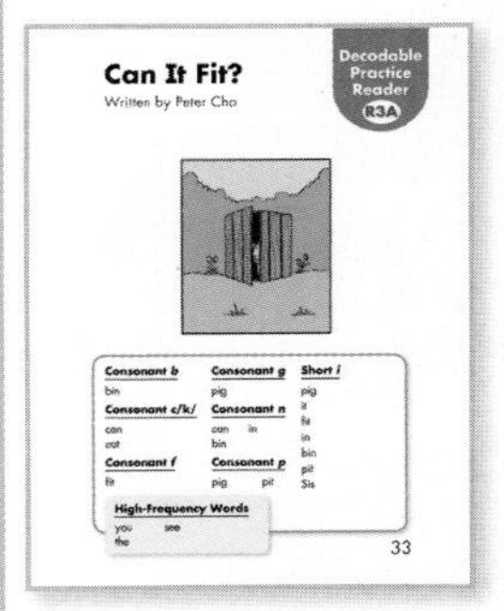

Decodable Practice Reader R3A

COMMON CORE STATE STANDARDS

RF.1.3 Know and apply grade-level phonics and word analysis skills in decoding words.
RF.1.3.b Decode regularly spelled one-syllable words.
RF.1.3.g Recognize and read grade-appropriate irregularly spelled words.
RF.1.4.a Read grade-level text with purpose and understanding.

Lesson 13

Phonemic Awareness

Initial and Medial /i/

INTRODUCE Show the Picture Card *igloo.* Say the picture name with me and listen to the sound at the beginning of the word: *i-gloo.* Let's make that sound: /i/ /i/ /i/. This is the short *i* sound. Show the Picture Card *six.* Say the picture name with me: *six.* What sound do you hear in the middle? Yes, the short *i* sound. It can be the beginning or middle sound of a word.

PRACTICE Listen as I say a word. Then say the word with me. Listen for the short *i* sound. Raise your hand if you hear the /i/ sound at the beginning. Clap your hands if the /i/ sound is in the middle of the word. Use these words: *inch, is, mix, in, fit, zip, insect, it, if, tip, itch.*

Phonics

Short *i*: *i*/i/

INTRODUCE Display Sound-Spelling Card 11. Point to *i.* The letter *i* stands for the sound /i/, which you hear at the beginning of *insects.* Have children say /i/ several times as you point to *i.*

PRACTICE Write *in.* In this word, the letter *i* stands for the sound /i/. Write the word *pin.* Listen as I say the sounds in the word: /p/ /i/ /n/. Say the sounds with me: /p/ /i/ /n/. Follow this procedure to model *sit, tip*, and *big*. Have children complete p. 35 in the *Reader's and Writer's Journal.*

APPLY Write these words: *fin, bib, sip, fit.* Have children say each sound in a word and then blend the sounds with you to read the word.

COMMON CORE STATE STANDARDS

RF.1.1 Demonstrate understanding of the organization and basic features of print.

RF.1.1.a Recognize the distinguishing features of a sentence (e.g., first word, capitalization, ending punctuation).

RF.1.2.c Isolate and pronounce initial, medial vowel, and final sounds (phonemes) in spoken single-syllable words.

RF.1.3 Know and apply grade-level phonics and word analysis skills in decoding words.

RF.1.3.b Decode regularly spelled one-syllable words.

RF.1.3.g Recognize and read grade-appropriate irregularly spelled words.

RF.1.4.a Read grade-level text with purpose and understanding.

Continued Instruction

High-Frequency Words

SAY AND SPELL Display the High-Frequency Word Cards for the words at the right. Some words we learn by remembering the letters. Have children say and spell each word, first with you and then without you.

HIGH-FREQUENCY WORDS	
look	the
like	I

DEMONSTRATE MEANING Have children write the words and then say sentences using them.

Decoding

Short *i*: i/i/

PREVIEW Distribute *Decodable Practice Reader R3B.* Ask children to read the title and words on p. 41. Then have children preview the story. Remind them that they will read words with *f, b, g,* and *i.* Ask children to turn to p. 43 and review how to read the sentences from left to right and top to bottom. Then review the features of each sentence, pointing to the capital letter and end punctuation.

DECODING IN CONTEXT Have pairs of children read the story, switching readers after each page. Monitor as they decode.

FLUENCY Have children reread *Decodable Practice Reader R3B* to develop automaticity decoding words with consonants and short *i.*

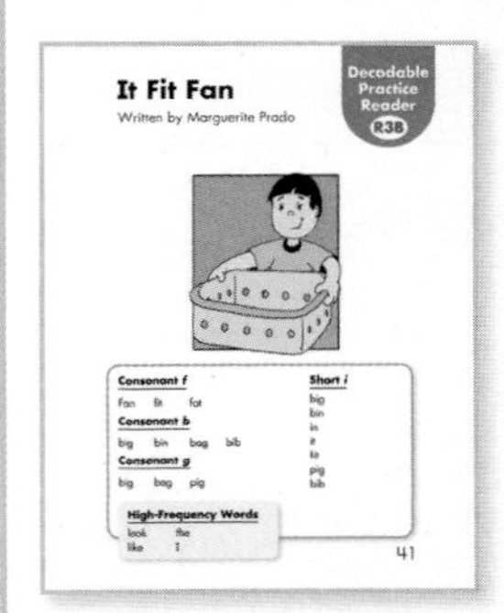

Decodable Practice Reader R3B

Continued Instruction

Review and More Practice

CONSONANTS *f, ff/f/; b/b/; g/g/* Use Sound-Spelling Cards 7, 2, and 8 to review /f/ spelled *Ff,* /b/ spelled *Bb,* and /g/ spelled *Gg.* Then write these words: *bag, fab, gig.* Ask the class to blend the sounds to read each word.

SHORT *i* Use Sound-Spelling Card 11 to review short *i.* Then have partners use the *f, b, g, t, p,* and *i* Letter Tiles to spell the words *bit, fit, big,* and *pig.* Then have them try to spell their own words using the Letter Tiles.

FLUENCY Have children reread *Decodable Practice Readers R3A* and *R3B.*

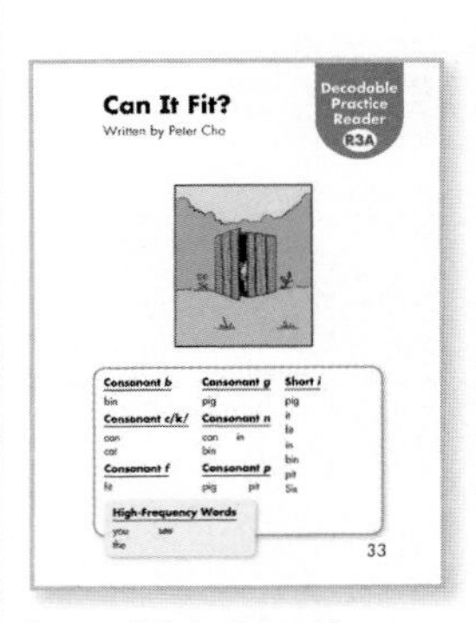

Decodable Practice Reader R3A

SKILLS

- consonants *d*/d/; *l, ll*/l/; *h*/h/
- short *o: o*/o/

OBJECTIVES

- Isolate and pronounce /d/, /l/, and /h/ in spoken words.
- Isolate initial and medial /o/ in spoken words.
- Decode and read words with consonants *d*/d/; *l, ll*/l/; and *h*/h/.
- Decode and read words with short *o*.
- Read and spell high-frequency words.

Lesson 1

Phonemic Awareness

Distinguish /d/, /l/, /h/

INTRODUCE Show the Picture Card *dog*. Say the picture name with me and listen to the sound at the beginning of the word: /d/ *-og*. Let's make that sound: /d/ /d/ /d/. Repeat this procedure for /l/ with the Picture Card *leaf* and for /h/ with the Picture Card *hat*.

PRACTICE Listen as I say the beginning sound of the word *dog:* /d/ /d/ /d/. Say the sound with me: /d/ /d/ /d/. I am going to say a word. If you hear the /d/ sound at the beginning of the word, raise your hands. Use these words: *desk, mop, doll, duck, carrot.* Continue the activity for /l/ with these words: *lion, nose, letter, pen, learn.* Use the following words for /h/: *house, hall, tent, horse, happy.*

Phonics

Consonants *d*/d/; *l, ll*/l/; *h*/h/

INTRODUCE Display Sound-Spelling Card 5. Point to *d.* The letter *d* stands for the sound /d/ that you hear at the beginning of *dime.* Have children say /d/ as you point to *d.*

PRACTICE Write *dig.* In this word, the letter *d* stands for the sound /d/. Segment *dig* and have children blend with you: /d/ /i/ /g/, *dig.* Continue with Sound-Spelling Card 14 for the letter *l* and the word *lid.* Repeat with Sound-Spelling Card 10 for the letter *h* and the word *hat.* Have children complete p. 40 in the *Reader's and Writer's Journal.*

APPLY Write the word pattern *_id.* I will say a word. Listen to the beginning sound. Raise your hand if you know the letter that spells the beginning sound. Say the word *lid.* Call on children to name and write the missing letter. Repeat the *_id* pattern with *did, hid,* and *bid.* Continue with these word patterns: *_ad (lad, had, dad, mad, sad, pad*), *_ip (lip, dip, hip, sip, tip*).

COMMON CORE STATE STANDARDS

RF.1.2.c Isolate and pronounce initial, medial vowel, and final sounds (phonemes) in spoken single-syllable words.

RF.1.3 Know and apply grade-level phonics and word analysis skills in decoding words.

RF.1.3.b Decode regularly spelled one-syllable words.

Decodable Practice Readers | Letter Tile Drag and Drop
Foundational Skills Games | Sound-Spelling Cards

PEARSON realize

High-Frequency Words

SAY AND SPELL Display the High-Frequency Word Cards for the words at the right. Some words we learn by remembering the letters. Have children say and spell each word, first with you and then without you.

IDENTIFY FAMILIAR LETTER-SOUNDS Point to the *l* in *look.* What is this letter and what is its sound? (/l/)

DEMONSTRATE MEANING Have children write the words and then say sentences using them.

HIGH-FREQUENCY WORDS

was look
I

Decoding

Consonants *d*/d/; *l, ll*/l/; *h*/h/

PREVIEW Distribute *Decodable Practice Reader R4A.* Ask children to read the title and words on p. 49. Then have children preview the story. Ask children to point to the first word of each sentence. Remind them that they will read words with consonants *d*/d/, *l*/l/, and *h*/h/.

DECODING IN CONTEXT Have pairs of children read the story, switching readers after each page. Monitor as they decode.

FLUENCY Have children reread *Decodable Practice Reader R4A* to develop automaticity decoding words with consonants *d, l,* and *h.*

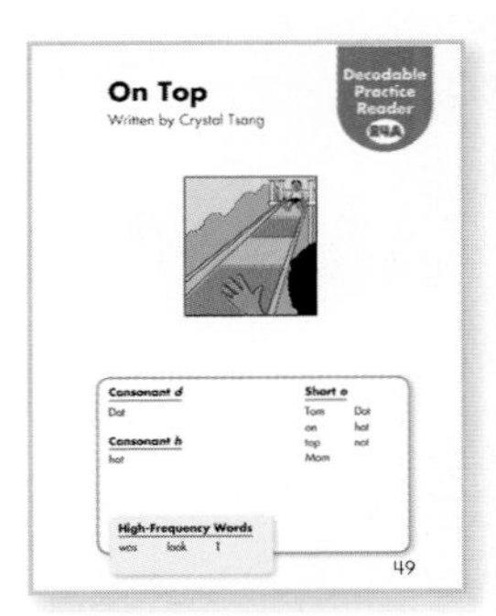

Decodable Practice Reader R4A

COMMON CORE STATE STANDARDS

RF.1.1.a Recognize the distinguishing features of a sentence (e.g., first word, capitalization, ending punctuation).
RF.1.3 Know and apply grade-level phonics and word analysis skills in decoding words.
RF.1.3.b Decode regularly spelled one-syllable words.
RF.1.3.g Recognize and read grade-appropriate irregularly spelled words.
RF.1.4.a Read grade-level text with purpose and understanding.

Lesson 3

Phonemic Awareness

Initial and Medial /o/

INTRODUCE Show the Picture Card *octopus*. Say the picture name with me and listen to the sound at the beginning of the word: *o-ctopus*. Let's make the sound at the beginning of the word: /o/ /o/ /o/.

Say the word *hot.* Segment the sounds: /h/ /o/ /t/. This word also has the short *o* sound. Say the word with me: *hot,* /h/ /o/ /t/. Where did you hear the /o/ sound? Yes, the sound is in the middle.

PRACTICE Listen as I say a word. Then say the sounds with me. Raise your hand if you know whether the /o/ sound is at the beginning or in the middle of the word. Call on a volunteer to tell whether the sound is at the beginning or in the middle of the word. Have children segment the sounds in these words with you: *on, ox, hop, pot, cot, rock, top, dot, odd, not.*

Phonics

Short *o: o*/o/

INTRODUCE Display Sound-Spelling Card 17. Point to *o.* The letter *o* stands for the sound, /o/, that you hear at the beginning of *octopus.* Have children say /o/ several times as you point to *o.*

PRACTICE Write *ox.* In this word, the letter *o* stands for the sound /o/. Write the word *hop.* Listen as I say the sounds in the word: /h/ /o/ /p/. Say the sounds with me: /h/ /o/ /p/. Follow this procedure to model *top, pot,* and *hot*. Have children complete p. 46 in the *Reader's and Writer's Journal.*

APPLY Write these words: *got, top, dot, lot*. Have children say each sound in a word and then blend the sounds with you to read the word.

COMMON CORE STATE STANDARDS

RF.1.2.c Isolate and pronounce initial, medial vowel, and final sounds (phonemes) in spoken single-syllable words.

RF.1.2.d Segment spoken single-syllable words into their complete sequence of individual sounds (phonemes).

RF.1.3 Know and apply grade-level phonics and word analysis skills in decoding words.

RF.1.3.b Decode regularly spelled one-syllable words.

RF.1.3.g Recognize and read grade-appropriate irregularly spelled words.

RF.1.4.a Read grade-level text with purpose and understanding.

Lesson 4

High-Frequency Words

HIGH-FREQUENCY WORDS	
you	we

SAY AND SPELL Display the High-Frequency Word Cards for the words at the right. Some words we learn by remembering the letters. Have children say and spell each word, first with you and then without you.

DEMONSTRATE MEANING Have children write the words and then say sentences using them.

Decoding

Short *o*: o/o/

PREVIEW Distribute *Decodable Practice Reader R4B.* Ask children to read the title and words on p. 57. Then have children preview the story. Remind them that they will read words with short *o.*

DECODING IN CONTEXT Have pairs of children read the story, switching readers after each page. Monitor as they decode.

FLUENCY Have children reread *Decodable Practice Reader R4B* to develop automaticity decoding words with consonants and short *o.*

Decodable Practice Reader R4B

Lesson 5

Review and More Practice

CONSONANTS *d*/d/; *l*, *ll*/l/; *h*/h/ Use Sound-Spelling Cards 15, 21, and 23 to review /d/ spelled *Dd,* /l/ spelled *Ll,* and /h/ spelled *Hh.* Then write these words: *lot, doll, hot.* Ask the class to blend the sounds and read each word.

SHORT *o* Use Sound-Spelling Card 17 to review short *o.* Have children use Letter Tiles to spell the following words as you say them: *dot, hot, hop, top, mop.*

FLUENCY Have children reread *Decodable Practice Readers R4A* and *R4B.*

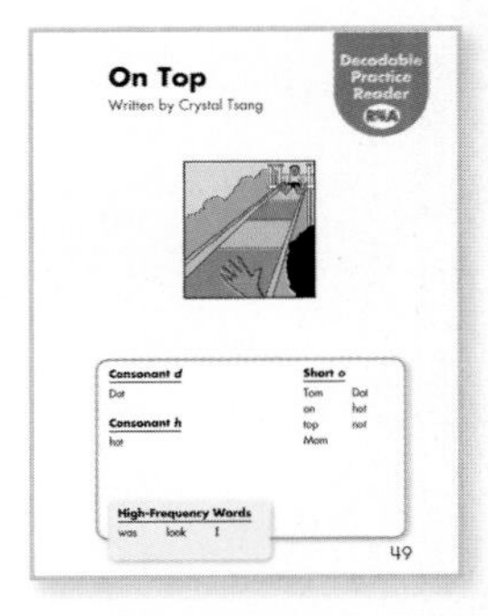

Decodable Practice Reader R4A

SKILLS
- consonants *r*/r/, *w*/w/, *j*/j/, *k*/k/
- short *e*: *e*/e/

OBJECTIVES
- Isolate and pronounce /r/, /w/, /j/, and /k/ in spoken words.
- Isolate initial and medial /e/ in spoken words.
- Decode and read words with consonants *r*/r/, *w*/w/, *j*/j/, and *k*/k/.
- Decode and read words with short *e*.
- Read and spell high-frequency words.

Lesson 6

Phonemic Awareness

Distinguish /r/, /w/, /j/, /k/

INTRODUCE Show the Picture Card *rug.* Listen to the sound at the beginning of the word: /r/ *-ug.* Let's make the beginning sound: /r/ /r/ /r/. Now let's say the picture name: *rug.* Repeat this procedure for /w/ with the Picture Card *web,* for /j/ with the Picture Card *jam,* and for /k/ with the Picture Card *kite.*

PRACTICE Listen as I say two words: *red, bed.* Say the words with me: *red, bed.* Tell me which word has the same beginning sound as the word *rug*. Yes, the word *red* begins with the same sound as the word *rug.* Use these word pairs: *pen/rake, net/rock.* Continue the activity for /w/ with *web* and these word pairs: *wig/bell, lamp/window.* Use these word pairs for /j/ with the word *jam: bus/jet, juice/sun.* Use these word pairs for /k/ with the word *kite: kitten/boot, log/key.*

Phonics

Consonants r/r/, w/w/, j/j/, k/k/

INTRODUCE Display Sound-Spelling Card 20. Point to *r.* The letter *r* stands for the sound, /r/, that you hear at the beginning of *rocket.* Have children say /r/ as you point to the letter *r*.

PRACTICE Write *rat.* In this word, the letter *r* stands for the sound /r/. Segment *rat* and have children blend with you: /r/ /a/ /t/, *rat*. Continue with Sound-Spelling Card 26 for the letter *w* and the word *wig.* Repeat with Sound-Spelling Card 12 for the letter *j* and the word *job* and Sound-Spelling Card 13 for the letter *k* and the word *kid.* Have children complete p. 54 in the *Reader's and Writer's Journal.*

APPLY Write the word pattern *_ig.* I will say a word. Listen to the beginning sound. Raise your hand if you know the letter that spells the beginning sound. Say the word *wig.* Call on volunteers to name and to write the letter to complete the word. Repeat the *_ig* pattern for the words *jig, pig, big,* and *dig.* Continue with *_it* (*kit, hit, bit, fit, pit, sit*) and *_an* (*ran, can, fan, pan, man, tan*).

COMMON CORE STATE STANDARDS

RF.1.2.c Isolate and pronounce initial, medial vowel, and final sounds (phonemes) in spoken single-syllable words.

RF.1.3 Know and apply grade-level phonics and word analysis skills in decoding words.

RF.1.3.b Decode regularly spelled one-syllable words.

Lesson 7

High-Frequency Words

SAY AND SPELL Display the High-Frequency Word Cards for the words at the right. Some words we learn by remembering the letters. Have children say and spell each word, first with you and then without you.

IDENTIFY FAMILIAR LETTER-SOUNDS Point to the *d* in *do.* What is this letter and what is its sound? (*d*/d/) Repeat with the *s* in *see.*

DEMONSTRATE MEANING Have children write the words and then say sentences using them.

HIGH-FREQUENCY WORDS	
the	do
you	see

Decoding

Consonants *r*/r/, *w*/w/, *j*/j/, *k*/k/

PREVIEW Distribute *Decodable Practice Reader R5A.* Ask children to read the title and words on p. 65. Then have children preview the story. Ask children to choose a sentence in the book and identify the first word and end punctuation. Remind them that they will read words with consonants *r*/r/, *w*/w/, *j*/j/, and *k*/k/.

DECODING IN CONTEXT Have pairs of children read the story, switching readers after each page. Monitor as they decode.

FLUENCY Have children reread *Decodable Practice Reader R5A* to develop automaticity decoding words with consonants *r, w, j,* and *k.*

Decodable Practice Reader R5A

COMMON CORE STATE STANDARDS

RF.1.1.a Recognize the distinguishing features of a sentence (e.g., first word, capitalization, ending punctuation).
RF.1.3 Know and apply grade-level phonics and word analysis skills in decoding words.
RF.1.3.b Decode regularly spelled one-syllable words.
RF.1.3.g Recognize and read grade-appropriate irregularly spelled words.
RF.1.4.a Read grade-level text with purpose and understanding.

Lesson 8

Phonemic Awareness

Initial and Medial /e/

INTRODUCE Say the word *end* and ask children to listen to the sound at the beginning of the word: /e/ *-nd.* Let's make that sound: /e/ /e/ /e/. This is the short *e* sound. Say the word *bed.* What sound do you hear in the middle? Yes, the short *e* sound. It can be the beginning or middle sound of a word.

PRACTICE Listen as I say a word. Then say the word with me. Listen for the short *e* sound. Raise your hand if you know whether the /e/ sound is at the beginning or in the middle of the word. Call on a volunteer to tell whether the sound is at the beginning or in the middle of the word. Use the following words: *bell, edge, desk, net, elk.*

Phonics

Short *e: e*/e/

INTRODUCE Display Sound-Spelling Card 6. Point to *e.* The letter *e* stands for the sound, /e/, that you hear at the beginning of *elephant.* Have children say /e/ several times as you point to *e.*

PRACTICE Display the Picture Card *net.* Say the picture name with me: *net.* Let's say the sounds in the word: /n/ /e/ /t/. Who can write the first letter? Have a volunteer write the letter *n.* Continue with other volunteers writing the middle and final letters in the word. Let's spell the word together: *n-e-t*. Now let's read the word: *net.* Have children complete p. 59 in the *Reader's and Writer's Journal.*

APPLY Display the following Picture Cards: *bed, hen, jet, web, ten.* Have children name the pictures with you. Then provide time for them to segment each word into its sounds and then write the letter that spells each sound. Choose a volunteer to write each picture name. Have children check their words.

COMMON CORE STATE STANDARDS

RF.1.2.c Isolate and pronounce initial, medial vowel, and final sounds (phonemes) in spoken single-syllable words.

RF.1.2.d Segment spoken single-syllable words into their complete sequence of individual sounds (phonemes).

RF.1.3 Know and apply grade-level phonics and word analysis skills in decoding words.

RF.1.3.b Decode regularly spelled one-syllable words.

RF.1.3.g Recognize and read grade-appropriate irregularly spelled words.

RF.1.4.a Read grade-level text with purpose and understanding.

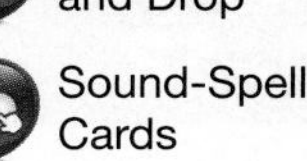

Decodable Practice Readers

Letter Tile Drag and Drop

Foundational Skills Games

Sound-Spelling Cards

PEARSON realize

Lesson 9

High-Frequency Words

SAY AND SPELL Display the High-Frequency Word Cards for the words at the right. Some words we learn by remembering the letters. Have children say and spell each word, first with you and then without you.

IDENTIFY FAMILIAR LETTER-SOUNDS Point to *w* in *with.* What is this letter and what is its sound? (*w*/w/) Continue pointing out familiar letter-sounds in the other words.

DEMONSTRATE MEANING Have children write the words and then say sentences using them.

HIGH-FREQUENCY WORDS	
with	do
is	a
the	we

Decoding

Short *e*: *e*/e/

PREVIEW Distribute *Decodable Practice Reader R5B.* Ask children to read the title and words on p. 73. Then have children preview the story. Remind them that they will read words with short *e.*

DECODING IN CONTEXT Have pairs of children read the story, switching readers after each page. Monitor as they decode.

FLUENCY Have children reread *Decodable Practice Reader R5B* to develop automaticity decoding words with consonants and short *e.*

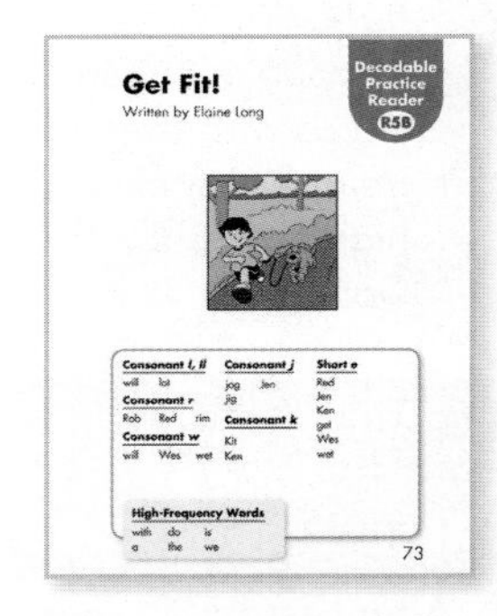

Decodable Practice Reader R5B

Lesson 10

Review and More Practice

CONSONANTS *r*/r/, *w*/w/, *j*/j/, *k*/k/ Use Sound-Spelling Cards 20, 26, 12, and 13 to review /r/ spelled *Rr,* /w/ spelled *Ww,* /j/ spelled *Jj,* and /k/ spelled *Kk.* Then write these words: *rip, wag, job, kid.* Ask the class to blend the sounds and read each word.

SHORT *e* Use Sound-Spelling Card 6 to review short *e.* Have children use Letter Tiles to spell the following words as you say them: *red, kit, wet, jet.*

FLUENCY Have children reread *Decodable Practice Readers R5A* and *R5B.*

Decodable Practice Reader R5A

SKILLS

- consonants *v*/v/; *y*/y/; *z, zz*/z/; *qu*/kw/
- short *u: u*/u/

OBJECTIVES

- Isolate and pronounce /v/, /y/, /z/, and /kw/ in spoken words.
- Isolate initial and medial /u/ in spoken words.
- Decode and read words with consonants *v*/v/; *y*/y/; *z, zz*/z/; and *qu*/kw/.
- Decode and read words with short *u*.
- Read and spell high-frequency words.

Performance-Based Assessment Time

After Lesson 12, your class will be working on the Performance-Based Assessment. You should plan your Foundational Skills instruction accordingly.

Lesson 11

Phonemic Awareness

Distinguish /v/, /y/, /z/, /kw/

INTRODUCE Show the Picture Card *van*. Say the picture name with me and listen to the sound at the beginning of the word: /v/ *-an.* Let's make the sound at the beginning of the word: /v/ /v/ /v/. Now let's say the picture name: *van*. Repeat this procedure for /y/ with the Picture Card *yak,* for /z/ with the Picture Card *zoo,* and for /kw/ with the Picture Card *queen.*

PRACTICE Listen as I say the beginning sound of the word *van:* /v/ /v/ /v/. Say the sound with me: /v/ /v/ /v/. I am going to say a word. If you hear the /v/ sound at the beginning of the word, raise your hands. Use these words: *fish, vet, vase, violin.* Continue the activity for /y/ with these words: *yarn, suit, yo-yo, yard.* Use these words for /z/: *zebra, zero, horse, zipper.* Use these words for /kw/: *quarter, quill, five, quack.*

Phonics

Consonants *v*/v/; *y*/y/; *z, zz*/z/; *qu*/kw/

INTRODUCE Display Sound-Spelling Card 25. Point to *v.* The letter *v* stands for the sound, /v/, that you hear at the beginning of *volcano.* Have children say /v/ as you point to *v.*

PRACTICE Write *van.* In this word, the letter *v* stands for the sound /v/. Segment *van* and have children blend with you: /v/ /a/ /n/, *van.* Continue with Sound-Spelling Card 28 for the letter *y* and the word *yet.* Repeat with Sound-Spelling Card 29 for the letter *z* and the word *zip* and Sound-Spelling Card 19 for the letters *qu* and the word *quit.* Have children complete p. 68 in their *Reader's and Writer's Journal.*

APPLY Write the word *van.* Have children change the initial consonant to make these words: *can, man, tan, Dan, fan, pan, ran.* Then tell children to read the words. Continue with the words *yet* (*vet, bet, met, get, jet, let, net, pet, set, wet*), *zip* (*dip, hip, lip, rip, sip, tip*), and *quit* (*bit, fit, hit, kit, pit, sit*).

COMMON CORE STATE STANDARDS

RF.1.2.c Isolate and pronounce initial, medial vowel, and final sounds (phonemes) in spoken single-syllable words.

RF.1.3 Know and apply grade-level phonics and word analysis skills in decoding words.

RF.1.3.b Decode regularly spelled one-syllable words.

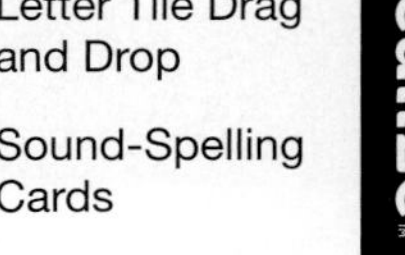

Lesson 12

High-Frequency Words

SAY AND SPELL Display the High-Frequency Word Cards for the words at the right. Some words we learn by remembering the letters. Have children say and spell each word, first with you and then without you.

IDENTIFY FAMILIAR LETTER-SOUNDS Point to the *f* in *for.* What is this letter and what is its sound? (*f*/f/) Repeat with the *d* in *do.*

DEMONSTRATE MEANING Have children write the words and then say sentences using them.

HIGH-FREQUENCY WORDS	
for	a
do	the

Decoding

Consonants *v*/v/; *y*/y/; *z, zz*/z/; *qu*/kw/

PREVIEW Distribute *Decodable Practice Reader R6A.* Ask children to read the title and words on p. 81. Then have children preview the story. Remind them that they will read words with consonants *v*/v/; *y*/y/; *z, zz*/z/; and *qu*/kw/.

DECODING IN CONTEXT Have pairs of children read the story, switching readers after each page. Monitor as they decode.

FLUENCY Have children reread *Decodable Practice Reader R6A* to develop automaticity decoding words with consonants *v, y, z,* and *qu.*

Decodable Practice Reader R6A

COMMON CORE STATE STANDARDS

RF.1.3 Know and apply grade-level phonics and word analysis skills in decoding words.
RF.1.3.b Decode regularly spelled one-syllable words.
RF.1.3.g Recognize and read grade-appropriate irregularly spelled words.
RF.1.4.a Read grade-level text with purpose and understanding.

Continued Instruction

Phonemic Awareness

Initial and Medial /u/

INTRODUCE Show the Picture Card *up*. Say the picture name with me and listen to the sound at the beginning of the word: /u/ *-p*. Let's make the sound at the beginning of the word: /u/ /u/ /u/. This is the short *u* sound. Say the word *mug.* This word also has the short *u* sound. Say the word with me: *mug.* Where did you hear the /u/ sound? Yes, the sound is in the middle of the word.

PRACTICE Listen as I say a word. Then say the word with me. Listen for the short *u* sound. Raise your hand if you know whether the /u/ sound is at the beginning or in the middle of the word. Call on a volunteer to tell whether the sound is at the beginning or in the middle of the word. Use the following words: *under, uncle, cub, us, mud, until.*

Phonics

Short *u:* u/u/

INTRODUCE Display Sound-Spelling Card 24. Point to *u.* The letter *u* stands for the sound, /u/, that you hear at the beginning of *umbrella.* Have children say /u/ several times as you point to *u.*

PRACTICE Write *up.* In this word, the letter *u* stands for the sound /u/. Write the word *cut.* Listen as I say the sounds in the word: /k/ /u/ /t/. Say the sounds with me: /k/ /u/ /t/. Follow this procedure to model *fun, bug,* and *rug.* Have children complete p. 75 in the *Reader's and Writer's Journal.*

APPLY Say these words one at a time: *run, mud, cub, sun.* Have children segment the sounds in each word and then blend the sounds with you to read the word.

COMMON CORE STATE STANDARDS

RF.1.2.c Isolate and pronounce initial, medial vowel, and final sounds (phonemes) in spoken single-syllable words.

RF.1.2.d Segment spoken single-syllable words into their complete sequence of individual sounds (phonemes).

RF.1.3 Know and apply grade-level phonics and word analysis skills in decoding words.

RF.1.3.b Decode regularly spelled one-syllable words.

RF.1.3.g Recognize and read grade-appropriate irregularly spelled words.

RF.1.4.a Read grade-level text with purpose and understanding.

Continued Instruction

High-Frequency Words

SAY AND SPELL Display the High-Frequency Word Cards for the words at the right. Some words we learn by remembering the letters. Have children say and spell each word, first with you and then without you.

IDENTIFY FAMILIAR LETTER-SOUNDS Point to *h* in *have.* What is this letter and what is its sound? (*h*/h/) Continue pointing out familiar letter-sounds in the other words.

DEMONSTRATE MEANING Have children write the words and then say sentences using them.

HIGH-FREQUENCY WORDS	
the	is
a	we
with	they
have	

Decoding

Short *u: u*/u/

PREVIEW Distribute *Decodable Practice Reader R6B.* Ask children to read the title and words on p. 89. Then have children preview the story. Remind them that they will read words with short *u.*

DECODING IN CONTEXT Have pairs of children read the story, switching readers after each page. Monitor as they decode.

FLUENCY Have children reread *Decodable Practice Reader R6B* to develop automaticity decoding words with consonants and short *u*.

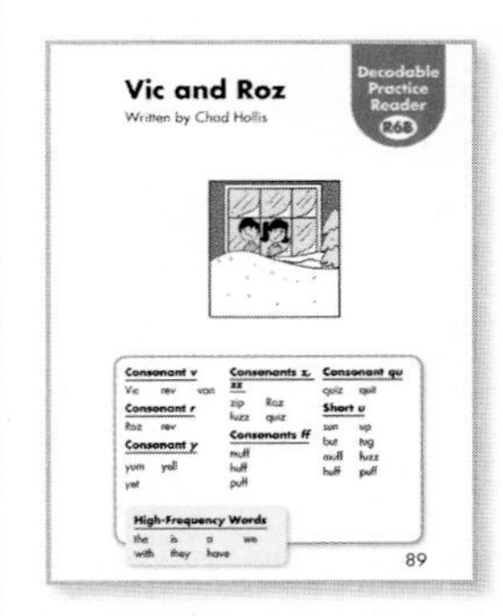

Decodable Practice Reader R6B

Continued Instruction

Review and More Practice

CONSONANTS *v*/v/; *y*/y/; *z, zz*/z/; *qu*/kw/ Use Sound-Spelling Cards 25, 28, 29, and 19 to review /v/ spelled *Vv,* /y/ spelled *Yy,* /z/ spelled *Zz,* and /kw/ spelled *qu.* Then write these words: *van, yak, zip, quit.* Ask the class to blend the sounds and read each word.

SHORT *u* Use Sound-Spelling Card 24 to review short *u.* Have children use Letter Tiles to spell the following words as you say them: *hut, up, buzz, yes, vet.*

FLUENCY Have children reread *Decodable Practice Readers R6A* and *R6B.*

Decodable Practice Reader R6A

SKILLS
- consonants
- short vowels

Check Progress

INFORM INSTRUCTION Use the reproducible pages that follow to assess children's decoding skills and their word reading in context, which includes high-frequency words. Make sure children understand that they should circle the word that names the picture. Use results to inform instruction.

SENTENCE READING Call on one child at a time to read aloud two of the High-Frequency Word sentences on p. FS29. Start over with sentence one if necessary.

ANSWER KEY for pp. FS27–FS29

Phonics

1. mop
2. sun
3. tub
4. cat
5. pin
6. net
7. fan
8. bus
9. dog
10. hat
11. rug
12. jet

High-Frequency Words

1. I, see, a
2. we, like, the
3. look, the
4. the, was
5. you, do
6. they, have, a
7. we, like
8. the, is, for
9. do, you, see
10. I, have, with, you

MONITOR PROGRESS

If . . . children have trouble reading words with consonants and short vowels,
then . . . reteach the lesson that targets the skill children have difficulty with.

If . . . a child cannot read the high-frequency words,
then . . . reteach the high-frequency word sections of each lesson and have the child practice reading the words with a fluent reader.

Name ______________________________

PHONICS

Read the words. Circle the picture name.

1.		log	kid	mop
2.		van	sun	bug
3.		mom	tag	tub
4.		cat	wet	zap
5.		pet	pin	quit
6.	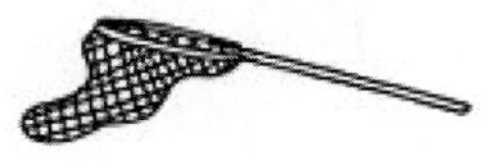	get	net	rob

Name ______________________________

7.  fan nap fin

8.  sit bus leg

9.  dig cup dog

10.  hat yak hen

11.  wig rug gum

12. jet vet job

Name ______________________________

HIGH-FREQUENCY WORDS

Read the sentences.

1. **I see a bus.**
2. **We like the fat cat.**
3. **Look at the dog run.**
4. **The bug was big.**
5. **You can do it!**
6. **They have a tan van.**
7. **We like red jam.**
8. **The bat is for Quin.**
9. **Do you see it?**
10. **I have fun with you.**

ReadyGEN®

Teacher RESOURCES

- Routines
- Graphic Organizers
- Text Complexity Rubrics
- Handwriting
- Leveled Text Instructional Plans
- Acknowledgments

Contents

Think-Pair-Share Routine

THE ROUTINE

1. Introduce the Think-Pair-Share Routine to children. You might begin by saying: In your head, think about how you might answer a question I ask. When I signal it's time to pair up, you'll get together with a partner and share your ideas. I'll give you a reminder to make sure each partner has a chance to share. Then, pairs can volunteer to share their ideas with the class.

2. Remind children of the rules for discussions, such as listening to others with care and speaking one at a time (taking turns). Then pair children randomly with classmates sitting nearby, or in ability-focused pairs.

3. For successful conversation between partners, have pairs sit in close proximity and engage in eye contact with each other. Remind children that they should attend closely to what their partner is saying.

4. Pose an open-ended question to ensure an engaging conversation. Specific text-related questions are suggested in the teaching lessons. Be sure children find evidence in the text to support their answers.

5. Invite pairs to take turns responding to the question. Model ways in which children may respond to their partners by saying: I agree with you. I thought something similar when ___. or I don't agree with you because I remember reading ___. or I think the author is trying to tell readers ___ because the text says ___.

6. After a minute or so, remind children to make sure each partner has had a chance to contribute. You might say: Now is a good time to make sure each partner has shared an idea.

7. Monitor children's conversations by listening briefly to each pair. Offer prompts to focus their attention on or encourage them to look at the text to find evidence to support their answers. For example: Explain your thoughts more. What part of the text helped you to draw that conclusion? or Find the words the author used to describe the character.

8. When pairs have had time to explore the question, have children in each pair choose a spokesperson. Have them rehearse briefly one key point that they would like to share with their classmates. You may ask them to write this key point. Then have volunteers present their pair's key idea to the class. Keep track of the children who act as spokespeople so you can encourage different children to act as spokespeople with each pairing activity.

Rationale

TEAM TALK Think-Pair-Share provides a structure for pairs of children to think and talk together in collaborative conversations. The name aptly describes the stages of children's participation:

- **Think**—Children have time to think about a topic or a text read aloud.
- **Pair**—Children take turns expressing key ideas with a partner.
- **Share**—Children present their formulated ideas to a group.

The Think-Pair-Share Routine provides children with structured support as they engage in text-reliant conversations. Ask children thought-provoking questions to get them involved in richer and more rigorous text-based discussions, such as: What is the main topic? What parts of the text help you know the main topic?

Implementing for Success

Use the following suggestions to guide children as they become familiar with the Think-Pair-Share Routine:

- Model how to do a Think-Pair-Share. Verbalize how you think through your ideas before stating them and how you support your ideas with text evidence.
- Model these best practices for speaking and listening, and have children use them during their Think-Pair-Share opportunities:
  - Ask and answer questions about key details stated by your partner to clarify understanding of what was said.
  - Use key vocabulary when responding.
  - Produce complete sentences and speak clearly when expressing your thoughts, feelings, and ideas.

Going Deeper

Once children are familiar with the routine:

- Incorporate retelling. Provide time for partners to repeat back what was said.
- Encourage higher-level thinking. Ask the listener to frame his or her thoughts in response to the speaker, making connections.

Whole Class Discussion Routine

THE ROUTINE

1 Introduce the Whole Class Discussion Routine to children. Here is an example: We are going to talk about this book together. Let's focus on _____. If you have something to say about this, raise your hand. Listen carefully to what your classmates say so that when you add to our discussion, you can add new ideas.

2 Remind children of the rules for discussions, such as listening to others with care and speaking one at a time (taking turns). Then state the focus of the discussion and any time parameters you have set, such as: We're going to talk about ____ for the next 10 minutes.

3 Pose an open-ended question to ensure an engaging conversation. Specific text-related questions are suggested in the teaching lessons. Give children time to think before they respond, and remind them to find text evidence that supports their responses. For successful Whole Class Discussions, remind children to wait for others to finish talking before they share their thoughts.

4 As children add to the class discussion, act as moderator rather than leader.

- Ask for more information after a response. This helps children develop their contributions more fully. For example: Tell me more about what you are thinking.
- Ask children to point out text evidence that substantiates their responses. For example: What words in the text help you know that? This helps children internalize the text and understand that it is important to support what they say with evidence from the text.
- If children provide an opinion, ask other children to share their opinions in response. For example: What do you think about that opinion? What is *your* opinion? Encourage children to support their opinions with valid reasons.

5 As you near the end of your allotted discussion time, invite children who have not participated to add their thoughts to the conversation. You might say: If you have not shared your thoughts, please share them with us now. You may have a different way to look at this text.

6 Summarize one or two of the most important points discussed. Reviewing the conversation for children in this way will help strengthen their new or revised understandings about the text.

Rationale

Whole Class Discussion provides an opportunity for the class to collaborate together. Thoughtful conversations about texts and topics provide opportunities for children to expand their oral vocabulary as they interact socially with their classmates. Engaging children in Whole Class Discussions allows them to share their own ideas and respond to each other's ideas. Whole Class Discussions result in a collective knowledge about texts and topics, repairing children's misinterpretations.

Implementing for Success

Use the following suggestions to guide children as they become familiar with the Whole Class Discussion Routine:

- Set a five-minute time limit for the class discussion.
- State a specific focus for the discussion to help children respond in appropriate ways. If children get off topic, restate the discussion focus.
- Model these best practices for speaking and listening, and have children use them in their Whole Class Discussions:
    - Refer to the text or topic during the discussion.
    - Build on the conversations of others.
    - Ask and answer questions about key details stated by a partner to clarify understanding of what was said.
    - Produce complete sentences and speak clearly when expressing thoughts, feelings, and ideas.

Practice by engaging children in Whole Class Discussions throughout the day about a variety of topics.

Going Deeper

Once children are familiar with the routine:

- Ask children to restate what the previous participant said before adding their own thoughts to the discussion.
- Encourage higher-level thinking by asking children follow-up questions to their responses.

Small Group Discussion Routine

THE ROUTINE

1. Introduce the Small Group Discussion Routine to children. Here is an example: You are going to work together with a few other children to talk about the text we just read. I will give you a question or two to think about and discuss. Each of you will have a role to play in your group.

2. Remind children of the rules for discussions, such as listening to others with care and speaking one at a time (taking turns). Then organize children into groups of three or four. Grouping can be in the form of ability grouping, interest grouping, or random grouping.

3. For successful Small Group Discussions, have children sit in a circle so that they can see and hear each other. Have them establish eye contact.

4. Introduce Small Group Discussion roles. These roles encourage all children to be active participants in the group. Group roles may include:
   - **Group Organizer:** introduces the task and keeps the group on target
   - **Clarifier:** restates what a group member has said to clarify and confirm
   - **Elaborator:** follows up with questions after a group member shares a response
   - **Reporter:** reports about the overall group discussion

5. Pose an open-ended question to ensure an engaging conversation. If the question relates to a text, remind children to find evidence to support their answers. Tasks may include using the text and a graphic organizer to record their thinking.

6. State parameters, such as: Talk in your groups for the next 10 minutes.

7. As group members take turns responding to the discussion question or the task outlined, remind them to respond appropriately. For example: I agree with you. I thought something similar when ____. or I don't agree with you because I remember reading ____.

8. Stop by each group to monitor children's conversations. If children aren't engaged in rich discussion, offer conversation prompts. For example: Show me the part of the text that supports your opinion. or Tell me about the character. What words does the author use to describe the character?

9. As the end of the allotted time nears, remind children of the task. Encourage the Reporter to rehearse what he or she will say.

Rationale

Small Group Discussion provides a supportive and safe structure for groups of three or four children. Small Group Discussions allow individuals to practice and expand their oral vocabulary as they engage in thoughtful conversations about topics or texts. Children collaborate with classmates in an intimate setting, allowing all group members to be actively involved.

Implementing for Success

Use the following suggestions to guide children as they become familiar with the Small Group Discussion Routine:

- Set a time limit for the Small Group Discussion and for children to add their thoughts.
- State a clear focus for the Small Group Discussion.
- Model these best practices for speaking and listening, and have children use them in their Small Group Discussions:
    - Build on the conversations of others.
    - Ask and answer questions about key details stated by a classmate to clarify understanding of what was said.
    - Produce complete sentences and speak clearly when you express your thoughts, feelings, and ideas.

Engage children in Small Group Discussions often. Discussions may revolve around subject matter, classroom situations, or literature. Provide feedback as children participate.

Going Deeper

Once children are familiar with the routine:

- Add a Fact Checker to the roles of a small group. Have the Fact Checker flag text evidence as children share text details in their responses.
- With the children, brainstorm a list of questions that the Elaborator might ask during group discussions. For example: What made you think that? What more can you tell us about that event?

Read Aloud Routine

THE ROUTINE

1. Introduce the Read Aloud Routine to children. Here is an example: I'm going to read aloud this text. Your job is to listen carefully for where this story takes place and how the author describes the setting. I'll stop from time to time for us to talk about what I've read.

2. Gather the group in a comfortable, intimate setting. If possible, gather where children can partake in the visual aspects of the text as well as hear you easily.

3. Before reading the text aloud, explore the text with children. Provide a synopsis of the text. Explain the genre. Give children knowledge that they may need to understand before hearing the text read to them, such as: This text is broken into different parts. Each part will tell us about a fruit or vegetable. Suggestions for exploring the text are found in the teaching lessons.

4. During the Read Aloud, stop briefly to monitor children's understanding of the text. Engage children in brief conversations by asking questions, such as: What do we know about the main character now? You may also model your own thinking aloud. For example: I learned something new. I did not know that grasshoppers had five eyes.

5. After completing the Read Aloud, give children an opportunity to talk about the text. Ask engaging, open-ended questions that draw them back into the text. For example: In what part of the book did we learn about pumpkin plants? or How did Alex react when his grandma surprised him? Ask questions to confirm understanding, such as: What happened in this part? You could also model how to clarify understanding. For example: I was a bit confused in this part of the book. I'm glad I continued to read on. The next page helped me understand Uncle Ron's reaction.

Rationale

Read Aloud opportunities provide children with the chance to listen to a proficient reader model fluent reading. When children have the opportunity to listen to texts being read to them, they can focus solely on listening to the message and language of the text. Children are free to listen and take in new vocabulary that often goes beyond the scope of what they would use in most oral language conversations.

As you plan for a Read Aloud, decide on the focus. Read Alouds are excellent opportunities to expand children's vocabulary and can consistently be used for teaching new words and concepts. Additionally, the focus could be to expand children's knowledge of subject content, to follow the development of a character, or to determine the structure of a text. Also, plan for places in the text that provide natural stopping points for brief, text-based discussions.

Implementing for Success

Use the following suggestions to guide children as they become familiar with the Read Aloud Routine:

- State a clear focus for the Read Aloud.
- Identify key words in the text for children to listen for, and ask them if they can figure out what the author means by these words.
- Remind children to listen carefully to the text being read aloud.
- Model how to refer back to the text as you stop for brief conversations.

Engage children in Read Alouds often. Read Alouds can be as quick as reading a poem or as long as 15 minutes to engage in a rich piece of literature.

Going Deeper

Once children are familiar with the routine, encourage higher-level thinking. Ask children questions that require them to think specifically about the text or make connections to other texts. For example: *In what ways does the main character remind you of a character in another book?*

Shared Reading Routine

THE ROUTINE

1. Introduce the Shared Reading Routine. For example: *We're going to read this text together. As we read, your role will be to follow along and help me with the character dialogue. As we read, let's look for words or phrases the author uses to describe the characters.*

2. You may gather the group in a comfortable, intimate setting to promote a sense of working together through the text.

3. During the Shared Reading, point out print conventions. Besides unlocking text meaning, this is an opportunity to model how text works. For example, reading from top to bottom and left to right, navigating text features, and attending to punctuation.

4. Stop briefly to monitor children's understanding of the text. Engage children in brief conversations by asking questions, such as: *What is something new that you learned?* or *Where does this story take place?* Model your own thinking aloud, helping children understand how a proficient reader navigates text and overcomes challenges. Upon subsequent similar challenges, invite children to model their thinking. This allows you to assess children's understanding of what you previously modeled and their abilities to overcome challenges as they read.

5. After completing the Shared Reading, discuss the text's overall meaning or main idea. Then ask open-ended questions that focus on more specific elements, such as setting, characters, or text structure. Have children use text evidence to support their responses.

Rationale

The Shared Reading Routine provides children with the opportunity to engage in the shared responsibilities of reading text. This opportunity falls in the middle of the gradual-release model (the instructional practice in which the responsibility starts with the teacher and is gradually transferred to the student). During Shared Reading opportunities, the teacher's role is to support children as they engage with the text.

The Shared Reading Routine is effective in a whole class or small group setting. The text is usually familiar to children but provides some language or text structure challenges. The familiarity provides comfort as children tackle the text challenges. Determine what opportunities you will take to demonstrate effective reading strategies.

Implementing for Success

Use the following suggestions to guide children as they become familiar with the Shared Reading Routine:

- State a clear focus.
- Remind children that you are reading the text together, so they are active readers along with you.
- As children unpack key vocabulary, encourage them to think aloud about how they come to understand that vocabulary. Model appropriate strategies, such as using illustrations and context clues, reading on, or rereading to understand the terms.
- As children respond to the text, remind them to listen to one another carefully. Then they may state their opinions and support them with reasons and text evidence.

Engage children in Shared Reading opportunities during all subject-matter lessons to give them the experience of engaging in more challenging text in a highly supported way.

Going Deeper

Once children are familiar with the routine:

- Have pairs discuss their "Aha!" moments as they read the text.
- Provide them with an open-ended question to discuss.

Independent Reading Routine

THE ROUTINE

1. Launch the Independent Reading Routine with the class. For example: Independent Reading provides a time for you to choose books or other materials *you* want to read. These texts should help you to practice some of the things we have talked about during our reading lessons. The texts should be interesting to you, but they should not be too easy or too hard. For more information about how to introduce Focused Independent Reading to children, see the Implementing for Success section on pp. TR14–TR15.

2. Monitor children as they choose their Independent Reading texts. Assist individuals in finding appropriate materials as needed. For more information about how to guide children in self-selecting texts, see the Implementing for Success section on pp. TR14–TR15.

3. Announce and display the Process Focus and Strategy Focus for the day. Define them in a way children can understand and give examples to illustrate their meanings. Some definitions and examples are provided in the chart below. Remind children that they should apply *both* focus points to their self-selected texts.

PROCESS FOCUS	DEFINITION	EXAMPLE
Engagement and Identity	developing and self-assessing one's reading preferences and behaviors	Children select familiar or preferred texts.
Stamina	sustaining one's reading over time	Children read for a period of time.
Independence	reading without assistance	Children reread familiar texts without help.
Community (see the **Text Club Routine** on pp. TR20–TR23)	participating in collaborative conversations about texts	Children talk about texts in groups and share with the class.

STRATEGY FOCUS	DEFINITION	EXAMPLE
Vocabulary Knowledge	related to the lesson's Benchmark Vocabulary or Language Analysis instruction	Children apply vocabulary and language strategies to read new words and navigate text.
Decoding and Word Recognition	related to the lesson's Foundational Skills instruction	Children recognize high-frequency words and apply phonics strategies to decode new words.
Fluency	reading steadily without starts and stops	Children read familiar texts smoothly.
Critical Thinking	applying higher-order thinking skills to texts	Children examine what they read and make connections.
Comprehension	related to the lesson's Reading or Language Analysis instruction	Children apply text-analysis strategies to understand what they read.

4 Once children have selected their Independent Reading texts and have a clear understanding of the focus points, they should find a comfortable place in the room and begin reading.

5 For Independent Reading accountability, confer with 2–3 children to discuss their self-selected reading. Ask probing questions to assess whether they are reading appropriately leveled texts. Remember that Independent Reading is an opportunity for children to practice what they have learned with texts they can handle. It is not a time for them to face significant challenges on their own. Also, ask children open-ended questions to determine whether they understand what they are reading and to gauge their progress with the day's focus points.

6 At the end of Independent Reading time, call on volunteers to share what they read or what they learned from their reading.

Independent Reading Routine

Rationale

Independent Reading is reading that children do on their own using self-selected texts. By empowering children to choose texts that correspond to their own reading levels and personal interests, Independent Reading builds motivation, engagement, and stamina. It also helps children develop key literacy skills—such as word recognition, decoding, vocabulary, fluency, comprehension, and content knowledge—by providing opportunities to apply what they learn in the reading lessons to texts of their own choosing. As children's reading abilities improve over time, so will their facility with increasingly complex texts.

Providing regular opportunities for children to read independently is an essential part of daily reading instruction. The whole-group reading lessons provide models of proficient reading and engage children in rich conversations about text. Children then transfer understandings from those experiences to their own reading through the Focused Independent Reading lesson and the Independent Reading Routine.

Implementing for Success

To prepare for Independent Reading:

- Ensure your classroom library contains texts that address a wide range of reading levels, interests, authors, and genres.

To introduce Focused Independent Reading to children:

- Explain that it is an important part of their reading instruction.
- Emphasize that it is an opportunity to choose texts *they* wish to read.
- Explain that they will read their chosen texts and examine them in different ways. Doing so will help them gain knowledge, pleasure, and skills from the reading experience.
- Point out that independent reading occurs at the same time as small group instruction. Since you will be busy working with small groups or conferring with individuals, teach children how to help themselves while you are unavailable. For example, they could ask a classmate for assistance or wait until you are moving between groups.

To guide children in self-selecting texts, encourage them to ask themselves the following questions. Model asking and answering these questions through a think-aloud.

- Do the cover, title, and pictures seem interesting?
- What do you think this text is about? Do you want to read about the people and places in it?
- Look inside the text. Do the words look "just right"—not too easy and not too hard? Use the Five-Finger Rule: Read the second page. Hold up one finger for each word you don't know or are unsure of. If you hold up more than five fingers, the book is probably too hard.

During Independent Reading:

- Children will read self-selected texts, concentrate on the two focus points for the day, and connect their texts to key ideas in the module or unit.
- Teachers will lead small group instruction, assess oral reading fluency, monitor and support **Text Clubs** (see pp. TR20–TR23) and other reading activities, and confer with individuals to gauge their reading progress (see the **Independent Reading Rubric** and **Independent Reading Continuum** on pp. TR16–TR18).

Going Deeper

Once children are comfortable with the Routine:

- Encourage them to read texts of greater complexity, about different topics, and in a wide variety of genres.
- Ask them to reflect on their reading through drawing, writing, or the **Independent Reading Log** (see p. TR19).
- Give them opportunities to talk about their reading with classmates in **Text Clubs** (see pp. TR20–TR23).

Independent Reading Rubric

ENGAGEMENT AND IDENTITY Developing and self-assessing one's reading preferences and behaviors

DATE	EMERGING	DEVELOPING	ADVANCING	AVID
	Reluctant to read; does not view self as a reader	Reads if required; selects favorite texts that may lack sufficient challenge	Enjoys reading; is developing text preferences	Eager to read and share texts; conscious of personal preferences

STAMINA Sustaining one's reading over time

DATE	EMERGING	DEVELOPING	ADVANCING	AVID
	Unable to read for a period of time; is easily distracted	Struggles to sustain reading over time; may be distracted by others	Reads for the allotted time with eyes on text	Would continue reading beyond allotted time

INDEPENDENCE Reading without assistance

DATE	EMERGING	DEVELOPING	ADVANCING	AVID
	Needs considerable help to progress through texts	Progresses through famliar texts; needs help with new texts	May need help with new texts or challenging sections of text	Rarely needs help

VOCABULARY KNOWLEDGE Related to the lesson's Benchmark Vocabulary or Language Analysis instruction

DATE	EMERGING	DEVELOPING	ADVANCING	AVID
	Struggles to read many of the words in a text; has difficulty navigating text	Reads most words in a text with support; navigates through familiar texts	Reads the words in a text with little or no support; navigates through texts	Reads and understands the words in a text; navigates through texts well

DECODING AND WORD RECOGNITION Related to the lesson's Foundational Skills instruction

DATE	EMERGING	DEVELOPING	ADVANCING	AVID
	Struggles to recognize high-frequency words; skips new words	Recognizes high-frequency words; is beginning to decode new words with guidance	Reads high-frequency words; applies lesson to help decode new words	Reads high-frequency words and new words accurately

FLUENCY Reading steadily without starts and stops

DATE	EMERGING	DEVELOPING	ADVANCING	AVID
	Reads haltingly; often needs cues; is easily frustrated	Reads at a slow pace; may need cues; may become frustrated	Reads steadily at a slow pace; may need cues	Reads familiar texts smoothly

CRITICAL THINKING Applying higher-order thinking skills to texts

DATE	EMERGING	DEVELOPING	ADVANCING	AVID
	Has great difficulty examining texts; does not ask questions about texts	Examines texts with guidance; is beginning to ask questions about texts	Examines texts; asks basic questions about texts	Examines texts; makes connections; asks questions about texts

COMPREHENSION Related to the lesson's Reading or Language Analysis instruction

DATE	EMERGING	DEVELOPING	ADVANCING	AVID
	Struggles to understand self-selected texts; has difficulty answering questions about texts	Understands self-selected texts with support; is beginning to answer questions about texts	Uses lesson to help understand self-selected texts; answers basic questions about texts	Understands self-selected texts; answers questions about texts

Independent Reading Continuum

GRADES	ENGAGEMENT & IDENTITY	STAMINA	INDEPENDENCE	VOCABULARY KNOWLEDGE	FLUENCY	CRITICAL THINKING	COMPREHENSION
K–1	Explores familiar texts; chooses texts matching interests; identifies favorite texts; sets one reading goal	Reads (through pictures and/or words) in increments of 5–15 minutes; reads longer with multiple texts	Engages with texts read aloud; reads familiar texts independently and unfamiliar ones with assistance	Recognizes familiar words; reads around new words	Rereads familiar texts multiple times for smoothness	Makes basic text-to-self connections; asks text-dependent questions	Demonstrates basic understanding of text read; responds to text-dependent questions
2–3	Chooses texts at independent and instructional levels; tries unfamiliar texts; identifies favorite authors and genres and why they are favorites; chooses texts that match level and interests; sets basic reading goals	Reads in sustained increments of 15–30 minutes; reads longer with multiple texts	Reads familiar texts and ones at independent and instructional levels on own; reads challenging texts with assistance	Applies knowledge of phonics and language to work through new words	Rereads familiar texts for smoothness; reads texts somewhat evenly on first try	Makes text-to-text and text-to-world connections; asks inferential questions	Demonstrates understanding of text's story or topic; responds to inferential questions
4–5	Reads new texts of challenging level or interest; discusses texts; recommends texts to others; identifies and self-assesses own reading behaviors; sets reading goals	Reads in sustained increments of 30 minutes or more; gets "lost" in the reading	Reads a variety of text types at different levels without assistance	Applies word-analysis strategies and content knowledge to tackle new words	Reads familiar and unfamiliar texts smoothly and at a consistent pace throughout	Makes high-level connections across texts and contexts; asks beyond-the-text questions; evaluates texts based on success of author's purpose	Demonstrates understanding of text's theme or purpose; responds to beyond-the-text questions

Independent Reading Log

Name ____________________

Date and Minutes	Title	What I Read About Today	Enjoyment	What I Will Do Tomorrow
____ date ____ minutes			__ I love this! __ I like this. __ I do not like this.	
____ date ____ minutes			__ I love this! __ I like this. __ I do not like this.	
____ date ____ minutes			__ I love this! __ I like this. __ I do not like this.	
____ date ____ minutes			__ I love this! __ I like this. __ I do not like this.	
____ date ____ minutes			__ I love this! __ I like this. __ I do not like this.	

Text Club Routine

THE ROUTINE

1. Introduce children to Text Clubs. For example: During Text Club time, you will work with your classmates to read and talk about books and other texts. You will read a text. Then you will meet with your Text Club to talk about it. Every group member will have a different job to do.

2. Define, model, and assign Text Club roles to children. Sample roles include:
   - **Leader:** leads the group's discussion and keeps everyone on task
   - **Word Wizard:** writes down new or important words from the text
   - **Questioner:** poses questions about the text for the group to discuss
   - **Recorder:** records answers to the questions discussed in the group
   - **Illustrator:** draws pictures to describe the text or clarify the group's ideas, thoughts, or feelings

3. Assign children to Text Clubs and preview the texts they will read. Be sure to include a variety of text levels so that all children may be successful. Each group member should have a copy of the text.

4. Children read the text. Initially, you may wish to have them read as a group with their Text Clubs. Children can preview the text on their own first and then move into their groups to read and discuss. Depending on their abilities, children should eventually be able to read the text independently.

5. Children meet in their Text Clubs and carry out their assigned roles. As they discuss, sit down with each group to assess children's comprehension. Encourage them to ask each other questions to clear up confusion, get additional information, or clarify something they do not understand. Help them build the conversation through multiple exchanges by responding to each other's comments. If needed, model such an exchange for the group. For example:

   (child 1) How did the main character feel at the beginning of the book?
   (child 2) He felt sad because he didn't have any friends.
   (child 1) He was lonely. I would have felt lonely too.
   (child 2) Me too, but I felt happy later on.
   (child 1) Why?
   (child 2) Because then he made friends.

6. Have members of each Text Club share what they read and discussed in their groups with the class. For example, they may act out a story, describe in detail what the text was about, or clearly express the group's ideas or feelings about the text. Remind children to speak in complete sentences using standard English.

7. Debrief with each Text Club. Ask children to reflect on how successful they were in examining the text as a group. Have them think about their discussions and record their thoughts by writing or drawing in a reading journal or notebook.

Text Club Routine

Rationale

Text Clubs provide a flexible format in which four to six children become part of a temporary reading community with their peers. The groups are fluid and can be formed in a variety of ways, with each variation centering on a different aspect of reading and including a different grouping of children. Text Clubs provide opportunities for children to read and discuss texts with classmates of varying abilities. By working together in this way, children develop an understanding of different text types and gain practice in participating in group discussions.

Implementing for Success

To prepare for Text Clubs:

- Determine the aspect of reading around which the Text Clubs will be formed, such as topic, character, setting, or plot sequence. Choose different aspects over the course of the year.
- Consider the reading abilities and interests of children. It is important to gather sets of texts that will allow all readers to be successful.
- Model how to participate in conversations about texts through read alouds and shared discussions. Children are more likely to succeed with Text Cubs if they have had experience with collaborative text discussions.
- Determine the groups and roles to which you will assign children. Be sure to vary the assignments throughout the year.

During Text Clubs:

- Make sure children understand their assigned roles. Display role definitions to ensure children know what to do and how to complete their respective tasks.
- Remind children to follow the rules for discussions, such as listening to others with care and speaking one at a time about the topic or text.

Going Deeper

Once children are comfortable with the Routine, choose from the following activities to help them explore Text Clubs more deeply:

- Ask children to reread the same text with the same Text Club members but take on different roles in the group. Doing so will allow children to experience the text from different perspectives.
- Have children from each group "jigsaw" with children from other groups to share an element of the text they read. This engages all children in all texts being read in the class.

Benchmark Vocabulary Routine: Informational

THE ROUTINE

1. Introduce the Benchmark Vocabulary Routine for Informational Text to children. For example: As we read informational text, we will come across words that we have not seen or heard before. Sometimes the author gives us the meaning of the words right in the text. Other times we might have to read on to understand what a new word means, or we might have to look at a diagram in the text to understand the word.

2. Write or display the sentence or passage containing the new word. Say the word aloud, and have children repeat the word. Use the word in another sentence, providing children with a similar context in which to hear the word used. For example, "Leaves sprout on the trees" is found in the text. You might share this sentence: Young plants sprout from the ground.

3. If there are context clues to help establish the meaning of the word, have children share those. Help children understand how the word relates to other words. For example, in *Supermarket* by Kathleen Krull, the text states, "Behind all the eggs, milk, yogurt, and cheese is a refrigerated area keeping everything cold." The word *refrigerated* is defined further on in the sentence with the words *keeping everything cold*. Point out that *refrigerated* is similar to the word *refrigerator,* which most children are likely familiar with.

4. If the word is boldface in the text, show children how to find the glossary in the book and read the glossary definition aloud. If not, you might want to look the word up in a children's dictionary. However, be aware that sometimes definitions of technical words are not helpful if children do not have some foundational knowledge regarding the concept.

5. Create a semantic map with children. This helps children see and make connections between the unknown word and known words and/or concepts.

6. Encourage children to refer to the semantic map to help them use the word in a sentence. They can turn to a partner and have a quick one-minute conversation using the word. Have volunteers share their sentences with the class so that you are better able to assess children's understanding.

7. As children develop their conceptual vocabularies, point out opportunities for them to use new terms when writing in response to informational text.

Rationale

Informational texts provide opportunities for children to develop subject-matter concepts and build connections between words that are unique to those concepts. Children must be taught needed vocabulary so that they can understand the text, and strategies so that they can determine word and phrase meanings. As children build their subject-matter vocabulary, it is important that they can call on their understandings of affixes, inflected endings, and root words, as well as learn to derive meaning from text information, such as pictures, charts, and context. This generative approach to vocabulary instruction empowers children to apply knowledge of how words work when they encounter new words in complex texts.

In informational texts, some of the critical vocabulary is more technical. Readers have a greater challenge comprehending specialized vocabulary because the words rarely have synonyms and they represent new and complex concepts. Children are less able to use their background knowledge to help comprehend specific text. It is important to provide children with opportunities to experiment with and develop conceptual vocabularies so that they move through the grades with a foundation of such words.

Consider providing opportunities for children to engage with the vocabulary through experimentations as well as conversations. This can lead to deeper understanding and correct usage of terms. Rigorous vocabulary instruction helps children expand their domain-specific vocabularies.

Tips and Tools

TERMS TO KNOW

affix An affix is a word part, either a prefix or a suffix, that changes the function or meaning of a word root or stem. For example, paint/repaint; friend/friendly; excite/excitement.

inflectional ending An inflectional ending expresses a plural or possessive form of a noun, the tense of a verb, or the comparative or superlative form of an adjective or adverb. For example, *dogs/dog's; skipping/skipped; faster/fastest.*

root word A root word is a word that can't be broken into smaller words. For example, *port*, meaning "carry," is the root word of *report, portable,* and *transport.*

Benchmark Vocabulary Routine: Informational

Implementing for Success

Use the following suggestions to guide children as they become familiar with the Benchmark Vocabulary Routine for Informational Text:

- Pronounce the new word and then have children repeat it two times. Read aloud the passage in which the word is found.
- Discuss the word's meaning through context clues, text features, a glossary, or a children's dictionary.
- Create a semantic map of the word so that children see the connections between the word and related words. Have children use the map to create sentences and internalize the word.

As children engage in Benchmark Vocabulary discussions, their word knowledge will grow. The more words children know, the more words they can read and understand in text and use in their speaking and writing. In addition, the more children know about how words work in texts, the more they will increase their ability to comprehend complex content-area texts by applying this knowledge when encountering new words.

Tips and Tools

Word Maps

Semantic mapping is a word-mapping strategy to engage children in thinking about and discussing word relationships within a set of connected concepts and ideas. Using a graphic organizer, the ideas most central to a concept are displayed closest to the main topic, and details are added and linkages are formed to display interconnectedness within the concept. There is no perfect or "correct" semantic map. You may wish to adapt either the Web A or Web B graphic organizer, as in this example.

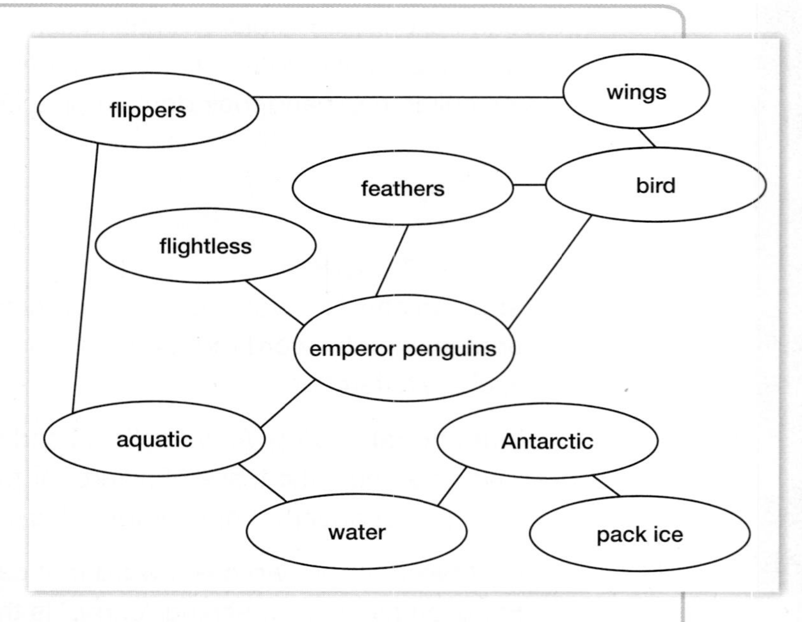

Going Deeper

Once children are familiar with the routine:

- As you read an informational text, sort specialized words into categories to create connections for children. For example, a book about seasons includes words such as *autumn, spring, summer,* and *winter,* which you can use as categories. Within each season, there are words specific to that category, such as *harvest, bloom, humid,* and *snow.*
- Have children create word poems. They may draw a meaningful shape to represent the new word and then list words that connect to it around the outline of the shape. For example, an outline of the sun might have the words *rays, heat, bright,* and *star* around it. An outline of a camel might have the words *desert, hot, sand,* and *hump* around it.

Tips and Tools

Teaching Tip

Children are often challenged by the vocabulary of informational texts because the words are unfamiliar and represent complex concepts. By creating word maps, children have access to a visual network of words that leads them to see how ideas are connected. Teaching words as a network of ideas, teaching word parts, teaching examples and non-examples related to a new word, and helping children connect new vocabulary and their prior knowledge are strategies that foster understanding of how words work and prepare children to unlock meaning as they read increasingly complex texts.

Benchmark Vocabulary Routine: Literary

THE ROUTINE

1. Introduce the Benchmark Vocabulary Routine for Literary Text to children. For example: As we read narrative text, we will come across words that we have not seen before. Authors often give us clues to understand those words. Sometimes we need to look closely at the new word and break it into word parts. Sometimes we need to look in a children's dictionary for the definition of the word. Let's look at how words work.

2. Write or display the sentence or passage containing the unfamiliar word. Break the word into syllables and pronounce it. Have children repeat the word and share context clues about its meaning. This brings children back into the text. Help children understand the part of speech of the word in question. For example: *Snug* is a describing word. We call it an adjective.

3. Model looking up the word in a children's dictionary and then read a simple definition. Relate the meaning to its use in the text to ensure comprehension. For example: *Snug* can mean "providing physical comfort; comfortable" or "firmly positioned in place and difficult to dislodge; tight." The use of *snug* in the first sentence fits the first definition: "He had felt safe and snug in his shell." The use of *snug* in the second sentence ("But now it was too snug.") fits the second definition. Now the word *snug* means that Hermit Crab's shell is tight, not that he is too comfortable in his shell.

4. Use the word in other ways; for example: After washing and drying my sweater, it was snug on me. Then discuss the word in more depth. For example: Why do you think Eric Carle used *snug* instead of *tight* to explain Hermit Crab's shell?

5. Help children list synonyms for the word. Then compare and contrast the word with those synonyms. How is *tight* different from *snug?* How is *comfortable* different from *snug?*

6. Encourage children to practice using the word in a sentence. They can turn to a partner and have a quick one-minute conversation using the word. Have volunteers share their sentences with the class so that you may assess children's understanding.

7. As their word knowledge expands, guide children to carefully consider word choice and nuances in word meaning as they incorporate new vocabulary when writing in response to literary text.

Rationale

As children develop their oral and written vocabularies, they will encounter many words that they have not read before or used in their oral language. It is imperative to help children understand strategies to address and comprehend new vocabulary in texts. Children need to learn foundational skills in letter-sound knowledge and develop an understanding of the complexities of affixes, inflected endings, root words, and multiple-meaning words. Children need to recognize the features and functions of words and begin making connections among words. This generative approach to vocabulary instruction will enable them to unlock the meanings of unknown words as they are presented with increasingly complex texts.

In narratives, vocabulary may center on categories of words, such as motivations, traits, emotions, actions, movement, communication, and character names. The words in these categories are often new labels for known concepts. It is important to address these kinds of words so that children understand the text and how to tackle similar unique words in other literary texts.

Teaching vocabulary words with lively routines develops vocabulary and stimulates an interest in and awareness of words that children can apply in their independent reading. Also, rigorous vocabulary instruction helps children expand their oral vocabularies so that they "own" the new words.

Tips and Tools

TERMS TO KNOW

affix An affix is a word part, either a prefix or a suffix, that changes the function or meaning of a word root or stem. For example, *happy/unhappy; friend/friendly; excite/excitement.*

inflectional ending An inflectional ending expresses a plural or possessive form of a noun, the tense of a verb, or the comparative or superlative form of an adjective or adverb. For example, *dogs/dog's; skipping/skipped; faster/fastest.*

root word A root word is a word that can't be broken into smaller words. For example, *act,* meaning "do," is the root word of *action, actor,* and *react*.

Benchmark Vocabulary Routine: Literary

Implementing for Success

Use the following suggestions to guide children as they become familiar with the Benchmark Vocabulary Routine for Literary Text:

- Pronounce the new word and have children repeat it. Read aloud the passage in which the word is found.
- Discuss the word's meaning within the context. If necessary, rephrase the meaning in language that is easier for children to understand.
- Have a volunteer use the word in a sentence that is related to the passage. Then have a volunteer use the word in a new context. Talk about the different usages.
- Discuss synonyms for the word. Reread the passage, substituting synonyms for the word. Talk about why the author may have chosen that word rather than one of its synonyms.

As children engage in Benchmark Vocabulary discussions, their word knowledge will grow. The more words children know, the more words they can read and understand in text and use in their writing. In addition, the more children know about how words work in texts, the more they will be able to approach unfamiliar words with the confidence and knowledge to comprehend complex texts.

Going Deeper

Once children are familiar with the routine:

- Create word webs and post them around the room for children to refer to when they write. Add synonyms of the word, such as *comfortable* and *tight* for *snug*, or add morphological family members of the word, such as *fright* and *frighten* for *frightening*.
- Engage children in word hunts during read alouds, shared reading experiences, or independent reading time. Have them look for words that may be similar to or opposite from the featured words in the Benchmark Vocabulary instruction for the day.
- Have children suggest words to add to the classroom word wall.

Tips and Tools

Word Walls

Effective classroom word walls for literary texts are ongoing and organized around categories of words, such as motivations, traits, emotions, actions, movement, communication, and character names. As you add to the word wall, consider adding subcategories of words. For example, words that denote emotion could be further categorized as happy words, sad words, fear words, and so on. Involve children in organizing the word wall to engender rich oral vocabulary development.

TERMS TO KNOW

synonym A synonym is a word that has almost the same meaning as another word.

morpheme A morpheme is the smallest unit of meaning in a word. Morphology, or the study of word structure, explores how words are formed from morphemes. Introducing a morphological family rather than a word in isolation prepares children to make connections between words and determine word meanings.

Cause and Effect

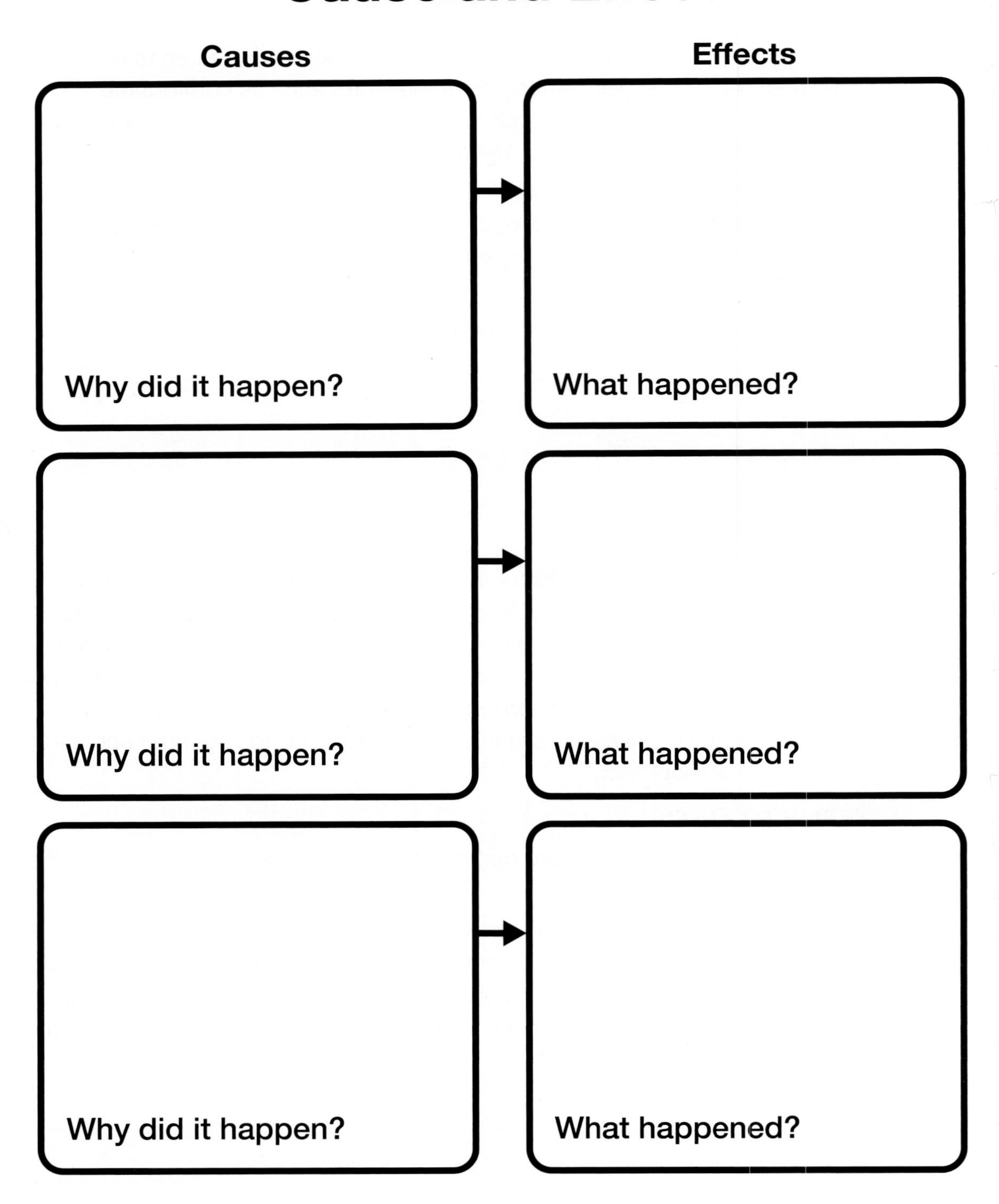

Compare and Contrast

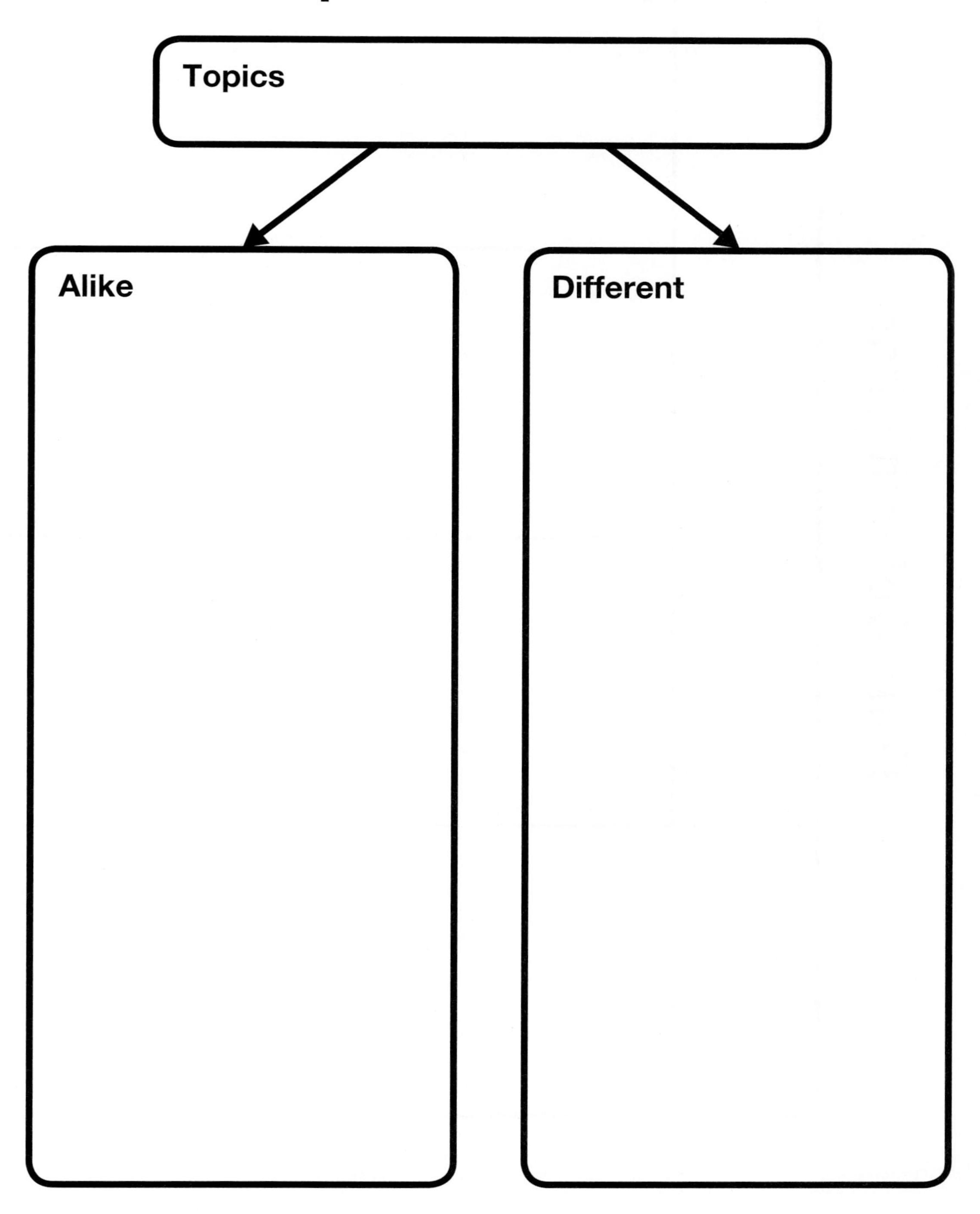

Graphic Organizers

Four-Column Chart

K-W-L Chart

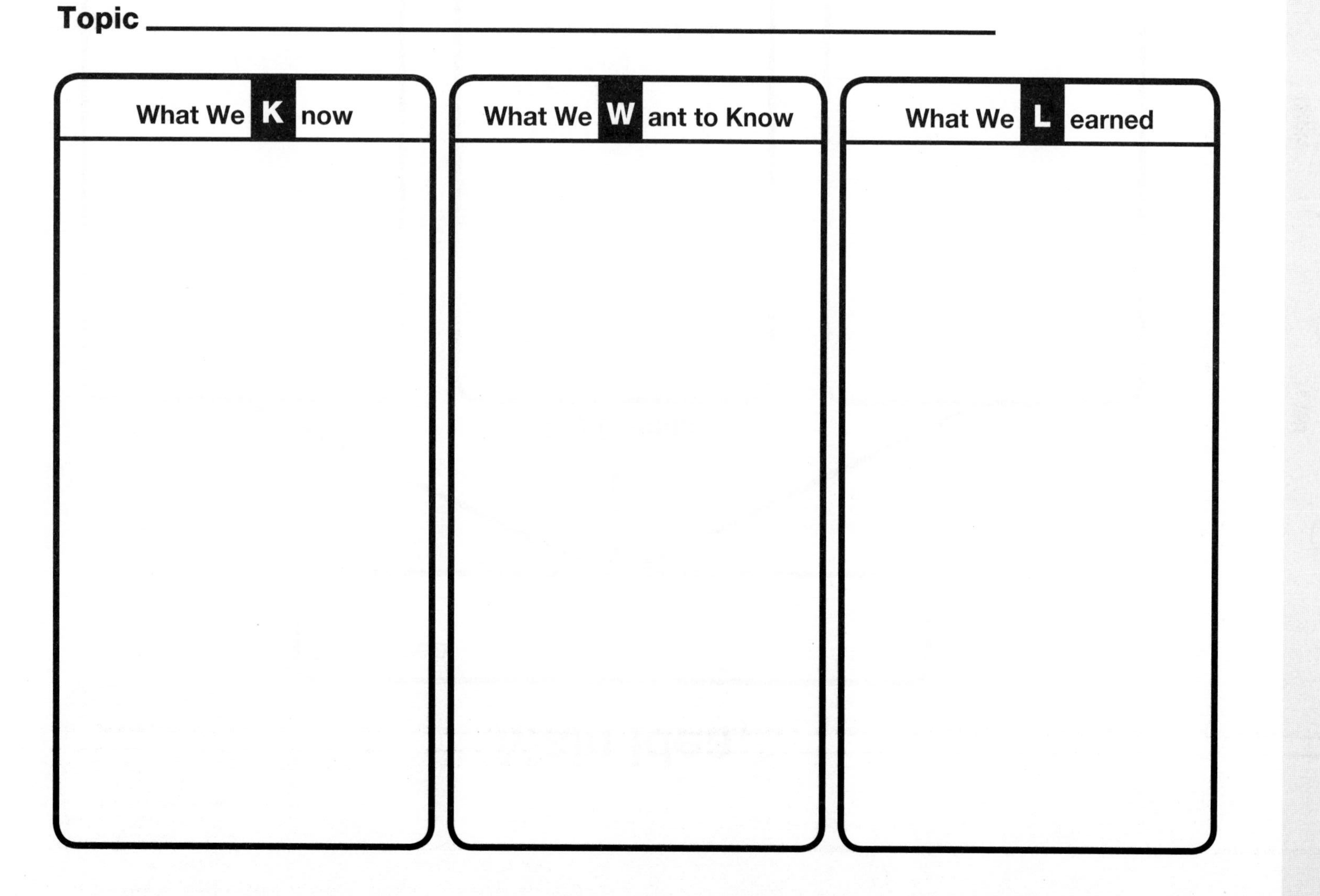

Graphic Organizers

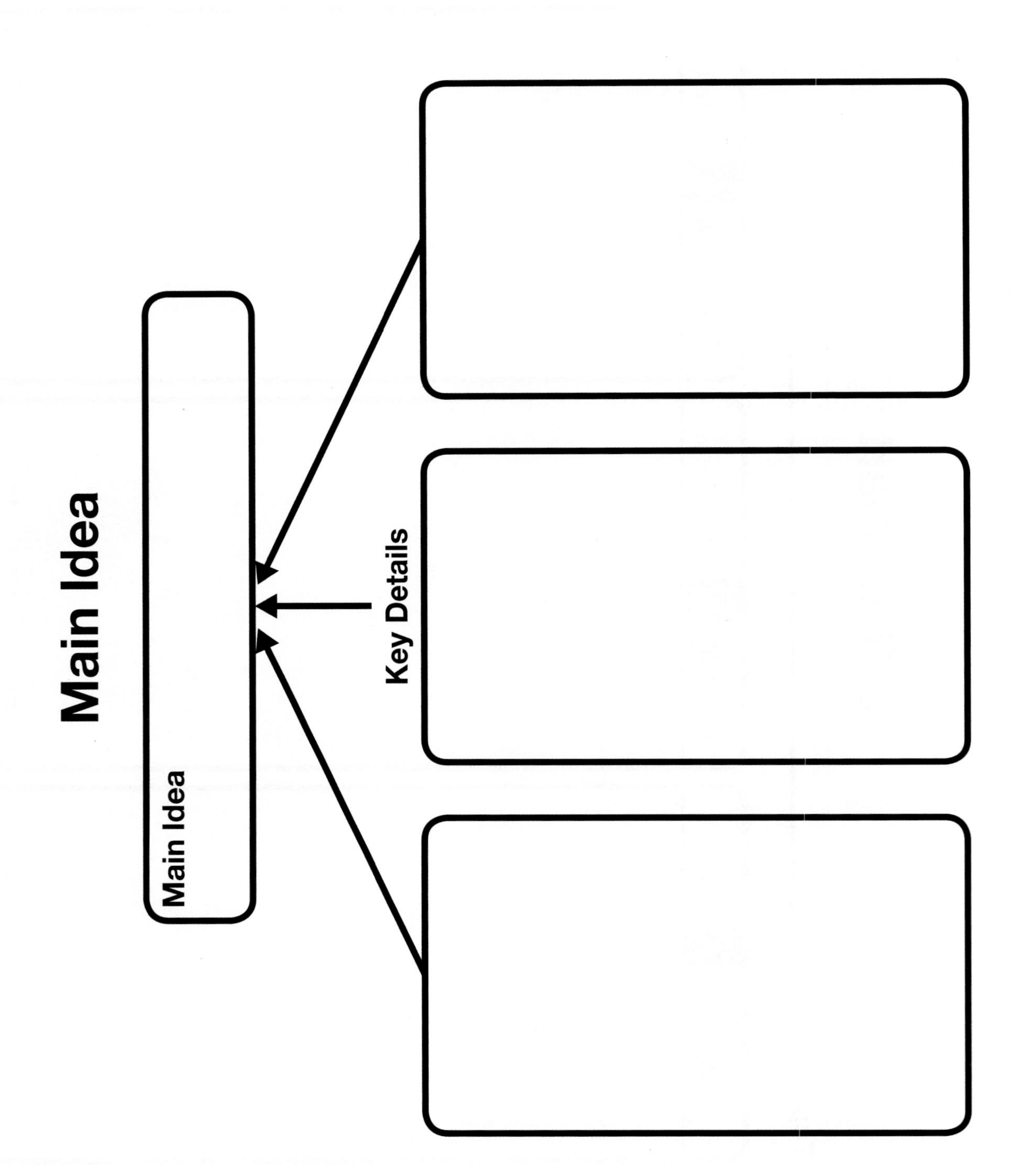

Story Sequence A

Title ______________________________

Beginning

↓

Middle

↓

End

Story Sequence B

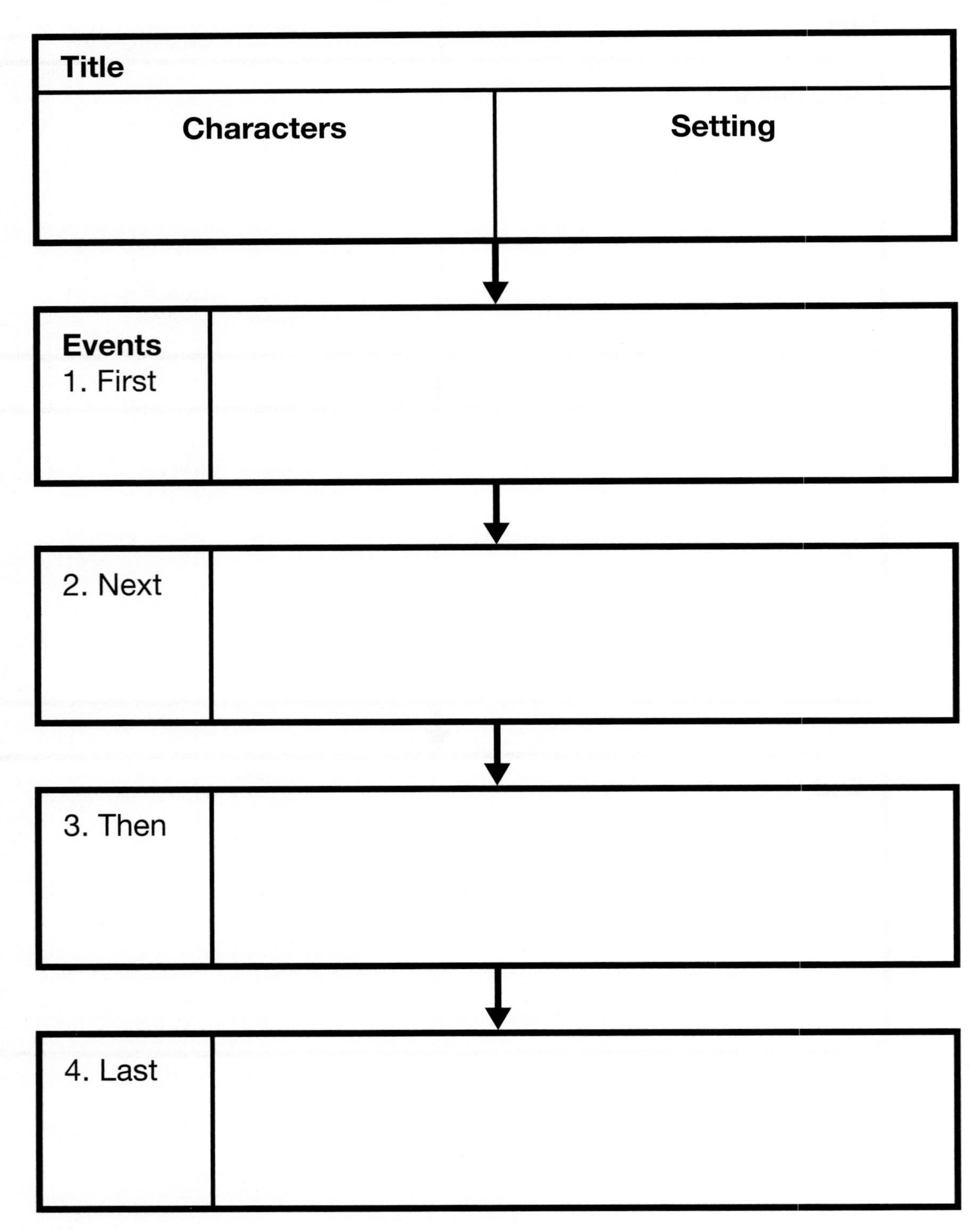

T-Chart

Three-Column Chart

Three Sorting Circles

Two Sorting Boxes

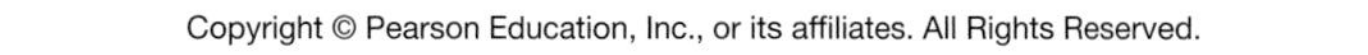

Venn Diagram

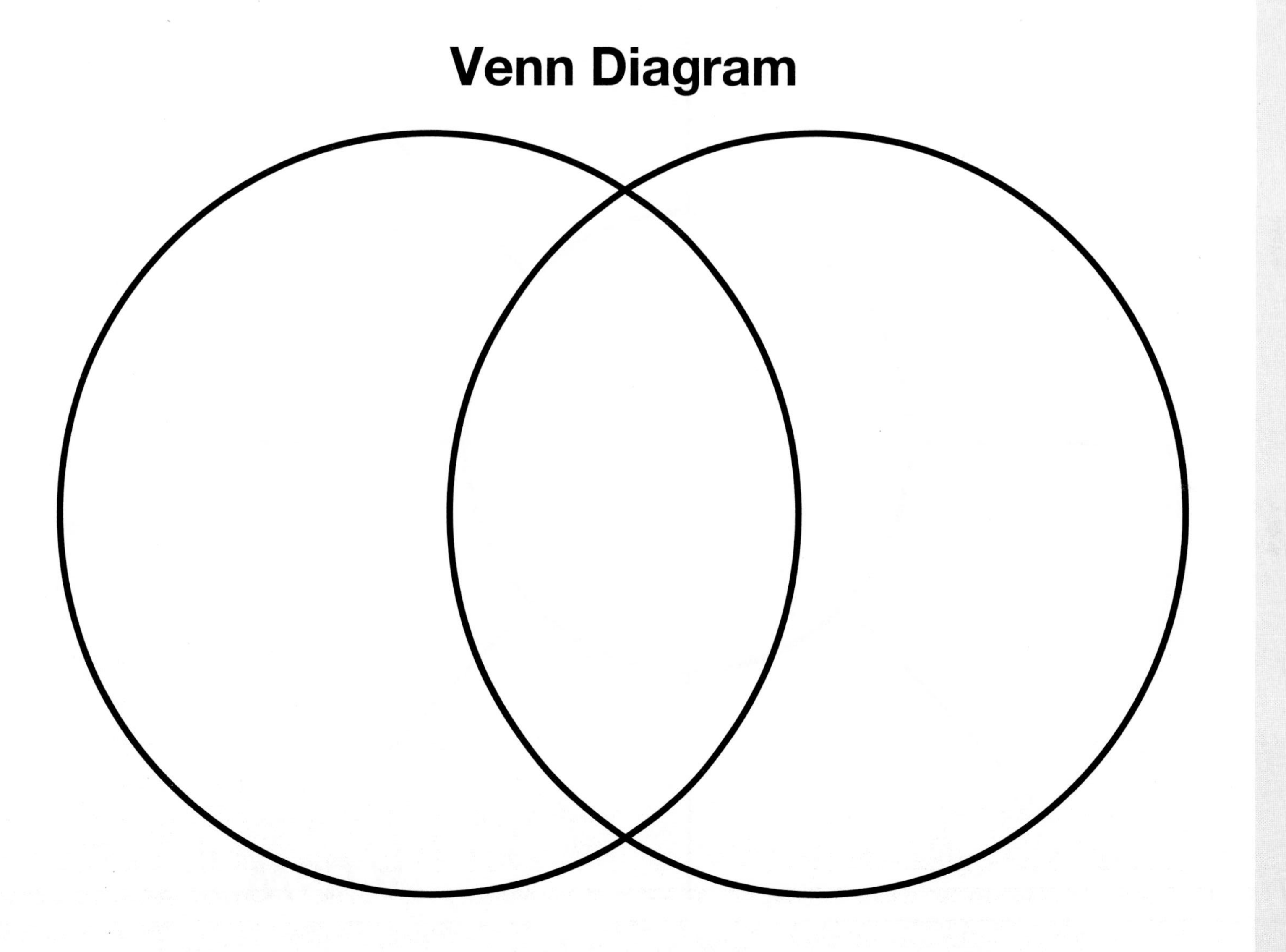

Graphic Organizers

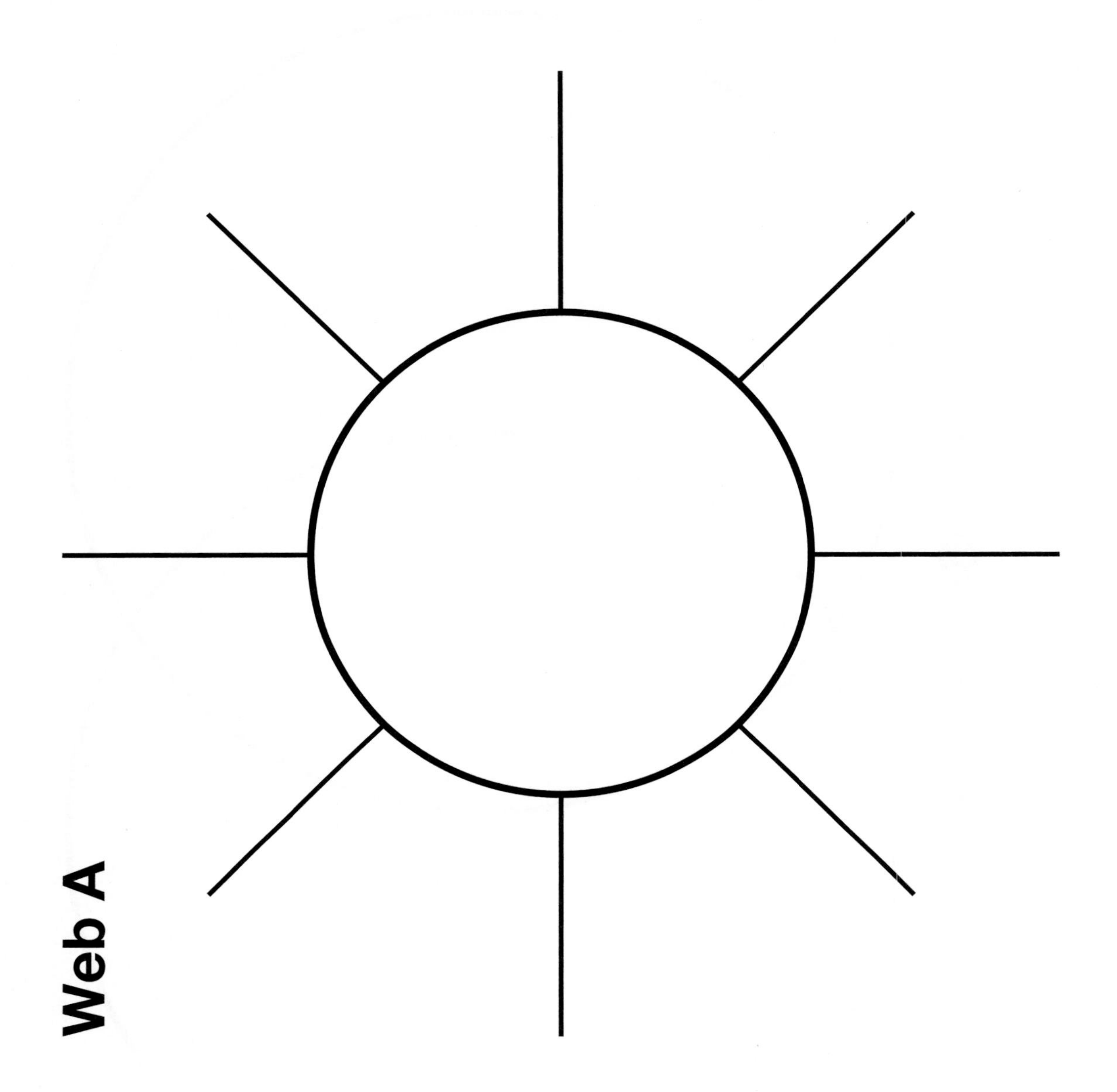

Web B

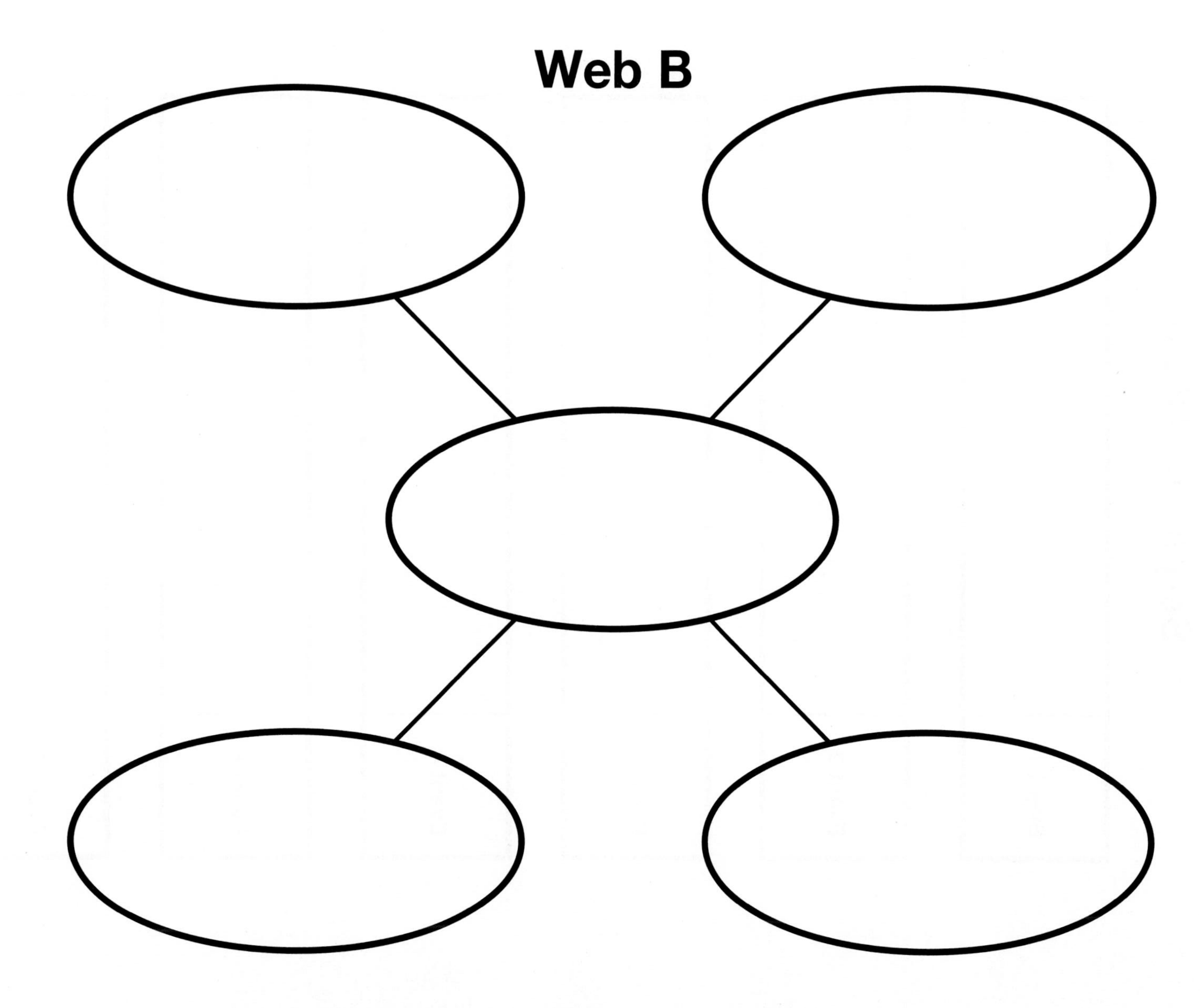

Sequence Chart

Event 1	
Event 2	
Event 3	
Event 4	
Event 5	
Event 6	

Text Complexity Rubrics

Text Complexity Measure

Use the rubric to familiarize yourself with the text complexity of ***Stellaluna***.

QUANTITATIVE MEASURES	
LEXILE	550L
AVERAGE SENTENCE LENGTH	8.03
WORD FREQUENCY	3.36
PAGE COUNT	48

QUALITATIVE MEASURES	
LEVELS OF MEANING	accessible, literal meaning about a lost bat who lives with birds for a time; more complex themes about survival through adaptation, the nature of friendship, and appreciating differences
STRUCTURE	conventional narrative structure with informational notes about bats at end
LANGUAGE CONVENTIONALITY AND CLARITY	some advanced vocabulary *(sultry)*; occasional complex and compound sentences
THEME AND KNOWLEDGE DEMANDS	some basic information about bats and birds helpful; an understanding that lessons about animals may also apply to humans

READER AND TASK SUGGESTIONS

PREPARING TO READ THE TEXT	LEVELED TASKS
Invite children to share what they know about bats and birds. Build background as needed.	Help children create a Venn diagram that compares and contrasts story information about bats and birds. Lead them to see how the animals cared for each other despite differences, and invite discussion about what humans can learn from the story.

Text Complexity Measure

Use the rubric to familiarize yourself with the text complexity of **"Dragons and Giants" from *Frog and Toad Together.***

QUANTITATIVE MEASURES	
LEXILE	460L
AVERAGE SENTENCE LENGTH	8.03
WORD FREQUENCY	3.69
WORD COUNT	313

QUALITATIVE MEASURES	
LEVELS OF MEANING	accessible concept about testing physical bravery; more subtle, inferred message about how sharing fears can be brave
STRUCTURE	conventional narrative; sequential
LANGUAGE CONVENTIONALITY AND CLARITY	mostly simple sentences with occasional compound and complex sentences
THEME AND KNOWLEDGE DEMANDS	a developing understanding that bravery can be defined in a variety of ways

READER AND TASK SUGGESTIONS	
PREPARING TO READ THE TEXT	LEVELED TASKS
Discuss with children their understandings of what it means to be brave. Invite them to name someone who is brave.	Work with children to create several definitions for the word *bravery.* Help them find and discuss pictures of people showing bravery in unconventional ways.

Text Complexity Rubrics

Text Complexity Measure

Use the rubric to familiarize yourself with the text complexity of ***Time to Sleep.***

QUANTITATIVE MEASURES	
LEXILE	140L
AVERAGE SENTENCE LENGTH	6.34
WORD FREQUENCY	3.73
PAGE COUNT	16

QUALITATIVE MEASURES	
LEVELS OF MEANING	accessible concept (how animals and people sleep); explicit main idea
STRUCTURE	main idea and key details structure organized into sections supported with illustrations and photographs; text features include contents, headings, and a picture index
LANGUAGE CONVENTIONALITY AND CLARITY	mainly simple sentences with some and complex sentences and questions; includes content-area vocabulary such as *time, sleep, bats, branches, dolphins, tuck, feathers, koalas;* some multiple-meaning words; common language
THEME AND KNOWLEDGE DEMANDS	familiarity with animals and how people sleep; the meaning of Zs in the pictures

READER AND TASK SUGGESTIONS	
PREPARING TO READ THE TEXT	LEVELED TASKS
Ask children to discuss where and when they sleep.	Turn to the picture index on p. 16. Explain to children that readers can use an index to find important information in a book. Model how to use the picture index by locating the listing for the word *bat* in the index and then turning to page 4. Invite children to work with a partner to practice using the picture index. Ask pairs to identify and locate the remaining animals listed.

Text Complexity Measure

Use the rubric to familiarize yourself with the text complexity of ***What Do You Do With a Tail Like This?***

QUANTITATIVE MEASURES

LEXILE	620L
AVERAGE SENTENCE LENGTH	11.97
WORD FREQUENCY	3.67
WORD COUNT	467

QUALITATIVE MEASURES

LEVELS OF MEANING	accessible, literal concept about how animal anatomy aids function
STRUCTURE	compare-and-contrast structure conveyed through art and text; question-and-answer format contains main ideas and supporting details
LANGUAGE CONVENTIONALITY AND CLARITY	visual context clues for most content-specific vocabulary; repetitive sentence structures
THEME AND KNOWLEDGE DEMANDS	an understanding that animals are built to help them survive

READER AND TASK SUGGESTIONS

PREPARING TO READ THE TEXT	LEVELED TASKS
Discuss with children how humans use noses, ears, eyes, mouths, and feet to help them in their daily lives.	Help children create a list of reasons why animals have tails. Work with them to draw conclusions about how animals' features allow them to survive.

Text Complexity Rubrics

Text Complexity Measure

Use the rubric to familiarize yourself with the text complexity of **"How Polar Bears Hunt."**

QUANTITATIVE MEASURES	
LEXILE	260L
AVERAGE SENTENCE LENGTH	5.80
WORD FREQUENCY	3.49

QUALITATIVE MEASURES	
LEVELS OF MEANING	accessible content; one level of meaning
STRUCTURE	clearly presented factual information; images supporting the text
LANGUAGE CONVENTIONALITY AND CLARITY	simple sentence structure; all capital letters to show emphasis
THEME AND KNOWLEDGE DEMANDS	a basic knowledge of polar bears and where they live; addresses scientific concepts of prey and predators

READER AND TASK SUGGESTIONS	
PREPARING TO READ THE TEXT	LEVELED TASKS
Discuss with children what makes polar bears different from other types of bears. Help children make a list of what they think a young polar bear needs to learn.	Reread the text with children and help them identify the relationships among the animals and their surroundings. To help children share what they have learned, provide sentence frames or sentence starters, such as the following: *Polar bear cubs need ______. Seals ______ polar bears. Polar bears ______ seals. Animals in cold places ______.*

Text Complexity Measure

Use the rubric to familiarize yourself with the text complexity of **"A New Family."**

QUANTITATIVE MEASURES

LEXILE	350L
AVERAGE SENTENCE LENGTH	6.95
WORD FREQUENCY	3.68

QUALITATIVE MEASURES

LEVELS OF MEANING	narrative fiction; factual information delivered in fictional text
STRUCTURE	dialogue; events happen chronologically; diagram with arrows
LANGUAGE CONVENTIONALITY AND CLARITY	academic language; natural, conversational language; images support the text; signal words for sequence
THEME AND KNOWLEDGE DEMANDS	text assumes little prior knowledge; text addresses scientific concepts

READER AND TASK SUGGESTIONS

PREPARING TO READ THE TEXT	LEVELED TASKS
Say the words *nest, eggs, chick,* and *feather.* Ask children how these words are connected, and ask them to suggest other related words. Children may look for these words as they read the selection.	Review with children the images on the right page. Talk about how the arrows are useful in understanding the story's sequence. Work together to create another set of sequenced pictures to retell events from the story.

Text Complexity Rubrics

Text Complexity Measure

Use the rubric to familiarize yourself with the text complexity of **"A Happy Ending."**

QUANTITATIVE MEASURES	
LEXILE	360L
AVERAGE SENTENCE LENGTH	6.57
WORD FREQUENCY	3.54

QUALITATIVE MEASURES	
LEVELS OF MEANING	figurative language: personification; realistic and unrealistic events
STRUCTURE	chart; images support the text
LANGUAGE CONVENTIONALITY AND CLARITY	clear, conventional language; quotation marks to call out words
THEME AND KNOWLEDGE DEMANDS	addresses scientific concepts; text assumes some familiarity with the topic; reference to another literary text

READER AND TASK SUGGESTIONS	
PREPARING TO READ THE TEXT	**LEVELED TASKS**
Invite children to describe a swan and a duck. Record their responses on a two-column chart.	Reread the selection together. Ask children to tell how the chick changed as it grew. Help them find words in the text that describe the changes. Ask if the words describe a swan, a duck, or both.

Manuscript Alphabet

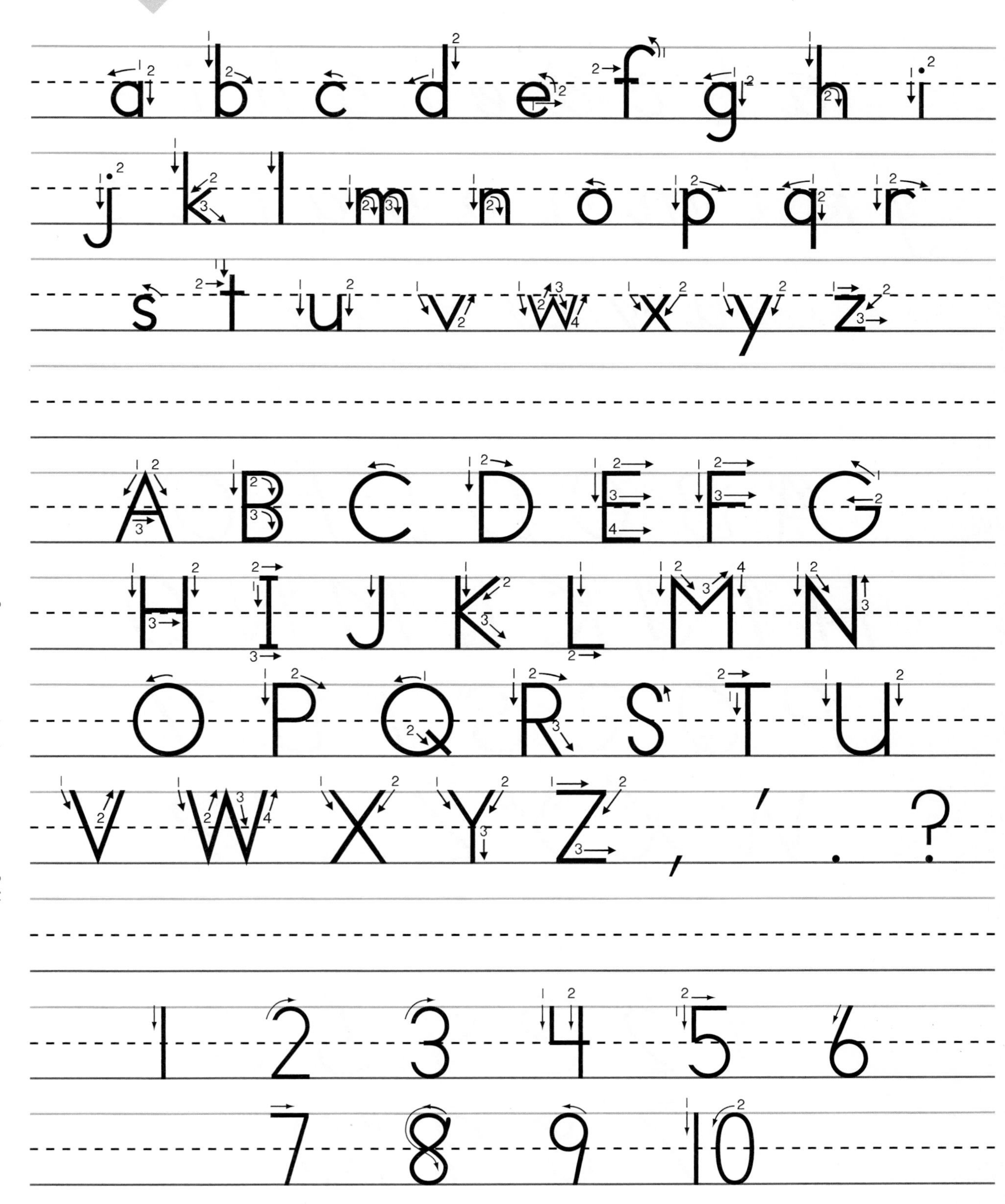

D'Nealian™ Alphabet

Leveled Text: Informational

Use leveled readers in combination with your classroom instruction to help children develop self-extending reading and thinking strategies as they become active, independent readers and writers, and as they deepen their understanding of and engagement with unit themes and topics.

Before Reading

Get Ready to Read Informational Text

The activities in this section are designed to help you gauge children's knowledge of the ideas and vocabulary they will encounter in an informational leveled reader and to provide support as needed. You will want to customize text selection and instruction to accommodate your children's needs and motivations as well as the challenges of the text.

UNDERSTAND TEXT TYPE AND PURPOSE Discuss with children the characteristics of informational text (It contains facts about a topic; its purpose is to inform readers; it may contain photographs and other text features to help readers understand the topic). **Ask:** How can you tell that a book is informational text and not a story? (The text gives facts rather than tells about characters and events; it might have maps, charts, or other text features that connect to the topic; information might be organized under specific headings that connect to the topic.)

PREVIEW AND PREDICT Point to and read aloud with children the title of the selection and key words in the text. Call their attention to important text features, such as headings, photographs, and captions. Flip through the pages together, and have children describe what they see in the text and text features. **Ask:** What topic do you think you will learn about in this informational text?

EXPLORE VOCABULARY Based on the topic children determine from previewing the book, build background around concept vocabulary. **Say:** Based on the title and pictures, here are some words we'll want to talk about before we read. For example, if the book is about making choices about money, you may want to explore words like *goods, services, consumer,* or *income*.

During Reading

Access Text

The activities in this section are designed to help you provide targeted instructional support before children read and to help you model the active-reading process as you engage with children in a preliminary reading of the text. Choose activities that are appropriate for your children and the text.

FOCUS ON CONCEPTS OF PRINT Point to and read aloud the title and the name of the author and/or illustrator. **Ask:** What does the author of a text do? (write the words) What does the illustrator do? (draw the pictures) Remind children that you will read from top to bottom and from left to right.

FOCUS ON PHONICS Help children decode unfamiliar words in the leveled reader by reviewing a previously taught phonics or word study lesson. For example, review vowel and consonant sounds, or ask children to locate word patterns they already know. Focus on a vowel team, a word family, or a compound word. Model how to decode a specific word in the leveled reader.

FOCUS ON INFORMATIONAL TEXT Provide a targeted mini-lesson that addresses these questions:

What does the text say?

- ask and answer questions about key details
- find the main topic and retell key details
- describe connections between pieces of information

How does the text say it?

- ask and answer questions about unfamiliar words
- locate key facts using text features (headings, menus, icons, etc.)
- distinguish between information in pictures and in text

What does the text mean?

- identify key ideas using both illustrations and text
- identify reasons an author gives to support points
- identify similarities and differences between two texts

Consider the following questions when determining the lesson focus:

- Which aspect of this leveled reader will be most challenging?
- Which aspect of this leveled reader must children understand to understand the text as a whole?
- Which reading strategies will help children internalize the process of reading actively?
- Which understandings about text and structure must be reinforced as children interact with other types of informational text?

Mini-Lesson

1. **FOCUS ON A GOAL.** Choose an instructional goal that best helps children understand the text. For example, to help children identify the main topic of an informational text, explain that finding the **main topic** means looking at all the sentences in a paragraph or a selection to decide what the text is mostly about.
2. **FOCUS ON WHY IT MATTERS.** Explain that active readers explore a selection closely to understand what the text is about, why an author is writing, and why the information is important. Is the author writing to inform, explain, or persuade? For example, help children understand that the **main topic** of a text helps point them to the most important ideas the author wants to inform readers about.
3. **FOCUS ON MODELING.** Read the leveled reader for the first time aloud as children follow along in their books. Have children point to each word in their books as you read. Model the mini-lesson focus. For example, to model finding the **main topic,** pause occasionally after sentences or paragraphs and **say:** These sentences are mostly about ________. I'll read on to see if______ is the main topic of this book.
4. **FOCUS ON SUPPORT.** Provide an activity that will reinforce the instructional goal. For example, in a mini-lesson about finding the main topic of an informational text, direct children's attention to a text previously read in the unit. Reread the title and a few pages of the book with children. **Ask:** What did you see and read about on each page of this book? How are these key details alike? Then ask children to restate the main topic of the book in their own words.

Leveled Text: Informational

Close Read

The activities in this section are designed to help children become more successful independent readers by first working in comfortable partnerships. Choose activities that are appropriate for your children and the text. As children progress, you may decide to have them engage in these activities independently.

PARTNER LISTEN Have children listen to a recording of the leveled reader and point to each word in the text as it is read aloud. Ask partners to help each other hold the book correctly and follow the words from top to bottom and from left to right.

PARTNER READ Have children take turns reading the leveled reader aloud to their partners.

- Remind children to begin by pointing to and/or reading aloud the title and the names of the author and/or illustrator.
- Encourage children to use the phonics or word-study strategy you modeled to decode another challenging word in the text.
- Have the children who are listening point to each word their partners read.

PARTNER SHARE Have partners practice using the informational text mini-lesson focus to interact with the leveled reader more closely. Ask them to work together to

- ask a question and use the text to answer it.
- identify a key detail they think supports the main idea.
- use context or picture clues to figure out an unfamiliar word.
- identify a text feature and explain how it helps readers understand the text.
- identify a reason the author gives to support a point.

After Reading

THINK ABOUT IT The activities in this section are designed to help children consider how the leveled reader enhances their understanding of the unit topic. Have children focus on the following questions:

- How are the ideas (illustrations, description, etc.) like other books I have read in this unit?
- How are the ideas in this text similar to another book I have read in this unit?
- What new things did I learn about the topic from reading this book?
- What is the most interesting part of this book? Why?

TALK ABOUT IT The activities in this section are designed to help children develop their understanding of the unit topic and enhance their listening and speaking skills by engaging in a group discussion. Give children sentence frames to help them express their ideas in a group setting.

- This book is like the other texts in this unit because ________.
- The ideas in this text are similar to/different from the ideas in ________ because ________.
- One new thing I learned about the topic from this book is ________.
- The most interesting part of this book is ________ because________.

WRITE ABOUT IT In this section, children demonstrate their understanding of the text and its connection to the unit topic through a brief writing activity. Possible activities might include the following:

Draw a picture of something important or interesting in this book and label it.

Write a brief summary.
This book was about ________.

Answer a question.
I found the answer to my question about _______ by going back to the text and reading that___________.

Find two things that are alike from this book and another book. Then draw and label them.

Write a brief comparison or contrast sentence.
This book was like another book I read because ________.
This book was different from another book I read because ________.

Leveled Text: Literary

Use leveled readers in combination with your classroom instruction to help children develop self-extending reading and thinking strategies as they become active, independent readers and writers, and as they deepen their understanding of and engagement with unit themes and topics.

Before Reading

Get Ready to Read Literary Text

The activities in this section are designed to help you gauge children's knowledge of the ideas and vocabulary they will encounter in a literary leveled reader and to provide support as needed. You will want to customize text selection and instruction to accommodate your children's needs and motivations as well as the challenges of the text.

UNDERSTAND TEXT TYPE AND PURPOSE Discuss with children the characteristics of literary text (It tells a story, or a narrative; it often has illustrations that show characters, settings, or events). **Ask:** How can you tell that a book is literary text and not informational text? (The selection tells about characters and events; it has a setting, plot or problem, and a resolution or solution; it often contains a message about life the author wants to share.)

PREVIEW AND PREDICT Point to and read aloud with children the title of the leveled reader. Call children's attention to key words in the story. Flip through the pages together, and have them point to and describe what they see in the illustrations. **Ask:** What do you think this story will be about?

EXPLORE VOCABULARY Work with children to understand the literary language of the text, such as words relating to character, setting, plot, and theme. **Say:** Here are some words we'll want to talk about before we read. Choose words that are important to comprehension or that will ultimately help students uncover the theme or message in the text.

During Reading

Access Text

The activities in this section are designed to guide you as you provide targeted instructional support before children read and to help you model active reading strategies as you engage with children in a preliminary reading of the text. Choose activities that are appropriate for your children and the text.

FOCUS ON CONCEPTS OF PRINT Point to and read aloud the title and the name of the author and/or illustrator. **Ask:** What does the author of a text do? (write the words) What does the illustrator do? (draw the pictures) Remind children that you will read from top to bottom and from left to right.

FOCUS ON PHONICS Help children decode unfamiliar words in the leveled reader by reviewing a previously taught phonics or word study strategy. For example, review vowel and consonant sounds, or ask children to locate word patterns they already know. Focus on a vowel team, a word family, or a compound word. Model how to use the strategy to decode a specific word in the leveled reader.

FOCUS ON LITERARY TEXT Provide a targeted mini-lesson that addresses these questions:

What does the text say?

- ask and answer questions about key details in the text
- retell narratives, and demonstrate understanding of the central message
- describe characters, settings, and major events, using the text

How does the text say it?

- identify words and phrases that suggest feelings or appeal to senses
- explain differences between books that tell stories and those that give information
- identify who is telling the story at various points in the text

What does the text mean?

- use illustrations and details to describe characters, setting, or events
- compare and contrast experiences of characters in a story

Leveled Text: Literary

Consider the following questions when determining the lesson focus:

- Which aspect of this leveled reader will be most challenging to children?
- Which aspect of this leveled reader must children understand in order to understand the text as a whole?
- Which reading strategies will help children internalize the process of reading actively?
- Which understandings about narratives must be reinforced as children interact with other types of literary text?

Mini-Lesson

1. **FOCUS ON A GOAL.** Choose an instructional goal that best helps children understand the text. For example, to analyze **character,** explain that the characters in a story perform the action. We know what they are like from what they say and do and from what others say about them.
2. **FOCUS ON WHY IT MATTERS.** Explain that active readers explore a selection closely to understand what happens in a story, why a character behaves in a certain way, and what message or observation about life the author wants to share. For example, if a **character** changes his or her behavior after losing a valued friend, the author may want readers to understand that friends are more important than possessions.
3. **FOCUS ON MODELING.** Read the leveled reader for the first time aloud as children follow along in their books. Have children point to each word in their books as you read. Model the mini-lesson focus. For example, to model identifying the **main character** and **story problem, ask:** Whom is this story about? What problem or difficulty does this person face?
4. **FOCUS ON SUPPORT.** Provide an activity that will reinforce the instructional goal. For example, in a mini-lesson about the **main character** in a story, direct children's attention to a text previously read in the unit. Reread a few pages of the book with children. **Ask:** Who in this story is facing a problem? What details does the author give about this character? What does the character say and do? What do others say about this character? How do you know? Then ask children to describe the main character and story problem in their own words.

Close Read

The activities in this section are designed to help children become more successful independent readers by first working in comfortable partnerships. Choose activities that are appropriate for your children and the text. As children progress, you may decide to have them engage in these activities independently.

PARTNER LISTEN Have children listen to a recording of the leveled reader and point to each word in the text as it is read aloud. Ask partners to help each other hold the book correctly and follow the words from top to bottom and from left to right.

PARTNER READ Have children take turns reading the leveled reader aloud to their partners.

- Remind children to begin by pointing to and/or reading aloud the title and the names of the author and/or illustrator.
- Encourage children to use the phonics or word study strategy you reviewed as a class to decode another challenging word in the text.
- Have the children who are listening point to each word as their partners read.

PARTNER SHARE Have partners practice using the literary text mini-lesson focus to interact with the leveled reader more closely. Ask them to work together to

- ask and answer questions about key details in the text.
- retell narratives, and demonstrate understanding of the central message.
- describe characters, settings, and major events, using the text.
- identify words and phrases that suggest feelings or appeal to senses.
- identify who is telling the story at various points in the text.
- use illustrations and details to describe characters, setting, or events.
- compare and contrast experiences of characters in a story.

After Reading

THINK ABOUT IT The activities in this section are designed to help children consider how the leveled reader enhances their understanding of the unit theme. Have children focus on the following questions:

- How is the story like other books I have read in this unit?
- What new things did I learn about the unit theme from reading this book?
- What is my favorite part of the book? Why?

TALK ABOUT IT The activities in this section are designed to help children develop their understanding of the unit theme and enhance their listening and speaking skills by engaging in a group discussion. Give children sentence frames to help them express their ideas in a group setting.

- This story is like the other texts in this unit because ________.
- The message in this story is similar to/different from the message in ________ because ________.
- One new thing I learned about [state unit theme] from this book is ________.
- My favorite part of the book is _______. I like it because ______________.

WRITE ABOUT IT In this section, children demonstrate their understanding of the text and its connection to the unit theme through a brief writing activity. Possible activities might include the following:

Draw a picture of something you liked in this book, and label it.

Write a brief summary.
This book was about ________.

Answer a question.
I found the answer to my question about _______ by going back to the text and reading that___________.

Find two things that are alike from this book and another book. Then draw and label them.

Write a brief comparison or contrast sentence.
This book was like another book I read because ________.
This book was different from another book I read because ________.

Acknowledgments

Illustrations
Cover: Joey Chou

Photographs
Photo locators denoted as follows: Top (T), Center (C), Bottom (B), Left (L), Right (R), Background (Bkgd)

xiv (T), xviii, xx (T), 6 (T), 12, 13, 15, 17, 19, 21, 22, 23, 25, 27, 29, 31, 32, 33, 35, 37, 39, 41, 62, 63, 65, 67, 69, 71, 72, 73, 75, 77, 79, 81, 82, 83, 85, 87, 89, 91, 92, 93, 95, 97, 99, 101, 102, 103, 105, 107, 109, 111, 112, 113, 115, 117, 119, 121, 132, 133, 135, 137, 139, 141, 143, 145, 147, 149 Houghton Mifflin Harcourt Publishing Company; xiv (C), xx (C) "Dragons and Giants" by Arnold Lobel from FROG AND TOAD TOGETHER. Text Copyright © 1971, 1972 by Arnold Lobel. Illustrations copyright © 1971, 1972 by Arnold Lobel. Used by permission of HarperCollins Publishers.; xv (C), 150 (C) WHAT DO YOU DO WITH A TAIL LIKE THIS? by Steve Jenkins and Robin Page. Copyright © 2008 by Steve Jenkins and Robin Page. Reprinted by permission of Houghton Mifflin Harcourt Publishing Company. All rights reserved.